CRISIS OF THE

BRITISH EMPIRE

TURNING POINTS AFTER 1880

David Nicholson

HALSGROVE

First published in Great Britain in 2017

British Library Cataloguing-in-Publication Data
A CIP record for this title is available from the British Library

ISBN 978 0 85704 320 7

HALSGROVE
Halsgrove House,
Ryelands Business Park,
Bagley Road, Wellington, Somerset TA21 9PZ
Tel: 01823 653777 Fax: 01823 216796
email: sales@halsgrove.com

Part of the Halsgrove group of companies
Information on all Halsgrove titles is available at: www.halsgrove.com

Printed and bound by Parksons Graphics, India

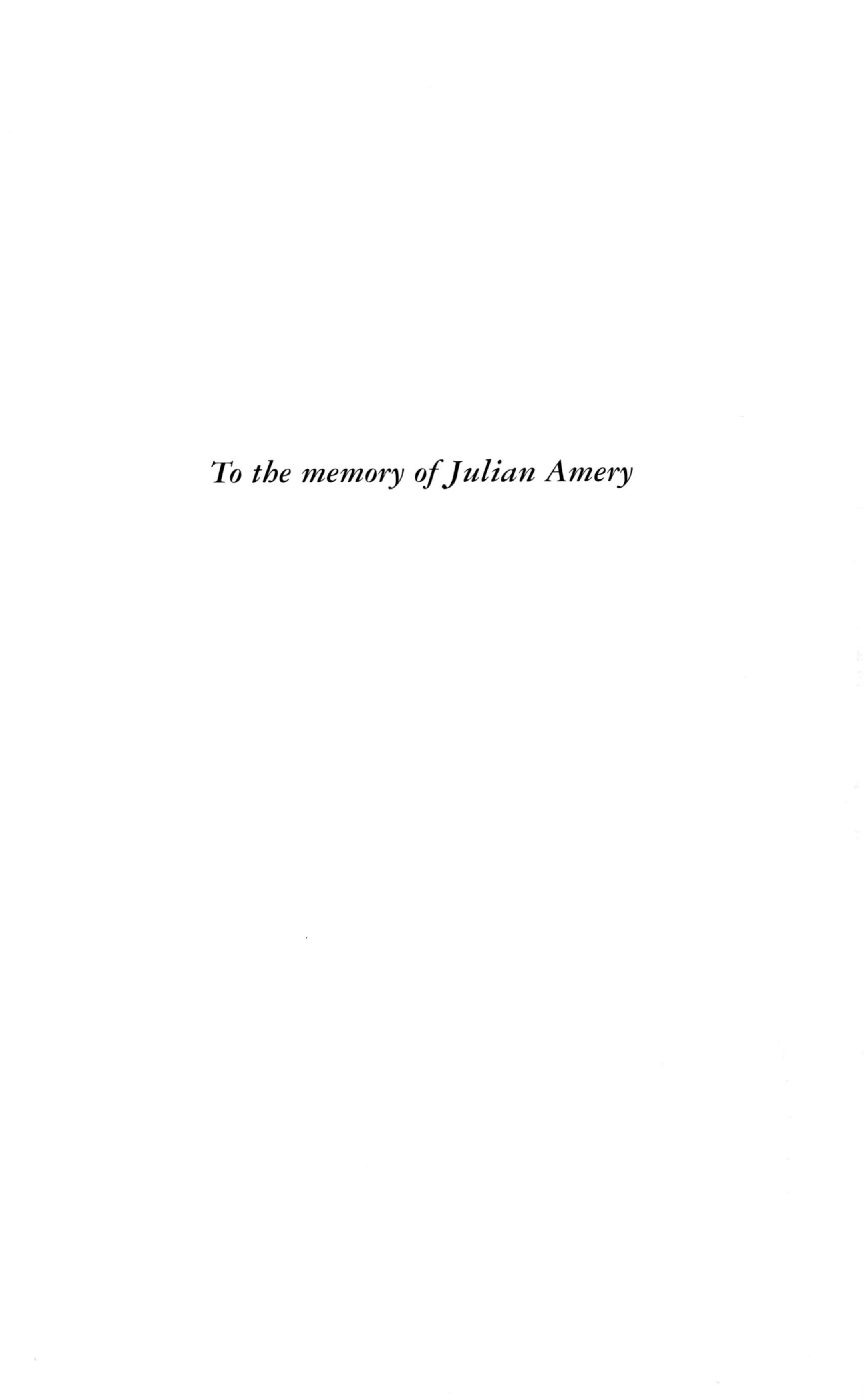

To the memory of Julian Amery

The various coloured cartoons, including the back cover, are taken from *The Stuwwelpeter Alphabet* by Harold Begbie, illustrated by F. Carruthers Gould, Grant Richards, 1900.

The black and white cartoons of Lord Hugh Cecil, the Bülow-Chamberlain clash of 1902, and the Anglo-French Entente, are from *F.C.G.'s Froissart* 1902 and 1903–6, T. Fisher Unwin.

IMAGE CREDITS subjects are italicised

Front cover: *Sir Austen Chamberlain*, Philip de Laszlo, 1920; *D. Lloyd George*, A. & R. Annan & Sons; *Anthony Eden*, William Little, c 1943, in the UK National Archives.

Inside book: *W. E. Gladstone*, J. J. E. Mayall; *E. Carson*, Liborio Prosperi, *Vanity Fair*, 9 November 1893; *J. C. Smuts*, Harris & Ewing collection at the Library of Congress; *Paul Kruger*, Portrait Gallery of the Perry – Castañeda Library of the University of Texas; *Lord Milner, Baron von Eckardstein, Sir Edward Grey, Count Mensdorff,* all by Leslie Ward ("Spy"), *Vanity Fair*, 15 April 1897, 21 July 1898, 5 February 1903, 21 December 1905; *Sir Mark Sykes*, by W. Hester, *Vanity Fair*, 26 June 1912; *Bonar Law, von Bülow, Sir D. Haig, King Feisal, Talaat Pasha, S. Baldwin* (by Walter Stoneman), *Sir H. Samuel, Ramsay MacDonald, P. Snowden, Sir W. Fisher*, all in George Grantham Bain collection at the Library of Congress; *A. Chamberlain*, The Norwegian Nobel Institute 1925; *W. Churchill*, Lynn Ott; *L. Amery,* Walter Stoneman, under licence from National Portrait Gallery; *The Kaiser*, T. H. Voigt, 1902; *Bethmann-Hollweg*, F. Brant; *Dr Weizmann,* Chaim Topol; *Enver Pasha,* Nicola Perscheid; *Dr T. Herzl*, Karl Pietzner; *R. Bennett*, Library and Archives Canada/C-000687; *N. Chamberlain*, Wellcome Images; *Hirota Koki* Rekidai Shusho tou Shashin, Japan,1936; *Yoshida Shigeru,* Japan, c. 1950; *E. Bevin,* UK government 1940s; *A. Eden*, www.number10.gov.uk

Apart from those of the Sykes-Picot agreement, the Japanese occupation of China, and the Treaty of Sèvres, all maps are from The *World-Wide Atlas* published by W. & A. K. Johnston Ltd, 1914.

Contents

Author's Foreword and Acknowledgements

"The historian can record ... what went wrong, but – in his feckless and unhelpful way – he is not necessarily there to tell them how they could have got it right."

(Alistair Horne, *A Savage War of Peace,* p545.)

I have been asked many times, by many different people "who is this book for?" The answer that occurred to me as it was finalised was: "It is for people like me, who are interested in all kinds of history, who are not specialists on any particular period or subject, but have a reasonable background knowledge of people and events, and would like to know whether there were any possible alternatives to the ways in which certain matters were handled." The subjects treated in this study include Home Rule for Ireland, the Scramble for Africa and subsequent events in South Africa, the road to, and through the First World War, how Britain came to dominate the Middle East in the early 1920s, how we gradually fell out with our first 20th century formal ally, Japan, and how it all unravelled after 1939.

And I have inflicted upon readers two chapters about Tariff Reform, because it was important in its time, and brought about mighty political turbulence then. Since most historians dismiss Tariff Reform, denying that it made a positive contribution to a cohesive British Commonwealth, I have yielded to the temptation to argue the contrary view. That view will be relevant, and even counter-balancing, as our world moves into unknown political territory in the face of Trumpism and Brexit. And there are a few paragraphs on how certain wise French, German and other leaders sought a democratic form of European unity on the eve of the Collapse of 1931 and the coming to power of Adolf Hitler, with his more sinister alternative.

Indeed, this book is replete with counterfactual challenges. *Pace* Horne, quoted above, I at least try, on occasion, to suggest how it might have been got right.

It might be said that "certain issues are left in the air, with various implications and nuances not developed or spelt out." That is, mostly, deliberate: I was taught by Lord Patten of Barnes some forty years ago not to resort to hammer blows in party political discourse, but to proceed more subtly. I am not an expert on the subjects I have described or debated, and have preferred, on the whole, to quote views and judgements, which I tend to support, by those who are more expert or were participants. On occasion, of course, I have indicated my own view, making remarks about how well, or how badly, something turned out.

So this book does not begin to attempt to describe how the modern world should be organised. I take responsibility for my choice and selection of quotations and judgements from secondary sources and for the sometimes unconventional conclusions these point towards. In this volume will be found discussion of such matters as a federal structure for the UK to solve the "Irish Question" of a century ago; the hopes for a *via media* in South Africa during the first half of the 20th century; the various ways in which Britain might have avoided being drawn into the First World War; the "case for" the much maligned Sykes-Picot agreement over the Middle East, and the warnings which were raised in the 1920s about the risks, all too evident over the past sixty years, flowing from a one-sided interpretation of the Balfour Declaration, whose centenary falls this year. It is worth nuancing that last sentence; in 1956, a crucial year in the period of Imperial decline, we saw the case for the State of Israel acting as a counter to our enemies.

Regarding another even greater event whose centenary is about to pass, on which I have frequently agonised as this book went forward: the First World War. What has increasingly struck me is how the most recent historians – Christopher Clark, Sean McMeekin, Dominic Lieven, John Charmley (albeit in 1999) – all chip away at the conventional view that France and Russia were necessarily the goodies and Germany and Austria-Hungary, while undoubtedly inept in July 1914, the fundamental baddies. And just as this book was being copy edited, I read David Owen's *The Hidden Perspective: the Military Conversations 1906-14* (published 2014). Some telling points from it are added to footnotes to Chapter Four. Two others, most unconventionally, I make here. First, those military conversations "between Britain and France" were obviously known to Germany (if only from a secret agent, p91), and were therefore "bound to have a profound influence on German behaviour ..., convincing them that Britain had made its decision to back France" (p80).

And on 7 April 1907, in the absence of the fanatically pro-French ambassador in Paris, Sir Francis Bertie, the Prime Minister, Sir Henry Campbell-Bannerman, met the then French premier, Georges Clemenceau, and made it clear that he did not consider Britain committed. This produced an explosion from Clemenceau about "CB", "*Quel père imbecile, quel idiot*". As Owen commented, Bannerman "had a message which he felt honour-bound to deliver ... and he delivered it in plain English" (op cit , pp92, 95). The French would have to wait for more of a green light until "CB" retired or died (he did both in April 1908).

Various good friends have helped me by suggesting books I should read, occasionally questioning my conclusions, and even criticising my style! I hope that I show that I have taken their points to heart. They include John Barnes (with whom I co-edited the Leo Amery Diaries), Sir Roger Carrick, Professor David Coleman, Professor David Dutton, Joe Egerton, Michael Jones, Neil Kerr, Jackie Krendel, Edward Russell-Walling, and Patrick Storer. I have spared other busy friends the task of reading and commenting. I take responsibility for all contentious conclusions, any silly factual mistakes and any surviving stylistic horrors. And I have checked and sought to avoid infringements of copyright, but apologise if any have inadvertently taken place.

I hope the choice of subjects speaks for itself: it is by no means an A to Z of Imperial or foreign history during this period. A fuller discussion and description on how the

British handled India during the period would make this book too long. I regret having to omit such a discussion, not only for its own sake, but because the diaries of Leo Amery, mentioned above, include those for the time he was Secretary of State for India, 1940 to 1945, and also because my late father-in-law served as an officer in the Indian Army during the 1920s and 1930s. I have, however, yielded to the temptation to produce some counterfactual lines which might set some hornets buzzing.

I am grateful to Halsgrove for letting this book see the light of day and would like to thank Steven Pugsley, Sharon O'Inn and my daughter Eleanor for their assistance in its production. And I should not forget the staff of the London Library for their help and guidance over several years.

I have used traditional spelling of Chinese and Indian place and personal names (including the Wade-Giles system), because this was used in the correspondence of the time and in many of my secondary sources. I have also used the traditional Japanese practice of putting surnames first, and the word "Unionist" to describe the Conservative party from 1886 up until about 1918-22, when it once again tended to be termed "Conservative". I have tried to keep pace with the British habit of names changing as statesmen etc ascended the social scale and I have also tried to ensure which member of the Chamberlain or Amery family, for example, is being featured, sometimes using only a first name. I have not otherwise indulged in the modern tendency of unnecessarily emphasising first names, but I attempt to remedy this in the Index.

The dedication of this book to the memory of Julian Amery is not only on account of the use I have made in it both of his father's diaries and his own masterly three final volumes of the *Life of Joseph Chamberlain.* Julian greatly enhanced and broadened my historical interest by asking me, in 1968, to work on his father's papers, in the interest of a further volume of biography or, as it transpired, editing the Diaries. This was in return for access to these papers for a thesis which I was embarking on at the time on the "Protectionist Lobby in the Conservative Party 1922-29". The latter was never completed and has been overtaken by other works, notably that by Robert Self. Julian also was anxious for me to pursue politics and enter Parliament. I well remember his inimitable voice saying, in early 1969, "David, you must stop writing history for a while, and come and make history"- this being his successful by-election for Brighton Pavilion in March 1969. My own political career was, probably to his disappointment though he never showed it, delayed, abbreviated and not entirely pursuing all the objectives he had set himself. The current volume, especially the Epilogue, is an attempt to set that balance right.

Authors usually at this point thank their wives and families for tolerating their monastic seclusion during the time of writing. This did not happen in my case as my attention and writing was in "spurts" over the past seven years, and I hope I did not during that time neglect family, friends and other tasks and pursuits. While most friends were not obliged to read drafts, I hope they will read, enjoy and learn from the published version.

Allshire, March 2017

Introduction

"It is a party shackled by tradition; all the cautious people, all the timid, all the unimaginative, belong to it ... Yet the Conservative Party is the Imperial Party ... *you* must work with it if you are to achieve even a part of your object."

(Salisbury to Milner, quoted R. Shannon, *Crisis of Imperialism*, p229, without primary source or date but c. 1890.)

"The British Empire is like some of those early vertebrated monsters-its backbone is bigger than its cranium."

(Crupp, a character in H.G. Wells's *The New Macchiavelli* based on L.S. Amery.)

This book studies various potential "turning points," or crucial decisions, affecting the development of the British Empire from a peak of stability during its time of supremacy in 1880 up to 1939-41, after which, however heroic her efforts, Britain saw her international power steadily withering. During this period, Britain's rulers took decisions, or failed to take them, encouraged trends, or sought to prevent them, which had negative consequences for the strength and cohesion of the then Empire.

No other people, not Rome, nor Spain, nor Russia, whose conquests and colonies were either of adjacent territories, or of one vast sub-continent, spread their power and their people so substantially over all five continents as the British did. One of the most recent Imperial historians emphasises the irregularity of our achievement: it "had no logic at all. It looked like the booty of an obsessive collector ..." The result by the mid 19th century was a collection of "beachheads and bridgeheads, half conquered tracts, half-settled interiors, mission-stations and whaling-stations, barracks, cantonments and ... treaty ports."[1]

This book principally concerns the development and maintenance of what another historian has called "Greater Britain" – the Empire, later the Commonwealth, of settlement. "Greater Britain was a relatively short-lived entity, with a life-span of ... , say, 1880s-1960s. But it was big and powerful in its day, a virtual United States, which historians of the period can no longer ignore, nor dismiss as a failed idea."[2] And a third historian states: "the first fifty years of the twentieth century encompassed the apotheosis of the British Empire ... when it ... was a more unified, coherent and powerful world system than at any other time in its existence."[3] And a moot question arises: if it had not failed, would Britain have been so attracted after the early 1960s by the lure of membership of, rather than just external support for, the European Community?

Perhaps nothing could have prevented India from ultimately taking a separate course. While some Imperial thinkers sought to contrive a means, including

"Federation", by which Britain herself and the white-settled Dominions might have worked more closely together, each one demanded self-government and a separate identity. Australia and New Zealand remained closest in sympathy with Britain. Canada was always going to be difficult, partly because of her French population, and partly on account of her proximity to the United States.[4]

South Africa posed an even greater problem; the 19th century Imperial historian Froude, in his *Two Lectures on South Africa,* said of it "It is a conquered country, which we have occupied in our own interest against the wishes of the people to whom it belongs. Some English colonists have settled there since then, but South Africa is Dutch."[5] No amount of British emigration there enabled them to outnumber the Boers, still less the black races, and there was inevitable Dutch hostility towards Empire cohesion. Despite the writing on the wall from at least 1914 indicating South Africa's separate and sad destiny, the country enjoyed a huge status in Britain in the early 20th century: its importance as an export market, the exertions of the Boer War and the idealism of reconstruction after it, the distinguished contributions thereto and subsequent careers of the "Milner kindergarten", even the fiction of one of these, John Buchan, with its admiration of South Africa. Or perhaps it was simply the glamour of gold and diamonds and the attractions of the Cape and Natal to upper-class winter holiday makers.

In recent years there have been a variety of "critiques" of the Empire, some aiming at a more "popular" market. Dr Ronald Hyam's works[6] are very thorough: describing British Imperial administrators, he states that "probably a majority of them were circumsized". Indeed, his studies of sex in the Empire (a hundred pages in *Understanding the British Empire* – 2010 – and an entire book *Empire and Sexuality: The British Experience)* open new vistas for the student, with sideways glances at other enthralling authors. How far this changes our conclusions on the British Imperial experience is debatable; similar studies of French, Russian or Spanish colonialism would provide comparisons and contrasts, perhaps with more brutality and less homosexuality.

More recently, there have been works by Sir David Cannadine, Jeremy Paxman and Kwasi Kwarteng MP.[7] Cannadine has an issue with the landed aristocrats and Oxbridge scholars who ran India and the other colonies; another study might speculate how benevolent and incorrupt the rule of mill-owners, steel makers or metal bashers might have been, assuming these could be spared from their homeland tasks. Paxman produces a rollicking, somewhat debunking gallop from the pirates and privateers of the 16th century to the collective flag-lowerings of the mid 20th, G. A. Henty tempered by Lytton Strachey with a touch of BBC political correctness thrown in!

Thus the reader is obliged to confront slavery and the British foul treatment of the Irish and other peoples at the sharp end of colonialism. The slave trade was a vile enterprise, but as a land-based operation, it goes back into the mists of time. African chiefs and elders collaborated in it, as well as Arabs, Moors and Turks; all the colonial powers, including the freedom-loving Americans, later indulged in it, while Britain played a significant role in terminating it. And anyone who has studied what little is known of the 5th century Anglo-Saxon invasions, then the Viking depredations, and then the Norman occupation, together with the rude relations with Scotland between the 13th and 18th centuries, should not be surprised that, as Paxman states, "some of the British behaviour was appalling" (as well as some being "admirable."). Paxman also acknowledges, if it had not been the British doing the colonising "it would almost certainly have been somebody else" and British government "was better than many of the other possibilities."[8]

Kwasi Kwarteng gives a comprehensive and penetrating analysis of the British impact on six very different countries, none of which were essential to the core Empire Project, and five of which saw a fairly unhappy aftermath to British rule. The six are: Iraq, Kashmir, Burma, Sudan, Nigeria and, the probable exception, Hong Kong. The British impact in each case involved neglect and premature independence, but Kwarteng reaches several telling conclusions relevant to the whole Imperial experience. Rightly, given certain of the main themes of this present book, he refutes Ferguson's claim that the Empire was the champion of free market liberalism and democracy; "benign authoritarianism", he thinks, "would be a better description" . In the context of Hong Kong, he declares "the British Empire had nothing to do with liberal democracy": "the reality of empire ... was a pragmatic affair, governed more by notions of intellectual and social elitism, deference and privilege than by any abstract ideal of democracy or political liberalism." So he vigorously backs the diplomats and administrators against the strange Whiggish alliance of Lord Patten and Lady Thatcher.[9]

The ruling elite's endorsement of the Empire project had not always existed. The early 19th century Liberal-Radical campaigner, John Bright, proclaimed "it will be a happy day for England when she no longer possesses a single acre of territory in Asia." The chief exponent of separation was Goldwin Smith, Professor of History at Oxford from 1858 to 1866 and then, perhaps appropriately, Professor at Cornell University, who wrote a series of letters in 1862 to the *Daily News* referring to the colonies as "useless dependencies", adding "The Colonies must go".[10] Sir James Stephen, the "real director of colonial policy", wrote in 1849 "it remains for the Canadians to cut the last cable which anchors them to us ... The same process is in progress in the Australian colonies", while smaller colonies like South Africa and New Zealand were "wretched burdens which in an evil hour we assumed and have no right to lay down again." Lord Melbourne, the Whig Prime Minister, sent Lord Durham to govern Canada, writing to him "The final separation of these colonies might not be of material detriment." In 1870 the Liberal Lord Granville and his successor at the Colonial Office Lord Kimberley "made public statements repudiating any desire to further the dismemberment of the empire"; the fact that this statement had to be made implied people believed the reverse.[11]

In his great speech setting out future Conservative policy at the Crystal Palace on 24 June 1872, in a passage rarely quoted, Disraeli repudiated all this Liberal-Radical thinking: "If you look to the history of this country since the advent of liberalism forty years ago, you will find there has been no effort so continuous, so subtle, supported by so much energy, and carried on with so much ability and acumen as the attempts of liberalism to effect the disintegration of the Empire of England. And ... of all its efforts this is the one which has been nearest to success." He condemned this thinking as "totally passing by those moral and political considerations which make nations great, and by the influence of which alone men are distinguished from animals".[12]

Disraeli went on prophetically to forecast the Imperial issues which would be dominant thirty and forty years later. "Self government" when conceded, should be "conceded as part of a great policy of Imperial consolidation ... accompanied by an Imperial tariff ... and by a military code ... by which, if necessary, this country should call for aid from the Colonies themselves. It ought , further, to be accompanied by the institution of some representative council in the metropolis (to bring) the Colonies into constant and continuous relations with the Home Government."[13] In fact, the Disraeli government of 1874-80 did not venture into the stormy waters of tariff policy, taking no other measure to "consolidate" the Empire than proclaiming Victoria "Empress of India", largely to enable her to look the European Emperors in the eye.

Some early expectations, particularly of demographic expansion, with implications for trade, were wholly unrealistic; the Imperialist writer (and Liberal MP), Sir Charles Dilke, thought Canada would support a population as large as the USA, while Australia might possess "a white population which may be counted by hundreds of millions".[14] Disraeli's reluctance to promote Imperial consolidation is understandable: he was aged 69, with only seven years to live, when he came to power in 1874. The Third Marquess of Salisbury, who dominated politics in the 1880s and 1890s, presided over much Imperial expansion, but did not reopen the Free Trade debate.

***

So what went wrong after 1880? This study aspires to address, in roughly chronological order, a series of counterfactuals or "turning points." In many of the questions raised, the verdict may well be "it seemed to be the right thing to do at the time."

1. Ireland. The key decision not to adopt moderate Home Rule took place in 1884-6, but there were further developments extending through to 1922 and beyond. The importance of Ireland to the security and cohesion of the whole United Kingdom, as dictated by geography, is obvious.

2. Over-extension in Africa in 1880-1902, and the gradual failure to secure a firmer base in South Africa after 1902.

3 . The failure to adopt Tariff Reform at an early enough stage, in the key period 1903-5. Further failure up to 1914 and in the 1920s also requires explanation.

4. How Britain failed to do a deal with Germany over their international rivalry, and then became more and more committed to Germany's potential enemies, both encouraging them and making Germany's rulers more prone to risk-taking.

5. The conduct of the 1914-18 War, with its strategic and tactical mistakes, the diplomatic failure to detach any of Germany's weaker allies until the end, and mistakes made in peace-making, including the start of the alienation of Italy and over-extension into the Middle East.

6. The final adoption of Tariff Reform and Imperial Preference, after further delay, in 1931-2 at the Ottawa Conference.

7. The road to 1941: especially the mistakes leading to Japan, as well as Italy, joining an alignment hostile to Britain.

The Epilogue will trace, along with some counterfactual questioning, the real damage done by the 1939-45 War, leading to the final collapse of British power in India, then the Middle East, and finally in Africa, as well as the weakening of the links with the "old Commonwealth" .

Certain of these themes require a fuller initial explanation.

Over-extension: Africa and the Middle East

Did the enthusiasm for Imperialism go to the head of British leaders in the 1880s and 1890s? Was it wise, and was it inevitable, for Britain to extend her full control across vast expanses of tropical Africa and, after 1918, doing the same across the Middle East? Every time in the 19th century her forces had been tempted to control Afghanistan, disaster had resulted. Could the classical and historical scholars who ruled in London have seen examples of restraint from other Empires? Rome, for example, under Augustus set a limit to expansion, then under Hadrian evacuated Mesopotamia and Armenia, and later Dacia and southern Scotland. Others might have drawn lessons from the failure of Philip II of Spain to rest his oars in, say, 1580, Louis XIV in the 1680s and Napoleon in 1810.

Lord Elton judged that the Scramble for Africa was "altogether alien to the tastes and traditions" of the British.[15] Lord Milner, speaking to the Royal Colonial Institute in 1908, pronounced "If I had to choose between an effective union of the great self-governing states of the Empire *without the dependent states*" or the retention of both the dependencies and "the distant communities of our own blood and language" together, "I should choose the former".[16] Despite these misgivings, the process of aggrandisement continued. By incorporating more non-European peoples in the Empire, expansion inevitably ended with their independence and separation when democratic claims were pursued.

Contrasted to that of the Americas and Australasia, the European colonisation of Africa was a failure. Nowhere were the numbers of settlers large enough to challenge the eventual assumption of "black majority rule". Even where settlement was most successful, in South Africa, there developed no "happy medium" between apartheid and exclusively black rule, although whether this was completely inevitable will be examined in Chapter Two.

No political group across the spectrum had clear alternative ideas in the late 19th or early 20th centuries on how the African colonies might be retained indefinitely in the Imperial network, but it was assumed they would be. Elton quotes the Labour leading figure, Herbert Morrison, post 1945: to grant African colonies self-government would be "like giving a child of ten a latch-key, a bank account and a shot-gun."[17] The tropical African colonies were rarely in the news between 1918 and 1950; between 1955 and 1980 they were rarely out of the news, these developments accompanying the final agonies of the Empire.

The First World War and Over-Extension into the Middle East

The emergence of united Germany as the most powerful state in Europe in no way made war between Britain and her inevitable. In the 1890s and early 1900s British military and naval chiefs were still planning in terms of war with Russia, as well as with Russia's improbable ally, France. The key to the irreversible decline of the British Empire, however, were the two great wars with Germany, and it is hard to resist the conclusion that the first one made the second inevitable. Was war in 1914 inevitable, and in particular, was Britain's involvement avoidable?

While this author accepts the conventional view of Britain refusing a deal with Hitler in 1940, and therefore disagrees with Professor John Charmley's implication that Churchill should (or even would) have detached himself from the war and let Hitler and Stalin fight it out, Charmley's arguments on pre-1914 hold more attractions. In *Splendid Isolation: Britain and the Balance of Power 1874-1914,* chapters 20 to 23, Charmley indicts Sir Edward Grey, Foreign Secretary after 1905, of virtually committing Britain to a military alliance first with France and then with Russia, without telling Parliament, or the Cabinet, or, until quite late on, the Prime Minister! If only half the allegations he makes against Grey can be sustained, the conventional view of Britain's slide to war in August 1914 would need radically to be revised. While he gives very little attention to the July 1914 crisis, he describes in some detail the exchanges between Russia, France and Britain during the "Scutari Crisis" of the spring of 1913 (when Austria-Hungary was preparing to interdict, by force if necessary, the Montenegrin occupation of

Scutari, later in independent Albania), implying that the tragic 1914 slide to war through alliance commitments might have occurred a year earlier.

What is clear, in Charmley and elsewhere, is that by 1913-4, not only were France and Russia militarily on a par with Germany and Austria-Hungary, but that the likely reactions of other powers and various Balkan states would be to the detriment of Germany. In these circumstances, France and Russia were more confident, and Berlin and Vienna somewhat fearful.

In his biography of Lord Salisbury, Andrew Roberts describes a most attractive counterfactual. "If Salisbury had had Gladstone's political longevity and had also stayed in office until he was eighty-four, he would have been Prime Minister in 1914 ... We cannot know, but must suspect, that Salisbury would have made more strenuous efforts to prevent the cataclysm." Roberts quotes Algernon Cecil, Salisbury's nephew, on how the great man would have handled the 1914 crisis, "very differently ... than it was by the Asquith government", by way of private letters of warning to Berlin, about restraining Austria, and St Petersburg, about restraining mobilisation, culminating in a Congress, paralleling that in Berlin in 1878 "with the British Foreign Secretary this time as honest broker."[18]

One consequence of the Allied victory in 1918 was the collapse of Ottoman Turkish rule over the Middle East. Britain, with France, moved into the vacuum – another episode of over-expansion. While the African colonies remained peaceful between the wars, there were revolts in Egypt, Iraq and eventually Palestine. Could this expansion have been avoided? The Suez Canal route was seen as crucial for military, commercial and settlement traffic to the East: faster and therefore cheaper than the Cape route.

Assuming occupation of the Middle East had become inevitable, could it have been handled differently? Was the Balfour Declaration a wise or desirable venture, or was its ambiguity and its administration, leading to its exploitation in ways few intended at the time, the real problem? Perhaps a case might be made, a century later, for the frequently condemned Sykes-Picot agreement of January 1916. Would not two of the Sykes-Picot provisions, first, for an Arab state in the hinterland of Syria, and second, for international control of Palestine, by Britain, France, probably Italy, and also Russia or the US according to the timing, been more satisfactory, certainly for Britain's later interests? In these circumstances, neither Arabs nor Jews in Palestine would have been led to entertain realistic hopes of sovereignty or statehood, and, perhaps, the tensions between these two peoples which developed in the Twenties and led to warfare in each of the next five decades, might have been avoided.

Tariff Reform

If, as this author believes, the essential and most permanent achievements of the Empire Project consisted of the acquisition, settlement and development of what were termed the Dominions, we need to study the history of a prolonged controversy in British politics – known at the time and referred to in these pages as Tariff Reform. The details of the arguments, involving incomplete statistics and dry-as-dust exchanges over trade policy, are unappetising to the modern reader, which is probably why recent historians of the Empire skim over it. But it dominated politics in the early 20th century and was seen by large numbers of its influential supporters as being crucial to the successful economic interdependence with Britain of the Dominions of settlement, as well as important to their development.

Launched by Joseph Chamberlain in 1903, rejected by the Liberal and the nascent Labour parties, adopted as Conservative party policy in 1910, rejected by the electorate in the two elections of that year, put on the back-burner in the face of still more pressing controversies, resurrected but again rejected by the electorate in 1923, a version of the Tariff Reform programme was finally implemented in 1931-32 in the aftermath of the economic cataclysm. Another reason why several recent Empire historians, such as Niall Ferguson, pass rapidly over the Tariff Reform controversy is that it essentially represents, to modern orthodoxy, economic and political heresy. As it involved Britain's introducing protective tariffs on imports, it was attacked at the time for jeopardising Free Trade on which Britain's commercial success of the 19th century was believed to depend. Legitimate doubts had arisen as to whether a free trading Britain could compete satisfactorily in a world, after 1870, in which other countries, having dabbled with free trade, had abandoned it, and like Germany and the USA, as well as France, Russia (and, indeed, the British colonies, soon to be Dominions), were building economic success behind national tariff barriers.

Tariff Reform did not mean only "insular protection" for Britain; the British trading bloc, established at Ottawa in 1932, competed strongly in power and economic strength with the USA. This was a prime reason why the USA strove to demolish it, eventually, after 1945, succeeding in this objective. Ottawa might not have given Britain, or for that matter the Dominions, all they desired – such agreements rarely do. But the positive effects of the Ottawa system have been recognised by some of the latest Empire historians. "Trade between Britain and the Dominions, already high, increased greatly … Between 1929 and 1938 the volume of British imports from Australia and Canada more than doubled", with the Empire's share of British imports by value rising from 27% to almost 40%. "We should not overestimate Ottawa, which consolidated rather than created the Greater British economic system … By 1939, Greater Britain was at its peak economically."[19]

Could Tariff Reform have been implemented earlier? Did delay matter? Perhaps Ottawa did come too late, as the early to mid Thirties coincided with the collapse of international collective security and the growth of challenges to the Versailles settlement.[20]

The Road to 1939-41

If the peace-makers at Versailles in 1919 had confined the operations of the League of Nations to Europe – the US would have objected but the US did not join the League – Britain might have been spared two misfortunes in the 1930s. She would not have had to go through the League's hoops over the Japanese annexation of Manchuria in 1931, and she would not, at the League's behest, have had to come close to war with Italy over Ethiopia in 1935. These episodes ensured that Japan and Italy joined Nazi Germany in 1940-1, posing a strategic and resources nightmare for Britain.

Like any other Empire, the British transcontinental hegemony would not long survive the decline of naval and military strength. Britain's rearmament after 1936 benefited the Navy and Air Force, but not the Army, so vital in 1940 if France was to have been saved. In the late Thirties, Germany and Japan massively expanded their armaments, usually to incorporate very modern and effective weapons, but both were running into problems with raw materials and economic overheating. Even in 1936 when British spending rose, its allocation was less than Italy's and one-third or one-quarter of Germany's, while the inadequacies in British industrial plant and shortage of skilled engineers slowed down production of tanks, aircraft and ships.[21] The greatest setback was with France; the French army and air force were both formidable at the start of the Thirties. A collapse in the French economy after 1933, then massive devaluation in 1935-6, together with the Popular Front government, meant a slump in armaments spending. This prevented the re-equipping of the army, but especially affected the air force, which by 1940 had become seriously obsolescent.[22]

Given the development of threats to Britain and her allies during the Thirties, America was the elephant in the room. Having refused to join the League of Nations, she failed during this period to translate her strength in resources either into armaments or alliances. If anything, her relations with Britain deteriorated. Tensions and even talk of possible war "flared up on two occasions, in 1920-1 and again in 1927-9". On issues ranging from the Middle East, Ireland, trade rivalry in South America or war debts, "the Anglophobes in the United States and the imperial isolationists in Britain directed policy and dominated the press."[23]

By the end of 1927, the British Prime Minister, Stanley Baldwin, was reported "to loathe the Americans so much that he could not bear meeting them." In 1929, Baldwin warned the Labour leader, Ramsay MacDonald, who was to defeat him a few months later, that "the American money power is trying to get control of some of the natural resources of the Empire. They are working like beavers."[24]

There is no doubt that the British Empire, virtually alone after June 1940, would suffer heavily from Japan, as well as Italy, putting her naval and air strength into the hostile balance. This would almost certainly not have occurred had France been able to stay in the war. So the most obvious counterfactual is to suggest that, if Britain had strengthened her Army before 1939 and placed a substantial proportion of it on the Continent in 1939, France would not have fallen. Baldwin argued for a Continental Army, but was overruled by Neville Chamberlain, supported in 1933-34 by Cabinet. They were influenced by the fact that Sir Basil Liddell Hart, military correspondent of The *Times,* was preaching that the involvement in the land war of 1914-8 had been a great mistake, and criticisms of the slaughter in the trenches were reaching their peak. Thus the Army was given lowest priority of all three services. Pressure from the French for troops led in February 1939 to Cabinet agreeing to develop a Continental Army of 32 divisions. No training facilities or armaments were available for such a force; indeed, the only troops available were two infantry divisions and one mobile division lightly equipped "for an eastern theatre."[25]

Britain's military weakness was one of the factors in producing the failure of the talks in the summer of 1939 designed to align the Soviet Union with Britain and France in defending Poland from Nazi aggression. Quite apart from the Soviet view of Poland (and the Baltic States), the British ambassador in Moscow found Litvinov, then Foreign Minister, "convinced that France was 'practically done for." Stalin told Churchill in Moscow in August 1942 that "he thought England must be bluffing; he knew we had only two divisions we could mobilise at once, and he thought we must know how bad the French army was ..."[26]

Building up forces and concentrating them across the Channel would have been risky: the phrase "eggs in one basket" comes to mind, and sceptics would argue that the option would have been doomed by weak political leadership, inadequate air cover and a mistaken tactical doctrine. And how rotten was France? If it had enabled France to survive, Italy would have stayed out, with consequences for the naval and air balance in the Mediterranean, and Japan would not have been led to occupy Indo-China. What is even clearer is that Japan only gradually and with a degree of political disunity gravitated towards the Axis, and her military and naval chiefs disagreed as to whether to strike north, against the USSR, or south, against the "Western" powers.

The humiliation at Singapore and the fact that Australia and New Zealand became dependent on American strength for their defence acted as fatal blows at the cohesion of the pre-war Commonwealth and Empire. A mere fifteen years saw the virtual end of the latter, while the former was transformed into a much larger, looser and very different entity. It became, to use Hobbes' epigram on the Papacy, "no other than the ghost of the deceased Roman Empire, sitting crowned upon the grave thereof."

***

During the British Raj, India must be seen as a most unusual possession of any Empire. Dwarfing its possessor in size and population, and contrasted in antiquity and complexity of civilisation, India was neither a territory of settlement nor one of the colonies gobbled up in one of the 1890s "scrambles". Throughout the 1880-1940 period, India was the keystone of the extended Empire, as well as attracting immense respect and occasional envy elsewhere. Yet, paradoxically, leading Imperialists such as Joseph Chamberlain, Lord Milner, and Leo Amery showed very little interest in it for much of their lives. Despite being born in India, Amery paid relatively little attention to the Raj until he battled with Churchill over Baldwin's India Bill of the 1930s, and then was appointed by Churchill as Secretary of State for India in 1940.

While Niall Ferguson acknowledges that the average Indian did not get much wealthier under British rule and much of the profits of Indian industry went to British sources of capital, he asks, would Indians have been better off under the Mughals (who would have returned to power, at least in name, if the 1857 Mutiny had succeeded), or under the Russians, or the Dutch? Even at end of 19th century, however, famines and epidemics of plague and other diseases carried off hundreds of thousands, while literacy, even in native languages, remained very low. On the other side of the balance sheet were the huge sums invested by Britain in Indian infrastructure, as well as key reforms in the health and social spheres. In Ferguson's words "it is hard to believe that there was not some advantage in being governed by as incorruptible a bureaucracy as the Indian Civil Service."[27]

Undoubtedly, the greatest gains under the Raj were civil peace and unity. The sub-continent had hardly ever been united; the Mughals never controlled the south. The failure to maintain unity when independence was attained not only involved the death and maiming of millions during "partition", but resulted in continuous tension between the successor states. Despite British pessimism in the 1940s, modern India has achieved exemplary success, both in preserving democracy and developing prosperity based on capitalism.

Ignoring this fortunate outcome for a moment, and reverting to the fears of the '40s, might some kind of British role have continued, after 1945, holding the ring in the face of religious conflict and thus averting the disaster of Partition? This will be examined in more detail in the Epilogue. As an introductory point, perhaps the British, inspired equally by Imperial conceit and Liberal-Christian benevolence, made from the 1830s the mistake of treating the sub-continent as a unity. In fact, it resembled Europe, not only in area and population, but in varying languages and cultures as well as divisions of religion and political status. If the British had made more of nurturing the various languages and cultures, and protecting minority religions, while devolving power to provinces, such as Bengal, the Punjab, Madras and the southern coastlands, and Sind, each reflecting those separate loyalties, they might more easily have been able to resist pressures for political-party-dominated democracy at the centre. Devoid of some at least of the trappings of Viceregal power, the centre would still have controlled the armed forces, composed of all races and religions. These would have been used when necessary for defence against external threats; the British tended to exaggerate these threats, which only appeared right at the end, in 1942-5, and have not recurred since independence. The forces would also have been deployed to ensure law and order and to protect religious and other minorities from persecution by their rivals.

This was implied by Lord Elton, analysing the position in 1945. There were 180 million, mainly Hindu, for whom Congress appeared to speak, he wrote, 80 million who would welcome a separate Muslim state, which was then vehemently opposed by Congress and the Hindus, 80 million who lived in the States and, as the subjects of the Princes, had an entirely different legal relationship with the British Raj, and 50 million, mainly in Hindu India, who were "untouchables" (Dalits or "scheduled castes") according to the Hindu caste system.[28]

While some Hindus and Muslims joined together in rebellion during the Mutiny of 1857, their relationship had not usually been a happy one. Northern India was subjected to devastating Muslim invasions and raids, killing and enslaving Hindus and destroying their cities and especially their temples, from the 10th century onward. Southern India was not spared; the magnificent city of Vijayanagar, which flourished between the 14th and 16th centuries, during the height of the power of that eponymous empire, suffered a tragic fate. In 1565, its armies were massively defeated by an alliance of the Deccan Muslim sultanates, and the capital was taken, razed and depopulated over a period of several months. It was not rebuilt nor occupied subsequently. By the 1930s, it was the turn of the Muslims to be fearful of the Hindu majority.

Nineteenth-century developments moved towards centralisation. Annexation of several princely states under Lord Dalhousie 1848-56, especially that of Oudh, helped to cause the "Mutiny". This was under the doctrine of "lapse", dropped after 1858 as part of reconciliation, thus helping to keep the Princes loyal during later nationalist agitation. While the Mutiny was savagely suppressed, Queen Victoria gave assurances of respect for other religions and missionaries were told to curb their zeal for conversion and concentrate on education.

Another centralising force consisted of the ambitions of western-educated Indians, who filled those posts in the civil service to which they could be promoted and were especially prominent in the law and other professions. They saw things from an All-India view. Tensions developed between the racial arrogance of the British official and business classes in India and the ambitions of this group.[29] An attempt to ensure that justice should be colour-blind in 1883, the Ilbert Bill, led to intense opposition in Britain and from British settlers in India, such as they were. It was enacted in 1884 in a severely weakened state. The episode led to the formation of the Indian National Congress in 1885.

The first four decades of the 20th century saw various events which increased tension between the British and the Indians: Curzon's proposed partition of Bengal, with no consultation, and eventually reversed after intense revolutionary activity and the boycott of British goods; the Dyer massacre at Amritsar in 1919, coinciding with the Montagu-Chelmsford reforms; Gandhi's attempt to bridge the communal gap by championing the Ottoman Sultan after 1918; and finally, in peacetime, Gandhi's salt tax *satyagraha* with tens of thousands arrested including the whole Congress Working Committee (June 1930).

What is certain is that, as the Second World War proceeded, Britain gradually and perhaps inevitably lost the will to hold on to her Indian heritage.

Of all the peoples in the United Kingdom, the one which made the greatest contribution to Britain overseas, as administrators, soldiers, businessmen, explorers, missionaries or settlers, in proportion to their total number, were the Scots. While pressure for Scottish devolution, separation or even independence did not start with the end of Empire, there is no doubt that each has been fanned by the termination of an enterprise which the Scots had pursued on almost equal terms to the vastly more numerous English. And while commitment to the Imperial mission was not exclusive to Conservatives (Lord Rosebery and Lloyd George played a mighty role), it certainly seems to have helped to woo the Scots for the Conservatives. In 1955, when at least the colonial empire in Africa and the Far East survived, alongside the semblance of Dominion cohesion and British hegemony in the Middle East, in an otherwise relatively narrow General Election victory, the Conservatives won their highest ever proportion of votes in Scotland, over 50 per cent (even higher, just, than the proportion in 1931). From then on, the tally progressively declines, with occasional pathetic rallies, until the considerable recovery of the 2017 General Election.

Et si monumentum requiris? Lapsing briefly into the first person, while the style of this work is intended to be objective, I cannot disguise my admiration for the "Empire project"; especially involving the "Empire of settlement" as distinct from the tropical "colonies." As noted above, attempts to extend the Empire of settlement failed in Africa. So Rhodesia became Zimbabwe and Salisbury became Harare, with statues of Cecil Rhodes now being demolished in South Africa. The Rhodesian dispute dominated the earlier part of my adult life, from 1960 to 1979. I can recall, in the summer of 1979, walking over the ruins of Graeco-Roman cities in southern Turkey, reflecting on the parallel with the then likely removal of the British element in Rhodesia-Zimbabwe. And as so often with the high hopes of western liberals, those resting on the "settlement" of 1979-80 swiftly turned to dust.

While British cultural, linguistic and commercial influence has steadily increased in recent decades, most facets of "Greater Britain" had largely vanished by the 1960s, with the Empire of settlement holding on in Central Africa until 1980.

But perhaps the last word in this Introduction might be left with that South African former opponent of the British, later a doughty champion of their enterprise. General Smuts, replying in May 1917 at a banquet in the Royal Gallery of the House of Lords in his honour, with Asquith and Churchill among those present, had avoided the word "Empire" in his speech, using on one of its first appearances, the expression 'British Commonwealth of Nations': "We are not an Empire. Germany is an Empire, and so was Rome, and so is India; but we are ... a community of states and of nations far greater than any Empire that has ever existed ... not only a static system ... but a dynamic system, growing, evolving, all the time towards new destinies."[30]

FOOTNOTES

1 John Darwin, *The Empire Project* (2009), pp2-3.

2 James Belich, *Replenishing the Earth – The Settler Revolution and the Rise of the Anglo-World 1783-1939* p472.

3 Keith Jeffery, *British Isles/British Empire; dual mandate/dual identity*, in *The British Isles 1901-51,* ed. Keith Robbins OUP 2002, p13.

4 An illustration of variations comes from a comparison of the proportion of the population of each Dominion in uniform during the First World War: 11% UK, 8.8% New Zealand, 6.9% Australia, 5% Canada and only 2.2% of (white) South Africans. Quebec with 30% of the Canadian population produced only 5% of its volunteers. Glen St John Barclay *The Empire is Marching* Weidenfeld and Nicolson, 1976 p80.

5 Quoted in Vladimir Halperin, *Lord Milner and the Empire* (1952) p34.

6 Notably *Britain's Imperial Century, 1815-1914: a study of empire and expansion* (1976, 3rd edition 2002) and *Britain's Declining Empire: the Road to Decolonisation 1918-68* (2007).

7 Sir David Cannadine, *Ornamentalism: How the British Saw Their Empire* (2001). Jeremy Paxman, *Empire: What Ruling the World Did to the British* (2011), and Kwasi Kwarteng, *Ghosts of Empire* (2011). All three of these indulge in occasional "Imperial Tatlerism", slightly mocking descriptions of the social and educational background of colonial officials. Even Kwarteng, an Old Etonian, discusses various contentious characters who turn out to be Old Harrovians (op cit, pp46-7, 92, 106, 196, 329)!

8 Paxman, op cit, p285.

9 Kwarteng, pp381, 389-90.

10 Quoted in Vladimir Halperin, *Lord Milner and the Empire* (1952) p28.

11 These various quotes from Sir Llewellyn Woodward *The Age of Reform 1815-70,* pp367-8. Lord Elton states: "Bright and the Radicals sneered at the (Canadian) Confederation (in 1867) and suggested that the Canadian provinces might ... .join the United States." *Imperial Commonwealth*, p429. Elton was a redoubtable historian and a Labour supporter, particularly of Ramsay MacDonald, who enobled him.

12 Halperin, op cit, pp31-2.

13 Elton, op cit, pp368-9.

14 Quoted Darwin, *The Empire Project*, p99.

15 Op cit, p516.

16 Elton, op cit, pp365-6.

17 Quoted in Darwin, *Britain, Egypt and the Middle East* (1981), p96, my italics.

18 Roberts, op cit, p845.

19 Belich, op cit, pp470-1.

20 Robert Boyce, *The Great Interwar Crisis and the End of Globalism* (2009), especially pp425-32.

21 Paul Kennedy, *The Rise and Fall of the Great Powers* (1987), pp317, 319, citing Barnett, *Collapse* p564.

22 Kennedy, op cit, especially pp310-14. It was estimated in autumn 1938 that the French did not have any aircraft capable of bombing Germany. *British Military Preparations for the Second World War* by Sir Michael Howard, in *Retreat from Power* Vol I, 1906-39, edited by David Dilks, p114.

23 D. Cameron Watt, *Succeeding John Bull: America in Britain's Place* 1900-75 (1984), pp50-1; otherwise passim pp37-68.

24 Ibid, pp52 and 60. The Baldwin warning, slightly misquoted, is from the *Thomas Jones Diary* II,

for 8 March 1929 (not the same day 1928, as Watt cites).
25 Dilks ed, op cit, pp110, 113, 115. Liddell Hart published *The Real War1914-18* in 1930, enlarged as *A History of the World War 1914-18* in 1934.
26 *The Moscow Negotiations* by Lord Strang, Foreign Office diplomat who was present at these negotiations: from Dilks ed., op cit, pp170-86.
27 Niall Ferguson, *Empire-How Britain Made the Modern World* (2003), pp 216-7. He points out that, while the cost of British administration was 1% of Indian net domestic product a year between 1868 and 1930, in the same period the Dutch drained between 7 and 10% from their East Indies empire.
28 Elton, op cit, p504.
29 Darwin, *Project* pp194-201.
30 Quoted in Halperin, op cit, p 161.

CHAPTER ONE

The Loss of Ireland

"Aren't they a remarkable people? And the folly of thinking that we can ever understand, let alone govern them."
(Asquith to Venetia Stanley after the failure of the Buckingham Palace Conference, July 1914, quoted RJQ Adams, *Bonar Law* p166.)

The handling of Ireland between 1880 and 1922 merits discussion, for two reasons. First, there were various attempts to advance alternatives to full-blooded Home Rule which might have avoided the alienation of the majority of the Irish. Second, Ireland was a "first": it became, in practice, the first "British" territory to secede since the loss of the American colonies in 1783, and it thus created a precedent for, and perhaps encouraged, further secession.

We are, hopefully, in the 21st century seeing the end of terrible events in Ireland and a new harmony in relations within the British Isles: Brexit, however, will not help. But the story of Ireland as part of the United Kingdom was an unhappy one. While relations between Scotland and England were worst when they were independent states, before 1603, the position of Ireland in relation to the Crown was never a stable one, even in the centuries after Henry II's invasion and before the Reformation. The latter added a new problem[1]; thus there was a lengthy civil war under Elizabeth and shorter (but more brutal) conflicts in the 1640s, 1650s, and 1690s. England's enemy at the time, Spain, obtained a significant but temporary bridgehead in Ireland during the course of the Elizabethan war, but France later failed dismally to exploit Irish discontent in the 1690s and 1790s.

The Dublin Parliament was almost as ancient as the English Parliament – the earliest records date back to 1264. However it had long been dominated by the English and their supporters. In 1691, Catholics were excluded. In 1779, Lord North's government contemplated a full Union, but backed away. Ireland in 1798 rose in rebellion supported by French forces. Following this, Pitt set out to obtain a Union, with abolition of the Dublin Parliament. With substantial expenditure on bribery and lavish creation of peerages, this came about in 1801. The concomitant plan for Catholic emancipation was only to be implemented in 1829.

The Irish question bedevilled politics throughout the nineteenth century, and was exacerbated in the 1840s by the Potato Famine. Both the complexity of the problem and the intended official solution were aptly expressed in an important exchange in February 1844, during an eight-day Commons debate on Ireland. Lamenting the failure to introduce Catholic emancipation in 1801, Benjamin Disraeli said: "... They have a starving population, an absentee aristocracy, and an alien Church, and, in addition, the weakest executive in the world. That is the Irish question." What would MPs say, he asked "if they were reading of a country in that position? They would say at once, 'The remedy is revolution.' .... What then, is the duty of an English Minister? To effect by his policy all those changes which a revolution would do by force ..."[2]

On the final day of the debate, the Prime Minister, Sir Robert Peel, gave the official response: "We have witnessed with the highest satisfaction the gradual improvement of trade, and we trust the revival of prosperity in the commercial and manufacturing districts will be permanent." In contrast with Disraeli's call for a proactive policy, the approach of the Whig government of Lord John Russell was epitomised in 1848 by the Chancellor of the Exchequer, Sir Charles Wood (later 1st Viscount Halifax): "The more I see of government interference, the less I am disposed to trust to it, and I have no faith in anything but private capital employed under individual charge."[3] A further example of crude fantasy is seen in this reaction of *The Times* to the expectation that British capital and English and Scottish farmers would flock to Ireland: "In a few years more, a Celtic Irishman will be as rare in Connemara as is the Red Indian on the shores of Manhattan."[4]

Measures to reform land tenure were defeated or abandoned; a series of bad harvests in the early 1860s caused serious distress. Paradoxically, it was Gladstone in his budgets of 1853, 1854 and 1855 who raised Irish taxation. The only exception to this sorry position was in Ulster, where the linen industry, engineering and shipbuilding were rapidly expanding and, as in mainland Britain, absorbing much of the redundant rural population nearby. Unaffected, the rest of Ireland saw the rise of the Fenian Brotherhood – an oath-bound secret society which believed that British power could only be overthrown by force. Like its 20th century successors, it obtained great support in the USA, and after the American Civil War hundreds of experienced Irish officers returned to Fenian activities in Ireland. These took the form of terrorist acts, sometimes persuading the English of the need for reform, sometimes provoking measures of coercion.

In one of the brief spells of Conservative government in the mid 19th century, in 1868, Disraeli planned concurrent endowment of both Roman Catholicism and Presbyterianism in Ireland – "to level up not down" and to set up a Catholic University in Dublin. He "kept in close and cordial contact" with Cardinal Manning, the new Archbishop of Westminster and believed Manning favoured this scheme. Gladstone suddenly proclaimed that the Anglican establishment in Ireland should be swept away, and Manning ceased all further contact with Disraeli. "The character of Cardinal Grandison in *Lothair* was Disraeli's revenge."[5]

Gladstone proclaimed "My mission is to pacify Ireland" in December 1868 at the start of the first of his four administrations. Not seriously opposed by Disraeli, he disestablished the Anglican Church in Ireland. His 1870 Land Act had little practical effect on tenants' conditions. His introduction of the secret ballot in 1872 removed much of the influence of landlords; thus, in the general election of 1874, Liberal MPs in Ireland were largely displaced by 59 MPs who described themselves as "Home Rulers". They were led by Isaac Butt, who had been for a time an Orange Tory Dublin councillor and then a Conservative MP.

In 1870, the Home Government Association had been formed to demand, in Butt's words, "full control over our domestic affairs". The Home Rule cause was powerfully reinforced by the return at a by-election on 22 April 1875 of a Protestant landlord from Co Wicklow: Charles Stewart Parnell. Butt died in 1879, and after the 1880 election, the Irish parliamentary party (now 61 in number) elected Parnell as its leader.[6] He exploited Parliament's rules of procedure to delay business. The tenant farmers of Ireland, some of the poorest in Europe, were severely affected by the bad harvests of the late 1870s. Many attacks on landlords or their agents occurred during this "land war", leading to pressure in London for coercive measures.

While he was still a Radical Liberal, Joseph Chamberlain's sympathies for English labour against landlords led him to favour the agrarian agitators in Ireland, and he saw, better than others, the link between agrarian hardship and disaffection to British rule in Ireland. He pressed for support for a bill to compensate Irish tenants evicted for non-payment of rent, against resistance from the leader of the Whig wing of the government, Lord Hartington; the bill was rejected by the House of Lords. Chamberlain supported Gladstone's proposal for Grand Committees for England, Scotland and Ireland, but the Whig majority in the Cabinet rejected this. Eventually, in 1881, the government decided to proceed with a combination of coercive and land-reforming legislation – the former to please the Whigs, the latter the Radicals. Parnell became president of the Land League, but he was dissatisfied with Gladstone's Land Act of 1881 and his provocative language resulted in his imprisonment in Dublin and suppression of the league. Seven months later, secret negotiations (the "Kilmainham treaty") led to his release, and to new legislation which helped tenants with arrears of rent. The land legislation of 1881 and 1882 reduced agrarian unrest, but Irish resentment was retained by the fierce Crimes Act of 1882.[7]

Irish politics were further transformed by Gladstone's Franchise Act of 1884 which extended the vote to poorer tenant farmers, thus increasing Parnell's Nationalist support to 86 MPs in the 1885 election.[8] Perceiving the likelihood of this at the end of 1884, Chamberlain, seen as the most favourably disposed member of the Cabinet to Parnell's concerns, discussed through intermediaries measures that would meet some Irish aspirations. However, at the same time, in a letter to a correspondent with good contacts in Ireland, he explained his fixed principles and priorities: "I can never consent to regard Ireland as a separate people with the inherent rights of an absolutely independent community. I shall not do this in the case of Scotland, or of Wales … Ireland by its geographical position and by its history is a part of the United Kingdom, and it cannot divest itself of the obligations or be denied the advantages which this condition involves … If nationalism means separation, I for one am prepared to resist it … Sooner than yield on this point I would govern Ireland by force to the end of the chapter."[9]

However, as Mayor of Birmingham he had seen how effective popularly elected local government could be, and was prepared to move in this direction, proposing in a memorandum circulated on 25 April 1885 to his Cabinet colleagues (*Local Government in Ireland*) the creation of an elective central board for Ireland with legislative powers to deal with specifically Irish questions that did not require reference to the UK Parliament, such as education, local railways and perhaps other public works. Parnell, however, saw this only as a stop-gap: it was no substitute "for the restitution of our Irish Parliament", and proclaimed in public "no man has the right to fix the boundary of the march of a nation". The Catholic bishops of Ireland, through Cardinal Manning, were sceptical of the value of Home Rule and attracted by Chamberlain's idea of a central board.[10] Gladstone also was sympathetic, though nervous of Chamberlain's radical proposals for England and his general ambition, and therefore, as Chamberlain's recent biographer states, he "was determined to hold Chamberlain, more than any other member of the cabinet, at arm's length." Furthermore, "Gladstone could have thrown his weight behind the central board and brought most if not all of the Cabinet to accept it", including Hartington but perhaps not Earl Spencer, the Lord Lieutenant of Ireland. When the Cabinet considered the scheme on 9 May Gladstone did indicate support for the idea, but did not lobby for it. Thus with all the peers except Granville opposed, but all the commoners except Hartington supportive, the Cabinet was deemed to have rejected it: in Gladstone's words, it had become as "dead as mutton". Chamberlain was bitter; a great opportunity "has been lost owing to the pedantry and timidity of the Whigs." [11]

Party politics descended into temporary confusion. Chamberlain's ally Dilke resigned over renewal of coercion, obliging Chamberlain also to resign. Gladstone's government was defeated on a clause in the Budget by the Conservatives and Irish and resigned (June 1885). Under a minority Conservative government, awaiting the registration of the new electorate before a general election could be held, Lord Randolph Churchill and the new Lord Lieutenant of Ireland Lord Carnarvon[12] drew Parnell towards the Conservatives: Chamberlain was told that Parnell had had "a higher bid". At the same time (mid July 1885), the Dilke scandal (he was cited as co-respondent in the Crawford divorce case), "expelled Dilke from the innermost councils of the Liberal party" and thus reduced Chamberlain's influence there. The coolness of Gladstone was increased by Chamberlain's "Radical Programme" (known as "the Unauthorised Programme"), his vigorous attacks on ship-owners, including Liberals, who were resisting his proposals to protect merchant seamen from the owners' negligence, and, not least, by huge posters describing Chamberlain as "Your Coming Prime Minister". Parnell (September) announced "a platform with one plank only ... national independence"; a month later Chamberlain told his leader " I would rather let Ireland go altogether than accept the responsibility for a nominal union." Meanwhile, Gladstone's election manifesto was "blandness" – "a slap in the face to Chamberlain."[13]

In this December 1885 Election, the Liberals won just under half of the House of Commons. Parnell advised Irish voters in England to vote Conservative: it is thought this cost the Liberals between 20 and 65 seats.[14] On Ireland, Chamberlain was clearly hardening his heart: he had made the Irish a good offer, with his central board scheme, only to be rebuffed by them. Rumours of a radical move over Home Rule by Gladstone – still in Opposition; he did not return to Government until early February 1886 – were indicated by his son Herbert on 12 December 1885 with a letter published in *The Times*: "... if five-sixths of the Irish people wish to have a Parliament in management of their own local affairs, I say, in the name of justice, and wisdom, let them have it." Despite disclaimers in the name of the old man, this became known as "the Hawarden Kite", after Gladstone's North Wales home.

Chamberlain warned him (19 December): "it is my belief that we should sustain a tremendous defeat" in any election on Home Rule: "The English working classes ... are distinctly hostile to Home Rule ... & I do not think it would be possible to convert them before a General Election." Gladstone's personality and in particular his style of party management at this time contributed to the catastrophe: he "wrapped himself in silence or ambiguity and ignored most of his colleagues ... said nothing in public ... refused to answer letters from colleagues until the end of the year, when he put them off with polite evasions".[15]

At the turn of the year we find Chamberlain musing on alternative solutions, for example giving separate legislatures to the other parts of the UK, including possibly Ulster, as well as southern Ireland, while leaving Imperial affairs to Westminster, with a supreme court to arbitrate conflicts. It is, of course, a tragedy for the Empire that this radical approach was not pursued further or, indeed, acted upon. Some kind of federal system for the United Kingdom, perhaps with a dual mandate, might have permitted those Colonies which were to become Dominions to secure representation at Westminster, mainly for foreign affairs and defence, without any question of them interfering in genuinely internal British affairs. This was a notion frequently to be advanced in the 1890s and 1900s, but was always to fall on stony ground.[16]

Marsh gives numerous examples of Gladstone's aloofness towards Chamberlain in particular, and also the former's skill in consolidating support for his Home Rule proposals from Morley, hitherto a close Chamberlain ally, but now appointed Chief Secretary for Ireland, and Harcourt, who might have been sceptical.[17] The Cabinet discussion in mid March made the breach apparent. Chamberlain drafted ideas for the editorials of the *Birmingham Daily Post:* "any scheme of the kind attributed to Mr Gladstone will lead in the long run to the absolute national independence of Ireland", with Britain sinking "to the rank of a third rate Power, and its Foreign Policy ... complicated by perpetual references to the state of feeling in Ireland."[18]

Gladstone's determination not to compromise with Chamberlain led to the latter's resignation. Chamberlain explained: " a much smaller scheme would have produced greater friendliness ... It would have built up things by degrees instead of taking a leap in the dark ... This scheme ... will make the Irish hostile to any smaller scheme."[19]

The Second Reading on 8 June 1886 saw the Bill rejected by 343 to 313, with 93 Liberals voting against it. In the election which took place during July, only 191 Gladstonian Liberals were returned, with 85 Irish Nationalists, opposed by 316 Conservatives and 78 anti-Home Rule Liberal Unionists.

Chamberlain's approach of building things up by degrees might have led to something approaching Home Rule which he and others (though not the Whigs) might have accepted. The Irish would have been disappointed but not alienated; they would witness some constitutional progress rather than thirty-odd years of frustration. Once, however, Gladstone had offered them the "whole loaf" they were not likely to accept any half measures, especially as he continued to lead the Liberals until March 1894, maintaining his commitment to Home Rule. The Election of 1892 produced a minority Liberal government under him, dependent on Irish Nationalist votes. He introduced a new Home Rule Bill, which was passed in the Commons at second reading on 21 April 1893 by 43 votes and at third reading on 1 September by 34 votes, but was killed by the House of Lords which voted against by 419 votes to 41 on 8 September.

Chamberlain never returned to his Home Rule sympathies. Salisbury, who led the Unionist coalition and dominated politics until 1902, appears almost intemperate in his hostility to the Irish. Although he accepted that they had been subjected to great historical wrongs, and he opposed both the intolerance of Orangemen and absentee landlordism, his early journalism shows, in his biographer's words, that "Cecil ... intensely disliked Ireland and the Irish". He wrote in 1857 "England knows Ireland as well as a man knows the corn that has afflicted his spirit from early youth ... She has given us foreign invasions, domestic rebellions, and in quieter times the manly sport of landlord shooting." He welcomed Irish emigration, hoping that this would leave places "to be filled up by a Scotchman or Englishman over whom the vicious tradition has no power."[20]

Despite this unpromising approach, Unionist government saw progress for Ireland. Salisbury put his ostensibly detached dilettante nephew, A.J. Balfour, in charge as Chief Secretary in 1887, and "Bloody Balfour" restored order. He instituted a public works programme to "kill Home Rule with kindness", and, more importantly, he and his colleagues sought vigorously to tackle the causes of social discontent by eliminating the excesses of landlordism through land purchase. Inevitably, his earlier efforts, in 1888 and 1891, were disappointing, but the final measure, Wyndham's Act, after George Wyndham the Chief Secretary, was passed in 1903 and proved satisfactory to both landlords and tenants. In that year there were still 500,000 tenant farmers; by 1909 some 270,000 purchases had been negotiated, with nearly 50,000 pending, and by 1922, when the Irish Free State was established, only 70,000 remained unpurchased. A recent biographer describes the Wyndham Act as "an extraordinarily ambitious policy ... demand(ing) large scale capital expenditure ... with the fundamental aim being to remove the Irish landlord class. Never in European and certainly not in British history had state intervention on this scale been devoted to such an overt act of social engineering ... By 1910, two-thirds of land in Ireland had changed hands." [21]

The Irish issue subsided, not even to be resurrected when the Liberals returned to power in late 1905. They did not raise the issue in the 1906 election and most Liberal candidates failed to mention it in the two elections of 1910; Asquith himself was initially lukewarm, as was Sir Edward Grey, and Lloyd George and Churchill were more interested in welfare reform. However, the Liberal determination to remove the Lords' veto, arising out of the Lords' rejection of the 1909 Budget, coincided with the insistence of the Irish MPs on removing this last impediment to Home Rule. After this had been achieved in the 1911 Parliament Act, the Government, now dependent on Irish support, turned to Home Rule in 1912. The progress of the following ten years towards *de facto* Irish independence was at times dramatic, at times tragic. It would not be complete without reference to the strange "Lloyd George Offer" of 1910, the attempt between 1910 and 1918 by Austen Chamberlain and others in both main parties to secure a Federal solution to the Ulster and Irish issue, and the underlying threat, and occasional reality, of violence and civil war.

During the summer recess of 1910, Lloyd George drew up a memorandum, dated 17 August, proposing the formation of a coalition government to deal with various crucial issues. His biographer gives a full account, arguing that this was very much in Lloyd George's character; in contrast to his rhetoric (the "Limehouse" speech) he disliked excessive party conflict. He had already suggested a Constitutional Conference, taking place during that summer. The only reference to Ireland in this initial document was in character: "the advantages of a non-party treatment of this vexed problem are obvious."[22]

Lloyd George's associate at the start was Churchill, who had become his key ally in the Government; unfortunately, on account of his defection, he was heartily disliked by many Unionists. They explained it privately first in early October to Churchill's great Unionist friend, F. E. Smith. Smith informed Balfour who "lunched or dined" with Lloyd George; Balfour did not reject it out of hand but wanted to discuss it with colleagues. "It was not a firm proposal and Balfour only passed on the broadest summary to his colleagues."[23] Nor was the memorandum shown to the Unionist leaders; it was only summarised orally.

The package involved the Liberals conceding a stronger Navy, an element of compulsory military service, immediate Preference on existing duties and the appointment of a Commission to advise within six months what further duties it might be in Imperial interests to impose. In return, the Unionists would accept a reduction in the Lords' powers, the disestablishment of the Welsh Church, some changes in Balfour's Education Act, and various measures of social reform to which

Tariff Reform radicals would be sympathetic. But only later, at the end of October, did Lloyd George produce a second memorandum which was more specific about the Irish issue, to be "settled on some similar lines as were sketched by Mr Chamberlain in his speech on the First Reading of the Home Rule Bill of 1886". This was thought to be part of a process in which Lloyd George, having impugned Joseph Chamberlain's honour during the Boer War, sought reconciliation (Chamberlain had been crippled by a stroke in 1906). Whether, as Grigg acknowledges, he would be able to persuade his Liberal colleagues to abandon Gladstonian Home Rule is a different question. During talks with Balfour in secret "Lloyd George departed from his own brief and placed increasingly heavy emphasis on the solution of the Irish problem by devolution or federation."[24]

Thus the Offer was designed to attract Austen Chamberlain, but Balfour did not inform him of it until after Austen had heard of it, dining with Bonar Law, in mid October. Lloyd George made no effort to see that the Chamberlains heard of it. Austen was definitely attracted and ready "to give the most attentive and even friendly consideration to these proposals."[25]

Alfred Lyttleton, the former Unionist Colonial Secretary, wrote to Balfour that October saying there was "a very great sympathy with Local Federation (sic) among our younger intellectuals ... F. S. Oliver, Brand, Kerr and Milner's kindergarten, Milner himself, and Garvin."[26] Garvin, since 1908 editor of the *Observer,* wrote to Balfour, copied to Austen "would not an Ireland under Federal Home Rule send a solid *majority* [his italics] of Conservatives to help defend in the Imperial Parliament nearly all we care for." And Austen wrote to F. E. Smith that "each one of us" recognised "the vast importance of the results which Lloyd George holds out to us", adding "I am assured, as you are yourself, that Lloyd George has made this proposal in perfect good faith ... What he calls Federal Home Rule for the United Kingdom and what I should call Provincial Councils ... adds to the value of the proposal and increases its possible advantages." No such proposal "has been made to us or even hinted at either inside or outside" the Constitutional Conference.[27] Balfour, however, was "deeply suspicious of the Irish and not at all impressed by the fuzzy thinking and vague generalities of the federalists." It was later seen as a weakness that the Federalists did not draft any tentative schemes or draw upon the plans of the Scottish and Welsh home rulers.[28]

Two years later, as the Irish crisis was worsening, Austen recollected and reflected on this episode in a letter to Lansdowne. "I know that (Lloyd) George several months later said to me that his idea was 'something on your father's lines' ... and that he stated to Balfour that if the Nationalists would not take what was offered he would break with them."[29]

From all that is known of Balfour's character and caution, it is unsurprising that he was not attracted either to the policy package or the notion of coalition. His first reaction to Austen was typically expressed: "I did not take up a *non possumus* attitude ... I think it quite possible, though perhaps improbable, that a *modus vivendi* might be arrived at on the substance of a common policy if the enormous initial difficulties of a coalition could be overcome."[30] Balfour, it seems, would have compromised on tariffs, temperance and the Welsh Church but not on the Union: the plan "foundered on the issue of Ireland", where Balfour was "more fundamentalist" than Austen.[31] In the 1912 letter to Lansdowne, Austen reflects on the episode with some coldness: Balfour's "whole history", he said, "forbade his being a party to any form of Home Rule". Balfour made it clear to Lloyd George when they met on 2 November 1910 that he could not see how federalism was compatible with maintaining the Union.[32]

It was an indication of the resistance that Chamberlain and other Unionists would encounter, in the thick of the Home Rule crisis of 1913-4, when they urged an alternative route. These others included F. S. Oliver, who had been promoting, between 20 October and 2 November, by letters to *The Times* under the pseudonym *Pacificus,* ideas about "Home Rule All Round" as a means of rescuing central government from overload.

In fact, the federation/devolution issue had not been silent since the Home Rule debacle of 1885-6. In the late 1880s the right-wing *National Review* carried an article advocating Imperial federation as a solution to the Irish problem. Ireland would obtain a separate legislature, as many colonies possessed, and Irish representatives like them would sit in an Imperial assembly: "The Irish would be contented, having secured for themselves the management of their own affairs, to remain part and parcel of that Empire in whose imperial business they had a voice."[33]

The main activity was on the Liberal side. In 1885 Rosebery introduced legislation to establish a Scottish Office headed by a Secretary for Scotland. Although the Gladstone government fell before Second Reading, the Salisbury government ensured it was passed before Parliament was dissolved. There was some agitation for Scottish Home Rule after this but Home Rulers were rarely in a majority in Scotland; however, "as many as 60 out of the 72 Scottish members favoured Scottish Home Rule."[34] On 9 April 1889 a motion on Scottish Home Rule was defeated by 200 to 79 with 22 of the 72 Scottish MPs voting against and only 19 in favour. The main argument deployed then and later by proponents was the neglect at Westminster of Scottish affairs like education, public health and police. Motions calling for Home Rule All Round were put forward in 1891 and 1892, but in 1891 the House was counted out and in 1892 the motion was lost by 74 to 54. On 3 April 1894 a motion calling for a Scottish legislature was carried by 180 to 170, but a year later another Home Rule All Round motion was lost by 128 to102. Henry Campbell-Bannerman, who was later to be Liberal Prime Minister, stated that Irish Home Rule would involve Scottish Home Rule "as sure as eggs is eggs".[35]

A federal scheme was high on the agenda of the Cabinet committee set up to prepare a Home Rule Bill in February 1911. While Birrell, the Irish Secretary, was the only one to oppose it because it might delay Home Rule for Ireland, Churchill, Haldane and Lloyd George were enthusiastic and Grey, Loreburn and Samuel were moderately supportive. The absence of any appetite for devolution in England came to be seen as the obstacle: Sir Courtney Ilbert, Clerk of the Commons, criticised Churchill's ideas, which were then quietly dropped. As Asquith wrote to C. P. Scott in July 1911 "we could not go back to the Heptarchy."[36]

The Irish leaders Redmond and Dillon wanted the 1912 Bill to keep to the earlier Gladstone models with no references to devolution to Scotland and Wales; these would lead to prolonged debates and the possible killing of the Bill. "The Scottish Liberals who favoured Home Rule All Round were bitterly disappointed but prepared to vote in principle for the Bill as a first step towards a more comprehensive scheme." In May 1912 a deputation of Scottish Liberal MPs urged Asquith to introduce a Scottish Home Rule Bill in the next session. Asquith could not promise this but said he would like to apply devolution to all parts of the UK "by appropriate methods". During the next six months these Scottish Liberals "proved a major worry to the Liberal Government."[37]

Some senior Unionists were thinking along these lines as a solution to the whole Irish problem and especially the problem of Ulster. After 1912, the readiness of the new Unionist leader, Bonar Law, to go to extremes in his support of Ulster is a matter of historical record; Balfour and the Cecils found the Ulstermen "deeply antipathetic".[38] However, Austen Chamberlain, who nearly became leader of the Party in 1911, found Law's attitude "rash" and his language "dangerous", and had doubts "about the desirability of indicating that ... opposition ... might go beyond the limits of ordinary constitutional action."[39] He was also concerned that the Government might well be forced to exclude Ulster from Home Rule, which would largely satisfy British public opinion but would break faith with Irish Unionists in the South. So he welcomed the idea of Home Rule All Round, which he told Lansdowne, "would be infinitely less dangerous than the present Bill even with Ulster excluded." Discussing the question with Churchill in November 1913, Austen also "got the impression that Churchill and several other Liberal ministers genuinely wanted a settlement, without themselves knowing how to achieve one."

In addition to Lansdowne, former Foreign Secretary and co-leader (as Leader of the Opposition in the Lords) of the Unionists from 1911 to 1916, Carson, the Ulster leader, was a potential ally and was believed to be sympathetic to the federal solution "if Wales, Scotland etc were being treated as an equal party with Ireland." However, "though privately sympathetic ....(he) could not publicly move from his stand upon Ulster." F. E. Smith believed in federalism but was "trusted even less by his own side than by the Liberals", while Balfour, as we have seen, "crucially ... believed in exclusion (of Ulster), not federalism, as the only viable solution to the present stalemate."[40] Unfortunately, Austen Chamberlain was abroad until late October 1913, so momentum was lost.

In November 1913 Oliver published his pamphlet *The Alternative to Civil War*, and by early December, the ministers Haldane, Morley, Lloyd George and Grey were affirming their enthusiasm for federation, with even Asquith now believed to be sympathetic. On the Unionist side, Lansdowne, Chamberlain, Selborne and Lord Robert Cecil were supportive, and a dinner between Chamberlain, Smith, Churchill, and Morley on the 8th carried high hopes. However, "what was also clear from these meetings was a hesitance on both sides to commit themselves." Little progress took place in meetings between Asquith and Carson on 16 December and 2 January 1914: the wider federal case "was not even raised". As Oliver sadly reflected to Milner "They don't seem to have realised or visualised what federalism or anything else means."[41]

If Asquith had accepted Home Rule All Round, it was believed that the combination of Chamberlain, Carson, Lansdowne, Balfour, Selborne and Curzon would have been "more than enough" to persuade Law. But by March 1914 it was clear that Asquith was against the idea, with Chamberlain declaring "the government have finally and deliberately shut the door on any federal solution."[42] Historians believe that Asquith had toyed with federalism as a method of delaying events, dividing the opposition and keeping his Scottish and Welsh MPs in line, while remaining fixed to orthodox Home Rule. Law saw federalism as a threat to his key political strategy of forcing an election which he hoped to win. And support for compromise weakened among the Unionists after March 1914 as a result of mounting extremism; for example, Milner and Amery were keen on federalism in 1912 and 1913 but by 1914 they were organising the British Covenant. Dates are significant: Asquith's compromise scheme for Ulster of excluding from Home Rule areas which would automatically come under it after six years was leaked to the *Daily News* on 9th March and immediately rebutted by Carson as "sentence of death with a stay of execution for six years."

There was a final pre-war splutter of the federalists on 5 May 1914, when Law, Balfour, Carson, Lansdowne and Chamberlain met, the last named said that he and Lansdowne "had from the first laid more stress than Carson and Law on the Imperial aspect of the Home Rule Bill and therefore had been anxious to prevent the impression growing that you only had to cut out Ulster in order to make the bill safe."[43] Leo Amery looked to Austen to make the wider case, having written to him the previous day "if there is to be a compromise on some form of federalism or devolution it cannot be by tinkering with this Bill ... but it does involve a start *de novo*".[44] However, not only would the Unionist leadership not press this line, but there was no sign of Asquith looking at it. Austen took no part in the Buckingham Palace Conference in July, the last attempt to avoid the clash of arms, as his father suffered two heart attacks leading to his death on 2 July 1914.

The alternative to these compromise efforts certainly seemed to be violence, if not civil war. The narrative in *The Ulster Crisis: Resistance to Home Rule 1912-14* by A. T. Q. Stewart describes the drift into the abyss. It shows the recruitment and drilling of military-style units of "volunteers", who eventually totalled around 90,000, officered by retired British Army officers and commanded by respected veterans (who at times communicated in Hindustani to avoid discovery). Two key

UK figures, fully aware of what was going on, were Major General Sir Henry Wilson, Director of Military Operations, an Irishman whose family had been given land in Antrim by William III, and Field Marshal Sir John French, the Chief of the Imperial General Staff. Both these were to have huge responsibilities imposed on them on the outbreak of the European War, the latter commanding the Expeditionary Force to France.

The Ulster leaders aimed to use these units to prevent Ulster being administered from Dublin under the Home Rule arrangement, and to establish a Provisional Government to ensure this. It was not so much an ethnic objection, with the descendants of Scots and English settlers wishing to resist domination by Irish of mainly Celtic ancestry; it was religious. In Stewart's words, "even better-informed Protestants believed the society of southern Ireland to be priest-dominated, and feared that an independent Irish administration would be dictated to by the bishops and that consequently their civil and religious liberty would in some way be curtailed."[45] Because they were confident of holding the territory of Ulster, these units and more particularly their leaders did not envisage fighting Catholic Nationalist forces, though there was always the possibility that they might have to. Their main fear was that they might have to fight the forces of the Crown, seeking to enforce the Home Rule Act. By no means did this create reluctance; considerable, well-financed, and well-organised efforts were made to import armaments. An indemnity guarantee fund to compensate supporters and their dependants for any loss or disability they might suffer on Ulster's behalf was opened and by 1 January 1914, pledges to this fund totalled over £1 million – an immense private sum for those days.[46]

As early as the summer of 1913 we see purchases of Maxim machine guns being made of Vickers in London, as well as of rifles and small arms ammunition. With complaints by the "Volunteer" units that they had insufficient arms, an amazing venture took place. This involved the successful transport, during March and April 1914, of 35,000 mainly new Austrian and German rifles, with around 3 million rounds of ammunition, first from Hamburg onto *SS Fanny* located by a Danish island, thence via Great Yarmouth, Lundy Island and North Wales to Tuskar Rock, off the east coast of Ireland; and thence, via a collier, to landings at Larne, Bangor and Donaghadee, all near Belfast. They were then distributed by motor car (the UVF, unlike the mainland army, appreciated the superiority of the motor over horse-drawn transport!). Local units of Volunteers, carrying out a "test mobilisation", occupied these ports while the arms were being landed and immobilised telephones and telegraphs, while peacefully ensuring non-intervention by police and customs.[47] By July 1914, the Volunteers were estimated to have 37,000 rifles.

Preparations were not confined to Ulster. In early 1914, Lord Milner initiated a British Covenant organised by the Union Defence League. Launched on 3 March, this stated that if the Bill was passed "I shall hold myself justified in taking or supporting any action that may be effective to prevent it being put into operation, and more particularly to prevent the armed forces of the Crown being used to deprive the people of Ulster of their rights as citizens of the United Kingdom." The first signatories included besides Milner, Field Marshal Lord Roberts, the "most distinguished British soldier alive", Kipling, Sir Edward Elgar and Professor A. V. Dicey. Two million had signed by the end of July 1914. Demonstrations and pledges of practical support came from the various provinces of Canada, from New Zealand and South Africa, and even from Australia where "the very strength of Nationalist support ... stimulated the Australian Orangemen into action."[48]

These preparations were not against an imaginary occurrence. The government in London had begun to prepare military measures. The 3rd Battle Fleet was ordered to Lamlash on the Ulster coast, and Churchill, First Lord of the Admiralty, on 14 March, made a menacing speech in Bradford, culminating in the well known declaration "let us go forward together and put these grave matters to the proof". On the 18th and 19th Sir Arthur Paget, Commander-in-Chief Ireland was told at a conference with Asquith, Seely, the War Secretary, and Churchill, to order the 3rd Cavalry Brigade (at Curragh) to seize the bridges across the Boyne, while the remaining troops in Ireland, assisted if necessary by an additional division from England, would advance into Ulster. The intention, clearly, was to overawe any resistance by the suddenness of the move and the concentration of forces. However, it led directly to what has become known as the "Curragh Mutiny", whereby 59 out of a total of 72 officers in the Cavalry Brigade said they would prefer to be dismissed "if ordered north". There is little doubt that officers in other units felt the same, and that they all carried the sympathy of their men. Thus by the 21st March it was clear that whatever was envisaged towards Ulster could not be carried out; the military and naval moves were stopped.

Modern readers would mostly disapprove strongly of much of this – the organising of militias and the gun-running – and recent historians reflect that disapproval.[49] It certainly has no parallel in British history since, perhaps appropriately, the "Glorious Revolution" of 1688, a recent west European parallel being the French army rising in 1958 which brought de Gaulle to power. Right or wrong, it must be accepted that the initiative towards violent resistance came from within Ulster itself – it was not hatched in Westminster. Of the Unionist leaders, fully committed to supporting Ulster, whatever ensued, all – Law, Balfour, Carson, Curzon – went on to hold high office during and after the First World War; Law, indeed, was to be Prime Minister. Nor did their involvement count against them electorally at the time: a total of 15 by elections were contested during 1913, in which the Unionists gained three seats, and in a total of 8 contested up to the end of May 1914, they also gained three seats.

Lloyd George and Churchill (despite the Bradford speech) had privately felt from the beginning that Ulster should be excluded from the Bill. The Government began to refer openly to the possibility of special treatment, and Churchill raised it publicly in October, but three days later Redmond declared his opposition: "Ireland is a unit ... the two nation theory is to us an abomination and a blasphemy." Secret meetings between Law and Asquith, first at Max Aitken's house on 14 October, and later in the year failed. Meetings and correspondence between Asquith and Carson over Christmas and New Year were also barren. Asquith was beginning to move towards the Ulster case, but what he offered was regarded by Law and Carson (and, indeed, the King, advising Asquith) as inadequate. There was no question of separate devolution to Ulster; Law was insisting that it remain represented by the Westminster Parliament.[50]

Why had Asquith been so reluctant to compromise? There was an element of determined principle, but that should surely have thawed in the light of the risks and the lack of enthusiasm of various of his colleagues. There was the survival factor: by the summer of 1914, as a result of by-election losses since December 1910, the Unionists had 287 seats, as against 257 for the Liberals, 42 for Labour and 84 for the Nationalists. If Asquith conceded Ulster's demands, the Government could no longer depend on Nationalist support, and it is conceivable that Labour would have turned against it. Would, however, the Unionists vote with these two latter parties and would Redmond turn Asquith out, thus dooming Home Rule?

After the Home Rule Bill had been carried for the third time on 26 May, with only Royal Assent between it and implementation, the Buckingham Palace Conference took place. Asquith and the Nationalists were prepared to give way on the time limit for exclusion, but would not say so until there was agreement over the geographical extent of the excluded area. This was never reached; they disagreed over Tyrone.[51] While the Liberals feared an election, the Unionists were hoping for one. That was the calculation of die-hards like Amery, who wrote to Neville Chamberlain on 25 July, after the failure of the Conference, "even the acceptance by the Government of the 'clean cut' for the whole province of Ulster would have led to a tremendous explosion of indignation from our Party against our leaders for bringing us into a position where we should virtually ... have accepted Home Rule for the rest of Ireland. I have never seen such a scene of anger in our Lobby as there was when the Conference was first announced, and it was only when assurances spread round that there was no likelihood of anything coming of it that feeling was in the least mollified ... We are now in a splendid position ... back on the broad ground of the maintenance of the Union and of the right of the nation to decide."[52]

Events were to dictate a more violent path, with near fatal consequences for any residual communal sentiments between the Nationalist Irish and their fellow UK citizens. They were further provoked by the delays in carrying through the Home Rule legislation. In opposition to the relative moderation of Redmond and his colleagues, Sinn Fein propaganda spread, exploiting the impatience of "young men who had lost faith in the middle-aged and elderly politicians of the parliamentary party"[53] to form the Irish Volunteers. Originally organised in Dublin in November 1913, by the following July, its numbers were up to 100,000. On

26 July, a small yacht, steered by Mrs Erskine Childers, landed 2500 rifles and 125,000 rounds of ammunition at Howth; there was a clash with troops, with some casualties.

Redmond also lost support by his endorsement of participation in the European war, but he also saw that the war created an opportunity for reconciliation between Ireland and Britain while promoting a distinctive Irish corps. Kitchener, however, regarded Nationalists as inherently disloyal and scarcely bothered to disguise his low expectations. Few leading Catholic Home Rulers were chosen by the authorities to serve as recruiting agents. Officers in Irish units tended to be Protestants while their men were often Catholic. Few Irish MPs were admitted into the Army.[54] Redmond wanted a specific Irish army corps that united soldiers from Ulster and Nationalist Volunteers; some of his most enthusiastic supporters among the Volunteers went to France and were killed, including his brother who died of wounds in June 1917. While Australian nationhood was strengthened by Gallipoli, Redmond was, unimaginatively, denied his vision, and his credibility suffered. Despite his contentious pre-war role, the First Coalition in 1915 saw Carson appointed Attorney General, while Redmond was not included. Asquith's offers to Redmond are well documented, whereas "Redmond's refusal of office was ... highly questionable, certainly when judged with the benefits of hindsight."[55]

A more extreme element, totalling only about 11,000, seceded from the main body of the Volunteers, and even among these were divisions over whether an armed rising was sensible. Contradictory orders ensured that the Easter Monday Rising of April 1916 was mainly confined to Dublin. The rebels surrendered after seven days of fighting, and initially were condemned by much of Irish public opinion, with Redmond denouncing them in Parliament. However, 15 of the insurgent leaders were executed and public opinion turned against the executions and to sympathy for the insurgents.[56] This further helped to explain the rise to dominance of Sinn Fein and the eclipse of Redmond's party; he died in March 1918.

The Government intended conscription in Ireland to sit alongside a new Home Rule Bill, to implement the recommendation for a single Irish Parliament in Dublin made by a Convention representing the nationalists, the Ulster Unionists and the Southern Unionists, under Sir Horace Plunkett. "The numbingly protracted sessions of the convention meant that the chances of a speedy settlement soon receded," while the death of Sir Alexander McDowell "may well have scuppered the possibility of a broadly based deal including the Ulstermen". A chasm opened up between Lord Midleton, the Southern Unionist leader, and the Ulstermen, while Lansdowne was seen to have been discredited by advocating peace with Germany in November 1917. Plunkett is criticised for delays and long debates, while Redmond's successor Dillon was much less consensual and more sympathetic to the aspirations of Sinn Fein.[57] And conscription was vigorously opposed by all Nationalist opinion, including the Roman Catholic bishops. Sinn Fein obtained the credit for the eventual decision not to extend conscription, while the Home Rulers, who had (after voting against it) withdrawn from Westminster in protest, "had virtually admitted their own impotence."[58] Thus , in the 1918 General Election in Ireland, Sinn Fein saw 73 candidates elected; the Unionists won 26 seats, and the late Redmond's Home Rulers only 6.[59] The Sinn Feiners ignored Westminster, met in Dublin in January 1919, proclaimed themselves the parliament of the Irish Republic and re-affirmed the declaration of independence of 1916. Now real civil war resulted.

During 1917 F. S. Oliver and Lord Selborne had continued work on the federal issue – helping to persuade Carson who told Plunkett that a federal solution was the only principle "upon which a settlement was possible". After the publication of Oliver's *Ulster and a Federal Settlement,* Carson wrote to Lloyd George on 14 February 1918 "the only possible solution seems to me to lie in a system of Federation for the whole United Kingdom". However other Ulster Unionists refused to take this plan seriously. A well attended meeting of Unionists on 24 April persuaded Amery that the federal concept was winning many adherents: he estimated, perhaps optimistically, that 150 Unionists would support a Federal Bill, which would carry with Liberal and Labour support. Lloyd George, nervous about the reluctance of the English to go down a federal track, and reluctant to disturb the party and constitutional balance during wartime, was unconvinced.[60]

Before this, the War Cabinet had set up yet another committee, chaired by Walter Long, Influenced by Long and Austen Chamberlain, this leaned towards the solution of a federal United Kingdom, but Balfour opposed this in discussion on 23 April 1918. By late June Long had drafted a Bill "for a federal system for the UK": the simultaneous establishment of national parliaments for England, Scotland, Wales and Ireland with the UK Parliament supreme but reduced to 350 members. In a Cabinet discussion in June Balfour and Curzon expressed disagreement with the attempt to "pull up the British constitution by the roots", and Lloyd George argued that unless a substantial majority of English representatives were in favour, on account of the size of England, it was idle to attempt it. Long regretted the delay and told Lloyd George that the old type of Home Rule was "as dead as Queen Anne. Federalism is the only substitute."[61]

With guerilla war now raging, another Cabinet committee, also chaired by Long, was appointed in early October 1919. The gist of its various reports between November 1919 and February 1920 was for the creation of one Parliament for the three southern provinces of Ireland and a second one for Ulster, together with a Council of Ireland composed of members of the two. However, the Cabinet on 24 February agreed on a bill setting up one Parliament for the six counties of the north and another for the remainder of the island – in fact, the structure for next 50 years. This bill obtained second reading on 31 March, then languished (as violence in Ireland outside the six counties did not abate) , and finally received Royal Assent in December 1920.[62]

The so-called Irish "War of Independence" lasted until a fragile truce in July

1921, with Lloyd George then in secret communication with De Valera. The Irish rebels "succeeded in making normal government impossible, but ... could not force the withdrawal of the British forces."[63] British public opinion, however, would never tolerate the effort and the bloodshed necessary to re-conquer Ireland systematically. In negotiations during October and November 1921, the principal Irish representatives, Michael Collins and Arthur Griffith, were thought to be prepared to accept that the Irish Free State should become a self-governing Dominion within the Empire, with the King as Head of State, but they insisted that Northern Ireland should be subject to the Dublin Parliament. Lloyd George put this to the Ulster leader, Sir James Craig, believing he would accept. Craig seems to have been firmed up by a visit from Bonar Law (who, having resigned office earlier in the year, had been recuperating in the south of France) and rejected the idea. Law was in fact prepared to break with Lloyd George over this, and the latter realised his dependence on a Unionist majority which would reject any coercion of Ulster. This was made clear at the annual Unionist party conference (appropriately enough, in Liverpool) a few days later.[64]

On 6 December the treaty was signed, with the Free State accepting the Empire and the King, but with the six counties separated, and the boundary to be determined. Britain retained responsibility for coastal defence and the maintenance of naval establishments in certain Irish ports. By 1939, these naval concessions had been surrendered; as Amery wrote in 1953 "We shrugged our shoulders somewhat regretfully at what the loss of most of Ireland meant in sunken ships and lost lives in this last war."[65]

The treaty, however, was sufficiently disappointing to many of the Nationalists that an Irish Civil War, between pro-treaty and anti-treaty forces, took place (June 1922-May 1923). The murder on 22 June 1922 of Field Marshal Sir Henry Wilson, recently elected MP for North Down, led to outrage in Britain and successful pressure on Collins to attack the Dublin rebels, who had occupied the Four Courts. This Civil War saw greater loss of life than the War of Independence, and during its last six months almost twice as many republican prisoners were executed by the Free State authorities as had been executed by the British during the whole period 1916-21,[66] while Griffith died of heart failure and Collins was assassinated.

The Irish "War of Independence" was the first such conflict to occur in the British Isles since the Wolfe Tone revolt of 1798. It was also, if the Indian Mutiny and the rather different Boer War are excluded, the first violent conflict that Britain faced as part of the process of retreat from Empire, and it has similarities as well as contrasts with later, post 1945, conflicts, in Palestine, Malaya, Kenya and Cyprus. Did the Irish experience show that the Imperial Colossus had feet of clay? Did it dispirit the British from fighting their corner? What is perhaps significant is that, until after 1945, no other part of the colonial Empire[67] followed the Irish example and resorted to violence and guerrilla activity – and by 1950 the international climate in which the Empire existed had changed completely.

FOOTNOTES

1 In the middle ages, Ireland was generally regarded as a Papal possession because the Donation of Constantine had given all Western islands to St Peter and his successors. The Donation is of course a forgery – but it was regarded as valid for some centuries after 1100.

2 Commons Hansard, 16 February 1844.

3 Quoted in J. C. Beckett, *The Making of Modern Ireland 1603-1923* p 352; Beckett comments "the Irish landlords were, as a body, too poor, too incompetent, too selfish, to initiate any general improvement themselves."

4 Quoted Beckett, p 353.

5 Robert Blake, *Disraeli*, pp 496-7.

6 Butt and Parnell were both firm parliamentarians; they were also "social conservatives" and there are signs that either might have co-operated with British Conservatives. Thirty years later, one of the proposers of a federal scheme, Earl Grey, said "The Catholic Celt is against Socialism, against secularisation and for Tariff Reform," Quoted in Jeremy Smith *The Tories and Ireland 1910-14* p29. And a "leaning" towards the Tories was "shared by a disparate group of Home Rulers, including T. M. Healy and perhaps Parnell himself, who was much closer on many issues and indeed in political temperament to Tory cynics like Randolph Churchill than to the principled radicals, pious Nonconformists and high-minded Gladstonians who comprised the Liberal front bench". Alvin Jackson *Home Rule – An Irish History 1800-2000*, p50.

7 Forster, the Chief Secretary for Ireland, had resigned over the Kilmainham change of policy; tragically, his successor, Lord Frederick Cavendish, younger brother of Lord Hartington, and an official who was the real target, were both murdered by terrorists in Phoenix Park, Dublin, in May 1882.

8 Significantly for future politics, the number of Irish members was not reduced from that established in 1800 and 1832, despite the dramatic fall of the Irish population as a proportion of that of the whole UK.

9 Letter of 17 December 1884 to a long-time Walsall supporter, quoted more fully in John Kendle *Ireland and the Federal Solution: The Debate over the UK Constitution 1870-1921* p25.

10 Compare "Concern for Crown and Empire (even if one was Protestant and the other British) had a surprisingly long tenure within the pre war Catholic establishment." Jackson, op cit, p102.

11 This episode, with quotations, from Peter T. Marsh, *Joseph Chamberlain: Entrepreneur in Politics*, pp193-8, also Kendle op cit, p28.

12 Carnarvon was largely responsible for federal self-government in Canada in 1867 and had later worked on similar proposals for South Africa. He favoured a similar approach to Anglo-Irish relations.

13 Marsh, op cit, pp205-208.

14 See Andrew Roberts *Salisbury: Victorian Titan* p332 for Salisbury's role in encouraging this: "more than willing to keep up the pretence ... perhaps cynical ... it worked spectacularly well."

15 Marsh, op cit, p221. Also Jackson, op cit, p64 "his infuriatingly legalistic and ambiguous statements ... were seemingly designed to mislead."

16 For example, Cecil Rhodes supported Home Rule for Ireland because he thought it would promote "imperial federation" (Beckett, op cit, p403 footnote).

17 Marsh, op cit, pp223-4, 232-33. Marsh explains how the breach was exacerbated by personalities: "Chamberlain had been driven to rebel more by Gladstone's treatment of him than by the proposals for Home Rule ... The old captain proceeded to treat the debate over Home Rule as a personal contest." Rather than "bide his time", Chamberlain "was too angry and too ardent to wait" (p236). In 1893, at dinner with Chamberlain, Rosebery recalled these last Cabinet meetings and remarked that, had it not been for Gladstone, "our differences might have been arranged" (p354). Marsh contrasts the bitterness of the Gladstonians towards Chamberlain, because the "disagreement was narrower", with their lesser hostility towards Hartington, whose opposition was "uncompromising" (p244). None of this is unique in politics!

18 Quoted ibid, p233.
19 Both quotes ibid, p235-6.
20 Roberts, op cit, pp52-55.
21 E. H. H. Green, *Balfour* p42.
22 John Grigg, *Lloyd George,* pp261-74. The 17th August Memorandum is on pp362-8. The Lloyd George Offer is discussed in Julian Amery's *Life of Joseph Chamberlain, Vol VI*, pp 955-6, Marsh, op cit, p657 and David Dutton, *Austen Chamberlain: Gentleman in Politics* pp71-3.
23 Amery, op cit, p955.
24 Grigg, op cit, p269-71; Kendle, op cit, p119.
25 Austen Chamberlain, *Politics from the Inside,* p283-4.
26 Kendle, op cit, p120.
27 *Politics from the Inside,* pp283-4. Garvin to Balfour, 20 October 1910; A. Chamberlain to Smith 21 October. Chamberlain's description "Provincial Councils" aptly pictures his unimaginative mind: one can hardly see the Irish Nationalists being seduced by the phrase.
28 Kendle, op cit, p123.
29 *Politics from the Inside,* p292; letter written 26 August 1912. Lansdowne, who had large landed interests in the South of Ireland, was sympathetic to Austen's view.
30 *Politics from the Inside,* p288; letter dated 22 October 1910.
31 Grigg, op cit, p272.
32 Quoted Dutton, op cit, p71; *Politics from the Inside,* p293.
33 Quoted Kendle, op cit, p37.
34 Patricia Jalland, *UK Devolution 1910-14: Panacea or Tactical Diversion?* English Historical Review No 94, 1979, pp757-85.
35 Kendle, op cit, pp66-7, 80-1.
36 Jalland, op cit, p765.
37 Kendle, op cit, pp147, 150.
38 Law was the son of a Presbyterian minister who had been born in Ulster and had died there, having spent much of the intervening period in Canada. Roy Jenkins, *Asquith,* pp275-6, sniffs at Law's "poor white" sense of inferiority.
39 Dutton, op cit, pp103-6 for this episode; the quotes are from his account.
40 Smith, op cit, p121; see p163-4 for Carson telling Oliver "If we were being treated similarly to all other elements of the UK we could hardly assert the right to resist by force something which was equally being given to all members of the community in which we live."
41 Ibid, pp130-1, 120.
42 Ibid, pp161, 164.
43 Austen Chamberlain to Mary Chamberlain 5 May 1914, quoted Dutton, p106.
44 *The Leo Amery Diaries Vol I* edited by John Barnes and David Nicholson, p100. In early 1912 Amery wrote 17 articles for the *Morning Post,* subsequently published as *The Case Against Home Rule.* He argued that it "flies in the face of all the facts of geography, of history, of economics ... Under the Union the common tariff of the United Kingdom and (its) market ... will be devoted to building up Ireland's agriculture and Ireland's industries." In a Commons speech in April 1912 he described the UK as "more compact than the island nation of Japan or the sea-girt nation of Italy." *My Political Life* I pp401, 405.
45 Stewart, op cit, p43.
46 Stewart describes documents which show detailed plans for disrupting transport and telegraph and telephone communications, capturing arms depots and "wherever possible the guns of any field artillery", as well as this: "All avenues of approach by road for troops or police into Ulster should be closed by isolated detachments of men occupying defensive positions commanding such roads". Ibid pp126-7.
47 Ibid, pp76-77.

48 Ibid, pp134-5, 138-9.
49 Roy Jenkins, op cit, and Ian Gilmour (*Inside Right* p33) link it in to the whole 1906-14 period of opposition: the latter stating that at this time the Conservative party "betrayed itself and came close to betraying its country". Adams, *Bonar Law* p109, cites others. However, a more subtle point is made by John Ramsden, *The Age of Balfour and Baldwin* (p79): "at bottom there was some democratic basis for the Unionists' case, for the Government was pressing on with a reform that they knew was not backed by the electorate."
50 Jenkins, op cit, p291. Adams refers to these "sterile discussions", which Law reported to Lansdowne, Balfour and Long, who was also concerned about the Southern Unionists. In December, Asquith tried to interest Law in the "long-cold" idea of UK-wide devolution which "continued to fascinate Churchill and (Austen) Chamberlain" who had been in touch on this subject. Law "impatiently brushed" this aside, (op cit, p141).
51 Adams, op cit, p 165. There is a peculiarly "Irish" element about the disagreement; the opposing leaders had very good personal relations. Asquith described their attitude; " Each said 'I must have the whole of Tyrone, or die, but I quite understand why you say the same.' " Neither would accept a proposal by the Speaker, following Solomon, of cutting the county in half. Jenkins, op cit, p321.
52 Barnes and Nicholson, op cit, p101. The Unionists attended the Conference out of deference to the King.
53 Beckett, op cit, pp430-1. Jenkins (op cit, p280) refers to Asquith's erroneous view of Redmond as having a "Parnell-like hold on the country".
54 Jackson, op cit, p145-6.
55 Ibid, p149.
56 Beckett, op cit, p441. Contrast one execution after the De Wet revolt in South Africa in 1914, see p53.
57 Jackson, op cit, pp179-83. Also pp189-90 critical of Plunkett.
58 Ibid, p445.
59 Support for Sinn Fein "was strong among the young and with women" both of which benefitted from the extension of the franchise in 1918. Jackson, op cit, p186.
60 D. G. Boyce and J. O. Stubbs *FSOliver, Lord Selborne and Federalism* in the Journal of Imperial and Commonwealth History 1976, pp53-81, especially pp68-73. Jackson (op cit, p188) cites the Government Whip, Freddie Guest, estimating 100 federalist Unionist sympathisers, and a total of nearly 200 in the other parties. But see Jackson p194 for a critique of Oliver, whose "quirky convictions" made his relationship with both main parties "often highly fraught."
61 Kendle, op cit, p207.
62 Adams, op cit, pp286-7.
63 Beckett, op cit, p448.
64 Adams, op cit, pp301-5, which quotes Law writing to his confidante J. P. Croal, editor of *The Scotsman,* setting out what he told the Prime Minister to say to Collins and Griffith: "If you form a constitution within the Empire and behave decently to Protestants there and make no attempt against Ulster, we will not interfere with you. We will allow trade to go on as at present ... If you don't behave decently we will spend no more British blood in Ireland. We will fight you by economic blockade."
65 *My Political Life,* I p399.
66 Beckett, op cit, p 459.
67 Apart from the exceptional circumstances of Arab and then Jewish violence in the Palestine mandate in the '30s and '40s, the Axis inspired Iraq revolt of April 1941 – by then in an independent country – and the "Quit India" revolt of August 1942.

CHAPTER TWO

Imperial Overreach: Britain and Africa

"If ten years hence, there are three men of British race to two of Dutch, the country will be safe and prosperous. If there are three of Dutch to two of British, we shall have perpetual difficulty."

(Lord Milner, about South Africa in 1900, quoted T.R.H. Davenport *South Africa – A Modern History* p151)

With the vast tracts of Canada, Australia and New Zealand all awaiting settlement and economic development, and with the huge population of India to govern, surely Britain would be reluctant to take on more extensive responsibilities. Warnings were given, not only by Gladstone and "Little Englanders". That doughty Imperialist, Leo Amery, linked colonial expansion to the prevailing economic credo of free trade, which he questioned: "Not being quite strong enough to keep the door open (ie for British exports) in Europe by threat of force, [Britain] tries to do so elsewhere by forcibly retarding the expansion of other Powers. This policy has increased our armaments and our territory enormously ..." With what became the Dominions in mind, he continued: " I believe that if we had gone in for Imperial Preference in the (18)40s we should now be a second United States ... both as regards prosperity and ... armaments, but we should not be holding Nigeria or Uganda."[1]

In twenty years, 1880-1900, one-third of the continent of Africa was added to the British Empire, which with other western European countries took part in the Scramble. The only countries to retain independence were Liberia and Ethiopia (Morocco fell to the French in 1911). Why did this happen? The factors drawing Britain on were, in roughly chronological order, first, before 1880, the missionaries and explorers, which created an appetite and sense of duty at home to combat the slave trade and Christianise, civilise and protect the population.[2] Second, but inevitably a twin, came material incentives, the ambitions of trading companies and exploiters. Some of these were the fantasy of *King Solomon's Mines,* published 1885, but appetites were stimulated by the reality of the discovery of diamonds (1867) and then gold (1884) in South Africa, and the exploitation of palm oil in Nigeria and minerals in Rhodesia and Katanga.[3]

These two factors attracted very little backing from Whitehall. But third, and most important after the mid 1890s, was a quasi-military desire to forestall European rivals (more often the French) and occupy territory. Linked to this, in the last two years of the century, came two major British military ventures – one, the "unfinished business" of the re-conquest of the Sudan from Muslim fundamentalists (which also ensured that Britain, rather than France, controlled the upper reaches of the Nile), and second, the enormously costly war to annex the two Boer Republics in southern Africa.

In these two decades little attention was given to developing in suitable parts of Africa a "British empire of settlement", nor did anyone have a clear idea of which parts were suitable, if any. Migration became important later, first in South Africa as a means of counteracting Boer numbers, and then in Rhodesia and Kenya. It largely progressed without any sense of urgency or deliberate planning and therefore proved inadequate.

In the mid-1870s, the only European areas of control, apart from Algeria, were the two Boer Republics, the British from the Cape to the Natal border, the French (up the Senegal), and the Portuguese (long standing but weakly held) inland from Luanda and up the Zambezi. The British appetite for colonial ventures in Africa received a temporary check in 1879-81. They had annexed the Boer Transvaal republic in April 1877: Disraeli's Colonial Secretary, Lord Carnarvon, was an advocate of confederation between the British colonies and the Boer republics, and he encouraged the new High Commissioner, Sir Bartle Frere, along this path. A combination of early settler excesses against the native tribes in Natal in 1874-5 and the folly of certain officials led to the Zulu War in January 1879.[4] If the alternative of establishing a protectorate in Zululand, similar to the other three protectorates on the borders of British South Africa, had been imagined and implemented, ensuring that Zululand, like the other three, never became administratively or demographically part of the South African state, the whole future history of the latter might have been different.

With Gladstone replacing Disraeli in April 1880, the Boers had reason to hope that their independence would be restored. Gladstone vacillated, the Transvaalers revolted and British defeats culminated in disaster at Majuba (27 February 1881) after which virtual Boer independence was conceded, under British suzerainty.

During the 1880s the French, under such commanders as Pierre de Brazza, were building up their strength in areas round the rivers Congo, Senegal and Upper Niger. Lord Granville, in charge during Gladstone's absence in 1883 "cared little for Africa least of all for its most pestilential part, the west coast from Gambia to the Congo."[5] Gladstone himself shared this reservation, but a powerful lobby was mounted by the National Africa Company led by Lord Aberdare, a former Liberal Home Secretary and a "front" for the real leader, the company's managing director, George Goldie Taubman, and others, for example James Hutton, a cotton trader, Liberal MP and President of the powerful Manchester Chamber of Commerce. Their aim was to establish a British monopoly on the middle to lower Niger and to stop the French establishing a French monopoly which would be defended by high tariffs. With Foreign Office support, in 1884 protectorate treaties were signed along the Niger coast.

In Germany, Bismarck had previously assured senior officials and personal confidantes that he was against Germany acquiring colonies. In 1884, he performed a *volte face*, not for the intrinsic benefit of colonies (they might well, as happened in Germany's case, consist mainly of relatively useless stretches of jungle or desert), but, as usual with Bismarck, as a tactic for internal politics.[6] However, "colony fever" was spreading in Germany through the *Deutsche Kolonial Verein*.

This led to the Berlin Conference in the winter of 1884-5. The Conference did not create the Scramble, but it set certain rules and decided certain issues. Probably the most important, and least recognised, of these was the "Principle of Effectivity": the agreement that a power could hold colonies only if it actually had treaties with local leaders, if it flew its flag there, and if it established an administration with a police force and made use of the colony economically. If it did not do these things, another power could take over the territory. This was directed at all Germany's competitors in Africa, especially Portugal, which had tended to seize coastlines and only feebly penetrate inland. Britain, for her part, wanted to minimise these obligations and bore the brunt of opposing Bismarck. The Lord Chancellor, Lord Selborne, carried a proposal distinguishing between "annexations" and "protectorates" – with the latter being recognised "as a perfectly legitimate, but much less complete form of government, exempt from any of the obligations imposed by the conference on occupying powers." However, this development was an unwelcome snub to Britain's ability "to exercise a sort of 'Monroe Doctrine' " over Africa.[7]

Much international tension over the next fifteen years – mainly between Britain and France – was caused by contests to control vast unpopulated and largely worthless areas, including much of the Sahara, the upper Niger basin, the Sudan and the Upper Nile. Before Disraeli bought the Suez Canal shares of the Khedive of Egypt, France had regarded Egypt as her sphere of influence; she had directed the construction of the Canal. In 1882, an Egyptian revolt threatened the lives of expatriates and, most important, the investments of the governments. Facing rumours that the French might reach agreement with the leaders of the revolt, Britain intervened (bombardment of Alexandria and battle of Tel-el-Kebir) and found herself in control of Egypt.[8] Trying to subdue a further revolt, by what we would today call "fundamentalists" under the Mahdi, in November 1883 Hicks Pasha and his mainly Egyptian army was wiped out at El Obeid, and the whole of Sudan was conquered by the Mahdi's Dervishes. General Charles Gordon was cut off in Khartoum where he was besieged from 12 March 1884 until it fell and he was killed on 26 January 1885. While this caused great anger in Britain (the Queen telegraphed hers uncoded), it mysteriously took thirteen years for Britain, acting for the Anglo-Egyptian condominium, to regain the Sudan.

The new Prime Minister, Lord Salisbury, who with short intervals was to hold that office (and that of Foreign Secretary) from 1885-92 and from 1895 to 1902, and the man who played a large role in expanding Britain's empire in Africa as head of the Colonial department, Sir Percy Anderson, "shared many of the same prejudices, among them a distaste for the African continent in general and for the kind of British businessmen ('buccaneers', Salisbury called them) who made fortunes there."[9]

The German government granted a charter to a colonisation company to establish a protectorate in East Africa in March 1885, and eventually an Anglo-German boundary commission in November 1886 agreed to partition East Africa into a British and German sphere of influence. The Germans had their own "buccaneer", one Carl Peters, who in early 1890 signed an agreement with the Bugandan king Mwanga giving Germany a protectorate over Uganda. Ugandan matters interested the Churches and missionaries; there were conflicts between French-sponsored Catholics and British-sponsored Protestants, and in 1885-7 there had been a barbaric persecution of native Christians by Mwanga[10], while in October 1888 the Dervishes penetrated up the White Nile only 100 miles away.

Fighting in Uganda, in which many Catholics were killed, produced a great French outcry to greet Gladstone forming his fourth government in August 1892. Lord Rosebery, then Foreign Secretary, was advised that if British left Uganda at the end of 1892 (as planned) the French would occupy and threaten the headwaters of the Nile, so Rosebery advocated annexation. Gladstone, in more familiar Gladstonian style, was scathing: "I see nothing but endless expense, trouble and disaster in prospect if we allow ourselves to drift into any sort of responsibility for this business."[11] He was supported by his Chancellor of the Exchequer and War Secretary, but Rosebery stirred up the mainly Tory press and encouraged letters to the press, while the Imperial British East Africa Company worked through the Chambers of Commerce in the large manufacturing towns and cities. When Rosebery succeeded as Prime Minister in March 1894, he declared Uganda a British protectorate.

And we see Salisbury, like Bismarck, varying his policy. *The Times* (22 August 1888) published a piece by "an African explorer" believed to represent Salisbury's views, calling for Britain to control a Cape-to-Cairo route, involving taking over the Sudan, Equatoria, and a corridor west of German East Africa, as well as what was then called Zambezia, a vast area in Central Africa.[12] This latter saw the biggest success for the biggest "buccaneer" of all, Cecil Rhodes, who established mineral rights in north-western Rhodesia in 1888, while Nyasaland became a British protectorate in 1891. Rhodes obtained a charter for the British South Africa Company to administer "Zambezia" in October 1889. "The government needed effective occupation by Rhodes in order to resist foreign encroachment ... Rhodes' s company could do all this without cost to the British taxpayer."[13] The Pioneers – 200 farmers and 500 Company police, set off from Bechuanaland in June 1890; on 12 September they reached and founded a fort at Mount Hampden, later Salisbury, now Harare. Three wars then took place in quick succession; first, against King Lobengula's Matabele warriors in 1893, in which the Company occupied Bulawayo. A ruthless policy of paying Company forces by expropriating the best land and cattle led to a Matabele revolt in March 1896: hundreds of whites were massacred. There were equally grim reprisals when in May they regained the upper hand. In June the Mashona rose but they were also crushed. However, Milner told Chamberlain with foresight (December 1897) "my guess is that it [Rhodesian development] is neither going to be a fiasco nor yet a rapid success". [14]

Meanwhile, real tensions had arisen in the desert wastes between the middle Niger and the Upper Nile. Sir George Goldie, chief of the Niger Company, used Sir Frederick Lugard in 1894-5 to secure treaties in the Niger hinterland, but this was countered by French expeditions with enough resources to build and garrison forts and establish "effective occupation". Despite disagreement with Salisbury, Chamberlain was determined "even at the cost of war – to keep an adequate Hinterland for the Gold Coast, Lagos and the Niger Territories"; these must not be "strangled". With Chamberlain's encouragement, Lugard infiltrated behind the French posts and in May 1898 the Niger talks in Paris concluded with the French surrender of Borgu. Although uninhabitable bush, it was the key to the Sokoto empire, now confirmed to be a British protectorate.[15]

Meanwhile what became known as the Fashoda Crisis was brewing. Gabriel Hanotaux, French Foreign Minister for most of 1894 to 1898, saw an opportunity of accomplishing the dream of General Louis Faidherbe, Governor of Senegal in the 1850s and '60s, of an empire stretching "from Senegal to the Red Sea". This would be established by expeditions marching from the Congo river on to the White Nile and then joining with Ethiopian allies.[16] In a Commons debate of 28 March 1895, after the Conservative Opposition pointed to this threat, Sir Edward Grey, Under- Secretary for Foreign Affairs made a reply (not cleared with Rosebery, who was unlikely to have disagreed) that he had no reason to believe that the French had such a plan, because to send "a French expedition under secret instructions, right from the other side of Africa, into a territory over which our claims have been known for so long ... would be an *unfriendly act* and would be so viewed by England." As Garvin stated: "There could be no question of partition... The naked alternatives would be withdrawal or war."[17]

This looming clash on the Upper Nile was linked to the destruction of the Italian invaders of Ethiopia at Adowa on 1 March 1896, with the French having largely armed the Ethiopians with modern rifles. Italy appealed to Britain to make a diversion, so both to confront Captain Marchand's force from Senegal and help Italy, Kitchener started then to build railways and advance up the Nile to crush the Dervishes.[18] British intelligence correctly expected several French expeditions to the Upper Nile – from Djibouti in French Somaliland in the east as well as from the west. This potentially grave threat was averted by bungling; for example, the expedition from Djibouti, not helped either by the hostility of the Governor of Djibouti, one Lagarde, who also acted as ambassador in Addis Ababa, or the ambiguity of Emperor Menelik, the intended ally, turned back in December 1897. Eventually only Captain Marchand reached Fashoda with a weak force on 10 July 1898.[19]

Having destroyed the Khalifa's army at Omdurman on 1 September 1898, Kitchener sailed further up the Nile with a powerful flotilla of gunboats; he reached Fashoda on 18 September. This confrontation saw both nations beginning to mobilise their home fleets. The French one was badly built and poorly organised. While British political leaders were united in firmness, in Paris people questioned the wisdom of war for such a remote area; the Dreyfus Affair was dividing France and her chief ally, Russia, was clearly indifferent. So the French government quietly ordered Marchand to withdraw on 3 November. "In Paris for a long time to come England was hated more than Germany had ever been." [20]

So, within a decade, with relatively little loss of (British) life or expense, the whole of what is now Nigeria, East Africa, the future Rhodesian Federation and the Sudan had fallen to British control.

The Boer War

The sorry story of the 1899-1902 war is too well known to merit detailed coverage here, but discussion of its causes and consequences is essential to our theme. In certain respects, the position of the Boer Republics resembled the recurrent position of Afghanistan. Britain did not want or need to occupy either, and attempts to do so, or in the case of Afghanistan, to impose a client regime, had met with bloody reverses. But, equally, Britain could not allow a potential enemy to occupy or secure bases in these territories. In the case of the Republics, there was the shadowy threat of German occupation (the Kaiser talked rashly about a "protectorate" after the Jameson Raid of 1895[21]), but the real threat was of an uprising among the numerous Cape Dutch, in collusion with invading Boer forces. For Britain, the loss of the Suez Canal would have been highly inconvenient and costly for maritime communications eastward; the loss of control at the Cape would have been fatal. Against this strategic background historians should read the nervous exchanges in 1898-99 between the Colonial Secretary in London, and the High Commissioner, Sir Alfred Milner,[22] in South Africa.

The Afghan comparison is complicated by two crucial factors peculiar to the Boer Republics: gold and Uitlanders. Vast gold fields in the Transvaal were discovered in 1886-this gold became crucial for Britain as the centre of international trade. Mining it required huge capital investment: hence the Randlords – Rhodes, Alfred Beit and Julius Wernher who funded the Jameson Raid – and whom both Salisbury and Chamberlain regarded as politically unsavoury. While the white population of the Transvaal was around 290,000, the bulk of the 50,000 living in the Johannesburg area were Uitlanders, mainly British.[23] The Transvaal Government, under President Paul Kruger, passed legislation to disenfranchise the Uitlanders from any meaningful political role, and this, together with high taxation and corrupt and inefficient public administration, gave rise to considerable discontent.

There had been hope that Kruger, who was 73 in 1898, might be replaced, but the Raid rallied support behind him; and in early 1898 he was re-elected President by a greatly increased majority. He then dismissed the republic's Chief Justice, for challenging the constitutionality of several acts of his government. Milner had hoped for a peaceful solution; he now reacted: "there is no way out ... except reform in the Transvaal or war". Tension rose further after the end of 1898, when a Boer policeman shot and killed a drunken Uitlander who resisted arrest – the policeman was acquitted of wrongdoing and commended by a Boer judge. 20,000 Uitlanders signed a petition to London. In face of London's apparent lack of interest in the Uitlanders' plight, Milner reacted by cabling in early May 1899 the "Helot Despatch": "The case for intervention is overwhelming ... the spectacle of thousands of British subjects kept permanently in the position of helots ..." The classical allusion, which would have been widely understood at the time, was to the slave population of ancient Sparta. [24]

There followed the Bloemfontein Conference (30 May-6 June 1899) between Milner and Kruger, and their teams, at the invitation of President Steyn of the Orange Free State, perhaps the last and best opportunity to avert a breakdown. Chamberlain encouraged Milner to include Prime Minister Schreiner of the Cape Dutch, but Milner used "the discretion thus left to him ... to reject this shrewd judgment."[25] Kruger went further than previously in offering concessions on the franchise (in a detailed Reform Bill), but these were accompanied by contentious conditions. Fearing Milner's impatience, Chamberlain telegraphed him: "I hope you will not break off hastily. Boers do not understand quick decisions ... I am by no means convinced that the President has made his last offer, and you should be very patient and admit a good deal of haggling ..."[26] Before this cable could reach Milner, he had returned to Cape Town.

Pressure from the Cape Dutch led Kruger to make, in mid July, what appeared to many to be a good offer, which Chamberlain publicly welcomed. The details, as described in a long memorandum by the able J. C. Smuts, then Transvaal State Attorney, were less promising and fuelled both a further appeal to London by the Uitlanders and Milner's own cynicism.[27] Chamberlain's response included a proposal for a joint Boer-British inquiry to investigate the details: Kruger rejected this as interfering in his "independence". A further apparently far-reaching offer from Smuts (mid-August) met hostility from Milner which Chamberlain described as "unnecessarily suspicious"; however, a few days later the Boers stiffened the accompanying requirements, as well as challenging suzerainty. This was a major reverse.

So, in late 1899, the countdown to war began. The massive Boer armament (Mauser rifles and ammunition – enough to equip every male of fighting age in the two Republics, as well as the expected reinforcements from the Cape Dutch – and quick-firing and heavy guns from Creusot and Krupps) was known to the British, but underestimated. They did not imagine that the heavy "Long Tom" guns in the Pretoria forts could be used as mobile field artillery. British forces in South Africa were weak in number. All along, Chamberlain hoped to avoid war (and few at a senior level seem to have envisaged the Boers striking first). He still thought of armed forces "as an intimidating tool in negotiation rather than for deployment in warfare".[28] Reinforcements from India were sent. And in a Birmingham speech on 26 August, Chamberlain made his impatience manifest: Kruger "dribbles out reforms like water from a squeezed sponge ... The sands are running down in the glass."

After this, it was a race between ultimata: hardly had Chamberlain got Cabinet agreement to his (emphasising franchise reform, going well beyond the Smuts proposals, but undertaking to guarantee "against any attack on the independence of the South African Republic"), than the Boers issued their own, outrageously requiring withdrawal (each to their previous locations) of British forces on the border, of those that had landed in South Africa since 1 June, and of those currently en route. It was easy for the Government to reject this, and it helped to swing Liberal support and also diminish French Canadian opposition to Canada's sending forces.

It is difficult to resist the conclusion that Milner at the very least missed opportunities for peace. He became a hero to the Imperialist group after 1900, and his prestige and their admiration for him lasted until his death in 1925 and beyond. It was well-deserved, but equally there can be little doubt that different handling might have avoided war in 1899.[29] His power and influence then should not be underestimated. He had a key ally as Under-Secretary for the Colonies in Lord Selborne who not only backed him but sent him a stream of private letters facilitating his handling of Chamberlain. Likewise George Wyndham, Under-Secretary to Lord Lansdowne at the War Office, was another ally, as were various editors and key journalists in newspapers across the political spectrum.

And the role of the "gold-bugs", Wernher, Beit and Percy FitzPatrick, should not be underestimated; they emphasised that if the pressure were kept up on Kruger, including military reinforcement, he would give way: Rhodes claimed that Kruger would "bluff up to the cannon's mouth". In fact, they knew that this pressure, and especially the despatch of British troops, would precipitate war.[30]

Whether it was Chamberlain's intention to avoid provocation, or whether it was simply that his colleagues were slow to move, the opening weeks of the war were "a very close run thing". The Transvaal mobilised on 28 September, the British troops sent from India only arrived in Durban by 9 October, just as the Orange Free State delivered its ultimatum, with their invasion of Natal beginning on the 11th. Fortunately for Britain, hesitations by the Free State "had cost the two Republics the whole of their crucial four weeks advantage".[31]

While some on the British side, like Milner, did not underestimate the difficulties of the conflict, many others initially had unrealistic expectations of overcoming the Boers. What were the Boer expectations? Smuts says that Kruger had decided war was inevitable by early September. In an eight page memorandum, dated 4 September 1899, Smuts called on the Boer chiefs to attack the British in Natal, destroy them before they could be reinforced, and then drive through to Durban and Cape Town, capturing "enormous quantities" of artillery and stores. With the Boers holding the coast against raids from the sea, they would then stir up revolt in India and elsewhere, while inciting Britain's enemies in Europe "to pull down the whole crazy structure of the British Empire." This from one who was to become a passionate and intelligent exponent of the international role of the British Empire; in 1899, he had an equally grandiose ambition "to build an Afrikaner Republic that would inherit British power from Cape Town to the Zambezi."[32] Smuts' great raid into Cape Colony in 1901-02 aimed at "a general revolution and declaration of independence ... the beginning of the deliverance of the whole of South Africa and the union of our people into a great nation from Table Bay to the Equator". And in a speech on 2 August 1901, Smuts repeats this ambition: "the flag of the great Republic would yet float from the Equator to Simonsbay."[33]

There was, however, no concentration of Boer forces for such a drive, and no determined attempt to take Mafeking, Ladysmith or Kimberley. In his *Memoir of the War* Smuts criticised this lack of offensive spirit in the Boer leadership in the early months, which he thought might have recruited large numbers of volunteers among the Cape Afrikaners[34].

For Britain, the war was a dismal experience. The defeats of the first months , which exposed her military weakness in terms of skill, tactics and the fitness of her troops, produced considerable hostile pressure from the public opinion of France, Germany and Russia, as well as threatening a revolt by the Cape Dutch. Only diplomacy, the caution of, for example, the French government, and, amazingly, the good will of the Kaiser, averted uglier consequences. British military successes in the spring of 1900 did not end this danger. With two years of guerrilla warfare to follow, with harsh repressive measures becoming necessary (blockhouses and barbed wire lines, and the sensationally reported use, though not the invention, of "concentration camps" for Afrikaner civilians), a large legacy of bitterness was sown.[35]

In the plus column of consequences of the war are at least two points. As a result of the experience of the British Army suffering "Black Week" in December 1899 and several other reverses, and the reforms that ensued, the "contemptible little army" that faced the might of Germany in 1914 gave an excellent account of itself.[36] Second, there was a massive response from the other white colonies to Chamberlain's call on them for help, and this achieved much in drawing the Empire together. Again, it was to stand in good stead, indeed be exceeded, in 1914. New Zealand made the best response, followed by the various Australian colonies but Sir Wilfrid Laurier, Prime Minister of Canada, initially vetoed a Canadian contribution. He later sang a very different tune; after Canadian forces captured Boer troops, he asked the Canadian House of Commons "is there a man whose bosom does not swell with pride ... that ... the fact has been revealed to the world that a new power has arisen in the west?"[37]

Reconstruction – Missed Opportunities 1902-14

If the war had been necessary to avoid a disaster for British power and prestige, first, what benefits did the conquest of the two Republics bring? And, second, how far did the post-war constitutional outcome prepare South Africa to address and avert the eventual stark outcome of what only became identified fifty or sixty years later as "exclusive black majority rule"?

In the short term, to answer the first question, the new South Africa saw an alliance between the English speakers and a large, but varying, proportion of the Afrikaners. This was to play a positive role during the First World War and in the development of the Commonwealth during the inter-war period.

There was a small pro-German revolt in 1914. The commander-in-chief of the Union Defence Force General Beyers resigned and gathered a force; along with those of General Maritz and General De Wet, this amounted to about 12,000. They were outnumbered by Prime Minister Botha's troops, many of whom were Afrikaners, and these moved fast. In October, Maritz was defeated and fled to the Germans; the Beyers commando was dispersed on 28 October, and De Wet was captured in Bechuanaland. In contrast to the reprisals after the Dublin Easter Rising, only one South African conspirator was executed.

A study of the second question would display a succession of failures, or inadequate policies, which led to South Africa gradually detaching herself from the remainder of the British world, becoming a Republic, and pursuing the slippery slope towards what became known as "apartheid," which alienated potential friends, cemented isolation, destabilised the country and failed completely to act as an alternative to "exclusive black majority rule".

The existence and prospects of the black majority population (together with those of the Cape Coloureds, the product of intermarriage and miscegenation, and Indian immigrants) hardly featured in the exchanges and negotiations preceding the outbreak of the war. The Boer attitude was always deeply suspicious of all people of colour: they regarded any employment in the war by the British of armed blacks as virtually a war crime. Since they usually shot the blacks in British service, armed or often unarmed, Kitchener armed those guarding blockhouses for their own safety. It is very likely that the British authorities avoided raising the "colour" question with the Boers as it would have brought heat rather than light to their negotiations. Thus the role of these communities was ignored; the "race issue" at the time of the Boer War was that between British and Afrikaners.

A letter from Leo Amery, the then *Times* correspondent in South Africa during the Boer war, to Sir Valentine Chirol, the foreign editor, saw Amery set out "my own idea", that of encouraging native self-government in local matters, leading up to a "House of Assembly, able to legislate on matters concerning natives, subject to a veto of the White House." Put into the context of his developing thoughts, this stark proposal appears somewhat less reactionary. He contrasted the fact that in the Basutoland protectorate "the natives practically have a sort of Parliamentary Government". He added "A white legislature would be much more tolerant and reasonable towards the just demands of a black assembly than a white electorate to (black) voters". He concluded "South Africa must develop as a white man's country under the guidance of white men ..."[38] Even so, the progress he envisaged would have been preferable to what happened.

Amery's views paralleled the Report of the South African Native Affairs Commission, chaired by Sir Godfrey Lagden and appointed by Milner, which sat in 1903-5, aiming at working out an agreed "native" policy for all southern Africa. Nearly all its members were English-speakers, but that did not prevent them proposing the separation of whites and blacks politically and territorially, with the whites running the legislatures and the land demarcated into white and black areas. The Lagden Report has been clearly seen as inspiring the segregationist policies of later years, in particular the period 1910-24 which saw "the first definitive legislative steps ... taken which placed 'Segregation' metaphorically on the cover of the statute book ... "[39]

Milner's original plan saw the interval after the war as time in which the British population of the Transvaal returned and increased. He told Chamberlain just before the war started "... once we [have] cleared the Augean stable ... thousands of people would at once swarm into the Transvaal, and the balance of political power ... would be rapidly and decisively turned against the Boer for ever."[40] He intended to withhold political power from the whites of the Boer Republics (now termed "new colonies") until British demographic ascendancy there had been secured: "If ten years hence, there are three men of British race to two of Dutch, the country will be safe and prosperous. If there are three of Dutch to two of British, we shall have perpetual difficulty."[41]

His plans were to bring the mines back to full production, get farmers back onto the land with restocking, and build up railway communications. Almost all livestock had been destroyed by war or by disease and there was massive white poverty in rural areas. While farmers were slow to adopt new methods, by the end of 1902 most people were back on the land, but rural recovery was made very difficult by drought during the period 1903-8. Milner wanted English speakers – he hoped 10,000 within a year – to migrate onto the land, bringing farming experience and capital. But he had limited funds for acquiring land and he lacked sufficient powers of expropriation. In fact only about 1300 English speaking heads of families settled on the land, while, ironically, Botha and Smuts both purchased a lot of land, as well as some of the barbed wire the British had been using against them.[42]

Mining returned to pre-war levels of production in 1904, but the mine owners showed little enthusiasm for substantially increasing the proportion of white workers; their economic interests lay in the opposite direction. While the government did employ large numbers of unskilled whites in public works, the employment on the railways of English navvies was abandoned by the Chief Engineer, because he had to face "so much opposition in carrying out my proposals". The historian's comment was "It seems obvious that the experiment lacked the approval of his superiors".[43] The solution for mining was to import labour from Asia – Chinese labour. It was clear that this was what the mine owners wanted: Sir Percy FitzPatrick, President of the Chamber of Mines, opposed Chinese labour; so at the Chamber's AGM in February 1903 he was replaced by Sir George Farrar, known to support it. "Farrar's gambit, of offering his employees a pro-Chinese petition to be signed as they turned up on pay day, must count as one of the cruder devices."[44]

The other issues, the gradual, or limited, enfranchisement of "natives", had featured in the peace negotiations. Milner was relying on British migration and did not consider the option of using the non-White communities as a counterbalance to the Afrikaners. Despite Chamberlain saying in 1899 "we cannot consent to purchase a shameful peace by leaving the coloured population in the position in which they stood before the war," and despite the fact that defence of the rights of the native population and also of the British Indian community in South Africa had "figured prominently in the official British rationale for the war,"[45] nothing was implemented. In one of the peace exchanges during the war, it had been proposed to exclude the grant of the franchise to non-Whites "before" self-government was granted to the annexed Republics.

At the Vereeniging peace negotiations, Milner, knowing "that these claims were intensely unpopular among the white population of the region, British as well as Boer",[46] proposed that they should not be considered "until after" self-government – though clearly once self-governing no Boer-controlled state would entertain them. The Permanent Secretary of the Colonial Office proposed to omit the word "after"; this was supported by Chamberlain.[47] Milner demurred ("there is much to be said for leaving question of political rights of natives to be settled by the colonists themselves"), but his original draft of peace proposals in May 1902 read "The Franchise will not be given to Natives until after the Introduction of Self-Government". That implied that it *would* be given to them then. Smuts in the negotiations brutally clarified it: "The question of granting the franchise to Natives will not be decided until after the introduction of self-government." Three years later Milner, writing to Lord Selborne, High Commissioner from 1905-1910, thought he had made the biggest mistake of his career in accepting the clause, but that comment "is at variance with his contemporary opinions".[48]

To the wider British world and, indeed, internationally, Smuts was a hero during the first half of the 20th century. He was not so regarded by his Afrikaner fellow citizens, as we shall see. What were his considered views on black political advancement? In a great debate in October 1908 with his more liberal friend John

Merriman, Smuts wrote: "I don't believe in politics for them {the natives} ... {it} would only have an unsettling influence. I would therefore not give them the franchise ..." At the same time he added "on the question of the Native franchise my mind is full of Cimmerian darkness and I incline very strongly to leaving that matter over for the Union Parliament."[49] As his biographer states, this "was an early manifestation of what was to be a life-long attitude to the native question...The explanation is that Smuts was never, at any time, ready to move in advance of public opinion."[50] In a major speech of 22 May 1917 in London, he declared: "In landownership, settlement and forms of government we are trying to keep them apart ... it may take a hundred years to work out, but in the end it may be the solution of our native problem. Thus ... you will have in the long run large areas cultivated by blacks and governed by blacks, while in suitable parts you will have your white communities which will govern themselves separately ... " There was no challenge to this early description of what was later known as apartheid from his London audience at that time, and he was able to cite the authority both of the revered Cecil Rhodes and of Lord Selborne, chairing that 1917 meeting.[51]

The "Coloureds" (those of mixed race) hoped for the extension of Cape precedents, where they had the vote, to the Transvaal. However, Milner could not help this "most respectable and ill-used class"; although sympathising with their point of view, he said they should be patient until white opinion was riper. "In short. Milner and his government did nothing for the Coloureds." Selborne tried to do better and in 1908 sent Botha and Smuts a memorandum proposing giving the Coloureds "the benefit of their white blood" and therefore not to classify them with Natives."[52] Nothing resulted.

Another issue on which, as it proved, the wrong decision was taken, was over the electoral system. The post-war Lyttelton constitution prescribed one vote one value, which favoured the English speaking community because they had a majority of adult males. Smuts persuaded the Liberal government to drop the Lyttelton constitution by threatening Premier Campbell-Bannerman in February 1906 ("You can have the Boers for friends ... You can choose to make them enemies, and possibly have another Ireland on your hands.") So the electoral system was skewed to "representation by population" taking account of the fact that the Afrikaners had a far higher proportion of women and children, and a faster birth rate. English speakers were concentrated in urban seats which were now under-represented in contrast to rural. In addition, the Cape Colony, where English speakers and moderate Afrikaners were strongest, was also under-represented. Paradoxically, Smuts and his moderate party, backed by English speakers, lost power in 1924 and were forced to compromise after 1933 in order to gain a share in government.[53]

These missed opportunities meant that Britain won the war only to lose the peace. When elections were held, Afrikaner parties won in Transvaal in 1907 and in the Orange River Colony in 1908. Churchill (now a Liberal) said of Milner "It is difficult to dispute the fact that Milner's presence and actions in the Transvaal tended to hasten the re-integration of the Afrikaners and the disintegration of non-Afrikaner unity."[54] Lyttelton told Balfour in January 1905 that Milner was not a good judge of men, as various chief officers all resigned or been retired. "It is hardly an exaggeration to say that every official was either incompetent, or believed himself to be so, or believed everyone else to be so."[55]

Some years later, in a letter to Lord Selborne, Chamberlain privately criticised the handling of South Africa after 1902. As well as strongly opposing the recruitment of labour from China, "I disapproved of Lyttelton's constitution. It went too far or not far enough." He was not surprised that the Liberals decided to repeal it. "I feel that the fear of a Transvaal which shall be like the Irish at home or the French in Canada is very real ... the fact that racialism [*sic* – this refers to anti-British Boer feeling] remains in Cape Colony after a hundred years of good government ... confirms my fear ... If the Dutch are in a majority over South Africa & they appear to be in the Transvaal, the ORC, & Cape Colony, are we sure that they will not make any effort to be supreme?" He asked Selborne whether "the natives" were to be represented in the new Parliament, not giving an opinion but stressing that in Cape Colony they "prize [it] very highly".[56] It was too late; the die had been cast.

Downhill 1910-39

In the first post self-government elections, in September 1910, there was little to distinguish between Botha and Smuts's South Africa Party (SAP) and the English-speaking Unionists – both wanted peace and tolerance between Briton and Boer, but both disapproved of racial miscegenation, regarding the idea of a black political majority as unthinkable, though the Unionists were less hostile to the retention of the Cape non-white franchise than the SAP. Both wanted African land ownership restricted to the Reserves, and African urban immigrants segregated.

The Boer chiefs showed their colours early in the new dispensation. Louis Botha, the first Prime Minister of the Union since 1910 (he died in 1919 and was succeeded by Smuts), resisted a single Imperial foreign policy at the 1911 Imperial Conference, while in 1912 Hertzog started a campaign for South Africa to control her own destiny. In November 1913 Hertzog and General de Wet walked out of the SAP congress in Cape Town, taking a few MPs with them. They formed a new Nationalist Party and this, at its Transvaal congress in August 1914, opposed South African participation in the war against Germany and any attack on German South West Africa. De Wet led a military revolt which Botha and Smuts put down with little loss of life. However, the rebellion consolidated Afrikaner forces behind Hertzog, whose Nationalists made impressive gains in the 1915 election, taking 16 out of the 17 OFS seats, 7 in the Cape Province and 4 in Transvaal.

The next election, in March 1920, made the Nationalists with 44 seats the largest party in the Assembly. With the SAP at 41 seats, the Unionists fell to 25, while Labour profiting from popular discontent during the post-war depression won 21 seats. Smuts failed to woo the Nationalists, on account of the latter's hostility to the Empire and because they had made republicanism a permissible article of faith. Then he persuaded the Unionists to dissolve, with its members joining the SAP on an individual basis. In an election the next year, the new SAP won 79 seats, mainly at the expense of Labour, against 45 Nationalists. One perhaps decisive consequence of the 1920 election result was that the Rhodesians, worried by the Nationalist advance, voted 8774 to 5989 against joining the Union. Their presence might have changed the direction of southern Africa, with more compromise with the blacks and less hostility to the British Empire.

Smuts was silent over native policy for several years. Two prominent liberals debated with him but wanted to go further than he. One, Jan Hendrick Hofmeyr (1894-1948), repudiated the dogma of racial inequality and upheld the colour blind franchise of the Cape. He also believed, as the majority of politicians in Britain still believed, that the right to vote was conditional on possession of specific educational capacities, which he thought only a small minority of South African natives possessed. The second, John Merriman (died 1926), was the last Prime Minister of Cape Colony before Union. He also championed a limited franchise which would deny the vote to poor and ignorant whites but would grant it to such non whites as might raise themselves to a certain standard of prosperity and education.

The early years of Union also saw a clash with the growing Asian community, predominantly Indian, which had from late 1870s migrated to Natal. These Gujarati traders set up shops which competed against the whites. One of them was Mohandas Gandhi, born in 1869 into a Hindu merchant caste family in Gujarat, educated at the Inner Temple in London, and then practising as an expatriate lawyer in South Africa. His experience of white bullying in Pretoria and Durban helped to politicise him. The British Indian Association of Johannesburg said "What the Indians pray for is very little. They admit the British race should be the dominant race in South Africa. They ask for no political power. They admit the principle of restricting the influx of cheap labour ..." Gandhi showed his loyalty to the Crown by serving with an Indian ambulance unit during a Zulu rebellion in 1906. The way in which it was put down, with over 3000 Zulus killed, shocked him: he described it as a "manhunt."[57]

In 1906 the Asiatic Law Amendment Ordinance, called by the Indians the Black Ordinance, was designed to close Transvaal against new Indian immigrants and clear it of all illegal ones. Gandhi started the first of his *satyagraha* protests against it, especially over the passes issue. Selborne confessed he had never anticipated such passionate resistance from Indians, and was concerned about the example this set to other communities. Sir Richard Solomon, the Agent General in London, told Smuts that this ordinance "was initiated and drafted by officials (Lionel Curtis etc) who though very clever do not understand human nature." Gandhi met Smuts several times and the two got on well together; however, not for the first time, there was a dispute over what they had agreed: "'Misunderstanding' is the appropriate description of what occurred."[58] This row had international reverberations: Indian members of the Viceroy's council in Delhi complained about the treatment of the Indians in South Africa. At the Imperial Conference in 1921 the latter asked for rights of citizenship. Other Prime Ministers were sympathetic but Smuts was opposed, arguing that if rights were given to Indians, they could not easily be denied to the natives.

Smuts faced fierce industrial clashes, and his handling of them did not add to his popularity. In January 1921 there was a serious strike in the gold industry. The Nationalists backed the strikers who were mostly Afrikaners. In February the strikers called on the "Pretoria Parliament" to set up a provisional government and proclaim a Republic. The government announced that strike commandos were unlawful assemblies and would be dispersed by the police; on 28 February police fired on one commando and killed three. On 10 March, faced by commandos holding the entire Rand, Smuts declared martial law. In three days of fighting he suppressed the insurrection. Hertzog was appalled: "Gen Hertzog went on to say that the Prime Minister's footsteps dripped with blood ... "[59]

In the 1924 Election, Nationalists made the issue one of stagnation versus progress, with pronounced racial undertones. Their slogan was "South Africa a huge black compound for the big capitalists or South Africa a prosperous white man's country," adding "If the present ... policy continues for another five years, it will be impossible ever to have a large white population. If you don't wish to save yourselves, save your children."[60] The swing was not large – the SAP vote was 5% down, Labour 3% up, Nationalists as before. But the SAP won more than half its seats in Cape Province, which had an abnormally high number of voters per constituency.

The system we recall as "apartheid" did not suddenly erupt after 1948. Those classed as "moderate" in previous decades took the many steps which built up the structure of apartheid. The 1913 Native Land Act defined the various tribal areas and prevented Africans buying land outside them. Additional areas outside the reserves were promised, but nothing was done for 23 years. So the black areas scheduled in the Native Land Act of 1913 could barely hold their existing populations, let alone hundreds of thousands of evicted squatters. By then, in 1936, there were desert conditions in many black areas, and more than half the country's 6.5 million blacks were working in so-called white areas.

Before Smuts' South Africa Party lost power in 1924 it made access to skilled trades safe for whites, by insisting on minimum educational qualifications for entry to apprenticeships. The 1920 Native Affairs Act and the Natives (Urban Areas) Act in 1923 sought to implement segregated political institutions for Africans, building on a system of district councils in areas where the African population predominated. These were able to levy a rate and spend the proceeds on certain specific agricultural, health and educational services. The 1920 Act also set up a Native Conference of African leaders to be nominated by the government and meet annually in Pretoria, together with an all-white Native Affairs Commission of experts who were to maintain contact with the African population through these leaders. The aim was to give Africans a constitutional outlet for grievances; but already the Nationalists wanted electoral separation and the abolition of the Cape's native franchise. The Commission proved dilatory in organising Native Conferences, with the first taking place in 1925. The Hertzog government reserved certain jobs in the mines and the railways for "poor" (or working class) whites as distinct from Africans. Most of these measures were highly unpopular among politically conscious Africans.[61]

In private conversations with Hertzog in February 1928, Smuts pushed him to consider "a common franchise all over South Africa, based on occupation and income or salary which was to apply to all, black and white alike." It would be high enough to exclude the bulk of the black population. There "might also be an education and civilisation test, applied to all non-Europeans in future". Hertzog "appears to have been attracted" by this but he did not follow it up, later telling Smuts that "opinion in the North was not ripe for it".[62] Months after, we see Hertzog's 1929 election manifesto "pouring scorn on 'the apostle of a black Kaffir State.' " Smuts was accused of "trying to make his country the miserable appendage to a mammoth Kaffir state". This referred to the British doctrine of paramountcy of African interests in Kenya, where the ethnic balance was very different, expressed by the Duke of Devonshire as Colonial Minister in 1923 and reinforced later. Smuts had a vision of "a great White Africa along the eastern backbone, with railway and road communications connecting north and south"; he had hoped to develop this, as a "highland backbone," seeing it as a necessary guarantee of the long term security of the white south. Thus he condemned the Sidney Webb (Lord Passfield) June 1930 "stupid White Paper on Paramountcy".[63]

East African settlement was a fantasy. After 1945, the settlers in Kenya determined to make it a "white man's country", pushing hard for the UK government to encourage immigration. With various land settlement schemes to bring in whites, between 1945 and the mid 1950s Kenya's white population rose from 17,900 to 55,700. With the Mau Mau campaign beginning in 1952: "Kenya would then discover the axiom sooner than Rhodesia: that all things being equal, few people prefer to move to a war zone."

Segregation was not an issue between the Nationalists and the SAP, and Smuts's Rhodes Memorial lectures at Oxford in November 1929 "laid special emphasis on the need to prevent the excessive integration of the black man in white society."[64] He starkly declared "... without large scale permanent European settlement on this continent the African mass will not be moved, the sporadic attempts at civilisation will pass, Africa may relapse to her historic and prehistoric slumbers ... (with) only mining holes and ruined forts (to) bear testimony to future ages of what once was."

Electoral developments showed the effect of earlier distortions imposed in the 1900s and saw new ones introduced. For example, the 1924 Election saw 63 Nationalists, under Hertzog, elected on 36% of the vote, as against 53 SAP members on 47%; the 1929 Election saw 78 Nationalists elected, on 40%, as against 61 from the SAP on nearly 49%. Smuts was thus out of office from 1924 to 1933. Might he have been braver in these decades of opportunity had the electoral arithmetic been more favourable? Instead, despite his presence, the governments of the Thirties ratcheted up the structure of apartheid.

In 1930 South Africa gave the vote to all women of European descent but gave no vote to any native or coloured woman, a further devaluation of the limited electoral power the latter communities had. Furthermore, the Cape's existing franchise laws had imposed a "civilisation" test on all men, including white men; because this test did not extend to women it was abolished in 1931. In 1929 7.5% of all voters on the Cape roll were natives – by 1935 the figure was only 2.5%.[65]

In March 1933 Hertzog and Smuts formed a coalition ministry with a platform including equal language rights between English and Afrikaans, acceptance of a "white labour" policy, and the maintenance of political separation for natives. In 1936 Hertzog passed, with only a demur from Smuts, a Bill removing Cape Africans from the common roll to a separate voters' roll which would return *white* members to the various legislative bodies. 169 members voted for this Bill, and only 11 against, including a few SAP liberals. One of them was Hofmeyr who, though a cabinet minister, had arranged with Hertzog that his opposition would not be construed as involving an issue of confidence. "He tore into the principle of communal representation on the ground that it involved inferior citizenship, and objected to the destruction of the 'vested right' of the Africans in the existing political system because it involved a breach of faith by the white man which was likely to destroy the trust of the black."[66] If only others had seen it this way, and acted accordingly.

The United South Africa Nationalist Party, usually known as the United Party, came into being in 1934. Dr Malan broke away with his more extreme Afrikaner followers to establish the Purified Nationalist party (HNP), which became firmly Republican. They rejected Hertzog's demand for sanctions on Italy after the invasion of Abyssinia and during the passage of the Aliens Bill in 1937 they asked for a ban on Jewish immigration. Malan's party in Transvaal and OFS excluded Jews from membership.

During the 1930s more legislation was passed which further built up what later was known as apartheid. Bills discriminating against Africans such as the Riotous Assemblies Bill, the Native Service Contract Bill, the Representation of Natives Bill, the Native Trust and Land Bill, and the Native Laws Amendment Bill. Further discriminatory legislation was passed relating to the growing Indian population: the Asiatic Bill, the Provincial Legislative Powers Extension Bill, and the European Women's Restriction of Employment Bill – designed to prevent Indian business owners from having white people in their employ and to restrict Indian land purchase in towns. Hofmeyr spoke out against most of these discriminatory laws, becoming more liberal as the government appeared to become more reactionary, although he was silent regarding the Native Laws Amendment Bill, to control the migration of black workers from rural areas into urban areas.

Hofmeyr said that "Smuts was weakly yielding to anti-semitism, colour prejudice and the other forces of reaction. He himself, he said, was ashamed of the government of which he was a member."[67] He might then have broken with Smuts, with unfathomable consequences, but politics was transformed by international developments.

Towards Isolation

Both Hertzog and Smuts were sympathetic to German complaints about the Versailles Treaty.[68] Hertzog was prepared to trust Hitler's undertakings right down to September 1939, while Smuts, who had previously preferred neutrality in a European war, felt unable to recommend it after the rape of Czechoslovakia in March 1939. He wrote on 28 August 1939 "With us there is no enthusiasm for Poland, and less for Dantzig and the Corridor;"[69] General Kemp said there would be a blood bath in South Africa unless it remained neutral.

On 3 September seven Cabinet members supported Smuts in joining Britain in declaring war, while six supported Hertzog, who had received a message from Malan saying he would back neutrality. The Assembly on the 4th saw Hertzog's neutrality motion get 67 votes while Smuts's amendment got 80. Hertzog asked the Governor General, Sir Patrick Duncan, for a dissolution but Duncan refused this on the grounds that a viable government could still be formed. On the 6th, Smuts formed this new government, with the cooperation of the Labour and Dominion parties (3 and 8 respectively).

Hertzog did not give up the struggle for neutrality, putting forward a motion on 23 January 1940, which was rejected by the same numbers as before, 67-80. He and his allies surprisingly ignored the fate of Holland in the spring of 1940 and when France fell Hertzog said Britain had lost the war and that South Africa should conclude a separate peace. C. R. Swart, later President of the Republic of South Africa, and one of Malan's chief lieutenants said "the signs, so far as we can judge, are that Germany has definitely won the war. The Nationalist Party is the only party that will be in a position to treat with the victor."[70] 37 Herzogites had crossed the floor to vote with Malan for neutrality. In December 1939 the two parties were united with Hertzog agreeing to a Republic outside the British Empire. One ugly phenomenon during the war was the operations of pro-Nazi Afrikaner militarist groups, the Broederbond and the Ossewabrandwag, with nearly 300,000 followers, which attacked men in uniform, helped escaping German POWs and engaged in acts of sabotage.[71]

Segregation apparently "slowed down" under Smuts's government post 1939: in May 1942 the Departments of Justice and Native Affairs agreed to restrain police from demanding the production of passes after there had been a large increase in the numbers of Africans arrested on the technicality of not having a pass; there had been a dramatic reduction of pass arrests in the second half of 1942. This may have been moderation, or it may have been a need to concentrate on pursuing the war.[72] However, many Afrikaners supported Smuts and the war; with Hertzog retiring from politics, the 1943 election gave Smuts 110 seats and Malan 43 (however, Malan had cut the UP's share of the Afrikaner vote from 40% to 32%).[73]

While Smuts played a major part in Allied strategy and inter-Allied conferences, at home his position became steadily more unhappy. When the Japanese navy invaded the Indian Ocean he declared on 11 March 1942 that if they invaded South Africa, he would arm the natives and the coloureds. Later, he wrote from the Prime Ministers' Conference in London in May 1944 that the time had come for arming the coloureds. Hofmeyr, as Deputy Premier, put this to the Cabinet, and recorded in his own hand the unanimous and strongly hostile view. The Natives Representative Council, set up in 1936, reached a deadlock with the Smuts government in 1946, encouraged by the African National Congress, over issues over pass laws, the recognition of African trade unions, and banishment without trial.[74]

A government decision in 1943 to set up a Coloured Affairs Department was opposed by coloured activists. African trade unionism, encouraged by Communists, was rapidly increasing. In August 1946, 70,000 African miners went on strike. This was combated and put down by the police at the cost of several lives and many injured; the arrest and trial of leading Communists followed. Issues had also arisen with the Indians over property in Natal and Indian squatting especially in Durban. "It was unfortunate for the United Party, but fortunate for the Nationalists, that the development of robust opposition by African, Coloured and Indian elements should have occurred at the same time as the beginning of the Government's serious difficulties on the international front. Together they created the strong impression that the Government could not control the situation ..."[75]

Smuts was seen as "grooming Hofmeyr as his successor." Hofmeyr, in his turn, was seen "as a man of dangerous liberal purposes". The Nationalists claimed that "a Hofmeyr government was incompatible ... with the survival of White South Africa". For the election of May 1948, the positive Nationalist slogan was "apartheid"; the two bogeymen were Hofmeyr and Communism.[76] This election was won by Malan's Nationalists by 70 to 65 for the UP, plus 9 for the Afrikaner party and 6 for Labour. Smuts, despite his great international prestige was defeated in his own constituency. The Nationalists were better organised, with an active cell system against the relatively inactive local organisation of the UP. Even so, the UP led in terms of votes: including estimates for uncontested seats, Malan had

462,000, Smuts 620,000. Once again, the different weights for urban and rural votes and the "piling up" of UP votes in urban seats counted against the UP. This time it proved to be decisive and irreversible.

The triumphant Nationalists removed the coloured voters from the common roll. In 1949 the representation of Indians, provided for in a Smuts Government Act of 1947, was abolished. Also in 1949, South West Africa was incorporated, and the six seats added, very lightly populated, largely by Germans; all went to the Nationalists. Smuts died in 1950 and Hofmeyr had died in December 1948: the United Party became a weakened Opposition. The Nationalists (still a minority Government in 1953) were to hold power until apartheid itself came to an end after 1990. All the attributes of elective dictatorship began to appear after 1948: the "Afrikanerisation" of the army led to 122 officers resigning in 1954-56 – 13% of the total. The armed forces increasingly were used in the suppression of internal resistance (the Sharpeville Massacre occurred in March 1960); press censorship and curtailment of civil liberties was increased. The Group Areas Act of 1950, built upon subsequently, established complete residential and other (in churches, schools, all forms of leisure) segregation: it was followed by the self descriptive Mixed Marriages Prohibition Act and the Immorality Act.

In addition, South Africa moved steadily into international isolation, with gradual hostility building to English-speaking whites and to British immigration, and gradual moves towards a Republic, eventually attained in 1961 only after a narrow victory in a whites-only referendum. The rift with Britain widened, with a decisive point in the attitude of the British Government being marked by Harold Macmillan's "Winds of Change" speech in Cape Town in February 1960 and simultaneous British decolonisation in the rest of Africa. The next thirty years were difficult and disagreeable, and the eventual outcome, in 1994, of a black-ruled state, was inevitable in the circumstances. It was better by far than the anarchy that might have arisen, albeit far from the aspirations of those idealists who worked to establish the Union in the first decade of the 20th century.

It is thanks to the patience and statesmanship of Nelson Mandela and F. W. de Klerk that revolutionary violence was largely avoided in the 1990s. Was there ever a happier medium between apartheid and uncurbed black sovereignty? Both for South Africa and for Rhodesia – and success in one might well have influenced the outcome in the other – the solution might have been a constitutional process which gave a role to the black majority, increasing by degree, but also with cast-iron guarantees to protect the interests of the whites, the Asians, and the coloureds.[77] And "cast iron" does not just mean a scrap of paper – we have seen where that ended in other African countries. Some kind of military check, linked to a constitutional court and possibly to a federal central government, might have been necessary. The advice of the 17th century political theorist Thomas Hobbes is compelling: "Covenants, without the sword, are but words, and of no strength to secure a man at all."

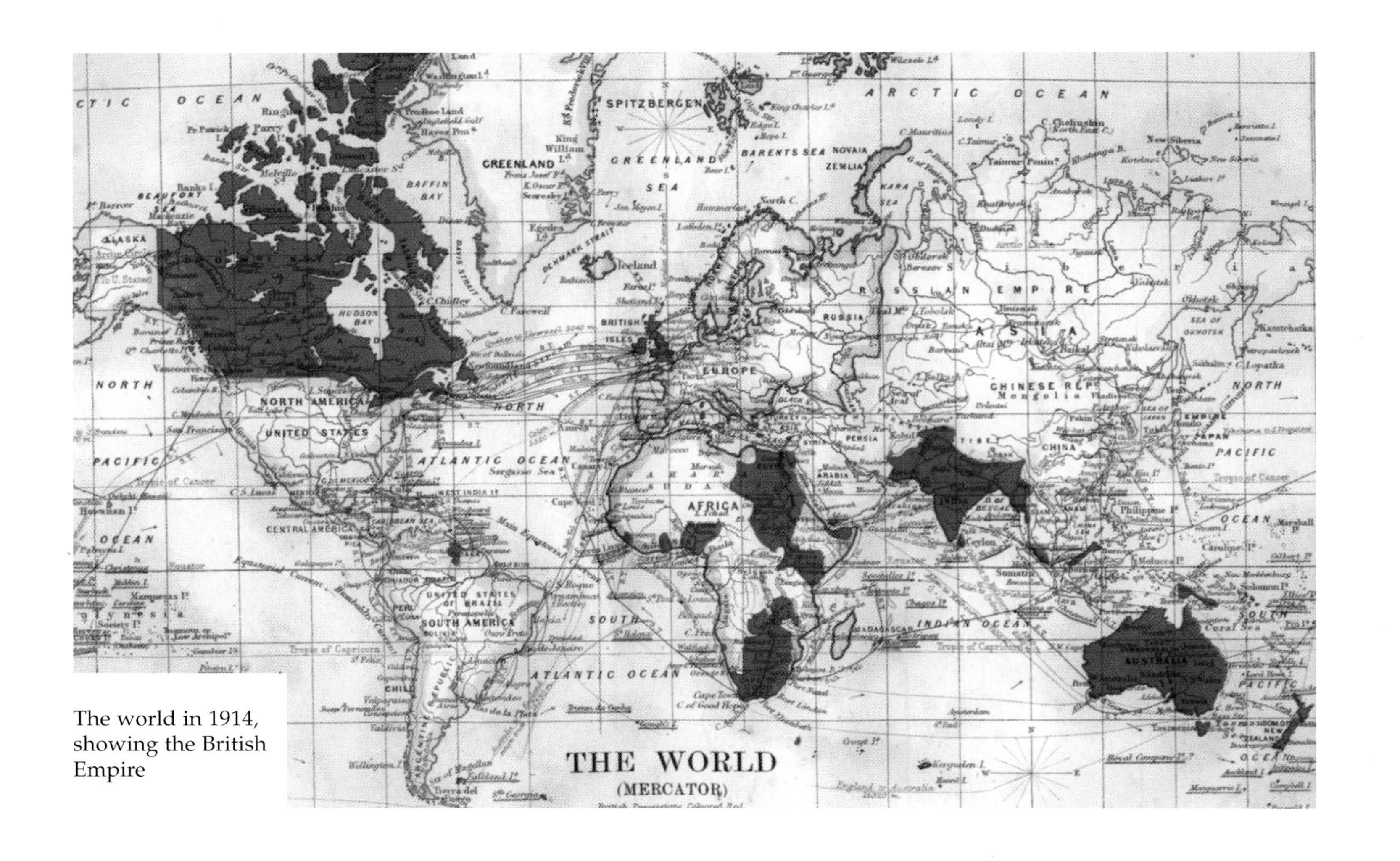

The world in 1914, showing the British Empire

Benjamin Disraeli

W. E. Gladstone

Edward Carson

General Jan Smuts

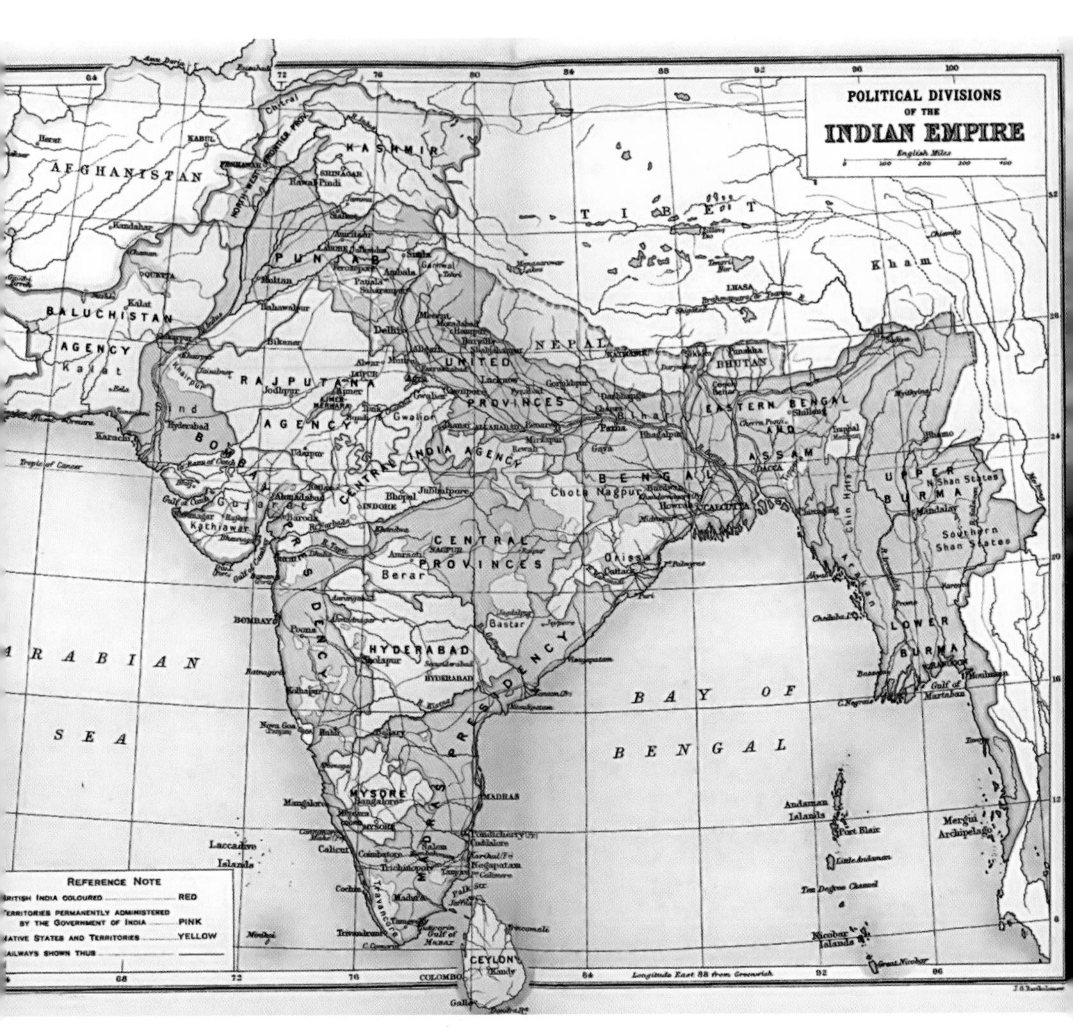

India, showing native and Princely States (coloured in yellow)

Joseph Chamberlain (and Jesse Collings) from *Struwwelpeter Alphabet*

Lord Curzon as Viceroy from *Struwwelpeter Alphabet*

Kaiser Wilhelm II from *Struwwelpeter Alphabet*

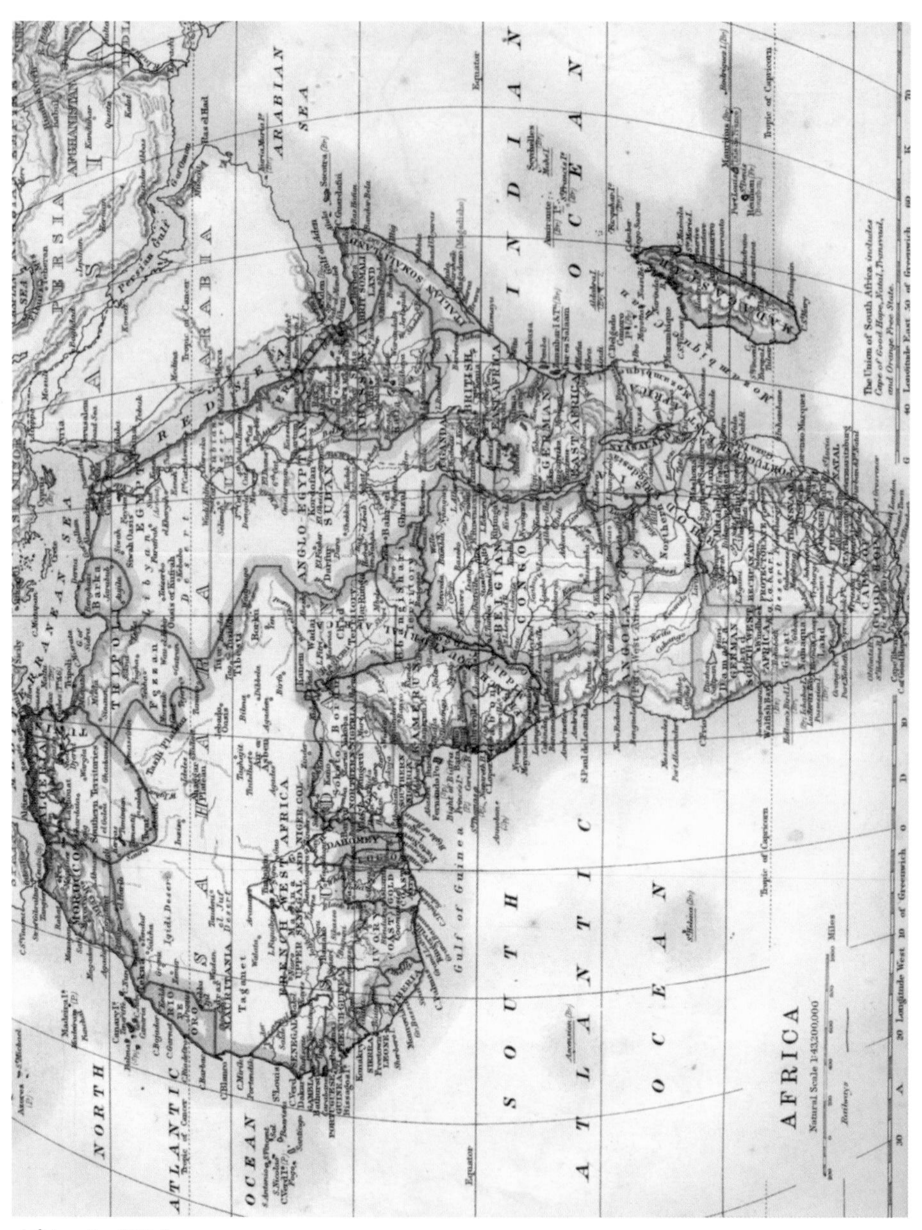

Africa in 1914

Cecil Rhodes (Jim being Jameson) from *Struwwelpeter Alphabet*

Lord Salisbury from *Struwwelpeter Alphabet*

Paul Kruger

General James Hertzog

Lord Milner

Andrew Bonar Law

FOOTNOTES

1 Amery to Milner, 20 June 1903, Barnes and Nicholson, op cit, p47. Compare Milner's view on p13.

2 David Livingstone started exploring in 1841 and was followed by Burton, Speke, Grant (expeditions 1857-9), and others, especially Henry Stanley (1874-77). They "discovered" the Great Lakes and the courses of the Congo and the Zambezi, and tried to find the sources of the Nile.

3 Chamberlain made the exaggerated claim in 1898 that the Ashanti lands, which he finally secured through the Fourth Ashanti War in 1895-6, contained "one of the richest goldfields in the world"; his recent biographer says "he was dazzled by any prospect of gold" (Marsh op cit, p427) and had high hopes of British exports.

4 Lawrence James, *Empires In The Sun: The Struggle for the Mastery of Africa*, pp58-9 for these mistakes.

5 Thomas Pakenham, *The Scramble for Africa*, p182.

6 His aim was to stir up temporary tension with Britain, in order to diminish the influence of the Anglophile Crown Prince Frederick (married to Queen Victoria's eldest daughter Vicky), who was now close to succeeding his 87-year-old father.

7 Sybil Crowe, *The Berlin West Africa Conference,* pp178-9; "Monroe Doctrine" in John Charmley, *Splendid Isolation: Britain and the Balance of Power 1874-1914,* p193.

8 James, op cit, pp81-3 is critical of Gladstone's role, as is Charmley, op cit, pp183ff. The absence of the French was caused by negligence, but this did not prevent them over the next 20 years expressing resentment at Britain's action. Equally, the correspondence between Cairo and London, and various statements by Gladstone and succeeding British Ministers, bears witness to Britain's reluctance to stay in Egypt. In 1886 Salisbury publicly stated that no date could be set for evacuation (Charmley, p214).

9 Pakenham, op cit, p279.

10 He had burnt to death young pages (some canonised in 1964) who refused to be sodomised by him.

11 Pakenham, op cit, p 430.

12 Ibid, p338.

13 Marsh, op cit, p318. Rhodes did not have it all his own way in London. He wanted direct control over what was Bechuanaland and became Botswana. Rosebery, who "liked and admired" Rhodes, conceded this in principle; Rhodes then tried to extract it in practice from Chamberlain, Colonial Secretary in Salisbury's government of 1895, who liked him less. On 6 November 1895, an "indaba" between the Bechuana chiefs and Rhodes, saw Chamberlain "taking a blue pencil, marked out on the map ample tribal reserves to be entirely under the Crown." Rhodes was furious: "They think more of one native, at home, than the whole of South Africa." J. L. Garvin, *Life of Joseph Chamberlain* III, pp31-35, p50.

14 Marsh, opcit, p449; Garvin, op cit, p355.

15 Marsh, op cit, pp429-32; Garvin, op cit, p211 for "strangled". James (op cit, p91) refers to the earlier pact in 1890 by which Britain would control Sokoto and France obtained Madagascar, Timbuktu and Chad.

16 Garvin, op cit, pp205, 225-9.

17 Ibid, p225.

18 Ibid, pp169-71.

19 Pakenham's account of all this is in op cit, chapters 29 ("The Race to the Middle of Nowhere") and 30.

20 Garvin, op cit, p236.

21 Garvin (op cit, p 93) quotes the diary of Marschall, the German Foreign Minister, on 3 January 1896 after the Raid: "His Majesty develops rather amazing plans. Protectorate over the Transvaal, from which I dissuade him straight away."

22 "Milner saw further than most men but he saw narrowly. He despised the evasions and compro-

mises inherent in political life ..."(Shannon, op cit, p329.)

23 The Uitlanders mostly fled at the outbreak of the war and therefore played no part in undermining Boer resistance.

24 Garvin describes it as "volcanic and devastating ... Official style it threw to the winds ... [Milner's] whole pent up soul and charged intellect went into ... an incitement which reads still as living and sweeping oratory" (op cit, pp394-6).

25 Garvin, op cit, p404.

26 Pakenham, *Boer War* p68; Garvin, op cit, pp405-8.

27 Milner used "the same blocking tactics as he had used ever since Bloemfontein". He sent a "snubbing cable" to Conyngham Greene, the British Agent in Pretoria, who was negotiating with Smuts, warned Chamberlain that the new offer was "full of traps and pitfalls" and arranged (though this may have been an accident) that Greene's despatch, commending the offer to Chamberlain, was sent by sea mail. (Pakenham, *Boer War,* p86.)

28 Marsh, op cit, p470. Marsh prepares us for the initial military fiasco: Chamberlain had previously failed to persuade his colleagues to strengthen the forces in South Africa; Britain's political elite had a "craft of leadership (which) was essentially civilian."

29 Pakenham, op cit, pp100-1: "The gap which remained to be bridged at the end of August was actually small enough ... Here lay the underlying tragedy of the war; the narrowness of the margin by which the peace was lost ... Kruger rejected the chance of compromise because he did not realise it existed."

30 Ibid, pp88-90.

31 Ibid, p103; Garvin, p466.

32 Sir Keith Hancock, *Smuts – The Sanguine Years 1870-1919* pp104-5, Hancock's words quoted.

33 Ibid, pp126, 133.

34 Donald Denoon, *The Grand Illusion; the failure of Imperial policy in the Transvaal colony during the period of reconstruction 1900-5* p16.

35 As Chamberlain pointed out in his controversial Edinburgh speech (see p109), the British measures were not as harsh as those practiced by France and Russia in their colonies. They were, indeed, far less outrageous than the repressive measures used by the Germans in East Africa in 1905-6 or the near genocide of the Hereros in South West Africa in 1904-6.

36 However, as Pakenham points out (*Boer,* p574), the main lesson was that the smokeless, long-range, high velocity bullet from rifle or machine gun, plus the trench, "had decisively altered the balance against attack and in favour of defence" – a lesson only slowly learned by the British (and the French and Italians) in 1914-7.

37 Marsh, op cit, pp473, 489.

38 Barnes and Nicholson, op cit, Vol I, pp36-7. The word "native" was generally used in exchanges of that time, and histories since, as describing black Africans. It was inaccurate, of course, as a growing number of whites were also "natives".

39 T.R.H. Davenport, *South Africa – A Modern History*, p332.

40 Quoted Hancock, op cit, vol I, p96.

41 Davenport, op cit, p151.

42 Ibid, p151. In addition, the information and other resources of the new Agriculture Department were reserved only to white farmers, and the Native Affairs Department refused to allow agricultural officers into African areas even in pursuit of animal diseases.

43 Denoon, op cit, p140.

44 Ibid, p147.

45 Marsh, op cit, p 521.

46 Ibid, p521.

47 Davenport, op cit, p15.

48 Hancock, op cit I, pp158-9.

49 Denoon, op cit, p25. In Milner's "Watchtower Speech" in the Transvaal in 1903, he argued that white civilisation should be defended, but that defence should be based "on the firm and inexpugnable ground of civilisation as against the rotten and indefensible ground of colour." Ibid, p104. This was not, alas, sufficient motive for franchise progress.
50 Hancock, I p257. As early as 1904, Smuts and Merriman coined the word "Commonwealth" to describe the British nations.
51 Bernard Friedman, *Smuts – A Reappraisal,* pp18-9, 30-1.
52 Denoon, op cit, p111; Hancock, op cit, I, p317.
53 Davenport, op cit, pp160-1. Thus the 1909 Act perversely provided for a "loading" of urban seats and an "unloading" of rural seats so that the number of voters needed to elect a MP could be a third fewer in a rural seat than in an urban one. Since the Nationalists were strong in the rural areas, and moderate Afrikaners and English-speaking voters stronger in urban areas, this favoured the extreme Nationalists and after 1948 saw them entrenched in power.
54 Denoon, op cit, p237.
55 Ibid, pp200, 203.
56 Letter dated 26 March 1908; Amery, Vol VI, pp927-9.
57 Hancock, op cit I, p324-8.
58 Ibid, p336.
59 Hancock, op cit, II p84, Military casualties were 176, including 43 killed, police 115 including 29 killed; revolutionaries and suspected revolutionaries 157, including 39 killed; innocent civilians: white 87 including 18 killed, non white 152 including 24 killed.
60 Ibid, p163.
61 Davenport, op cit, pp173ff.
62 Hancock, op cit, II p213, Davenport, op cit, p207.
63 Davenport, op cit, pp190, 208, Hancock, op cit, II, pp224, 229.
64 Davenport, op cit, p209.
65 Hancock, op cit, II p261.
66 Davenport, op cit, pp215, 221-2, 333.
67 Hancock, op cit, p292.
68 In a letter to his wife of 20 May 1919 Smuts said "Germany is being treated as we would not treat a kaffir nation." He feared/hoped the Germans would refuse to sign the Treaty. Hancock, op cit, I p524.
69 Hancock, op cit, II, p314 .
70 Patrick van Rensburg, *Guilty Land*, a Penguin Special 1962, p83.
71 Davenport, op cit, p236, James, op cit, pp250.
72 Davenport, op cit, p238-9.
73 Ibid, p238.
74 Hancock, op cit, II, pp480-5. 488-9. After this the NRC did not meet until January 1949 when it was told by the Malan government of its abolition, to take effect in 1951.
75 Davenport, op cit, pp244-5, 251. The "international" dimension refers to the views of other Allies, especially the USA, and the foundling UN.
76 Ibid, p252, Hancock II, p500.
77 The South Africa 2011 census showed whites at 9%, down from 14% in 1991, coloureds 9%, and Asians 2.6%. The coloured and Asian population of Rhodesia was much smaller but the principle remains.

CHAPTER THREE

Tariff Reform to 1914

"Tariffs! There are the politics of the future, and of the near future. Study them closely, and make yourselves masters of them, and you will not regret your hospitality to me."

(Joseph Chamberlain speaking to some young Unionist MPs in early 1902, as recalled by Winston Churchill; quoted Marsh op cit, p520.)

"Look here, Chamberlain, your policy is all very well but all the economists are against you."

(Duke of Devonshire, summer 1903; on 5 August 1903 14 professors had signed a letter to *The Times* condemning Tariff Reform; Amery V p291. History repeated itself in 1981!)

The most notable contribution to Greater Britain in the 20th century by Joseph Chamberlain and his followers can be summed up in two words – Tariff Reform. Launched by him in 1903, it was not to be finally adopted by the Conservative leadership until the economic crisis of 1931. So this economic system had only eight years of peace before the war and the post war American Challenge began to stifle it. Chamberlain's programme had two aspects: external, the creation of commercial bonds, through trade preferences, to strengthen Imperial trade and development; and internal, the protection of British industries and thus the creation of revenue to finance social reform.

Apart from the "cause" itself, its impact on the politics of the time has fascinating lessons for students. No other issue, not even Europe in the final third of the 20th century, saw such reverberations in relations between politicians in the same party and between them and constituency activists. In both cases the Conservative party was split, from the Cabinet down to the grass roots. Salvos of speeches were made by the combatants – in the 1900s to audiences of thousands, reported in detail in the press, in the 1990s to audiences of dozens, reported even in the quality press only in slogan form. Both battles were also fought out on the floor and the division lobbies of the House of Commons.

The party leader in both cases, Balfour or Major, gave chief priority to preserving unity, and thus each failed to satisfy the contending factions. While the feuding in the 1990s saw hardly any "de-selections" achieved, though some were attempted (and some Tory MEPs were purged after 1997), back in the 1900s things were much fiercer. Some MPs, like Winston Churchill, "crossed the floor" of the Commons over this very issue, and several others, like Lord Hugh Cecil, highly respected but not sharing the Chamberlainite views of their constituency activists, were driven from their seats.

What of the merits of Tariff Reform? While there were risks in the "full

Chamberlain programme", there can be little doubt that a moderate version, which with firm leadership might have passed through Cabinet in 1902-3, was very much in the interest of Britain and the Empire. That version would have included, first, effective retaliation against high tariff competitors – which Balfour agreed to in 1903 but never developed in detail or attempted to implement while he had the power. Second, it would have involved sufficient preference, at least on the corn and the retaliatory duties, to assure the Colonies, as they were then termed, especially Canada, that Britain believed in reciprocity.

If the Cabinet had accepted such modest proposals in 1902-3, these could have been built on as public hysteria decreased. In fact, Retaliation became the most popular part of the programme and might easily have been justified by the fact that every other major country, including the Colonies (about to become Dominions), used tariffs. Why did this not happen? Apart from party politics, various members of the Cabinet, deeply committed to Free Trade almost as a form of theology, would have resisted, and the political events of the summer of 1903 show their success in limiting Chamberlain's impact. It is because Balfour did not want to endure difficulty or part company with the resisters that nothing useful proceeded and the Unionist Party was wrecked, for the time being, on the reefs of disunion.

In fact the "leadership" issue provides another parallel with the 1990s. In each case, with the party having held office for a long period, a hugely dominant leader left office – Salisbury by retirement in 1902, and Thatcher in 1990 as a result of a coup. Each Titan was followed by a very different style of leader. And in particular Salisbury's sons, Lords Hugh and Robert Cecil, who played a substantial part in the resistance to Tariff Reform, deplored what they affected to see as Chamberlain's "materialism".[1]

Prelude: A Slow Start

In contrast to the United States, which from the start had federal unity, and which, thanks to the Louisiana Purchase and the Mexican wars, had made great advances by 1860, British colonial development had proceeded at a snail's pace. The British North America Act of 1867 set up a federation of Upper and Lower Canada, which British Columbia joined in 1871. The description of another future great Dominion in the 9th edition in 1875 of *Encyclopaedia Britannica* began with the unpromising title "Australia, or New Holland". Settlements had been made outside New South Wales in order to forestall Napoleon's French who were showing an interest, but British authority was not claimed over the whole continent until 1829.

The early development of New Zealand was even more fragile. When a Belgian, Baron de Thierry, having served in the British Army, suggested a colony, the Colonial Office told him (1823) that New Zealand was not a British possession. Thierry then applied to Charles X of France. The Revolution of 1830 cut short a

French plan to send missionaries as precursors of colonists. Facing later French threats, the British government ordered Captain Hobson, the senior naval officer in Australian waters, to treat with the Maoris: hence in February 1840 the Treaty of Waitingi.

In the course of his biography of Chamberlain, Julian Amery powerfully advanced his own counterfactual to the conventional economic history of the 19th century.[2] He argued the case for those economic doctrines, suitably updated (as they were under William Huskisson before his premature death in 1830), which preceded the Repeal of the Corn Laws and the various measures to install free trade adopted by Peel and his Whig-Liberal successors. This present volume does not need to engage in 19th century economic controversies. As background, however, Amery notes the "catastrophic consequences" for Canada of the dropping of the preference on Empire timber in 1860, and the "fatal blow" struck at the "flourishing wine industry of the Cape" by Cobden's commercial treaty with France in 1860. Given the paucity of mid-century Imperial markets, John Darwin tells of "Free Trade Imperialism," usually accompanied by "gun-boat diplomacy", and often directed at China. In the 1930s, Britain finally paid the price for her entanglement in China through the Opium Wars of 1840 and 1856, not the most attractive phase of our Imperial history.[3]

As a Liberal, during Gladstone's 1880 ministry, Chamberlain was sympathetic to his friend Charles Dilke's proposal for a preferential "Zollverein" (like that which helped to unite Germany) between Britain and the Colonies. He and his followers also had an ambitious social programme, with his real ambition, inspired by Bismarck's legislation, in the field of old age pensions. He was the "first political leader in Britain" to raise the subject when he did so in 1890.[4] Progress was slow: he succeeded by 1899 in getting the government to make a commitment, while his ally, Henry Chaplin, chairman of a parliamentary committee on pensions, said the only feasible revenue source would be from tariffs. But the cost of the Boer War doomed this; Sir Michael Hicks Beach as Chancellor refused to allot money in 1901-2.

At the same time, we see pressures from parts of the Empire. At the first conference of Colonial Prime Ministers in 1887, Hofmeyr of Cape Colony proposed a 2% implicitly preferential tariff between Britain and the Colonies to provide funds for the Navy. Nothing came of this, but after the USA introduced the McKinley tariff of 1890, a Colonial Conference in Ottawa in 1894 proposed a preferential customs union. Chamberlain, upon taking office in July 1895, let the Colonial Office staff know he was "seriously contemplating the possibility and expediency of giving Colonial produce a preference over foreign produce."[5]

The Opening of the Tariff Reform Campaign – 1902-4

The whole question was indeed to be thrust forward by the costs of the Boer War. In 1900 Hicks Beach raised income tax and borrowed heavily. In April 1902 he imposed a low registration duty of 2*s* per quarter (designed to raise £2,650,000 – not a small sum) on imported wheat. He disclaimed any protectionist or preferential intentions but Laurier, Prime Minister of Canada, saw it as giving Britain the opportunity of reciprocating Canada's preference to Britain (made at 25% in 1897 and raised to 33⅓% in 1900), by exempting Canadian wheat from the tax. Chamberlain suggested to Laurier that in return for exemption from the corn duty Canada might exempt certain British textiles; Laurier seemed keen. The Unionists in the Commons showed considerable interest in reducing the corn tax in favour of Canada and Hicks Beach would not rule out that possibility. The Colonial Conference of summer 1902 devised a set of resolutions which were agreed by all the Colonial Premiers, to the effect that preferential trade would strengthen the empire and therefore every Colony should "give substantial preferential treatment to the products and manufactures of the United Kingdom". The Canadians let it be known that they expected early progress.

As with the crisis over Home Rule in 1885-6, the full drama of the launch of Tariff Reform and the consequent divisions in Balfour's government might have been averted. The new Chancellor, Ritchie, a "Fair Trader" in the 1880s, was now a vehement Free Trader. Chamberlain raised the question of remitting the Corn Duty in Canada's favour in the Cabinet of 21 October 1902; the discussion was general and inconclusive but not unfavourable.[6] However, resistance began to build, and Ritchie relied closely on the Treasury mandarins, notably Sir Edward Hamilton, who shared strong Free Trade predilections.

Before the Cabinet meeting of 19 November, Ritchie had weighed in with a memorandum prepared by Hamilton and critical of the Corn Duty. Despite this, "the Cabinet finally resolved that, as at present advised, they would maintain the Corn Tax, but that a preferential remission of it should be made in favour of the British Empire."[7] However, Ritchie persuaded them not to communicate this decision to Canada until his Budget of the following spring.

Chamberlain was touring post war South Africa during the winter, preaching development, reconciliation, and underlying it all, the cause of a Empire larger than individual or communal loyalties. Amery believes that during the opportunities for thinking, and encouraged by the "stormy enthusiasm" of the meetings, "the practical issue of Preference and the dream of a united Empire were integrated to become a policy". Both he and Marsh describe the curious "first hand account" of a conversation with Milner and Sir Percy Fitzpatrick, consisting largely of a monologue by Chamberlain ("he spoke like a seer"[8]) on the potential of the Empire to supply its own needs "which would take place under a defensive tariff against the outer world and a preferential abatement in favour of all parts of the Empire ... Other countries had armed themselves with their tariffs but we stood unarmed and defenceless."

Events dictated the next dramatic step. While Chamberlain was away, it seems that Lord Goschen, a former Chancellor and powerful representative of the commercial classes on the Whig wing of the Liberal Unionists, spoke to Ritchie: "Goschen regards any coquetting with preferential treatment as fatal to sound finance, and I see his advice has *taken.*"[9] Ritchie threatened to resign if the Cabinet insisted on the preference on corn.

Balfour was "perfectly horrified" at this threat. His brother, Gerald, then President of the Board of Trade, urged that Ritchie be allowed to resign; he (Arthur) rejected it, because he could not afford to make another change at the Exchequer so soon after the departure of Hicks Beach. Instead of calling a Cabinet meeting, reminding them of their decision in November, and accepting, with suitable surprise, the resignation of Ritchie and any others, he "hesitated with fatal consequences".[10]

Chamberlain returned to a triumphal welcome on 15 March. Ritchie put his budget to the Cabinet in two meetings towards the end of the month, proposing outright repeal of the Corn Tax. This was "coldly received". There was more support for Chamberlain's preferential proposal, but Ritchie was adamant, and possibly four or five members agreed with him. "With intense lobbying", Chamberlain might have reduced that number. However, he was ill and exhausted; he decided the issue was lost, and thus "insisted almost petulantly" on repeal as less offensive to the Canadians. The latter were bitterly disappointed by the Budget of 23 April.[11]

On 15 May 1903 Chamberlain spoke to his constituents, having asked his veteran constituency agent, Mr Vince, to predict local response to a major policy departure. Pointing out that at that time, 40 millions of Britons outnumbered 10 millions of white population in the self-governing Colonies, he continued "before the end of this century, we may find that our fellow subjects beyond the seas may be more numerous than we are at home." He spoke of the increased trade, in textiles and iron and steel manufactures, that Britain had done with Canada since the grant of preference and urged "a treaty of preference and reciprocity with our own children", warning that Canada might repeal its grant if Britain did not respond. He added a call for retaliatory tariffs. While acknowledging that "a discussion on the subject should be opened. The time has not yet come to settle it", he also indicated a degree of urgency: "You have an opportunity; you will never have it again ... whether the people of this country really have it in their hearts to do all that is necessary ... to consolidate an Empire which can only be maintained by relations of interest as well as by relations of sentiment."

Chamberlain attracted powerful followers, notably journalists, like J. L. Garvin at the *Daily Telegraph* and Editor of the *Observer* after 1908, and Julian's father Leo Amery at *The Times*. Others included W. A. S. Hewins, the first Director of the LSE on its foundation in 1895, who resigned in 1903 to work for Chamberlain. All three wrote leaders and articles in support of the policy. The bulk of the Unionist press supported him. Only the *Spectator* supported the Unionist Free Traders (UFTs). While Liberals like Sir Edward Grey and Lloyd George were privately sympathetic to Chamberlain's espousal of Imperial Preference, neither was going to break ranks publicly with their party's commitment to Free Trade.[12]

Balfour's options were complicated by the reaction from the Free Trade wing of his party. Powerful UFTs, like Hugh Cecil and Churchill, had made their opposition to Chamberlain clear, and this led to the foundation of the Free Food League on 13 July. Key to this was the position of the Duke of Devonshire, leader of the Liberal Unionist wing of the party, commanding long political experience and immense social eminence. In the words of Balfour's private secretary, Sandars, "The Duke always said that he never understood the economics of Free Trade but he was as politically incapable of persuading himself that he was not a Free Trader as that he was not a Whig".[13]

Alan Sykes is cynical: "whilst the positions of Balfour and Devonshire and Balfour and Chamberlain were not irreconcilable, the positions of Devonshire and Chamberlain were." If Balfour wished to retain Chamberlain "he had to propose a formula within which Chamberlain could advocate his full policy, however it might develop"; if he wished to retain Devonshire, the policy had to have "limitations so tight that Chamberlain would be held rigidly to the Government line, and no more."[14] The contortions, qualifications and nuancing in Balfour's exchanges with the main contestants at this time provide adequate explanation for the failure of a substantive form of the Chamberlain programme to be endorsed by the Cabinet and to begin to be implemented – after all, the Government had in theory about four more years to go before an election.

Chamberlain had increased the pressure by announcing on 7 July the dates for his autumn speaking tour. The last Cabinet meeting of the session, before the long summer and autumn recess, was fixed for 13 August, and a week before it Balfour circulated a document in two parts: the first part (published on 16 September as *Economic Notes on Insular Free Trade)* vaguely argued that the increase of foreign tariffs made it necessary for the Government to have power to force these down by retaliatory duties; the second, known as the Blue Paper, endorsed preference and even food taxes. In fact, like his future speeches on the subject, Balfour sought to cover himself by resort to ambiguity, involving confusion: "We intend to propose no tax simply for Protective purposes ... and any readjustment of taxation ... should be framed so as to avoid any material increase in the budget of the working man ..."[15]

In Cabinet on 13 August, Devonshire, Ritchie, and Lords Balfour of Burleigh and George Hamilton all objected strongly to the Blue Paper. In view of the opposition, Balfour decided to postpone a decision until the next meeting, scheduled for 14 September. He wanted to remove the three Free Trader members as they were obstacles to the policy he wanted the party to follow, but he wanted to retain Devonshire. So, with help from Chamberlain (who was to resign in order to campaign freely), he evolved a complex device to achieve this. Marsh describes it as "ill-considered on Chamberlain's part, deceptive on Balfour's, and for both (it) proved worse than the dual leadership" which had existed hitherto.[16]

Before the meeting of 14 September, Balfour carefully avoided disclosing to the three Free Traders other than the Duke either his reservations over preference or the proposed resignation of Chamberlain; both these had to be disclosed to the Duke. Balfour least wanted a situation "where he might lose Chamberlain and be left with Ritchie." So this meant "not closing the door altogether against Preference"; he was obliged to speak to his colleagues "in more than usually Delphic terms".[17]

In fact, he displayed a degree of ruthlessness with the three. After the meeting the Duke wrote to Balfour: "I never heard anything more summary or decisive than the dismissal of the two Ministers ..." On the 16th Balfour told the Duke that Chamberlain was likely to resign, but the Duke asked "that the other resigning Ministers be given a chance to reconsider their position. Balfour said such a course was impossible as they were irreconcilable ..." Balfour also explained that he was now prepared to come out against preference at the party conference at Sheffield. In the light of this, the Duke withdrew his own resignation, and only when this had been done, did Balfour accept Chamberlain's resignation, with Austen Chamberlain becoming Chancellor.[18]

Balfour's deal with Devonshire was based on fragile ground. We see Devonshire, feeling guilty about abandoning his Free Trade colleagues, agonising over whether the declarations to be made by Balfour at Sheffield "would be consistent with the opinion which I had formed that [he] did not intend to depart widely from the principles of Free Trade ..."[19] Meanwhile Chamberlain was "stung to the quick by a rather naive letter" in which the Duke admitted that the former's resignation made it possible for him to remain in office. Chamberlain riposted angrily, reminding the Duke of his mistakes over the 1902 Education Act and War Office reforms: "on both of which I warned the Cabinet and yourself especially that you were destroying your party." He meant the Liberal Unionists, and he referred to by-election reverses "all before the fiscal question was mentioned". Concluding, he lashed out "I, who for the sake of the Party, swallowed these camels, now find that you and others strain at my gnat! What did I ask of you before I went to South Africa? That you should retain the ... Corn Duty and give a drawback to Canada ... While I was slaving my life out you threw it over as of no importance ..."[20]

Balfour at Sheffield, consistent with the agreement with Chamberlain, committed himself to retaliatory tariffs, to be used in bargaining to lower foreign tariffs, adding that he could not propose Preference. This last was heard "in stony silence", but the largely Tariff Reform audience cheered his statement that he was prepared to "annul and delete altogether ... the doctrine that you must never put on taxation except for revenue purposes".[21] This triggered the Duke's resignation the next day.

At the time of Sheffield, Chamberlain felt committed to his deal with Balfour, but his problem was that he regarded the Imperial aspect as more important than the "retaliatory" one. Domestic protection, he felt, could wait but the UK needed to respond to Canada. If Balfour had been determined, it could have been done, if not in 1902, then in the winter of 1903-4. As one historian of this period concludes, rather than force the Free Traders in the Cabinet to accept that their views had been rejected, "he allowed them to believe that the issue was still open".[22]

Chamberlain's speech at Glasgow (6 October), the first of his autumn campaign, to an audience of 6,000 gave the outline of a Tariff Reform budget: 2 shillings a quarter would be imposed on foreign corn and flour; a 5% duty on meat and dairy produce (but not bacon). There would be a duty on foreign wines and perhaps fruit (to help South Africa). But there would be a reduction of existing duties: by three quarters on tea, by half on sugar, and corresponding reductions in the duties on cocoa and coffee. In all cases colonial produce would be exempt. This speech was followed by others,[23] also to vast audiences: in Greenock, Newcastle (with a raging headache), Tynemouth, Birmingham (to 10,000), Liverpool, Cardiff, Newport, Leeds and finally London on 19 January 1904. The Liverpool rally was under the auspices of Alderman Salvidge's Conservative Working Men's Association and "the meeting was probably the finest of the tour" , with the resolution of thanks moved by the young F. E. Smith, who said "when Free Trade was carried, the working classes were neither represented nor consulted."[24]

The political landscape was lit up by salvos from opponents in both parties. At the Queen's Hall London on 24 November three ex-chancellors, together with Churchill and Lord Hugh Cecil, combined for a rally, including another six ex-Cabinet ministers. All was chaired by the Duke of Devonshire, who claimed that while he did not understand Balfour's policy he completely understood Chamberlain's and was determined to oppose it.[25] The Free Food League of which the Duke had accepted the presidency campaigned against Alfred Lyttelton, Chamberlain's successor as Colonial Secretary, in his by-election in Warwick and Leamington: he survived by 190 votes having had a majority of over 800 in 1900. Meanwhile, Chamberlain swiftly took over the Liberal Unionist organisation, denying it to the Duke.

A weakness of the Imperial development aspect of the programme was the relative paucity of the market. While the "Colonies" had a higher average standard of living than the UK, their population was small: in 1901, Canada , the largest, had 5,371, 000 people, Australia 3,773,000 and New Zealand a tiny 773,000. These contrasted with the populations of Germany, around 70 million, and France, around 40 million, let alone the USA, with 76 million in 1900 and 123 million in 1930.

Chamberlain had deliberately avoided implying domestic protection in the 15 May speech but the enthusiastic reaction from the metal-manufacturers of the West Midlands made it impossible for him to ignore this aspect. Gradually he moved towards the protectionist theme, but the picture of a Britain suffering from unfair competition can be exaggerated. He is criticised for offering to protect backward sectors of industry instead of concentrating on newer industries which needed sheltering in infancy (the rationale behind the 1921 Safeguarding of Industries Act). British management, especially in iron and steel and coal, was inefficient. It was not inefficient in the cotton industry, where the problem consisted of other countries supplying their own needs. After 1900 the woollen textile industry reversed the downward trend of its exports, as did boots and shoes. Engineering faced severe competition from Germany: Britain was still superior in textile machinery, agricultural machinery, boilers and machine tools, while by 1913 Germany was superior in motor cars and cycles, and armaments. In electrical products, Britain recovered from a bad period after 1903 and ceased to be a net importer of electrical machinery. Chemicals and glass were suffering more from foreign competition. Cables and telegraphic equipment were sound, and shipbuilding and maritime industries retained "their overwhelming predominance" up to 1914.[26]

Few envisaged in 1903-4 a war of the intensity and duration that was to break out in 1914. Corelli Barnett has argued that if Britain had moved away from the Free Trade dogmas in the years before the war, she would have coped better. " The German submarine ... reminded the British government after 1914 that the price of cheap food from overseas under the policy of Free Trade had been the ruin of British farms and the terrifying vulnerability of the British population to starvation by blockade." British wheat production fell by 6 per cent in 1892-1912; she was dependent on imports for four-fifths of her wheat supplies, and 40 per cent of her meat supplies.[27] Barnett is scathing about the decline in, or non-existence or unpreparedness of, those industries more directly relevant to waging war: especially iron and steel, but also light engineering, machine-tools, ball-bearings, magnetos, internal combustion engines, scientific instruments and chemicals. This was immediately apparent in the "shells scandal" of 1915-6, but also held back the production of aircraft, motor vehicles, poison gas and drugs such as aspirin.[28]

An initial problem facing his campaign was that Chamberlain was sometimes badly briefed. He set out to tackle these weaknesses after Glasgow, getting Hewins to provide him with a weekly digest of opponents' speeches together with suggested replies. He used the influential network of Chambers of Commerce; in July 1903 the Birmingham Tariff Committee circulated a lengthy questionnaire to 102 Chambers, seeking evidence to support preference, combat foreign competition and dumping, and the effect of foreign tariffs on prices.[29]

Chamberlain, however, was no longer young. He "was racked by gout and the effects of high blood pressure". After his exhausting tour of speeches ending in January 1904, he went to Egypt for two months to recover (the doctor had prescribed four months); he "was completely exhausted, and never regained the vigour of his 1903 campaign." There were various signs of his declining health over the next two years: his memory sometimes failed him, attacks of gout, bad colds and 'flu became more frequent. At Gainsborough on 1 February 1905, he suffered a momentary blackout during his speech: his wife prompted him.[30] On 1

June 1905 he was unable to speak or write for a few moments. These were fore-warnings of the devastating stroke which crippled him in July 1906.

India was always an Achilles heel to Chamberlain, who largely ignored it. Curzon the Viceroy, wrote "I often wonder what would have become of him and us, if he had ever visited India. He would have become the greatest Indian Imperialist of the time".[31]

There were strengths, some of them unprecedented hitherto. The Tariff Commission was a remarkable development; the Departments of State, he thought, were "quite unprepared for so great a business as the framing of a tariff"[32] and there was a danger of endless haggling with Free Traders in the Government service, as well as differences between industries. Marsh describes him as "acting like a Prime Minister nominating a royal commission",[33] when he outlined the idea in the Leeds speech of December 1903. Its aim was to frame a general tariff for the UK. Members had sufficient prestige and funds so as to command the information necessary. The Chairman was Sir Robert Herbert, a former Permanent Under-Secretary at the Colonial Office. Others included Sir George Ryder who had just resigned as Chairman of the Customs Board, Sir John Cockburn a former Prime Minister of South Australia, and Sir Charles Tennant, Asquith's father-in-law. The total was 58, including seven MPs; it was light on the agricultural interest, but a sub-committee was subsequently appointed. There were, sadly, no representatives of the trade unions, as these had come out against Chamberlain; it is surprising that he was not able to seduce the support of one or two from the labour movement.

Three individuals in particular supplied the brains for Tariff Reform. W. A. Hewins, secretary of the Tariff Commission, derived his understanding of the process of tariff making from the German experience: the assistant secretary was Percy Hurd, subsequently MP for Frome and then Devizes, and grandfather of the Foreign Secretary of the 1990s. A second, who was to be the chief adviser on the financial aspects of the policy, was Sir Vincent Caillard, a director of Vickers and other companies. He later helped found the National Bank of Egypt and promoted the construction of the first Aswan Dam. The third was Professor William Ashley, who held the Chair of Commerce at the new Birmingham University, and was an expert on the US, Canadian and German economies – each of which was protectionist.

The other great advantage and innovation was a massive propaganda machine for the constituencies: the Tariff Reform League, chaired by Arthur Pearson, then owner of the *Daily Express* and many provincial newspapers, and amply funded from industry. Its immediate effect was the production of pamphlets exceeding anything since the heyday of the Anti-Corn Law League, but eventually it was to have a significant and unique effect on constituency organisation, leading to the removal of MPs with hostile views. By the end of November 1903, four leading UFTs – Hugh Cecil, Arthur Elliot, Churchill and George Hamilton – all faced pro-Tariff Reform resolutions from their constituency associations, and in each case, the process was to end in tears.[34] A total of 11 defected before the 1906 election, and

6 after it.

A major test of the popularity or otherwise of the Chamberlain programme lay in the by-elections during the 1900 Parliament. The trend clearly shows that the Government had become increasingly unpopular. With the reaction to the cost and length of the Boer War, and the unpopularity of the 1902 Education Act among Nonconformists, reverses must have been expected. The Government lost five seats among the seven contested between January and October 1903, with the other two seeing greatly reduced majorities.

Great attention was given to two by-elections in mid December 1903, in Dulwich and Lewisham. Neither seat had been contested by the Liberals in 1900, but now they hoped to win one and possibly both. In Lewisham the candidate was a vacillating Chamberlainite who easily beat the Liberal by 7709 to 5697. The contest in Dulwich aroused more Liberal hopes: the Unionist, Rutherford Harris, was a "whole hogger" – a supporter of the full Chamberlain policy – and also a controversial figure, having been censured by Parliament for his part in the Jameson Raid; the Liberal, C. F. G. Masterman, was a rising hope. Even so, the Unionists won well, by 5819 to 4382. The two results, halting abruptly the post war swing against the Government, delighted the Tariff Reformers and hugely disappointed the Liberals. Masterman himself later wrote "Of all the mistakes ever made by any party rendered blind by prosperity and ignorance, time may brand as the greatest the refusal of Mr Balfour to dissolve ... after the Dulwich and Lewisham elections."[35]

Could they have won an election at this time, Amery asks. His reply is that if Balfour, in early 1904, had declared for the Chamberlain policy, added the authority of the Government and the weight of the party machine to the enthusiasm Chamberlain had aroused, and gone to the country in February, they might have won. Haldane, Asquith and other Liberal leaders feared it. Amery, on reflection, doubts it: citing the various other causes of Government unpopularity and the almost certain loss of 20 or more Unionist Free Trade seats, plus the swing of the pendulum assisting the Liberals. But, he adds, the Unionists would have remained numerous and united in support of a clear policy. If the Liberals formed a government, they would have had to depend on the Irish MPs – bringing nearer the Home Rule threat.[36]

Balfour did not want an election then. He wanted to enforce the Education Act, consolidate Wyndham's Irish Land Settlement legislation, build on the new Committee of Imperial Defence while awaiting the Esher report on the Army, and bring the Entente negotiations with France to a successful conclusion. He despised the Liberal leaders especially in the fields of foreign and defence policy. So he aimed to hold on possibly to the end of 1906. And, leaving aside his loyalty to UFT friends, he believed that if he declared for the full Chamberlain policy, "he would be leader only in name."[37] The opportunity passed by.

To the resignation of the Balfour Government

Balfour's caution now appeared to be endorsed by various by-election reverses. In January and February 1904, the Liberals captured Norwich and Mid-Hertfordshire (St Albans), both uncontested in 1900; they also narrowly took Ayr.

Loosely defined, there were up to 80 Unionist Free Traders (UFTs). By no means would all consider joining the Liberals. In early January, when they feared an imminent election, the Liberals considered receiving the refugees, but after the by-elections, Liberal hearts hardened. The UFTs "miscalculated the extent of their own power", and the Old Whigs among them "never fully understood the degree to which the Liberal rank and file backed Campbell-Bannerman", with his support for Nonconformity and wish to help the rising Labour party. As they had no party machine, the UFTs had "either to ally with the Liberals or accept Balfour's lead. They did neither and oscillated ..." They failed to halt the advance of Tariff Reform; "consequently, they were eliminated by Chamberlain."[38]

In the following weeks there were a series of skilful Liberal-led Commons debates with the various aims of embarrassing the Government, exposing its divisions, provoking its leaders to dilute or deny aspects of the Chamberlain policy, persuading UFT dissidents to rebel, and – an extreme hope, given its majority of 91 – to defeat the Government. These succeeded in all respects except the last.

During the Debate on the Address in February 1904, despite a Front Bench statement that the Government was against food taxes, the majority fell to 51 with 26 Unionists voting with the Opposition and 12 abstaining or away unpaired. It was a shock to the party managers, who thought that the dilution of policy by the Front Bench would ensure the support of almost all the UFTs. The influence of the Duke of Devonshire and hard-liners like Churchill helped to produce this result.[39]

Meanwhile, the Tariff Reformers continued their advance. At the end of November 1903 elections to the Conservative National Union gave them a large majority, and in early December the Council of the Chamber of Agriculture passed a strong resolution in favour of the full policy. A classification[40] of Unionist MPs produced by Chamberlain and dated 13 April 1905 listed as Preferentialists "who have publicly expressed their support of the whole policy", totalling 172; Preferentialists "who would support the whole policy if it were recognised as being the policy of the Government", at 73, giving a total of the combined group of 245; "Retaliationists, many of whom would support Preference also, if adopted by the Government", totalling 98; and "Members totally opposed to any change in the fiscal system – most of whom are retiring at the next Election", at 27.

The economic interests represented by Free Traders and Tariff Reformers were predictable: the former having interests in the financial sector, shipping, or in industries still committed to Free Trade, like cotton and coal; the latter from iron and steel, building materials, glass and chemicals – all hit hard by German competition.[41] Tariff Reformers were not surprisingly dominant in the Midlands and

UFTs in areas like London, Lancashire and Glasgow. The UFTs tended to be "extremely conservative about social reform", with opposition not only to tariffs, but to most forms of state intervention including "collectivist" social reforms and to any concessions to the rising Labour movement. Rempel quotes St Loe Strachey, editor of the pro-Free Trade *Spectator*: "I did my very best ... to get the Lords to throw out the Old Age Pensions Bill and if they had not been a set of miserable funks they would have done it." Strachey believed that "Protection and Socialism are really joined at the base. Both involve State servitude ..."[42]

On 12 May 1904, again in Birmingham, Chamberlain summed up after one year. He dismissed the by-election results; "where we have candidates who have a little courage ... and supported ... wholeheartedly the policy in which they believe", these did better. In a letter in July, he feared the Liberals will get a "large majority" at the General Election. Candidates put forward by the Central headquarters "are all wobblers and half-hearted. Their defeat is a foregone conclusion." An election, which he clearly wanted in early 1905, "will rid us of most" of the "small but noisy minority" of UFTs.[43]

Austen Chamberlain suggested to Balfour (24 August 1904) that, at the National Union conference in October he should promise to call a Colonial Conference to consider Imperial trade and then put what was necessary to Parliament. Sandars, often the evil genius, tells Balfour: "Joe has failed. Austen's letter shows that he knows he has, and that he wants to save what he can at some price. But why should we damage ourselves by paying that price?"[44] Balfour delayed a reply until Austen was about to depart on holiday; he then (10 September) indicated that he would need the support of the electorate for summoning a Colonial Conference and then would need to submit the conclusion to another election. Thus began the "two elections" policy which created havoc during the final 14 months of the Parliament.

Knowing Chamberlain was to speak at Woburn on 7 October, Balfour, with only three days' notice, accepted an engagement to speak at Edinburgh on 3 October. He spelt out his "two elections" policy, and urged his Party not to press him too far: "I individually am not a Protectionist ... For this country in its existing circumstances Protection ... is not the best policy." If the party took up such a policy "I do not think that I could with advantage in such circumstances be its leader". After Sandars had explained the two elections policy to him, Hicks Beach commented that "both he and Joe would be under ground before anything could be done".[45]

In his Woburn speech, Chamberlain dismissed a second election as "very inconvenient and very unpopular" and involving a long delay; if it was insisted on "I think the Colonies would be justified in accusing us of insincerity." Then he departed on six weeks holiday in Italy, while the Tariff Reformers triumphed completely at the National Union meetings on 28 October in Southampton. As Chaplin told Chamberlain, the Free Traders tried to delete part of the Tariff

Reformers' resolution and insert a clause approving Balfour's Edinburgh speech. "They got exactly 13 votes out of the whole of the meeting, a whole forest of hands going up for us with tremendous applause and cheering"; the main resolution was carried intact with only 2 against it. Unfortunately for them, this coincided with the "Dogger Bank incident" where the Russian Baltic fleet, en route for its demise at Tsushima, fired on British fishing trawlers mistaken for Japanese torpedo boats: thus Balfour devoted his entire speech to the international crisis and did not refer once to the fiscal resolution.

Chamberlain and Balfour had hardly met since his resignation. They dined alone on 17 February 1905. According to Chamberlain's note of their conversation that same night, Balfour insisted on the two elections, and this occupied much of their time; there was "no time" for discussion of his plans for putting flesh on the retaliation policy.[46] Despite Balfour's plea at this meeting for Lord Hugh Cecil, Chamberlain was ruthless. The Greenwich constituency association had already adopted I. H. Benn as candidate. Balfour made Acland-Hood, the Chief Whip, write to the Greenwich members praising Cecil's qualities and asking them to reconsider. Chamberlain wrote to them to support Benn, and put the League's machinery at Benn's disposal. Cecil contested the 1906 election without the support of his association and against Benn – the Liberals won the seat.

The Liberals then obtained four evenings for Private Members' time in the Commons, and carefully crafted four resolutions attacking the whole range of Unionist proposals for fiscal reform.

The Cabinet met on the 20th and 21st March 1905, as the first debate was on the 22nd. Austen, as Chancellor, was considering resignation, and Balfour himself threatened resignation unless the Cabinet were unanimous. This produced a novel compromise "humiliating in the extreme to both sides, but equally so"[47] – to abstain *in toto*. So Resolution 1 was carried by 254 (including 35 Unionist Free Traders) to 2.

Chamberlain now suggested that Balfour should call the Colonial Conference for 1905; the results could not be submitted to the present Parliament but might be made the subject for a mandate at the General Election. To impress Balfour with his strength, on 14 April he led a deputation of 142 MPs to request clarification of ambiguities ("precisely what Balfour wished to avoid"). On 15 May Chamberlain met Balfour again, who according to Sir Herbert Maxwell, a close Chamberlain lieutenant who was also present, said "whatever happened, Tariff Reform, including Colonial Preference, must be *the* foremost article in the programme" for the election. Maxwell added "He accepted as part of that programme, the principle of an all-round tariff on imports."[48]

The usual succession of incidents disrupted matters, although there seems to be a preciseness and sensitivity about words which might seem strange to modern politicians. Brodrick, the Secretary of State for India, speaking on 12 May at Farnham referred to the Colonial Conference meeting "next year". In Parliament, the Liberals asked whether the Government were contemplating such a Conference before an election, and Balfour replied, stating the fact, that the Conference was due to meet again in 1906. Amid Liberal uproar, Campbell-Bannerman moved to adjourn the House, alleging the breaking of pledges at Edinburgh. Typically, Balfour put up Lyttelton to reply instead of himself (22 May) and the UFTs added to their esteem by saying they would not support the Government if there were any question of holding a Conference to discuss Preference in the lifetime of the Parliament. Chamberlain and Balfour met on the 26th; Maxwell who only arrived towards the end wrote "All had gone wrong." Balfour had told them that "owing to the construction put upon his Edinburgh speech by some of our party, he felt debarred from allowing the Conference to assemble before the General Election. He explained that, when he made that ... speech, he had never contemplated the possibility of the Government remaining in office through 1906 ..." Maxwell described Chamberlain as "much depressed."[49]

Balfour spoke at the Royal Albert Hall on 2 June 1905. The vital points agreed between Austen and his father for insertion were diluted or, in Austen's words, "wholly lost in the mass of intervening matter". The Tariff Reformers got their main point – that Preference was the most urgent part of the policy. There was, however, no mention of an all-round tariff.[50] This marked the end of Chamberlain's attempt to secure a common front with Balfour before the election. As Marsh acknowledges "The way that Balfour jerked Chamberlain back and forth, often from a distance through intermediaries, was bound to infuriate him." To Northcote Chamberlain wrote on 13 June "it seems impossible for Arthur Balfour to dot the i's and cross the t's so that his own opinions and decisions can be understood by all alike."[51]

In his pre-recess speech to the Parliamentary party on 18 July, Balfour, largely on grounds of foreign policy, said he opposed an early dissolution. Chamberlain was by then strongly in favour of an autumn dissolution: the Government had had a net loss of twenty seats since 1902 through by-election defeat or defection and he could not stomach Balfour having to appease the UFTs to keep his majority.

Balfour's priorities changed after his last major achievement in foreign affairs, the signing of a strengthened treaty with Japan in September. Civil relations between him and Chamberlain were greatly disrupted by a speech on 1 November at Sunderland by Balfour's "least intelligent"[52] supporter in the Cabinet, the Lord President of the Council, Lord Londonderry, who claimed that Chamberlain's fiscal proposals had been discredited and that the party should now reject them in order to recover its unity. Chamberlain fired back at Birmingham (3 November), indicting the Prime Minister ("the apathy which has been born of timorous counsels and of half-hearted convictions") without mentioning him by name: "I wish an election because the great Unionist party is marking time when it ought to be fighting the enemy ... I would infinitely rather be part of a powerful minority than a member of an impotent majority." On 11 November Balfour, staying with Londonderry, gave a speech devoting much praise to Chamberlain's assailant.

On 8 November Chamberlain told Lord Ridley that he "confidently" expected dissolution at the beginning of February 1906. What then changed? At the annual Conservative Conference at Newcastle on 14 November the Tariff Reform resolution was carried by 698 to 2, an amendment asking the Conference to declare instead "its cordial support of the policy of the Prime Minister" having been rejected by an "overwhelming majority" (it obtained 8 votes[53]). Balfour's speech, however "was anything but the clear lead" Chamberlain had called for: he "went out of his way to defend the policy of abstention from the fiscal debates of March", adding, 'I was not afraid of the Opposition; I was afraid of my friends'. "[54] He made no reference to the resolution.

A few days later, in the train to Windsor to meet the King of Greece, Chamberlain said "I tell you, Arthur, you will wreck the party if you go on. You should have dissolved two years ago." Balfour at length replied ; "Well, I suppose you are right."[55] The final straw may have been Chamberlain's speech to the Liberal Unionist conference at Bristol on 21 November, where he stated: "No army was ever led successfully to battle on the principle that the lamest man should govern the march. You must not go into the battle which is impending, with blunted swords, merely in order to satisfy the scruples of those who do not wish to fight at all."[56]

Balfour's decision to resign, rather than dissolve, arose from a misplaced hope. Rosebery had rejected any "step-by-step" approach to Home Rule, which was the compromise agreed with Campbell-Bannerman by Asquith, Grey and Haldane. Balfour hoped that these three Liberal Imperialists would refuse to serve under Campbell–Bannerman, who therefore would not be able to form a Government. They decided to serve, however; he did form his Government, and then asked the King for a dissolution.

From the 1906 Election to 1914

The Unionist catastrophe in the January 1906 election decisively postponed the implementation of Tariff Reform – in the event, for 25 years. If 1906 had been a "normal" defeat, on the scale of 1880 or 1892, the Unionists might have expected, on "the swing of the pendulum", to return to power five or six years later. But they failed to break through in the two elections of 1910 and though the outbreak of war in 1914 saw them, through by-election gains, as the largest party, they were outnumbered by the Liberals and their allies, Labour and the Irish.

Several Unionists blamed the Tariff Reform campaign for the extent of the defeat of 1906. As always after an electoral disaster, the entrails of the corpse are carefully examined. In two ways the workings of the electoral system had damaged the Unionists. The party won 43.4% of the vote (to 48.9% for the Liberals); such a proportion produced Conservative majorities later in the 20th century. In 1906 these votes produced 401 Liberal MPs to 157 Unionists. While this disparity is partly explained by unopposed returns, an important factor was the electoral cooperation between the Liberals and Labour which continued in the two 1910 elections. Then, the Unionist vote increased to 46.9%, but this only gave them 272 or 273 seats – in 1892 47% of the vote had given them 314 seats.

Furthermore, in those days, polling was "staggered" over nearly three weeks. The first results in 1906 were the defeat of Balfour and every other Unionist in the six Manchester seats. Did this contribute, however slightly, to a "Gadarene" effect? Sadly for Chamberlain, the Birmingham poll (where the Unionists triumphed once again, holding all seven seats) was much later and so could not set an example. Otherwise, Tariff Reformers did well only in Liverpool (the Protestant Salvidge machine held its own) and in Sheffield, where their policy appealed to those involved in metal manufacturing. While the rural results were very disappointing, those in Scotland, Lancashire and London were dreadful. In these and other areas the previously Unionist working class vote turned away, influenced by the "dear food" cry and even more by the Taff Vale onslaught on trade union rights and the very potent smear of "Chinese slavery."[57]

The 56 Unionist Free Trade candidates obtained just over 240,000 (4.5%) of the total cast. Eleven seats were contested by both Tariff Reformers and UFTs, allowing three Liberals to win. Only two UFTs who faced Tariff Reformers held their seats; five of the most vigorous including Lord Hugh Cecil were defeated owing to split votes.

The figures usually given for the break-down of the 157 surviving Unionist MPs are: 109 Chamberlainites, 32 Balfourites, 11 Unionist Free Traders and 5 "uncertain".[58] While pointing out that the composition of each faction was not clear, Marsh calculates that almost 40% of the Chamberlainites and of the UFTs had survived, compared to only 20% of the Balfourites.[59] Despite this, Chamberlain did not use Balfour's temporary exclusion from the House to seek the formal leadership (Balfour was returned by a large majority in a by-election for the City of London on 27 February).[60] The two met for dinner on 2 February, in the presence of Mrs Chamberlain and Austen, with Chamberlain expecting Balfour to "advance in his direction". Balfour was hostile to food taxes and a general tariff and, it seems, even more so to having a party meeting dictate policy.[61] Chamberlain wanted a party meeting which with reluctance Balfour eventually agreed to.

What policy was to be put to the meeting? The Chamberlains drafted a resolution designed to avoid controversy between them and Balfour while excluding Free Traders. It was drawn "almost verbatim" from Balfour's speeches. Hugh Cecil told the Duke of Devonshire on 11 February, after a talk with "AJB" staying at Hatfield: "What he said is anti-Joe and I do not think he will move in Joe's direction at all. But I doubt whether he will depart from the region of mist where he has lived so long."[62]

Balfour then met the two Chamberlains, accompanied by his allies, including his brother Gerald and Lord Lansdowne. Discussions were sticky on 13 and 14 February, with Balfour seeing a resolution as trespassing on his leadership prerogatives. At length, Austen suggested turning it into an exchange of letters between

Balfour and his father and attempted to draft one for Balfour. This was then approved by the others and accepted by Balfour (on the 14th).[63]

It stated that "Fiscal Reform is, and must remain, the first constructive work of the Unionist Party ... to secure more equal terms of competition for British trade and closer commercial union with the Colonies; ... *while it is at present unnecessary to prescribe the exact methods ... I hold that though other means may be possible, the establishment of a moderate general tariff on manufactured goods, not imposed for the purpose of raising prices or giving artificial protection against legitimate competition, and the imposition of a small duty on foreign corn, are not in principle objectionable, and should be adopted if shewn to be necessary* for the attainment of the ends in view or for purposes of revenue." Chamberlain's reply agreed with the policy statement and pledged his support to Balfour as leader.

To those familiar with Balfourian speeches, the potential for "wriggle" appeared immense (the present author has italicised vulnerable sections).[64] The party meeting on the 15th passed unanimously a resolution of confidence in Balfour as leader. Chamberlain's supporters saw the exchange – the Valentine Compact, given the date – as a victory for Chamberlain, while the Cecils saw it, in the words of Salisbury, as "a surrender by Arthur (while) Arthur thinks it is a surrender by Joe."[65]

As Austen later wrote, Balfour's letter contained nothing which he had not said before "but by bringing together in half a dozen lines what was scattered over ten times that number of columns in the newspapers, ... give ... that clearness and precision which was so terribly lacking in his previous utterances."[66]

Speaking to the annual meeting of the Liberal Unionist Club on 11 May, Chamberlain menacingly referred to an Old Testament story, with which his audience would be familiar: "There may be some of the party ... who refuse to accept this concordat ... We have a right to put that shibboleth to every candidate for our favours, and to say 'Do you accept this? This is the official minimum'. If a candidate refuses, at least let it be understood that he is not on this point in unison with the vast majority of his party."[67] But the Tariff Reform movement was about to suffer its biggest single blow of the pre-war decade.

Chamberlain was almost 70. The strain of the past three years had taken their toll. In mid June, he complained of "unusual tiredness" and a sharp attack of gout followed. On his 70th birthday, 8 July 1906, the City of Birmingham had celebrated both this and his 30th anniversary as a Birmingham MP, and major speeches were required. On the 9th he spoke to 10,000 people at Bingley Hall from all over the country. On the 11th, in London, he went to a meeting of the Tariff Commission and told Hewins "I am a wreck."[68] Later that day, he suffered a stroke which paralysed his right side. His family concealed his illness for months. Some recovery took place; he was able to walk with assistance; his brain was unimpaired, and his speech, though varying in quality, enabled him to dictate. But he could not write, he gave no more speeches, and did not attend the House of Commons except to take the oath after the 1910 elections.

Paradoxically but understandably, as the threat by Chamberlain to his leadership evaporated, Balfour appeared to became more compliant towards Tariff Reform. The downturn in the economy in 1907-8 also played its part. Balfour saw much of Hewins and took a "new and unexpected interest" in the Tariff Commission's work, while Chamberlain pressed "whole-hog" tariff reformers to curb their hostility to Balfour. By the summer of 1908, Acland-Hood was refusing assistance from party headquarters to candidates refusing to accept Preference and a general tariff.[69]

Chamberlain's illness left a huge vacuum: "the flow of funds to the Tariff Commission had dried up" as soon as it was perceived to be grave.[70] Some tried to encourage Lord Milner to fill the gap. Leo Amery lunched with him on 28 September 1906 and "hammered away hard at the necessity of his coming out into the open ... He conceded the necessity but was evidently very unwilling." F. S. Oliver wrote about Milner a few weeks later: "I read his speech very carefully ... and it seemed to me that he must hate speech making very much ..."[71] In these circumstances, Chamberlain's successor could only be Austen. He lacked his father's skill and genius to inspire. Garvin (who in 1910 was to apostatise) wrote "his mind is wrapped deep in the cotton wool of platitudes, and in his will or insight I have no longer one particle of faith." Dutton judges: "Deep down, [he] probably wanted to play the role of mediator between the extremes of opinion within the party, rather than take the lead ..."[72]

Input from Hewins ensured that Balfour's speech to the National Union on 15 February 1907 at the Savoy Hotel was well received. Describing "a safe, sound, sober policy of fiscal reform", he rather apologetically linked it to the need to broaden the basis of taxation which "would be absolutely necessary if we were the only commercial nation in the world, and we did not have a single colony." This and other speeches marked "the beginning of a process which ... especially [his] most hostile critics, found incredible, the emergence of Balfour as a tariff reform leader." The development continued during 1907, until the party conference at Birmingham: it was this that "finally reconciled the extreme whole-hoggers to support of (his) leadership and the Birmingham programme which became the official party policy."[73]

After the mass meeting at the end of the Birmingham party conference, (Joseph) Chamberlain wrote to Maxse, "Balfour no longer shies at the prospect of a moderate duty on corn & meat which I think essential for our negotiations with the Colonies ..." Regarding free fooders like Hugh Cecil, he added, "the best thing ... is to leave these people strictly alone."[74]

The methods of the more extreme Tariff Reformers disturbed this growing harmony. The Confederacy came to the fore only after the 1906 election. The *Nation* saw it as "a kind of political Mafia".[75] Rempel describes it as "this extraordinary phenomenon in English politics – a secret society with all the trappings of oaths, threats and codes". With its main object to purge the party of free traders, it was formed out of a meeting of at the Isthmian Club in Piccadilly in December 1906 and soon expanded to over fifty members, thirty of whom became MPs. By 1909 one of their leaders, Sir Henry Page Croft, was able to boast that they had put such fear into all Conservative Associations that no Unionist Free Trader could be adopted. For example, in January 1908 the Confederates forced the free fooder Lord Henry Cavendish Bentinck to accept Chamberlain's policy without reservations in order to be selected as candidate for Nottingham South – despite his having been MP for this seat from 1895-1906.[76]

Another constituency example, which demonstrates the new line from party headquarters, came over the threat to run a Confederate against William Joynson-Hicks (later Home Secretary) in Manchester North West. Hicks started as a free trader and rashly agreed to use his influence to secure Lancashire seats for UFTs. Then Acland-Hood "sent for him – sworn that they would not recognise him if he fought on (these) lines ... Apparently now the official leaders of the party have joined the Confederacy."[77] Hicks gave in, and without UFT support, narrowly defeated Churchill, who had won the seat as a Liberal in 1906 and was contesting a by-election in April 1908 after appointment to office.

At the start of 1909 the "fiercest attack to that date" was launched by the Tariff Reformers on their surviving opponents, with the *Morning Post* of 18 January publishing a "black list" of MPs suspected of being hostile to the official policy. Thus negotiations over East Marylebone, Norwood and East Hertfordshire, collapsed; the three Free Traders had to abandon each of those constituencies.[78] Meanwhile, the Unionists made substantial advances in by-elections. After two gains in 1906, and one in 1907, their advance took off in 1908, which saw seven by-election gains, including the defeat of Churchill. Rising unemployment (it approached 10% during 1908) suggested a reason to working men for fiscal change.

Budgetary pressures now caused radical departures. Asquith, Chancellor at the time, "thought he had made provision for old age pensions", in the 1908 Budget, but "had miscalculated both arithmetically and politically" and by early 1909 considerable sums were needed to cover the deficit. Balfour had been warned that fiscal reform was necessary as the "only effective argument against the spoliatory schemes of taxation which will be put forward ...", and an all-round moderate tariff was the obvious alternative to "confiscatory proposals".[79] Leo Amery's diary also points to the crossroads ahead: "Hewins convinced the Government cannot find a Budget and will go to the country on any pretext as soon as Parliament meets." Hewins's office "had been working away at a tariff ... everything is perfectly ready for running it through on this year's Budget if required."[80]

However, a series of episodes were now to begin, lasting beyond 1914, which would absorb the fighting instincts of the Unionists and distract them from their commitment to the Tariff policy. The first was Lloyd George's 1909 Budget. His biographer, John Grigg, believed Lloyd George did not want to risk much of what happened – a Lords' veto, a general election, possibly losing both power and the Budget, and otherwise becoming dependent on the Irish.[81]

Whatever the intention, the Budget on 29 April 1909, with new taxes on major landowners and hikes in income and inheritance taxes on the wealthy, provoked an outcry from country landowners and urban landlords. But instead of solely emphasising the tariff alternative, Chamberlain "failed to keep his distance from the property defence associations which sprang up during the summer".[82] Various by-elections showed a swing to the Unionists of half that recorded during the previous twelve months. Lord Winterton told Maxse in August that Unionist leaders across the Midlands and North wished to "choose any battleground rather than that of coronets and landowners against the Budget."[83] And, perversely, Unionist Free Traders, who anyway tended to the Right, preferred to risk Tariff Reform: Strachey wrote "I have three political enmities – Home Rule, Protection and Socialism – and I mean to fight the one which is the greatest danger of the moment." He meant "Socialism".[84]

The January 1910 election was the only one (of the two that year) fought on the full Tariff Reform programme – adulterated, if that be the word, by the issue of Peers versus People. However, the case for Tariff Reform was not put at its strongest and subtlest, first, because its main champion was silenced and second, because in this vacuum, Balfour, whose speeches never swayed the public, reigned supreme. He used Tariff Reform as the best " defence of the propertied classes against higher direct taxation", and devoted his own election address (regarded until the 1950s as equivalent to the Party Election Manifesto) "almost entirely to the constitutional position of the Lords". Winterton feared that "whatever we may say now, the fight in the mind of nine out of ten working men will be 'Coronets and landowners against the people's Budget.' "[85]

So the results were disappointing. While the massive Liberal majority of 1906 was overthrown, they retained 275 seats against a Unionist total of 273 (although the latter won 250,000 more votes), and this, with 40 Labour MPs and 82 Irish Nationalists, guaranteed them government. The Unionist gains, predominantly in the south of England, owed more to a natural swing of the pendulum. They were unable to break the Liberal hold on the still prosperous textile areas of east Lancashire and west Yorkshire, and the results in working class areas of London were also disappointing. As Sykes argues, in these areas, where the Unionists failed to return to anywhere near their pre-1906 position, "the dominating factor was class". In Scotland, the Lords were "hated ... particularly for their social and economic position and for their activities as landlords."[86]

As Tariff Reform appeared to triumph and then to wane, we see the final disappearance of most of the Unionist Free Traders. Lord St Aldwyn (formerly Hicks Beach) wrote to Robert Cecil that "a man may be a Free Trader by reason and conviction ... but if he has anything to lose ... he will certainly prefer an indefinite T.R. [sic] policy to the fiscal policy which is initiated by the present Budget."[87] Pressure in the constituencies was the real deciding factor, however. Ousted from London, Robert Cecil and Gibson Bowles had stood as UFTs in the more friendly territory of Blackburn, but receiving no outside assistance were defeated, while Hugh Cecil stood for Oxford University, where possible opposition from the great archaeologist (and Tariff Reformer), Sir Arthur Evans, was diverted through the good offices of Lord Milner. Cecil was elected unopposed. Other less active Free Traders now ran with Tariff Reform support, retired, or stood as Independents or Liberals.

The death of King Edward VII led to a party truce over the Lords crisis, followed by a Constitutional Conference in June to explore a way forward. This led to the strange episode of the Lloyd George Offer which, because of its implications for averting the crisis over Home Rule, has been discussed in Chapter One. One aspect of this, showing that the Chancellor "recognised that simple reaffirmation of free trade was an inadequate response to tariff reform", lay in the speech which in mid October he gave to the Liberal Christian League; he praised Chamberlain for the "outstanding service" rendered "to the cause of the masses" by seeking a remedy to social ills "not in voluntary effort, but in bold and comprehensive action on the part of the State." He directed rather ambiguous praise at Chamberlain for converting the Unionist party to Tariff Reform.[88]

Could the Lloyd George Offer have saved Tariff Reform in 1910? Whatever compromise agreements might have been reached over other items in the Offer, it is highly unlikely that many Liberals would have swallowed any significant element of Tariff Reform. Chamberlain's state of health prevented him playing any part in the Constitutional Conference, and would have prevented him both from, to use Julian Amery's words, "[striking] the hardest bargain he could with the Liberals and then [using] all his energy and skill to carry the bulk of the Unionist party." So Marsh is unfair when he states: "In allowing Lloyd George's offer to slip through his fingers, Joe lost the best chance he ever had to bring tariff reform into effect".[89]

The *denoument* was swift. On 10 November Asquith announced that the Conference would not sit again; Parliament was dissolved on the 28th. The link between the Lords veto and unimpeded progress to Home Rule was clearly apparent, and Balfour told Austen on the 12th that many Unionists were now advising a "temporary dropping" of food duties to concentrate on opposing Home Rule and thus win votes. What was particularly alarming was that much of the panic was coming from those previously most stalwart, notably Garvin, who "seemed to be offering the support of the whole Unionist press except the *Morning Post* and the *Birmingham Daily Post*" for a diluted policy.[90]

Lansdowne had produced a Bill for reform of the Upper House, including provision for a referendum in cases of deadlock between the two Houses. In the debate on it, on 23 November, Lord Crewe, the Liberal Lords' leader, suggested Tariff

Reform be subject to a referendum. Bonar Law had met in Manchester on the 26th one Edward Marsden, Unionist editor of the influential *Textile Mercury*, who found Law open-minded on the subject of a referendum. Marsden telegraphed to Garvin "Lancashire can be won only if Balfour" submitted the Tariff to a referendum. Garvin then "trumpeted the idea" in the *Observer* on the 27th, adding the very attractive challenge to the Liberals to make a similar pledge on Home Rule (which would almost certainly be lost in a UK-wide referendum).[91]

After resisting these pressures for a while, on 29 November, four days before polling began, Balfour declared in a speech at the Albert Hall (before a crowd of ten thousand) that, in the event of a Unionist victory, "I have not the least objection to submitting the principles of Tariff Reform to a referendum." It was unconditional – no response from the Liberals over Home Rule was required, and while he told Austen that "all the colleagues I have been able to see were strongly in favour", in fact he "consulted few colleagues and made little effort to find them ... perhaps because he feared that he would not have been able to get his way if his colleagues had been consulted more fully."[92] His closest associate, of whom he saw much in the two days before the 29th, was Lansdowne, "an enthusiastic convert to the idea of a referendum as part of House of Lords reform." Balfour conveniently but dishonestly described it to Austen as "Bonar Law's proposal".[93]

Austen Chamberlain said he was "broken-hearted" ("The worst disappointment that I have suffered for a long time in politics"), but as an habitual loyalist he gave the policy his reluctant support on 1 December. While polling was continuing, he then at Buxton (15 December), in his last speech of the campaign, stressed that Balfour's pledge had been for one election only and was dependent on the Government agreeing to a referendum on Home Rule. This, perhaps predictably, provoked outrage from Lord Derby (leader of Unionism in the North West, and a notable Free Trader), who said of Austen's father that he was "tired of being dictated to by a paralytic old man."[94]

Despite this major sacrifice in policy, the result of the December election saw no change in party numbers (Liberals 272, Unionists 272, Irish 84 and Labour 42). Leo Maxse started his drum-beat: "I calculate that Balfour's Albert Hall speech cost us 40-50 seats. It is unpardonable. Balfour must go ...".[95]

Various die-hards, including Selborne, Milner, Carson, Wyndham and the newly elected (in May 1911) Leo Amery formed a "Halsbury Club", of which the declared objects were: full support for Tariff Reform and Imperial Preference, including the withdrawal of the referendum pledge, compulsory National Service, elected Second Chamber and total opposition to Home Rule, all contributing to the undermining of Balfour. Maxse directed his "Balfour Must Go – B.M.G." campaign that autumn to the local constituency chiefs who would dominate at the party conference at Leeds. Balfour vacillated. With resolutions of censure coming in from local parties, he suddenly cancelled an engagement on 8 November and told a "hurriedly convened" meeting of his constituency executive in the City of his decision to resign as leader.

Tariff Reform did not significantly feature in the leadership contest of November 1911. The candidates, who "emerged", on account of their seniority, were Austen and Walter Long. They stood for totally different social elements. Long, Wiltshire landowner, honorary Student of Christ Church, Oxford, "a country squire with impeccable credentials to represent the traditional land-holding influence", was "recognised by most of his senior colleagues to combine limited intellectual ability with an unstable temperament." Austen had the allegiance of the majority of Tariff Reform MPs, as well as the Party Whips and most of the Shadow Cabinet, but would suffer from the Birmingham and Nonconformist association. Thus neither "was likely to receive overwhelming backing, nor were the supporters of each ... likely to acquiesce willingly in the victory of the other."[96]

The emergence of a third candidate was rapid. At the urging of Edward Goulding , MP for Worcester, and Max Aitken, MP for Ashton- under-Lyne, Bonar Law announced his candidature on 9 November, four days before the planned party meeting at the Carlton Club on 13 November. After intervention by Balcarres, the Chief Whip, concerned at the possibility of deadlock, both Austen and Long agreed to stand down in Law's favour.

The priorities of Law were crucial to the future of the Tariff Reform campaign. He was reputed staunch for the cause, but he had been ready to support the referendum policy in 1910. Marsh adds, "all along it was the protective rather than the imperial side" which attracted him.[97] More significantly, Law gave priority to opposing Home Rule or securing an "opt-out" for Ulster. He faced an early, and in the event, decisive, political crisis over Tariff Reform. He told Austen in January 1912 that "he is beset by letters asking him to abandon Food Taxes". Law had made his then perception of the matter clear in a letter to Salisbury in February 1910: "The whole Imperial side ... is bound up in the mind of the public with the food duties ... For us to give up the food duties after we had definitely accepted them as part of our programme, would seem to the Colonies like the abandonment of the only side of the Tariff Reform movement which could be of value to them."[98]

At the first meeting of the full Shadow Cabinet since his election on 29 February 1912, Law "left the initiative" to Lansdowne who argued that dropping food duties would lead only to accusations of "poltroonery." At first, several were silent, but Law supported Lansdowne's view and urged the position of Canada, which would never agree to preferential progress without food duties. At this, the Shadow Cabinet "endorsed their leaders' position: the Referendum Pledge was dead, and food duties now an integral part of the programme." Only Lord Londonderry opposed, but Sykes characterises the decision as "taken reluctantly and without conviction." From a wish not to embarrass Balfour, Law advised that it would be best to delay any announcement.[99] This proved fatal.

Law was awaiting the visit to London in mid July of the Canadian Prime Minister, Sir Robert Borden, from whom he wanted a public statement of how necessary a British tariff programme, including food duties, was. Borden agreed to stress that failure by Britain to move would create an "irresistible pressure" for Canada to make terms with other countries – obviously the USA. Meanwhile, the party got restless at rumours that the Balfour Pledge was to be dropped. Derby wrote in March "reversing the reluctant assent he had given at the Shadow Cabinet". It was agreed that Lansdowne would make the announcement about the Pledge at the party conference on 14 November at the Albert Hall; he unambiguously withdrew the Pledge, stating that when the Unionists took office, they would do so with a free hand to deal with tariffs.

A panic then ensued, with the *Daily Mail* denouncing this action and the Unionist Associations in Lancashire and Yorkshire expressing grave concern. Even Archibald Salvidge, the powerful Liverpool party chief, and an early supporter of the Chamberlain programme, claimed that the leadership had erred in failing to consult the constituencies. With the Lancashire associations scheduled to meet on 21 December, chaired by Derby (whom Law "certainly knew that he neither trusted nor particularly liked"[100]), Law arranged to speak at Ashton-under-Lyne, Aitken's constituency in the heart of Free Trade territory. In this speech on 16 December, he stressed that no food taxes would be introduced until the Colonial Governments, at a Colonial Conference, had made specific proposals. While this policy was not objectionable to Tariff Reformers, "the stress which Law laid on it suggested that he was on the defensive and so encouraged his opponents." Leo Amery's diary, written up several days afterwards, described these crucial passages as "absolutely inexplicable", adding "All through the Christmas holidays the stampede seems to have continued in the columns of the papers and at country houses."[101]

Amery told Austen Chamberlain that the Ashton speech "far from clearing the air ... seems only to have made confusion worse ..." He was anxious to ensure that "food" in the speech only referred to bread and meat "and that we are not precluded from protective as well as preferential duties on barley and oats, fruit, hops, poultry and ... dairy products ... all the more vital in view of the Irish situation. If Home Rule is to be killed for good and all ... it must be by a really rapid economic development in Ireland following our return to power ..."[102]

Austen told Amery that "it was the most serious stampede there has ever been on the question. So many people had been at Bonar Law that BL was beginning to doubt the possibility of carrying on." A conversation with Balcarres the following day, saw Amery assured that "90 per cent of the party were on the scuttle and that they could not be stopped." F. E. Smith believed that Lancashire Unionists threatened a major revolt; he told Amery "that the whole policy might well have been carried if the rot had not been precipitated by the Ashton speech, but (he) considered that some jettison was now inevitable." A talk with Law himself followed: "he seemed very nervous and hesitating; declared it was out of the question for him to change his policy, but feared that he could not hold the party for long."[103]

At the Lancashire Unionists' meeting on 21 December, held in private, food duties were condemned but Derby "would not let them come to a vote", knowing what it would have stated. They agreed to an adjournment until 11 January and he invited Law to a lunch at his house in Lancashire on the 10th for MPs, candidates and "a few of the influential political leaders of the county," meanwhile circulating a "mischievous questionnaire." Law wrote that "Derby is the sole cause of all the trouble, as I suspected", and he declined the invitation, but met the Lancashire Unionists on 2 January at the House of Commons and threatened to resign unless they passed a motion of confidence in him and dropped any resolution on food duties. Balcarres, himself a Lancashire MP (for Chorley), calculated that by this point no more than 40 MPs actively supported abandoning the Balfour Pledge.[104]

Hearing that Law envisaged resignation, a movement began on the backbenches, headed by Carson, who was desperate to retain a united party to oppose Home Rule, to persuade Law to abandon food taxes but keep the leadership. He and his associates approached all backbenchers for signatures to a "Memorial", drafted in collusion with Bonar Law, but involving "long and hard negotiation among the partisans on both sides of the tariff issue ..." This paid tribute to Law's leadership qualities, "begging him to harmonise the party and to accept the tariff compromise."[105] Within two days, 231 of the 280 Unionist MPs signed it: the Speaker and 27 Frontbenchers were not invited to; most other non-signatories were either ill or away from London. Only eight actually refused to sign, including Leo Amery, George Lloyd and Lord Winterton.

Typical of Austen Chamberlain's loyalty ("he always played the game, and always lost it" as F. E. Smith cattily said of him), he refused to give his support but promised not to dissuade others. According to Leo Amery, Smith's telling strong Tariff Reformers of Austen's wish not to dissuade influenced a number to sign.[106] Austen wrote to Mrs (Joe) Chamberlain (7 January 1913): "... I have done my best, but the game is up. We are beaten and the cause for which Father sacrificed more than life itself is abandoned! ... The Whips' report is that though fifty or sixty Members would gladly support Law if he determined to stick to his guns, not more than 25 wished him to do so. Law says that so good a Tariff Reformer as Page Croft confirms this estimate. Three weeks of hesitation have destroyed the chance of a successful fight."[107] And as Leo Amery told Borden in Canada: "There has always been a large element in the party of members who, while in a general way in favour of the whole policy of Imperial Preference, have through laziness or timidity never had the courage to argue the case properly to their constituents, and with whom the disinclination to do so has increased rather than diminished."[108]

On 13 January Law wrote to Balcarres; although he did not repudiate food taxes, he passed the onus of asking for them to the Colonies, and undertook to submit such a request to a second general election. This had been a crucial episode, as Tariff Reform would now remain off the Unionist agenda for another ten years. Inevitably, there was, and is, a certain amount of "what if" speculation. Leo Amery believed that if Austen had held out and urged his followers to reject the Memorial, a large number would have done so. This, as Dutton points out, "is almost certainly not the case".[109] It is also contrary to all that we know of Austen's character, caution combined with loyalty, that he would have attempted this somewhat risky and extreme course.

Lord Selborne remarked about the party after his return from South Africa in 1910 "I saw a want of faith, a vacillation, an opportunism which disgusted me". Most Tariff Reform League campaigners were exhausted after ten years, and more immediate and politically more unifying challenges beset them.[110]

On 15 January 1913 the Commons debated the Third Reading of the Home Rule Bill, and passed it; the Parliament Act 1911 ensured that the Lords veto would be over-ridden. Politics in Northern Ireland and the UK generally started to accelerate down a dangerous slope. As Milner, a keen supporter of the tariff programme, but a Die-hard on Ulster, wrote to F. S. Oliver in October 1913: "To my mind, there is only one road of salvation for Unionists now, and it is to shout 'Ulster, Ulster', all the time ... no mention of tariff reform ..."[111]

FOOTNOTES

1 Cf Lord Robert Cecil to Balfour, 25 January 1906: "It is their whole way of looking at politics ... utterly sordid and materialistic, not yet corrupt but on the high road to corruption." (Richard Rempel *Unionists Divided: Arthur Balfour, Joseph Chamberlain and the Unionist Free Traders* p109).

2 Julian Amery, *Life of Joseph Chamberlain,* IV published 1950; the final two volumes, V and VI, were published in 1969. This from Volume V, pp196-222. J. L. Garvin wrote Vols I-III.

3 Darwin, op cit, pp39-41. With British capital and migrants going to develop the USA rather than the British territories, Amery quotes Lord Elgin, Governor-General of Canada: "All the prosperity of which Canada is robbed is transported to the other side of the line ..." (Op cit, pp205-6). Darwin shows (p 42) that in the decades between 1841 and 1901 the proportion of all British migrants with the USA as destination varied between 65% and 72%.

4 Shannon, op cit, p330. During the recession of the 1880s, a Fair Trade League was founded (1881) and in 1887 the annual Conservative conference voted overwhelmingly in favour of a protective tariff.

5 Marsh, op cit, p372.

6 With no minutes or even conclusions of Cabinet discussions, Amery quotes from Balfour's routine report to the King (21 October): "there is a very great deal to be said in favour of this proposal. But it raises very big questions indeed ... On the whole Mr Balfour leans towards it ..." Ibid, IV, p518.

7 Amery, op cit, IV, pp523-4 from Balfour's letter to the King of 19 November (also Rempel, p24).

8 These quotations from FitzPatrick's own account, parts of which appeared in *The Times* of 28 November 1923. Accounts of the episode are in Amery, op cit, pp529-32; also Marsh, op cit, pp549-50.

9 From Hamilton's diary, his italics; quoted Rempel, op cit, p26.

10 Amery, V p155-6.

11 Marsh, op cit, p561.

12 Rosebery had given an initially friendly reaction but "withdrew from the brink" after Asquith, Grey and Haldane refused to budge (Shannon op cit, pp 360-1). A few prominent Liberals did support: the Dukes of Sutherland and Westminster, Halford Mackinder, the "father of geopolitics", Saxon Mills, former editor of the *Daily Chronicle,* and Sir Charles Tennant, the industrialist. (Amery, V p305.)

13 Amery quoting "unpublished papers of Sandars" op cit, V p237.

14 Alan Sykes, *Tariff Reform in British Politics 1903-13,* p46.

15 Rempel, op cit, pp49-50.
16 Marsh, op cit, p575.
17 Amery, V p398, referring to hurt letters from Ritchie and Hamilton, after their resignation, that they did not know about Chamberlain's resignation.
18 Amery, op cit, p403; Shannon, op cit, p356; Rempel, op cit, pp57, 59.
19 Devonshire's speech in the Lords, 19 February 1904.
20 Amery, op cit, pp431-2.
21 Rempel, op cit, p60.
22 Ramsden, *Age of Balfour and Baldwin,* p8.
23 Chamberlain deployed his homely wit: to Asquith's claim that dumping "is at a loss and can't go on for ever," he jibed "I don't suppose I could hold Mr Asquith's head under water for ever but I can hold it there long enough to drown him". To the Duke of Devonshire, who said he was "not opposed to the Government's policy of retaliation but he hoped to be a drag upon the wheel", Chamberlain riposted: "I do not think I should much care to go down to posterity as a drag upon the wheel." (Amery, op cit, VI, pp507 and 504.)
24 Amery, op cit, VI, pp488, 493; Rempel, op cit, p44. For the Liverpool visit he stayed at Knowsley with Lord Derby, another Unionist Free Trader, who said, echoing King Agrippa in the *Acts of the Apostles*, "Almost thou persuadest me". Chamberlain replied "Almost, ... that might be the motto of the Stanley family." (Amery VI, p494.)
25 Rempel, op cit, p71.
26 Shannon, op cit, pp360-1.
27 Correlli Barnett, *The Collapse of British Power* p90.
28 Ibid, pp84-88.
29 Amery, V pp308-9, VI pp479-80.
30 Rempel, op cit, p65; Amery, VI p652. Beatrice Webb, a former flame, wrote "He is obsessed with the fiscal question ... He looks desperately unhealthy." (Ibid p571.)
31 Ibid, V pp270-3.
32 Ibid, VI p 529.
33 Marsh, op cit, p492-3; AmeryVI pp529-34.
34 The first two contested their seats in 1906, facing Tariff Reform candidates, Churchill defected, and Hamilton retired. Cecil and his opponent were both defeated by the Liberal, while Elliot was defeated in a straight fight with the Tariff Reformer.
35 Quoted *National Review*, January 1906; Rempel, op cit, pp73-4.
36 Amery, op cit, VI p545.
37 Ibid, p547; Shannon, op cit, p354.
38 Rempel, op cit, pp92-3, his quotes.
39 The Duke's "advice ... to vote against the Government determined many of them; and the dramatic way it was given ... was engineered by Winston." (Sandars papers; quoted Rempel p88.)
40 Amery, op cit, pp693-6.
41 Rempel, pp99-103.
42 Rempel, op cit pp112-3 and Sykes. op cit, pp149-50. The last two Strachey quotes are from letters to Hugh Cecil (10 April 1907) and Rosebery (22 July 1907).
43 Amery, op cit, pp572-3, Sykes, p82.
44 Amery, op cit, p619.
45 Rempel, op cit, p124.
46 Amery, op cit, p655.
47 Amery, op cit, p681.
48 Sykes, op cit, p88, Amery, op cit, p699.
49 Ibid, pp703-4.
50 Ibid, pp707-8.

51 Marsh, op cit, p619. Amery, op cit, p712. Sykes states that Chamberlain had, by mid 1905, "lost patience with Balfour's leadership." (Op cit, p95.)
52 Marsh, op cit, p624.
53 Rempel, op cit, p133.
54 Amery, op cit, pp753-4.
55 Amery, op cit, p755.
56 Ibid, pp756.
57 See p55. Jack Seely, a former Unionist MP who had defected to the Liberals on the fiscal issue, attributed his victory in a Liverpool seat to the Chinese issue, on which as he wrote many years later "I had special knowledge, for I may claim to have organised the agitation ..." He added "Most people think that the decision of the electorate was mainly against Mr Chamberlain and dear food. I do not believe this. I think a far greater factor ... was the decision to import Chinese labour into South Africa ... If there had been no Chinese labour I believe Mr Chamberlain would have carried the day for Colonial Preference, if not at once, at any rate within a year or two." *Adventure,* his autobiography, published 1931, p102.
58 Most of these details from Rempel, op cit, pp163-4 . The election had reduced the "hard core [Free Trade] activists" to "nine or ten" (Sykes, op cit, pp100-1).
59 Marsh, op cit, p632.
60 David Dutton, *Unionist Politics and the Aftermath of the General Election of 1906: A Reassessment, (Historical Journal* 1979, pp861-76) provides evidence that Chamberlain did consider the leadership, but felt even more, as he told a correspondent, that he would not join Balfour again without a more definite understanding on policy." (Cited p865.) The article contained two gems: St Loe Strachey on Chamberlain "Once a Jacobin, always a Jacobin" and Walter Long on Balfour, when newly returned to a Liberal-dominated Commons: "They laugh and jeer at him as if he was something let down from the skylight."
61 Amery, op cit, p813-4. In a letter to other Liberal Unionist leaders and to Garvin, Chamberlain stated: "He appeared to have hardened. He is opposed to a general tariff ... he would wish to keep the Cecils and all that that means."
62 Quoted Rempel, op cit, p169.
63 Amery, op cit, p846. Dutton, *Austen Chamberlain: Gentleman in Politics*, p54.
64 A Tariff Reformer scathingly summed it up a year later: "In the history of party politics, there are happily few examples of a more specious manifesto. Vague, indeterminate, elaborately guarded, it is susceptible of fully a dozen different meanings." ("The Unionist Leadership", *National Review,* February 1907, quoted Sykes, op cit, p111).
65 Rempel, p170, Sykes, op cit, p111.
66 Austen to Mrs Endicott, 20 February, quoted Dutton, op cit, p54.
67 The speech is in Amery, p850. "Shibboleth" originates in a very early example of ethnic cleansing. Pronunciation of the word distinguished Ephraimites from Gileadites. According to *Judges, 12*, after a battle, the surviving Ephraimites tried to escape. If anyone mispronounced the word on being challenged, he was clearly an Ephraimite, and was killed.
68 Amery, op cit, pp896, 901, 908.
69 Sykes, op cit, pp123-4; Marsh, op cit, p650.
70 Marsh, op cit, p649.
71 L. S. Amery diary, Barnes and Nicholson I, p55. Oliver to Amery, 17 December 1906; ibid p57.
72 Dutton, op cit, pp50, 52, 56. He quotes Lord Beaverbrook writing, years later, that Austen had "once confessed that tariff reform had been a millstone round the neck of his political career." (p52.)
73 Sykes, op cit, p131.
74 Letter dated 22 November 1907; Amery, op cit, p921-2.
75 Shannon, op cit, p362.
76 Rempel, pp176-7, 181-2, 184-5. Sykes, op cit, pp120, 158-9.

77 Sykes, pp166-7, quoting the report of a Manchester Free Trader to Strachey.
78 Ibid, pp179, 181.
79 Sykes, op cit, p119.
80 Barnes and Nicholson, op cit, p62; diary entry for 14 January 1909. The entry for 7 May shows Milner saying "in strict confidence that he, Austen Chamberlain, Bonar Law and Hewins were meeting and thrashing out every single item of a Tariff Reform Budget". (Ibid, p65.)
81 John Grigg, *Lloyd George,* pp179-80.
82 Marsh, op cit, p651.
83 Sykes, op cit, pp202-3.
84 Ibid, pp184, 187.
85 Marsh, op cit, p652; Sykes, op cit, pp206-7.
86 Sykes, op cit, pp207-8.
87 Rempel, op cit, p193.
88 Marsh, op cit, pp656-7.
89 Marsh, op cit, p657; Amery, op cit, p956. Sykes treats the episode in pp228-32.
90 Dutton, op cit, p74. Adams (op cit, p43) reports a late night meeting of Unionist chiefs in the Constitutional Club on 13 November (including F. E. Smith, Carson, Sandars, Garvin and Bonar Law) where Garvin dropped his bombshell: only Carson and Sandars supported him at the time.
91 Adams, op cit, pp43-6; Sykes, op cit, pp233-6.
92 Sykes, op cit, pp236.
93 Adams, op cit, pp44-6.
94 Dutton, op ci,t pp75-7; Sykes, op cit, p241.
95 Marsh, p658, Sykes, op cit, p239.
96 Dutton, op cit, p92 Also Adams, op cit, pp58-9.
97 Marsh, op cit, p660.
98 Quoted Adams, op cit, p77.
99 Adams, op cit, p79, Sykes, op cit, p255.
100 Adams, op cit, p86.
101 Diary, 17 December 1912; Barnes and Nicholson, op cit, I pp87-8.
102 Letter, 27 December 1912; ibid, p88.
103 Amery Diary, 31 December and 1 January 1913; ibid, p88-9.
104 Sykes, op cit, pp267-70; Adams, op cit, p88.
105 Adams, op cit, pp89-90.
106 Diary 7 January 1913, Barnes and Nicholson, op cit, p91.
107 (J) Amery, op cit, pp980-1.
108 Letter to Borden 6 January 1913, Barnes and Nicholson, pp89-90.
109 Dutton, op cit, p99.
110 Sykes, op cit, p288.
111 Sykes, op cit, p284.

CHAPTER FOUR

The Drift to War

"Chamberlain's last bid for a German alliance marks one of the great turning points in history. Had it prospered ... the golden era of the nineteenth century might have been indefinitely prolonged; and the advancing forces of civilisation might have continued to hold off the horsemen of the Apocalypse."

(Julian Amery, *The Life of Joseph Chamberlain, Vol IV* p161.)

"One day my dearest Nicky, you will find yourself *nolens volens* suddenly embroiled in the most horrible of wars Europe ever saw. Which will by the masses and by history be fixed on you as the cause of it."

(William II writing to Tsar Nicholas II, 26 September 1895, quoted Miranda Carter, *The Three Emperors,* p185.)

The First World War was the greatest man-made blow to European civilisation since the barbarian invasions. The cost is not only measured in terms of military dead and maimed, or in money. The First War made the Second almost inevitable. The British Empire, receiving two great shocks in the 20th century, was so weakened by the first that the second almost proved terminal. France was bled white, leading directly to her collapse in 1940. Further east, the consequences were more sinister. The poison directed into the German body politic by the circumstances of defeat in 1918, in conjunction with economic collapse, was to bear monstrous fruit after 1933. A gradually prospering and slowly reforming pre-1914 Russia was to see all this potential good swept away and replaced by the carnage, famine and all the other apparatus of 72 years of Communism. And the territory of the "ramshackle" Hapsburg dominions, supposedly an affront to liberal-nationalist reason, by its sheer instability after 1918 and by becoming, in the name of nationalism, the prey of fascists, irredentists, border rectifiers and ethnic cleansers, was for much of the next century to provide an even deeper affront to liberalism and reason.

"War Guilt"

All the powers had groups lobbying for war – either opportunistic or preventive, to forestall a potential enemy launching opportunistic war. These were mainly in the higher echelons of the armed forces but naturally included ideologues and propagandists. All the powers, equally, had their peace parties and it might have proved fortunate that, in the case of Germany and Britain, some peace keepers held key offices in the years immediately before 1914. In Germany's case, the Chancellor, Bethmann-Hollweg, was counter-balanced by the erratic Kaiser[1] and the professional General Staff. In Britain's case, the Liberal Cabinet had an anti-war majority until hours before Britain declared war. We shall see in this chapter how, in the decade before 1914, Britain made understandings ("ententes"), including military commitments, to Germany's two potential enemies, known to key Ministers and Army chiefs but concealed from the public, Parliament and, amazingly, from most of the Cabinet.

Underlying these factors was Germany's behaviour, especially in the final 48 hours, when the invasion of Belgium made war, for most people in Britain, the only decent decision.

Much of this chapter will seek to analyse Britain's relationship with Germany. First, a look is required at the evidence that other countries wanted or were risking war.

In the immediate circumstances of July 1914, following the murder of heir Franz Ferdinand and his wife, Austria-Hungary was powerfully attracted to violent revenge on Serbia. There was no question of the Hapsburg empire being able (or willing) to make war against Russia – she was relying on Germany to prevent that. Nor did the Hapsburgs have any particular territorial ambitions – the Hungarians did not want any more Slavs – but a victorious Austria would enable neighbouring countries each to take a slice of Serbia. As so often with Austria, mischief in objective was exceeded by incompetence in performance: while the Germans wanted her to act fast on Serbia, so as to present Russia with a fait-accompli, Austria did not present her ultimatum to Serbia until four weeks after Sarajevo. The Germans asked Berchtold, Austro-Hungarian Foreign Minister, to finalise a dossier of Serbian guilt before sending the ultimatum, and make sure of the support of Italy (to which both countries were bound in the Triple Alliance). Berchtold did neither.[2]

The countries which, on account of their territorial ambitions, seemed to have the most obvious motivations for war, were the members of the Dual Alliance, Russia and France.[3] During the 19th century Russia had been a habitual aggressor. Her expansionist plans, whether in the Balkans, towards Constantinople, in the Caucasus, in Central Asia or in the Far East, entailed risk of war with other powers (notably with Britain). Russian ambitions in the Balkans led to the Crimean War with Britain and France in 1854-6, and very nearly to another war with Britain in 1877-8, when Russian forces almost reached Constantinople. Russia could hardly seek much expansion in Europe – unlike even her position in the Communist era, she directly ruled both Finland and Poland, but like Stalin she sought Balkan "satellites" – sometimes Rumania and Greece, but mainly Bulgaria and Serbia.

In 1914, Rumania was allied to Germany and Austria, the King of Greece was the Kaiser's brother-in-law, and Bulgaria was seriously at odds with her three neighbours, having been resoundingly defeated by them and losing territory to each in the Second Balkan War in 1913. Serbia had become Russia's preferred satellite, following the brutal putsch in 1903 in which the Serbian King, Queen and Prime Minister were all murdered by army officers. The deposed dynasty had been close to Austria-Hungary, with foreign aspirations directed at Macedonia, rather than towards Austrian-held Bosnia and Herzegovina. After 1903 commercial relations with Austria cooled: Serbian armaments orders went to the French firm Schneider-Creusot instead of Skoda in Bohemia, and major loans were obtained from Paris rather than Vienna – to fund yet more armaments orders. In January 1914 another French loan amounting to twice the entire Serb budget for 1912 was arranged to cover this military expenditure. Nikolai Hartwig, the new Russian Minister to Serbia, as a strong slavophile pushed the Serbs into a more aggressive stance towards Vienna. While he often exceeded the instructions of the Russian Foreign Ministry, the latter did little to restrain him.

By 1900 France and Russia, which from opposite ends of the political spectrum took the unusual step of allying in 1892, were firmly locked together. France contributed the largest foreign investment in Russia, larger than that of Britain and Germany combined. We read of a "steadily intensifying mood of belligerence at the various Franco-Russian gatherings" in mid-1914. Over the Bosnia crisis in 1908, when Russia objected to Austria's annexation, France had expressed lack of interest. By November 1912 during the Balkan Wars, and with Poincaré in charge of policy, France recognised that "any territorial conquest by Austria-Hungary would constitute a breach of the European equilibrium and would affect France's vital interests."[4] In July 1914, when Sazonov, Russian Foreign Minister, "explicitly advised Belgrade not to accept a British offer of mediation", there are descriptions of an atmosphere of jubilation in St Petersburg and Paris over the opportunity of war.

Moreover, "Austrian, German, French and most of all Russian sources confirm that Russian mobilisation measures against both Austria and Germany were well advanced by 28 July", the date they were first made public. At a comparably early stage, Austro-Hungarian units were taking prisoners from Siberian and Caucasian units that, given Russia's transport problems, could only have reached the front if mobilised earlier in July. Sean McMeekin quotes an Austrian historian's view that "the Russians began mobilising towards the beginning of July".[5] And the Austro-Hungarian General Staff estimated that between 1907 and 1913 the number of Russian spies operating in Galicia increased tenfold.[6]

McMeekin describes Russia's war aims, developed at an early stage and in mid September 1914 put before Paléologue, the French ambassador, with Buchanan, the British ambassador, invited to sit in. In addition to Serbia and Rumania annexing the large areas of the Hapsburg dominions they in fact obtained by the post-war peace treaty, and Poland (almost certainly still under Russian control) obtaining Posen, Silesia and western Galicia, Russia herself would obtain East Prussia and eastern Galicia.[7] Her main ambitions, however, were outside central Europe, mainly at the expense of the Ottoman empire: Constantinople, the Bosporus and the Straits, and, it seems, all the land bordering the Sea of Marmara, together with the Aegean islands of Samothrace, Lemnos, Imbros and Tenedos. And if this were thought too modest, Russia wanted "Turkish Armenia" and "Kurdistan" as far as a line from Sivas to Mosul via Diyarbakir, and Persian Azerbaijan.[8]

So far as France was concerned, how far was she committed to "*revanche*" for 1870-1 and regaining Alsace-Lorraine? Practical people saw this as a lost cause; at times, there was far-fetched talk of offering Germany Indo-China or Madagascar in exchange. It was an undercurrent which affected key individuals like Poincaré, a Lorrainer. He was Prime Minister and Minister of Foreign Affairs from January 1912 to January 1913, and thereafter a very interventionist President of the Republic (the latter was not normally an important seat of power but Poincaré used it as such, in part by ensuring that his immediate successors as Foreign Minister were either weak, inexpert or shared his own outlook). In 1920 he wrote "in all my years in school ... I saw no other reason to live than the possibility of recovering our Lost Provinces."[9] Russian subsidies for Poincaré's election campaign in France and to keep him pro-Russian amounted to 2 million francs a year, as revealed by the Bolsheviks in 1920.[10]

Delcassé was appointed ambassador to Russia in early 1913, while Izvolski was Russian ambassador in Paris. Both had lost office as a result of German manoeuvres (in the two crises of 1905 and 1908, to be described); this reinforced their latent Germanophobia. "Delcassé performed a great disservice to European peace by supporting and pushing to the forefront Russian aspirations in the Balkans and the Straits."[11] He pressed the case for strategic railways in western Russia and oversaw negotiations for a massive French loan of 2500m francs in yearly instalments of 500m for 5 years for private railway companies on condition work was done in the western Polish salient to speed up Russian mobilisation.

The historian of French diplomacy at this time describes the role of Paléologue, ambassador in St Petersburg in 1914; he "epitomised the worst aspects of Germanophobia ... an ambassadorial dictatorship was established". The consequences were apparent in July 1914 when "Paris was either misinformed or kept uninformed" about Russian views. Paléologue's assurances "actively encouraged the Russians to adopt a bellicose attitude ... Both Russian moderation and German intransigence were exaggerated ... [While] he was the diplomat most closely listened to by St Petersburg ... at no time did he really use his influence to restrain Russia. Instead he encouraged the Russians to challenge Germany, even at the risk of war." The description of the way in which he had distorted, omitted and delayed the transmission of essential information, especially over military preparations amounting to mobilisation before it was publicly proclaimed, is particularly damning.[12]

In a series of conversations with Izvolski, Poincaré reassured the Russians that they could count on French support in case of a Austro-Serb quarrel. "Poincaré, Joffre (the French Commander in Chief) and Messimy (the War Minister) knew that Russia had resolved on war long before her general mobilisation was confirmed by Paléologue's 30 hours late telegram on Friday night" (31 July 1914). In all his messages to Paléologue on 30 and 31 July, the Prime Minister, Viviani, a peace supporter, did not endorse Russian mobilisation but made no request to halt it. And "the most recent research strongly suggests (although it does not prove) that Poincaré and Paléologue gave Sazonov verbal support for a strong line against Vienna during [the Franco-Russian] summit in St Petersburg" in July 1914.[13] McMeekin acknowledges that there is no evidence surviving from that summit, despite extensive research by both the French and the Soviets; the latter having normally shown no restraint in publishing the most incriminating material if they could find it. There are similar substantial gaps in the Russian correspondence with their envoys in Paris and Belgrade during July 1914.[14] What is clear is that the French were very anxious to hide from Britain the fact that Russia had mobilised first without military provocation from either the Germans or the Austrians; the Russians, like the French, were desperate for British support.

While Germany had no immediate territorial designs, and while the line up of strength in 1914 meant that a war, for Germany, was high risk[15], she seemed to be developing a wish for a preventive war – before she became even more relatively weaker. There are plenty of quotations from prominent people in Germany, military and civilian, arguing the case for a preventive war, all carefully assembled by a German historian, Fritz Fischer, in the 1960s. However, "had Reich leaders wished to advance expansionist aims through war, the military weakness of the Entente in the years immediately after the 1905 Russian revolution offered ideal yet unused opportunities."[16]

Part of Fischer's evidence, however, consists of the ambitious war aims proposed by Chancellor Bethmann-Hollweg after the battle of the Marne, and after hundreds of thousands of deaths in all armies. His objective was "security for the German Empire in the east and the west for the foreseeable future … France must be so weakened as to make its revival as a great power impossible for all time, Russia must be thrust back as far as possible from Germany's eastern frontier …".

In fact, all the powers, giving the price they were already paying, at an early stage evolved extravagant war aims. Britain decided before the end of 1914 to annex the German colonies, while France was planning to annex the Rhineland. Both powers wanted to partition the Middle East, and Russia's ambitions have already been described.

In July 1914, however, as we shall see, Germany did practically everything that ensured she appeared in the wrong. But one of the latest historians (2013), declares "There is no evidence – none – that either Bethmann or Kaiser Wilhelm II – the 'two old women' as German hawks called them – advocated *Praventivkrieg* before the Sarajevo incident nor, indeed, after it".[17]

British-German Relations 1895-1914 a) to the 1901-2 Turning Point

The way in which the "Sarajevo incident" led to war in Europe involving Britain was governed by the course of relations between these two major powers during the preceding twenty years. In his perceptive study[18], the late John Ramsden traces the ups and downs of the relationship at a more popular level. While the 19th century "was a period in which Germany became a country generally admired by British intellectuals", towards its end jealousy, suspicion and even hostility developed on both sides. The Germanophile Liberal leader Lord Rosebery sent his sons to school in Germany; they returned "rabid anti-Germans" because of the anti-British feeling they encountered. The Boer War encouraged this hostility in Germany, while the growth of the new German navy and powerful German commercial competition ensured a response in Britain. The press, notably the *Daily Mail,* poured oil on the flames, with its proprietor Lord Northcliffe, returning from a tour of German industry in 1909, saying "every one of these new factory chimneys is a gun pointed at England." Before 1900, France or Russia tended to be the villain in British invasion fiction; of the 31 such novels published after 1900, all except five had Germany as the invader. Notable was Erskine Childers' *The Riddle of the Sands*; in 1906 Northcliffe commissioned William le Queux to write *The War of 1910,* featuring a German invasion,which was serialised in the *Daily Mail* and became a best seller.[19]

Another historian refers to "the era of missed opportunities in Anglo-German relations" in the 1890s, arguing that various negotiations between the two "led Germany to the conclusion that the British were not prepared to concede anything of real value ... Ironically, perhaps tragically ... both sides seemed determined to win the other's friendship by making themselves as disagreeable as possible." This is echoed by Friedrich von Holstein, the key strategist in the German Foreign Office: "By acting in a friendly manner and speaking in an unfriendly one, we fell between two stools (for 'we' read 'Bülow')."[20] The turning point, as we shall see, involved episodes in 1901: after the "deeply ironic" row over the Edinburgh speech of the hitherto pro-German Joseph Chamberlain "relations were never the same again." Indeed, it was "downhill all the way to 1914."[21]

Given that both powers were anxious to deter Russian aggression in the Balkans, the Germans more from the aspect of protecting Austria-Hungary without having to fight Russia, we see Bismarck encouraging the First and then the Second Mediterranean Agreements (March and December 1887 respectively) between Britain, Italy and Austria. The Second provided that if Turkey resisted any "illegal enterprises" the three powers would defend her; if she connived at them, they would occupy such parts of Ottoman territory as they thought fit. This marks the first move from Britain's "splendid isolation", and was more formal than either of the Ententes with France and Russia in 1904 and 1907.

Rosebery, Foreign Secretary and then Prime Minister in the Liberal Government of 1892 to 1895, "accomplished practically nothing ... his troubles with the Cabinet made a coherent policy impossible." So far as joining the Triple Alliance or at least adhering to Salisbury's Mediterranean Agreements, Rosebery "believed these alternatives to be undesirable and unnecessary". In 1893-4 the Anglophile German ambassador in London, Hatzfeldt, "did everything he could" to transfer the understanding between the two powers "into an alliance", saying that if Russia came to control Constantinople she would control the world. But Rosebery knew that the Admiralty did not believe that Britain, even with Austrian and Italian support, could deny Russia access to the Straits if she were determined. Rosebery wanted Germany to deter France from helping Russia in the Mediterranean; the Germans were reluctant to commit to this.[22]

The main obstacle to an agreement, then and later, was that Germany wanted British support only in Europe, against France and Russia, which Britain, as a naval power, could not usefully give, whereas Britain wanted German support outside Europe where Germany was not interested: for example, German interests in the Far East were never significant enough to risk incurring the enmity of Russia there.

In the mid 1890s, a serious dispute arose between Germany and Britain, with an irresponsible reaction from Germany which reverberated in subsequent years. On 31 December 1895 Berlin heard about the futile Jameson Raid in South Africa. On 3 January the Kaiser sent the "Kruger telegram" congratulating Transvaal's President on preserving his independence "without appealing to the help of friendly powers". There is debate as to how concerned the Germans were. Germany was one of the biggest investors in the two Boer Republics, Krupps sold them guns and there was the occasional wild speculation about making the Transvaal a German protectorate. Alan Taylor, however, plausibly suggests that the Transvaal was not an important issue for the Germans and this judgement is borne out by Germany's albeit noisy inactivity during the real Boer War.[23]

The confusion in Berlin is shown by conflicting comments: on the same day as the telegram the Kaiser told his ministers to prepare invasion forces and warships. Marschall, the Foreign Minister, sent Salisbury a threatening formal note protesting at the "invasion" – a step usually regarded as one en route to declaring war. Hatzfeldt, hearing of Jameson's failure, snatched it off Salisbury's desk before it could be read.[24] Salisbury was told of an "unconfirmed intelligence report" of the despatch of German marines, which as he later told the Prince of Wales, would have meant war. According to Salisbury's biographer, the Kruger telegram was toned down by a threat of resignation from the German Chancellor, Prince Hohenlohe.[25]

On 10 April 1898 the first German Navy Bill was passed. It would enable the German fleet to contemplate challenging France or Russia, while remaining inferior to the Royal Navy. This did not alarm Britain at the time, but the Kaiser's insistence on constantly increasing the High Seas Fleet was to cause no end of trouble.

Despite the Jameson Raid episode and the growing naval issue, at various points the two powers got close to an agreement, almost an alliance. One key conversation took place on 25 April 1898 between Joseph Chamberlain, who was coming to the conclusion that Britain's "splendid isolation" was precarious, and Hatzfeldt: the former's account for his colleagues "failed to record to what extent he had once again pressed for a direct alliance with Germany". In this account, Chamberlain added: "I said I gathered that he thought any attempt to secure a direct defensive alliance ... was premature. He assented, but said the opportunity might come later. I reminded him of the French proverb '*le bonheur qui passe.*' " Hatzfeldt, on his part, reported that "Chamberlain had left him in no doubt that if Germany rejected a direct alliance with Britain he would do everything in his power to reach agreement with France and Russia."[26] Foolishly, the German policy makers remained convinced over the next few years that Britain would be unable to ally with France or Russia, seeing global tension between Russia and Britain as inevitable.

In a personal rather than Governmental capacity, therefore, Chamberlain advanced a detailed proposal at a meeting with Hatzfeldt at the house of Alfred Rothschild (very supportive of Anglo-German amity): in China, with European officers organising native defence forces, Germany would have Shantung, while Britain had the south and the Yangtze basin as spheres of influence. The difference in outlook between Salisbury and Chamberlain is shown by rhetorical salvos at this juncture: Salisbury's "Dying Nations" speech on 4 May 1898, in which he referred to "the jargon about isolation" (thought to be a reference to Chamberlain's ideas), followed a week later by Chamberlain, speaking to the Birmingham Liberal Unionists: "we must not reject the idea of an alliance with those powers whose interests most nearly approximate to our own ... [at present] we have had no allies – I am afraid we have had no friends".[27]

Meeting Lord Salisbury on 2 May Hatzfeldt asked for colonial concessions as solid evidence of Britain's desire for good relations (he presented a "bullish list of colonial demands").[28] It was in this context that Salisbury made his famous remark to Hatzfeldt (on 4 May 1898) "You demand too much for your friendship". Likewise Holstein wrote to Hatzfeldt on 31 May "a move towards England and a corresponding move away from Russia would create a storm in public opinion in Germany *today*. That is why the best method of treatment seemed to me 'friendly and dilatory'." This view was also expressed by the newly appointed German Foreign Minister, later Chancellor, Bernhard von Bülow: "we must remain independent between the two powers [Russia and Britain]; we must be the tongue of the balance, not the restlessly swinging pendulum."[29]

Thus there was no serious contemplation, on the British side, of "incentivising" Germany towards at least an Entente, both by offering her territory in Africa which Britain would otherwise control, and by using Britain's diplomatic influence to enable Germany to obtain land at least theoretically owned by others. In the first category would come, perhaps, much of Northern Rhodesia (now Zambia), into which British pioneers were beginning to penetrate, and in the latter, the province of Katanga (part of the Belgian Congo), and southern Angola. At least, partition of the Portuguese colonies was something the two powers at various times both definitely considered and made conditional agreements about. The wider offer just described would attract Germany as it would link her territory in East Africa with that in South West Africa. But would the economic and prestige gain for Germany, and therefore the goodwill to be derived, be worth the risk to Britain of having such a mass of German-controlled territory in the centre of Africa? In any event, the larger idea was never made by Britain, and given the brittle nature of public opinion on issues relating to Britain's prestige, the electoral consequences of making the offer might have been incalculable.[30]

Sir Frank Lascelles, then British ambassador in Berlin, sympathised with Chamberlain's desire for an approach to Germany. In August 1898 he made to the Kaiser a very sensible offer. Perceiving that Germany did not want war with Russia and that Britain could not help Germany against Russia in Europe, he proposed that if either England or Germany were attacked by two powers, the other would assist in defence. This was clearly aimed at France, and the Kaiser was favourably impressed; German historians have criticised their government for its hesitancy. In fact, as Lascelles later admitted, he had no instructions on this matter and Britain did not pursue it. In reporting to Balfour (in Salisbury's absence), Lascelles merely said that this idea existed "in some influential quarters." Bülow discouraged the Kaiser from further negotiations. "For once the Kaiser's marginal comments show he was not entirely duped by Bülow. (He) could see no reason why, provided China was excluded, an Anglo-German alliance might not be extended to other parts of the world."[31]

To the Kaiser and Bülow visiting London in November 1899, Chamberlain privately proposed an alliance which "would control the world" by confining "barbaric Russia to her proper bounds and compel turbulent France to keep the peace." Chamberlain's Leicester speech on 30 November 1899 "seemed to prove the sincerity of (these) private statements to the Kaiser and Bülow of his desire for an alliance." He proclaimed that no "far-seeing English statesman could be content with England's permanent isolation on the continent of Europe, " and advocated "a new Triple Alliance between the Teutonic race and the two great branches of the Anglo-Saxon race ... The natural alliance is between ourselves and the great German empire." Like other Chamberlain speeches, this fluttered the dovecotes. Its "particularly anti-French tone" upset some at home, while Hatzfeldt told Chancellor Hohenlohe of his suspicion that Chamberlain was pursuing "the object of precipitating a rupture with Lord Salisbury and of unseating him, in order to take his place".[32]

With such advice, it was not surprising that Bülow should respond coolly, but he was influenced mainly by internal German factors – German public hostility to Britain, and especially to Chamberlain, over the Boer War, which had just started,

German criticism of the Kaiser's State Visit to Britain at this juncture, and the need to get Reichstag support for the new Navy Bill. He over-reacted, however: speaking on the Bill on 11 December, he referred to Britain's "arrogant jealousy and growing hatred of Germany, and its shameful conduct in the Boer War" – to cheers: "Two years ago he could still have said that there was no danger of war with England, now he could say it no longer".[33] Chamberlain was appalled, as Holstein states some years later, Bülow's "pouring scorn on (Chamberlain's proposal) and on the whole idea of an Anglo-German alliance ... was as much a surprise to me as to the British Colonial Secretary, who was naturally outraged."[34]

Despite this, and despite a strong pro-Boer popular feeling, Germany was helpful during the Boer War by refusing temptations from Russia to join with them and France to force Britain to make peace. The impact of the Boer War on official Anglo-German relations could well have been worse: after it "German banks had no qualms about applying for a share in the post-war British Transvaal loan."[35] The Anglo-German China agreement of October 1900 recognised the economic partition of China into spheres of influence but, not surprisingly, the phrase "as far as they can exercise influence" meant that both Governments understood that Manchuria, a key Russian objective, was excluded. With Russian pressure increasing there, Bülow told the Reichstag "amid loud acclamation, and some irony at Britain's expense 'The Anglo-German agreement has no bearing on Manchuria ... What may become of Manchuria? Why, gentlemen, I really cannot conceive what could be more indifferent to us.' "[36]

The key element of the saga of missed opportunities leading to bitter resentment revolves around the various conversations which Baron Hermann von Eckardstein, a senior diplomat in the German embassy in London for much of this time, had, principally with Chamberlain himself. Eckardstein, married to the heiress daughter of Sir Blundell Maple MP, proprietor of Maple's furniture store in Tottenham Court Road, was very supportive of an alliance but tended to exaggerate to each side the interest of the other, so when each side discovered that he had been exaggerating, or even inventing, misunderstanding and resentment resulted. As Holstein's biographer put it: "both [Governments] confidently awaited generous proposals, and when no such proposals came they grew more mistrustful of each other than ever." In Charmley's words, "Eckardstein's meddling ... reinforced their impression that Chamberlain was prepared to run after the Germans."[37]

Hence Bülow and Holstein thought that Chamberlain and Lansdowne, now Foreign Secretary, had taken the initiative and that once Salisbury had fully retired, better terms would be offered. In May 1901 after an instruction from Bülow had been sent to London to "reactivate Britain's awareness of the desirability of a defensive alliance with Germany," Holstein wrote of it "By means of the Five-Power bloc (Britain, the Triple Alliance and Japan), England can push the Dual Alliance (ie France and Russia) about at will *without* war. But if England does nothing, according to Salisbury's formula, the Russians will take Manchuria and

France the southern provinces, including the upper waters of the Yangtze." He added (25 May): "If England ignores these weather signals, she will ... be professing an ostrich – like policy which has always been ... the policy of indolent and satiated nations." Yet on 29 May Salisbury wrote "a masterly statement of the principles of his own diplomacy to show why an alliance with Germany was unnecessary."[38]

With the Sultan of Morocco's authority breaking down, the British wanted to control Tangier (to complete the security of Gibraltar) and were ready to encourage Germany to take coaling stations on the Atlantic coast, in return for co-operation against France there. This offer, already made by Chamberlain in January, was "made rather more formally" in July 1901; Bülow was as slippery as ever, saying "in this affair, we must behave like the Sphinx".[39] How little the British understood the German position is seen from a paper on the alliance question drawn up at Lansdowne's request by Sir Thomas Sanderson, Permanent Under-Secretary of State at the Foreign Office, which "showed no comprehension at all of the idea that the alliance should come into effect only when one of the contracting parties was attacked by two or more great powers, and he failed to realise that it would apply to the British Empire as a whole". This "reveals a total failure of communication" between the two Governments. [40]

Holstein, who now supported the alliance idea, feared that if the negotiations were allowed to lapse they might never be resumed. On 19 December 1901, Lansdowne formally told Metternich, Hatzfeldt's successor, that the alliance proposal was at an end; however, he wanted the Germans to accept a declaration of common policy – in effect, an entente, similar on the surface to the one negotiated with France two years later. Metternich, cold about any close cooperation with Britain, replied that the German government would not be attracted by such a "minor proposal" – it was a case of "the whole or none," and he did not even report Lansdowne's suggestion to Berlin.[41]

Rich sums up, as the gravely ill Hatzfeldt, who had "for years enjoyed considerable confidence in England" was recalled in June 1901. The Alliance negotiations were "doomed to failure because of the misunderstandings about German policy created by the irresponsible activity of Eckardstein and the large fund of British suspicion and ill-will towards Germany generated by a decade of political blundering". Grenville concludes: "So, although there was a general agreement among the Kaiser's advisers that an eventual alliance between the Triple Alliance and England would benefit Germany, the golden opportunity had passed and neither Bülow nor Lansdowne recognised this at the time." He adds, significantly for the diplomatic revolution which was shortly to follow: "The cardinal error of Bülow's policy was not so much that he failed to negotiate an alliance with Britain as that he rejected out of hand the establishment of an Anglo-German entente". Rich adds "The entente, settling the outstanding colonial differences between Britain and France, was the type of agreement the Germans had long hoped to arrange with Britain as a prelude to a political-military alliance". Such an agreement "might well have been arranged if German policy had continued to inspire confidence in British leaders, as in Bismarck's day; if Germany had not indulged in such conspicuous naval and colonial rivalry; or if German diplomats had fully exploited every opportunity to establish closer diplomatic relations with Britain."[42]

As Amery comments, in appropriately purple prose "Chamberlain's last bid for a German alliance marks one of the great turning points in history. Had it prospered, the fate of mankind from that time to this [ie 1950] might have been altered immeasurably and for the better ... The golden era of the nineteenth century might have been indefinitely prolonged; and the advancing forces of civilisation might have continued to hold off the horsemen of the Apocalypse." He added: "If behind Eckardstein , there had stood a Bismarck, all might have been well ... But it was the tragedy of the situation that, from first to last, there was no responsible statesman in Germany on whom Chamberlain could rely."[43]

The *volte-face* was already under way. With the Boer War almost ended, in a speech in Edinburgh at the end of October 1901, Chamberlain defended the reputation of the British Army by comparison to "the action of those nations who now criticise our 'barbarity' and 'cruelty'." He did not name foreign armies, but the locations he gave made clear which he had in mind: "Poland, the Caucasus, Algeria, Tonking, Bosnia, in the Franco-German war". Extraordinarily, Russia and France, principally targeted, were silent: "the storm of indignation ... was confined to Germany alone" from leading dailies and public protest meetings. Bülow, through Metternich, asked the Foreign Office for an apology; Lansdowne refused, subsequently refusing to make even an expression of regret. Amery continues: "There was still time to make matters worse; and Bülow was just the man to do it." In the Reichstag on 8 January 1902, he hinted that the British had apologised – a lie – and then added a further rebuke. The actuality was trivial but as Amery states "Chamberlain was alienated for ever; and he had the whole country behind him." He received an Address from the City of London Corporation, and Sir Cecil Spring Rice (later ambassador to the USA 1912-18, and author of the hymn *I Vow To Thee My Country)* wrote to a correspondent on 17 April 1902: "You would be interested to see the effect created in England by the German treatment of us. .... Every one, in the (Foreign) Office and out, talks as if we had but one enemy in the world, and that Germany."[44]

Chamberlain was a bad enemy to have made. Noting the determination of the Unionist Opposition in 1914 that Britain should both declare war on Germany and despatch forces to France, was this hostility to Germany triggered in 1902? Chamberlain's latest biographer only briefly refers to, and tends to discount, his work on the Anglo-French Entente. As early as the beginning of March 1901 the French ambassador in London, Paul Cambon, suggested exchanging French fishing rights off the coast of Newfoundland for British territory in Gambia. Chamberlain found that both Lansdowne and Cambon "hesitated to advance at the pace" he desired, but Chamberlain had "lost some of his enthusiasm for great power diplomacy [and] the prospect of association with Russia as the ally of France repelled him."[45] So it is less likely that his antagonism towards Germany were key factors in determining the outlook of his younger supporters, like Leo Amery, who were in positions of greater influence in the party by 1914. Other factors, such as the influence of Army chiefs, like the very partisan Henry Wilson, and the Navy issue, played a key role.

That change in attitude between 1901 and 1902 is marked. Balfour stated in 1901 "It is a matter of supreme moment to us that ... Austria should not be dismembered, and ... that Germany should not be squeezed to death between the hammer of Russia and the anvil of France." The Admiralty began to assert its influence, with the First Lord stressing the German naval menace to Lansdowne, influencing him towards an approach to France. One historian wrote "In 1902 several within the Cabinet still favoured closer ties with Berlin; by 1904 the option was no longer acceptable nor even considered." Hugh Arnold-Forster, then junior minister at the Admiralty, was so impressed by what he had seen after a visit to Kiel and Wilhelmshaven that he drafted a Cabinet memorandum (September 1902): "Germany must be regarded as a possible enemy."[46]

A rather bizarre report from Eckardstein points to the change: on 8 February 1902, after a large official dinner, he is found eavesdropping on Chamberlain and Cambon conversing in the Marlborough House billiard room. They talked together "for exactly 28 minutes: I could not of course catch what they said and only heard the two words 'Morocco' and 'Egypt'." These were precisely the two key elements in the Anglo-French Entente of 1904. [47]

On his way to tour the newly pacified South Africa during the winter of 1902-3, Chamberlain stopped off in Egypt. After missing a meeting with the French *charge d'affaires*, Lecomte, he appears to have made a statement to Lord Cromer, High Commissioner in Egypt, to pass on to Lecomte. The latter reports to Delcassé (12 December 1902): Chamberlain had realised that Britain would have to count on the friendship of one or more of the Continental powers. "At first he had looked to Germany. It was not long ... before he realised that the violence of German Anglophobia, engendered by the Boer War and sustained by the jealousy and greed of Germany's rapidly expanding commerce, would make any understanding with that Power impossible for a long time ... From [Russia] there was nothing to be hoped for ... It was otherwise with France ... the French government's policies were not opposed to a conciliatory course ... French opinion, once so inflamed against England, seemed to have returned to a mood of calm ..."[48]

From the Entente to War 1902-14

All this did coincide with a new outlook in France. During 1901 and most of 1902 Delcassé, Foreign Minister from 1898 to 1905 (a long haul by French standards), was "undoubtedly right" in his view that Britain would not willingly agree to French rule in Morocco on almost any terms. After rebuffs from Lansdowne, Cambon favoured bartering the French claim to Egypt for any British interest in Morocco, where Chamberlain had already discussed with the Germans a partition agreement. Arthur Nicolson, then British Minister at Tangier, supported this idea, and the Quai d'Orsay "seems to have had wind" of it. Pressure built up during 1902 owing to the success of a Moroccan rebel which threatened the ruling dynasty.[49]

The French believed, with some justice, that the key figures in British foreign policy were King Edward, Chamberlain, and Lansdowne, and during the winter of 1902-3 Delcassé received "convincing evidence" that all three now favoured an understanding with France. His secret agent, Jules de Balasy-Belvata, sent an account written on 20 November of a private conversation with Chamberlain, in which Chamberlain "declared that the whole British people rejected any idea of association with Germany". Late in December, Lansdowne "suddenly and for the first time" told Cambon of his desire for an understanding.[50]

Various factors helped. The French colonial lobby now favoured an exchange of interests in Egypt and Morocco, while French chambers of commerce were afraid of Tariff Reform affecting their exports to Britain. The experience of the Boer War, in Cambon's view "bled Great Britain and made her wiser". And there was this new British hostility to Germany – noted by both French and German diplomats. Lansdowne described it early in 1903 as "furious and unreasoning". Metternich declared that he had never known such English animosity towards another country: the Anglo-French rapprochement "is the product of a common aversion to Germany ... Without the estrangement of England and Germany a mood of Anglophilia would have been impossible in France." The great success of King Edward's State Visit to Paris in May 1903 turned the pro-Boer hostility of the French public into admiration for the King's charm and skill. In conversations with the President and Delcassé, Edward "considerably exceeded the role of a constitutional monarch" in expressing support for a deal and suspicion of the Kaiser.[51]

The actual negotiations went more smoothly than might have been expected. Starting on 1 October, there was speedy agreement over Morocco, with provision for the neutralisation of most of its Mediterranean coast. The first draft was presented to Cambon on 16 March 1904. Delcassé objected to an article promising French support for future British policy in Egypt – this was resolved by an equivalent guarantee of British support for French policy in Morocco which was soon to have significant consequences. The agreement was finally signed on 8 April 1904.

Almost immediately, it was tested in the so-called First Moroccan Crisis.[52] Moroccan disorder caused French infiltration in 1904, and Germany challenged this. Starting with a visit to Tangier by a reluctant Kaiser at the end of February

1905, Germany built up a bullying attitude to France, especially towards Delcassé, with Bülow refusing at the end of April to negotiate directly with France but insisting on an international conference. In fact, Germany might well have benefited from the former approach, but she was convinced that the conference would take her side. With several of his colleagues, including his Prime Minister, scheming against him, Delcassé resigned on 6 June.

Germany's apparent victory was Pyrrhic in two respects. First, the conference which temporarily settled the crisis, at Algeciras in early 1906, saw Germany outnumbered and outmanoeuvred. More importantly, what the Germans believed was a clever device to drive a wedge between Britain and France had wholly the opposite effect. Lansdowne warned the German ambassador in June 1905 that if Germany made war on France "something which he did not believe possible, it was impossible to foresee the lengths to which public opinion ... would press the government to support France." Lansdowne asked Sir Francis Bertie, British ambassador in Paris, to tell Delcassé that Britain would offer "strong opposition" to any German demand for a port on the Moroccan coast; Bertie, typically, changed the emphasis from help over a specific and hypothetical issue to a general statement of support for French Moroccan policy.[53]

Most significantly, Franco-British military conversations were started. The Director of Military Operations, General Grierson, and his deputy, Colonel (later Field-Marshal) Robertson both believed war with Germany was inevitable and supported the idea of allying with France: at the start of 1905 both were playing war games on the deployment of British forces in northern France. Bertie worked at turning the Entente into an alliance, telling Paléologue, "It must be given muscles, it must be given the means to show its strength."[54] British naval ships visited Brest during Bastille week in 1905 and French ships came to Portsmouth in early August, with great public excitement on each visit.

Norman Rich comments "All that Germany had succeeded in doing was to alarm the rest of the world about her intentions and to dramatise herself as an international bully." He adds "The idea that Germany was looking for a quarrel with France over Morocco was widely held not only in America but amongst most of the states attending the [Algeciras] Conference."[55]

The situation was summed up on 20 February 1906 by the newly appointed Liberal Foreign Secretary Sir Edward Grey telling Foreign Office staff "If there is war between France and Germany it will be very difficult for us to keep out of it. The Entente and still more the constant and emphatic demonstrations of affection ... have created in France a belief that we should support her in war ... If this expectation is disappointed the French will never forgive us." While this might certainly be seen as a consequence of Germany's ineptitude over Morocco, in Charmley's view it also indicates a clear breach of continuity between Lansdowne's restrained idea of the Entente, and Grey's more committed approach. A problem in 1914, and before, regarding France, the Cabinet, Parliament, but also Germany, is that the nature of the unwritten British commitment was never clarified, mainly because of domestic political reasons, but perhaps because Grey did not want to be found out: thus he "acquiesced in a series of diplomatic nudges and winks which meant whatever the French wanted".[56]

Grey's policy was underpinned by a group of senior British Foreign Office mandarins. They included Sir Charles Hardinge, ambassador to Russia 1904-6 and then Permanent Under-Secretary until becoming Viceroy of India in 1910. His partnership with Grey has been described as "more one of equals than chief and subordinate" and was helped by a concurrence of their views over Germany and Russia.[57] He was followed, both in St Petersburg (1906-10) and as head of the Foreign Office (1910-16), by Sir Arthur Nicolson, father of Harold. When the fanatics for a firm French alliance were encountering resistance, Nicolson told Cambon on 10 April 1912 that the blame lay with "this radical-socialist Cabinet", supported by "financiers, pacifists, faddists and others" who wanted closer relations with Germany, adding, most improperly, that "the Cabinet will not last, it is done for, and with the Conservatives you will get something precise."[58] He feared Russian economic and military strength. "From this it followed that Russian loyalty must be bought at virtually any price." In the summer of 1912 he told the British ambassador in Vienna that Russian expansion into the Balkans was inevitable and should not be opposed by Britain.[59]

A third was Sir Louis Mallet, Grey's private secretary after 1905 and Under Secretary after 1907. He had urged Grey to "underwrite the French" at the Algeciras Conference and "was subsequently obsessed by the fear that the French or the Russians would take umbrage at any Anglo-German conversations." Having argued strongly for the Russian entente, he "was even more outspoken than Hardinge in his condemnation of talks with Berlin." A fourth was Sir Eyre Crowe, senior clerk in the Western Department, who in January 1907 produced an unsolicited *Memorandum on the Present State of British Relations with France and Germany* stating his beliefs that Germany wanted "hegemony" first "in Europe and eventually in the world", that she threatened the European balance of power in the same way that Spain and France before had done. He exaggerated the German subsidy to the foreign press, which "paled into insignificance" compared to the subsidy operations of Paris and St Petersburg, and "became one of Whitehall's most implacable opponents of a rapprochement with Germany." Even so, Crowe accepted that Germany's ambition to make herself so strong "was not deserving of moral censure. It inspires the policy of every Great Power worthy of the name..."[60]

Another of this group, Sir Francis Bertie, first Assistant Under- Secretary, then in 1905 ambassador to France, said that the best argument against a German alliance was that if one were made "we [should] never be on decent terms with France , our neighbour in Europe and in many parts of the world, or with Russia whose frontiers are co-terminous with ours or nearly so over a large portion of Asia."[61] The idea of "tidying up" these disputes was a principal Foreign Office impetus towards the ententes with both members of the Dual Alliance. Thus in April 1907 Grey started the negotiations which led to the Anglo-Russian agreement of August 1907.

The Anglo-French Entente came to resemble an irregular romantic affair, with France behaving as a jealous lover at any signs of friendly contacts between Britain and Germany. During 1906-7 there were mutual exchanges of visits by British and German mayors, newsmen and monarchs (even Edward and William had a better relationship). "But each step, indeed each hint, toward better relations with Berlin sparked recriminations from Paris and from the anti-German clique in the Foreign Office ..." Grey took a clear view, stating in January 1906, "the danger of speaking civil words in Berlin is that they may be interpreted in France as implying that we shall be lukewarm in our support of the Entente." In April 1910, he said to Edward Goschen, ambassador in Berlin: "We cannot enter into a political understanding with Germany which would separate us from Russia and France."[62]

The extent to which policy might have been distorted by this anti-German lobby is indicated by the existence, and relative sidelining, of prominent senior officials whose views were different. A recent historian tells that despatches from British envoys in Germany "that went against the grain of the dominant view, like those filed by Lascelles, De Salis and Goschen in Berlin, were plastered with sceptical marginalia when they reached London." Christopher Clark argues that "British policy could have taken a different course: had Grey and his associates failed to secure so many influential posts, less intransigent voices, such as those of Goschen and Lascelles or the parliamentary under-secretary Edmond Fitzmaurice, who deplored the 'anti German virus' afflicting his colleagues, might have found a wider hearing." Likewise Lord Stamfordham, private secretary to the King, wrote to Nicolson (23 July 1911) about his distrust "of French alliances and ... belief of a natural affinity of England to Germany." The most eminent critic was Lord Rosebery: speaking in Glasgow (13 January 1912): "No Glasgow merchant would do what we do in foreign affairs – that is, to engage in vast and unknown liabilities ... without knowing their nature and extent."[63]

The Anglo-Russian Entente dealt mainly with Persia (partitioned into spheres of influence and a neutral sphere), Tibet, and Afghanistan. The consequences were immediately apparent when the Kaiser, in the autumn of 1907, offered Britain a share in the Baghdad railway; the British replied that they could only discuss this in conjunction with France and Russia. The Germans were unimpressed, and withdrew the offer.[64] Ferguson is scathing over the Russian Entente. Referring to Grey's love of fly-fishing, he comments: "it was arguably Grey who was the fish others hooked." For years, Britain had sought to resist Russian expansion into Persia and Afghanistan; now this was dropped, and Grey supported cuts in spending on the defence of India to please the Radicals. What did not please them was the "Russian government's abysmal reputation for anti-Semitism and other illiberal practices." Ferguson concludes: "all this marked a clear break in British foreign policy ... [and] truly was appeasement, in the pejorative sense the word later obtained."[65]

Between two Morocco "crises" came one directly involving Russia. In Germany's junior partner, Austria-Hungary, in 1906, the warlike Conrad von Hötzendorff had succeeded the timid and pessimistic Beck as Chief of Staff, and the impatient Aehrenthal became Foreign Minister; both wanted to restore the prestige of the Hapsburg monarchy by a great *coup*. After the "Young Turks" revolt against the Sultan in the summer of 1908, on 5 October Austria-Hungary announced the annexation of Bosnia-Herzegovina. These provinces were largely populated by Serbs, under nominal Turkish sovereignty, and had been occupied militarily by Austria since the Congress of Berlin in 1878. The Russians were angry and the Serbs, demanding compensation, mobilised. The Germans wanted to strengthen Turkey and the Kaiser described the annexation as a "piece of brigandage", but Bülow persuaded him that this was a time for Germany to punish Russia for making the Entente with Britain.

It does seem that this was another bright scheme of Bülow's to weaken the Entente by humiliating Russia. On 21 March 1909 the Germans issued an ultimatum: Russia should unconditionally accept the annexation – "we expect a precise answer, Yes or No. Any vague, complicated or ambiguous reply will be treated as a refusal ... [and] we shall draw back and let events take their course."[66] Izvolski, Russian foreign minister, who thought he had done a deal with Aehrenthal, had to give way, and was demoted to the role of ambassador in Paris a year later. Russian public opinion was very angry, with the Octobrists, the largest party in the Duma, accusing the Government of betraying Russia's historic mission in the Balkans.

Significantly, the British Foreign Office had little sympathy for Izvolski over this matter, or for the "wretched Serbs". When it seemed possible that the Austrians would resort to force to check the Serbs, the Cabinet made it clear that it would not consider any role in a war arising from Balkan difficulties.[67]

The 1911 Moroccan Crisis resembled that of 1905, with Germany behaving clumsily. But "France, not Germany, initiated the second Moroccan Crisis," with French action flouting both the spirit and the letter of the 1906 settlement.[68] France occupied ruthlessly in succession Casablanca, Marrakesh, Rabat and finally the capital Fez. Italy, Spain and Britain had been squared – but Germany wanted compensation. On 1 July the German *Panther* (a "dirty old cruiser well overdue for the scrapyard")[69] anchored at Agadir.

The tension between Britain and Germany in the summer of 1911 involved a degree of smoke and mirrors. It seems to involve a fear – unsubstantiated, but frightening to some British navalists – that Germany wanted a Moroccan harbour on the Atlantic coast. In fact, the Admiralty had no objection to Germany acquiring Agadir , the German interest there was "only a passing whim" and it was too far south to affect Gibraltar. Thus Grey was authorised by the Cabinet on 19 July to tell the French that there were circumstances in which Britain might accept a German presence in Morocco; the French "angrily replied that British acquiescence on this point would amount to a breach in the Anglo-French agreement of 1904". Bertie in Paris first told the French that the British government would not allow a German acquisition; he then "had to pretend that he had not received Grey's instruction" in time! Bertie also exaggerated the German demands for compensation in the French Congo. Crowe was also dripping in his potent mixture, minuting Grey on 18 July: "If [German] demands are acceded to either on the Congo or in Morocco … it will mean definitely the subjugation of France." Confusingly, in view of the Cabinet decision on the 19th, but panicked by "the prospect of a German Atlantic port", Grey secured Cabinet approval for a private warning on 21 July to Metternich that Britain would be obliged to defend her interests if Germany meant to land at Agadir.[70]

Later the same day the same point was made in Lloyd George's Mansion House speech (given as Chancellor of the Exchequer) – "a gambit carefully planned by Grey, Asquith and Lloyd George" and pushed to ensure full coverage in certain newspapers. On the 24th Metternich assured Grey that Germany had no designs on Morocco, but on the 25th he strongly protested at the Mansion House speech. Grey then "stoked the fires of a naval panic," warning Churchill and Lloyd George that the German fleet was mobilised and ready to strike (in reality it was scattered and there were no intentions of concentrating it). The Royal Navy was moved to "high readiness." While the French made no war preparations, Bethmann wrote to Metternich that "Britain seems to have been ready to strike every day".[71]

The "crisis" was resolved by France taking over Morocco as a protectorate and Germany obtaining some sterile tracts of jungle on the borders of Kamerun. It had certainly encouraged Anglo-French military cooperation, which Henry Wilson's biographer describes as much closer than Franco-Russian or German-Austrian arrangements. Wilson was sent to Paris, agreeing the Wilson-Dubail memorandum of 21 July with the French Chief of General Staff; this stipulated the timing, units and planned location of British forces in France in case of war. Foch, returning from Russia in 1910 had told Wilson that France could not depend on Russian support in the event of a war with Germany; she therefore "must trust to England & not to Russia & that all our plans must be worked out in minutest detail …"[72] "Viator" declared in the *United Service Magazine* of February 1913 that the "theatre of war … will be Belgium, where our expeditionary force will take its place on the left flank of the French Army, with a view to arresting a German advance from the east." During these years, Wilson took cycling holidays in the expected war zone; hence the efficiency of his 1914 work in transporting the BEF and arranging its deployment.[73]

Another important decision, following the Agadir Crisis, was the crucial division of naval responsibility between the North Sea, now to be the responsibility of the Royal Navy, which was concentrated here, and the Mediterranean, the responsibility of France, where the French navy was to be concentrated. Although Churchill had to confirm in July 1912 that this did not "in any way affect the full freedom of action possessed by both countries", these were weasel words. As was discovered in July 1914, this naval arrangement had even more impact than the army staff talks – how were France's Channel and Atlantic coasts to be protected from German naval attack if Britain were neutral? [74]

After Agadir there was a reaction from Liberal ministers and backbenchers who did not share Grey's commitment to France. They demanded a Parliamentary committee to improve Anglo-German relations, and in two Cabinet resolutions of November 1911 ministers voted 15 to 5 demanding that Grey cease sponsoring military discussions between France and Britain without Cabinet knowledge or approval.[75] Lord Loreburn, the Lord Chancellor, wrote to Grey (25 August 1911) about French expectations of British naval and military support over Morocco "I believe you could not give it if you wished, in this which is a purely French quarrel. I believe you could not carry it in the present House of Commons except by a majority very largely composed of Conservatives and with a very large number of [Liberals] against you ..." In January 1912 he criticised Grey's "extravagant championship of France" and threatened that, if the Cabinet rejected his views opposing staff talks, he would resign. However, he was taken ill and resigned anyway in the summer of 1912.[76]

Almost certainly as a response to this political criticism, in February 1912 Lord Haldane, the Secretary of State for War, went to Berlin to propose a deal: Britain would consider Germany's colonial aims while seeking to reduce the naval arms race because of the cost. Bethmann was prepared to make concessions on the naval front. However, there was deadlock because Germany wanted a clear indication of British neutrality in a European war. Bethmann was in fact prepared to limit such an agreement to cases where Germany "cannot be said to be the aggressor". Various wordings were attempted; none satisfactorily.[77]

The French were nervous, with some pro-French chiefs in the Foreign Office telling them that there was no chance of an Anglo-German agreement. Bertie "worked hard to sabotage the agreement" by tipping off Poincaré and encouraging the French Foreign Office to apply pressure on London. More insidiously, he told Poincaré in March that the Anglo-German talks were perhaps not finished and that Grey was being "very weak".[78] By then it was clear that the Germans would reject any naval agreement without a neutrality pledge. Yet less than a year later (November 1912), Germany dropped plans for expanded naval building, in return for "an unprecedented growth in ... peacetime military strength", with recognition of her declining security position and Russian exploitation of the Balkan wars.[79]

Haldane warned Lichnowsky, now German ambassador in London, as reported by the latter on 3 December 1912 about "the conviction which is widespread here that the balance between the various groups [ie in Europe] must be more or less preserved. Britain could therefore in no circumstances allow France to be crushed." This caused the Kaiser to exclaim "what a nation of shopkeepers ... The final struggle between the Slavs and the Teutons will see the Anglo-Saxons on the side of the Slavs and the Gauls." It was " a dog in the manger attitude and fear that we might become too great."[80] In spite of this typical outburst, the period 1912-14 saw improvements in relations between Britain and Germany and growing tension with Russia over her renewed adventurism. Even a group of Unionists led by Lord Curzon felt that Britain had conceded too much in Persia. This was raised with Sazonov, Russian Foreign Minister, at Balmoral in September 1912 but it was clear that Russia would not abandon her forward policy.

With the simultaneous Chinese revolution Russia also saw an opportunity to move into Mongolia and Chinese Turkestan. Mongolia declared its independence and in October 1912 a Russo-Mongolian treaty gave Russia extensive economic privileges. That summer Russia had increased her consular guard in the capital of Chinese Turkestan, with the prospects of establishing a protectorate. These were also discussed at Balmoral "but with equally negative results". [81] Russia is seen as fomenting "unusual military activity" in Mongolia, Tibet and Chinese Turkestan. To counter this Hardinge as Viceroy arranged in the spring of 1914 a meeting at Simla between Chinese and Tibetan representatives, which agreed to increase British influence in Tibet. Sazonov, however, made it clear that he would not accept this without concessions in Afghanistan, Azerbaijan and the Gulf, while Grey rejected a Russian demand to station an agent in Herat.[82]

This Russian expansionism aroused concern in the British Cabinet, Parliament and the press, with Grey warning the Russian ambassador that Britain might have to issue public "disavowals" which might put the Anglo-Russian Convention at risk. In early 1914 Grey commented angrily on Russian plans for a strategic railway all the way to the Indian frontier, alongside Russian obstruction of British trading interests in Persia. And Russia refused to allow Britain to meet a Turkish request for British officers to organise a gendarmerie in Armenia. Even the Russophile Nicolson warned in the summer of 1914 that relations with Russia were approaching a point when "we shall have to make up our minds as to whether we should become really intimate and permanent friends or else diverge into another path."[83]

Grey was supported in his concerns by his private secretary, Sir William Tyrrell, who had earlier favoured a policy hostile to Germany but had later become "a convinced advocate of an understanding".[84] In Europe, the Balkan wars and the contention over Serbia and Montenegro's claims to parts of the new state of Albania, saw Russia behaving aggressively and Britain and Germany working together. They jointly sponsored the Ambassadors' Conference in London in the winter of 1912-13 to sort out Albanian borders. The Tsar and Sukhomlinov, Chief of Staff, were pressing for partial mobilisations on the Austrian frontier during this, while Kokovstov as chairman of the Council of Ministers, who regarded war as too great a risk, forced restraint.[85] Before July 1914 "the drift in British diplomacy was towards rapprochement with Germany and growing tensions with Russia ... Absent [*sic*] Sarajevo, this ... would have continued."[86]

This brief period of Anglo-German harmony took substantive form over discussions on the future of certain African colonies. The author of this particular research believes that these "efforts can be seen as the most significant contribution to the improved Anglo-German relations of the period from late 1911 to mid-1914." The two respective Colonial Ministers, Lewis Harcourt and Dr Wilhelm Solf, both favoured Anglo-German amity; the former "had a profound dislike of the foreign policy of the so-called Triple Entente". The British Colonial Office had, in contrast to the Foreign Office, a "traditional distrust of French colonial policy", and began to see the Germans as "desirable allies in Africa." Solf aspired to create a solid band of German territory across central Africa, seeing Germany's role, amazingly, as "England's junior partner". The collaboration would be cemented by a partition of Portuguese Angola and Mozambique, on which an Anglo-German convention had already been made in 1898; this would be formally modified in late 1913. Even Grey was sympathetic, writing in 1911: "these colonies are worse than derelict so long as Portugal has them: they are sinks of iniquity ... *But* how can we of all people put pressure on the Portuguese?"[87]

In March 1912 Harcourt asked his Permanent Under-Secretary, Sir John Anderson "to cast your mind and eye over the British Empire – especially Africa and the Pacific – with a view to seeing what we could give and what we want in exchange." These exchanges were abortive over the Germans seeking Zanzibar but proving unwilling to cede Ruanda, but significant changes were agreed in the proposed partition of Portuguese Africa.[88]

Both Foreign Offices were critical of the proposals – in London, Harcourt "was subjected to a stream of vicious criticism", principally from Nicolson, Crowe and Mallet. They were overruled by Grey who said that the Colonial Office was quite entitled to negotiate about colonies. The negotiations languished, however, with the German Minister in Lisbon describing Solf as "the only man in Berlin who zealously supported the Colonial settlement." After the paraphrase of the agreement had been initialled in August 1913 and the text in October, there were further delays in Berlin.

Hatton concludes that such agreements "were more realistic than they are usually given credit for", and these "diplomatic preparations ... for a repartition of Africa" recognised Germany's increased economic strength compared to 1884, and the "assumption that neither Belgium nor Portugal possessed the resources necessary to govern effectively their African colonies or to sustain their growing investment needs." Bethmann-Hollweg realised the wider issues at stake, writing to Lichnowsky on 16 June 1914 "Whether a European conflagration comes depends solely on the attitude of Germany and England. If we both stand as guarantors of European peace ... war can be avoided".[89]

Austria's Dilemma and the July 1914 Crisis

As stated at the start of this chapter, the Vienna government appears as the chief villain in turning the Serbian crisis of July 1914 into war. It is worth reflecting, however, that Austria-Hungary seemed somewhat isolated in these pre-war years, with only Germany to depend on. Her position in the Balkans deteriorated as a consequence of the 1912-13 wars: Serbia almost doubled in size, acquiring 1.5 million extra subjects. This worried Austria-Hungary because of Serb territorial ambitions. Was Britain open to criticism on account of Austrian vulnerability? Britain had no quarrel with Vienna, and very little sympathy for the Serbs. The Hapsburgs had been key allies of Britain against French aggression in 1689, 1702, 1740, 1792 and 1804-15, and Austria's threatened interventions against Russia at the end of the Crimean War and in 1878 had been decisive.

The evidence suggests that Britain became detached over the fate of Austria-Hungary. One historian argues that, from the mid 1890s, Britain urged Russia to concentrate specifically on the Balkans, rather than the Far East and Central Asia, both of which threatened British interests. "On the eve of the war," he argues, "the Foreign Office was aware of the fear prevalent in both Berlin and Vienna that Austria might collapse ... No thought of any action to help maintain Austria's independence and integrity was entertained." Furthermore, "Russia was not bound to be Austria's enemy; throughout the nineteenth century she had always found it profitable to seek a *modus vivendi* with Austria ... The danger regularly arose when Russia got tacit or open Western support for a forward policy, as she did before 1914." And Charmley points to evidence showing "recriminations and ill-will" between Britain and Austria after the Entente with Russia, "which in Vienna was seen as an abandonment of Britain's old policy."[90]

There is no doubt of France's hostility to Austria – she was busy building up Serb military power and from 1912 on was "determined not to allow an Austro-Serb or Austro-Russian rapprochement". Post 1919 history shows how justified were the warnings of this historian: "Only the presence of the Hapsburg monarchy holding down the Danube basin kept Germany or Russia from achieving mastery over Europe. With Austria there and determined to remain an independent great power, it was very difficult for either of them to fight each other, or dominate the other, or combine for aggressive purposes. Let Austria go under, and a great war for the mastery of Europe became almost mathematically predictable."[91]

Dominic Lieven's recent study also endorses the significance of Austria-Hungary: "in contemporary Asia, the existence of multinational states such as India, Indonesia and Iran is a reproach to anyone who believes that the triumph of European-style ethnic nationalism is an inexorable law of modernity." He praises the "the sterling performance" of the Hapsburg and Ottoman empires during 1914-8.[92] The next chapter will show the consequences of the fall of the Ottoman empire.

The sorry saga of the five weeks after the murders at Sarajevo is marked by several missed opportunities for saving the peace of Europe, more out of incompetence or lack of a sense of urgency than malignity. Even the Austrians do not seem to have wanted the full horror of a Europe-wide war. Austria was particularly reluctant to break with France or Britain.[93] Not only Austria, but other powers in those crucial weeks were indulging in brinkmanship, and were horrified when it was seen on this occasion to lead to the worst results.

There were British attempts at reconciliation, one made by Grey on 25 July for Britain, France, Germany and Italy to mediate. While the German minister Jagow replied in favour "of the four Powers working in favour of moderation at Vienna and St Petersburg", Russia's ambassador rejected the proposal immediately as it "would give Germany the impression that France and England were detached from Russia." Cambon, for his part, did not tell anyone in Paris about the proposal "which had struck him as so repugnant as to be beneath consideration."[94] The Kaiser's reactions to the Serb reply to the Austrian ultimatum are well known: "A brilliant achievement in a time limit of only 48 hours ... a great moral success for Vienna ... All reason for war is gone, and Giesl ought to have quietly stayed on in Belgrade" (referring to the Austrian envoy there). If he had received such a reply, "I should never have ordered mobilisation." A further proposal by Grey for German mediation in Vienna on the basis of the Serb reply, which coincided with a very similar proposal by the Kaiser, was described by Bethmann in a telegram to Tschirschky, German ambassador in Vienna, "it is impossible for us to reject this English suggestion *a limine*". This was sent just before midnight on 27 July; at 11.10 am the next day Austria declared war on Serbia.[95]

Clearly, if certain temporising acts had been taken even hours earlier the rush to war might have been halted: a further example comes from telegrams sent by Bethmann to Vienna during the night of 29-30 July, demanding that Austria resume direct talks with Russia. Described as "at last rescind[ing] the blank check [sic] he had foolishly offered Austria three weeks earlier", this also came too late.[96] Lieven refers to Germany's belated attempt to rein in Vienna, arising from the "dawning awareness" in Berlin late on the evening of the 29th from a Lichnowsky telegram passing on Grey's warning that Britain was unlikely to stand aside if war took place between Germany and France.

Bethmann had been traumatised by the death of his wife in May. Alexander Watson believes his sense of inevitability was caused not by this, but because he had "re-evaluated the threat posed by Russia", describing it as "looming above us as an increasingly terrifying nightmare". The "Great Programme" of rearmament passed the Duma in June 1914; it would add 500,000 men to the Russian army. Watson further believes that "what destroyed Bethmann's faith in British readiness to act multilaterally and continue restraining Russia was intelligence", obtained by a German agent in the Russian embassy in London, of secret Anglo-Russian naval discussions in May 1914.[97]

In fact, what caused these naval talks was nothing to do with the Baltic, the area of German concern, but Russian panic at the planned British provision of two

Dreadnoughts to the Ottoman navy in the Black Sea.[98] What Bethmann did not know in detail were the strains and suspicions, particularly in the Middle East, which formed a background to these naval exchanges.

As the Austrians and Russians, in particular, prepared for war, "the Germans had remained, in military terms, an island of relative calm throughout the crisis". The Kaiser was on his cruise and various other key Germans were on holiday. This was not an elaborate German feint to distract the world: "The internal memoranda and correspondence of these days suggest that both the political leadership and the military and naval commands were confident that the strategy of localisation (ie of the Serbian crisis) would work. There were no summit discussions among the senior German commanders and Moltke did not return from taking the waters in Carlsbad, Bohemia until 25 July."[99]

Once Germany decided that war with Russia could not be prevented, however, she became enslaved to her war programme (the so-called Schlieffen Plan). So, in order to implement this, even before attacking in the west through neutral Belgium, she put herself in the wrong by declaring war both on Russia and France. McMeekin, who hitherto had expressed sympathy with Germany, is merciless: "Germany's decision to violate Belgian neutrality – on M+3, two weeks before the concentration of her armies would be complete – was a political, diplomatic, strategic and moral blunder of the first magnitude ... For this colossal error in judgement, German leaders richly deserve the opprobrium they have been showered with ever since 1914."[100] Moltke was to blame for this, but, as Margaret MacMillan argues, Bethmann, Jagow or the Kaiser should have called him to account. She criticises the politicians for not knowing the military plans – the Chancellor was only told in 1912 – and for not insisting on alternative options. MacMillan thinks that if Kiderlen-Waechter had survived (he died suddenly at the end of 1912) in the summer of 1914 he might have countered the military. He had been succeeded by Jagow, known as "that little squirt" by the Kaiser, and too weak for this task.[101]

In fact, the military did have a shock, albeit briefly. On the basis of a telephone conversation with Grey and a conversation with Tyrrell, Lichnowsky telegraphed Berlin indicating that Britain would remain neutral if Germany did not attack France. The Kaiser was overjoyed, and called for champagne: "Now we can go to war against Russia only. We simply march the whole of our army to the east." Supported by Bethmann, Tirpitz and Jagow, he told Moltke to stop the advance into Luxemburg. Moltke demurred: the Kaiser replied "Your uncle would not have given me such an answer", adding "If I order it, it must be possible." In fact railway and mobilisation schedules could be and were altered all the time as information arrived and strategic objectives were modified especially after war actually broke out. According to his wife, Moltke had a mild stroke: he later wrote "Something in me broke and I was never the same again." When it became clear that Lichnowsky's telegram was "based on a misunderstanding", the Kaiser told Moltke "now you can do what you want."[102]

Clark questions Grey's consistency: he "appeared to be backing away from his earlier proposal" to Lichnowsky; his "communications with Lichnowsky, Cambon and various British colleagues during 1 August are so difficult to unravel that the effort to make sense of them has produced a sub-debate within the war origins literature ... Grey's ambiguities were on the verge of becoming open contradictions." McMeekin is more brutal. Referring to Lichnowsky's later chivalrous implication that he had misunderstood Grey, his friend, McMeekin describes two despatches sent by Grey to Bertie in Paris on 1 August which "give the lie to both men. Grey may not have been in his right mind [on] Saturday, but he did say what he said" ie to Lichnowsky.[103]

Grey was still on insecure ground in Cabinet, which on 2 August saw various Ministers resigning or threatened to resign over mobilising the Fleet or the guarantee to protect the French Channel coast following the 1912 agreement. Lloyd George expressed reservations and Sir John Simon claimed "The Triple Entente was a terrible mistake. Why should we support a country like Russia?" Lloyd George said to Grey "How will you feel if you see Germany overrun and annihilated by Russia?"[104]

Once the Germans delivered their crude ultimatum to Belgium and started their invasion, raw politics intervened in Britain.[105] One key to the Cabinet decision, and the rallying of "wobblers", was the Tory factor. Ferguson[106] argues that if the Government could not agree and broke up, the Unionists (by now the larger party by 288 to 260) would take power, with the Liberals breaking up into pro-war and anti-war sections. But the Tories would need significant Liberal support to obtain an overall majority since the Labour party and the Irish (totalling over 120) would not support them. An alternative would be through a dissolution and a Tory win – this would take six weeks. Britain might declare war in the interim, but it would be a divided nation that fought.

Clearly, the French diplomats in London were panicking that Britain might remain neutral: George Lloyd, Unionist diehard, had seen Cambon "The French regarded themselves as completely betrayed and were in an awful state of mind ... Cambon said quite straight to Lloyd that if we stood out and the French won they would gladly do everything to crush us afterwards, whereas if they lost we should naturally follow suit. He added that it would be worse for us even than Napoleon was."[107] Ferguson finds echoes of this: he thinks it "fantastic" [ie of fantasy, rather than admirable] for Grey to say to C. P. Scott that "if France is not supported against Germany she would join with her and the rest of Europe in an attack upon us."[108]

Cambon's threat is far-fetched. If France-Russia defeated the Central Powers, would Europe be content to see Russia on the Elbe and near Vienna, as was the case in 1945-90? Would a relatively exhausted France (having surely only won a Pyrrhic victory), with her demographic problem, be able to hold at bay 70 million angry Germans, as well as taking on a Britain very much stronger in population and economy as well as in Empire support than in 1800-15? If Germany won, since she had previously assumed that Britain was with the Entente, she would have been relieved, though Britain would need to continue re-arming and be prepared to adopt skilful diplomacy.

In fact, the Germans had an alternative, which we saw the Kaiser briefly discerning through the smoke. All powers in 1914 assumed a quick war-like the Balkan Wars. That is why the Schlieffen Plan took its form and why Germany was determined rapidly to identify and attack her enemies. The Russo-Japanese and Boer Wars, however, were relatively long and hard, and both showed the advantages that modern techniques – barbed wire, trenches, machine guns, even (in Boer hands) efficient rifles-gave to the defence.

If the Germans had evaluated these earlier contests, and then weighed the effect of Britain's strength – above all, her commercial and financial power – being thrown into the scale, she might have thought again. If she had concentrated her efforts on Russia, perhaps offering the Poles independence in a German protectorate (Russian Poles were far more oppressed than those in Austrian Galicia or German Posen), as well as protectorates for the Baltic states, she might well have inflicted on Russia in 1914 the defeats she was to inflict in 1915. There would have been no need to invade Belgium, and the attacking French would still have been slaughtered in the Vosges.

The realities of the conflict support this hypothesis. The Schlieffen Plan was riddled with logistical inadequacy. To march, almost without pause, resorting to eating unripe fruit, west of Paris (according to the plan) – no wonder Kluck's army was exhausted by the time it passed the Marne. To crush the French army in six weeks "was a breathtakingly audacious and, as it turned out, foolhardy aspiration." In fact, 73.5 German divisions were exceeded by 80 French, 6 Belgian and 6 British.[109]

In the East, without any German offensive capacity at the start, the Austrians invaded south Poland, with initial victories at the battles of Krasnik (23-25 August) and Komarow (26 August-2 September) – 20,000 Russian prisoners were captured in the latter. After this, Russian numerical superiority began to tell. "Conrad's indecision" and "Potiorek's selfishness" meant too many Hapsburg forces were in the Balkans rather than in Galicia. Without German support until several weeks later, with slow concentration, and with gross tactical mishandling, Conrad's "opening campaign had nearly destroyed the Hapsburg army," with huge losses of officers as well as of experienced and well motivated men. During August and September they suffered 100,000 killed, 220,000 wounded and 100,000 prisoners; by the end of 1914 these figures were 189,000, 490,000 and 278,000-nearly one million.[110] The numbers of dead and wounded show an initial capacity to fight well: the Hapsburg forces were never to match this vigour again in the East, though they performed well against the Italians, whom they despised, until the last weeks of the war. With a German concentration in the East in 1914, all might have changed.

If the Germans had not invaded Belgium, and left it to the French to declare war in support of Russia, it is very unlikely that Asquith could have rallied his Cabinet to war. It is equally unlikely that Britain would willingly have put blood and treasure into a contest largely being fought in Poland, this time with the Germans supporting the Poles! And with Britain neutral, Italy and Japan would hardly have joined the war on France's side. Without Germany occupying a large area of northern France (which prevented any worthwhile peace negotiations during 1914-8), a compromise peace would have been reached probably in 1915, with Russia likely to have been saved from revolution, and the Hapsburg empire from dissolution into feuding nationalities. And without the prolonged trench warfare of Ypres, Somme, Verdun, and Isonzo, hundreds of thousands of lives would have been saved.

One wonders if, at any time after Agadir, Asquith, Grey and a respected soldier (perhaps Kitchener) had visited Berlin and spelt out these home truths (no invasion of Belgium, no interference with the Channel ports, and respect for the integrity of France – though not necessarily that of her colonies if she provoked war), what might have been achieved. And the certainty of Britain's neutrality in 1914 would surely have restrained the war parties in Paris and St Petersburg.

FOOTNOTES

1 The history books are full of the Kaiser's frequent silly remarks, often directed at Britain. Not exclusively so, as displayed by the incident of him smacking the King of Bulgaria – later to be a German ally in war – on the bottom in public, making the King "white hot with hatred". (Margaret MacMillan *The War that ended Peace* p62). In fact, the Kaiser had a love/hate, admiration/envy attitude towards Britain. One aspect was his devotion to and awe of his grandmother Queen Victoria. "... For all his bluster and hysteria the German monarch was normally a force for peace and compromise within the German government." (Dominic Lieven, *Towards The Flame: Empire, War and the End of Tsarist Russia,* p101.)

2 Sean McMeekin *July 1914 – Countdown to War,* pp393-4. If they had attacked Serbia immediately, said Ion Bratianu, Rumanian Premier on 24 July, "then [you] would have had the sympathies of Europe on your side."

3 Even these two had their peace-seekers. In France, this was Prime Minister Viviani, countered by the war party in President Poincaré and others. In Russia, Kokovtsov, chairman of the council of ministers until the Tsar sacked him at the behest of Rasputin in January 1914 "dreaded war for Russia " because of lack of preparation and the danger of revolution.

4 Christopher Clark, *The Sleepwalkers – How Europe went to war in 1914,* pp297-8, 446.

5 C. Clark, op cit, p484; Sean McMeekin *July 1914 – Countdown to War,* p397; same author *The Russian Origins of the First World War* p61; hereafter *July 1914* and *Russian Origins* respectively.

6 Alexander Watson, *Ring of Steel – Germany and Austria-Hungary at War 1914-18,* p20.

7 Paléologue reported a conversation with a senior Russian minister, thought to be Krivoshein, the Germanophobe Minister of Agriculture. What would happen if Franz Joseph, the Hapsburg Emperor, died? "We would be obliged to occupy Galicia ... (it is) indispensable to the security of our frontier . And besides, it is basically Russian territory." (McMeekin, *Russian Origins,* p22.)

8 These demands were cemented in the Allied talks in early 1916 over the Sykes-Picot Agreement. (McMeekin, *Russian Origins,* pp90-1132, 206-7.)

9 Jack Beatty, *The Lost History of 1914 – How the Great War was not inevitable,* p232.

10 McMeekin, *July 1914,* p66.
11 M. B. Hayne, *The French Foreign Office and the origins of the First World War 1898-1914,* p266.
12 Hayne, op cit, pp269, 273, 294. Observing European diplomacy from London, Count Benckendorff, the Russian Ambassador there, concluded that "of all the powers France is the one which – I would not say actually wants war – but would see it come with least regret." (Lieven, op cit, p239.)
13 McMeekin, *July 1914* pp398, 399, 395 respectively.
14 Ibid, pp55-6.
15 The Dual Alliance was spending 10% of net national income on defence in 1914, while Germany and Austria-Hungary were spending 7%; thus the former fielded armies in 1914 of 2.5million, compared to 1.2 million for the latter. (Beatty, op cit, p10.) This arises partly from German spending on the navy – Falkenhayn exploded at Tirpitz that three battleships would have paid for 5 new army corps which would have won the battle of the Marne.
16 Watson, op cit, p61.
17 McMeekin, *July 1914* p387.
18 John Ramsden, *Don't Mention the War: the British and the Germans since 1890.*
19 Ramsden, op cit, pp67, 69. Le Queux had previously published another invasion fantasy in 1894: *The Great War in England in 1897*; significantly, this involved France and Russia attacking Britain. Eventually Germany comes to Britain's aid; the fruits of victory involve Britain obtaining Algeria and Central Asia, while Germany takes more of mainland France!
20 Gordon Martel, *The Limits of Commitment – Rosebery and the Definition of the Anglo-German Understanding* Historical Journal, Vol 27, 1984, pp387-404; MacMillan, op cit, p57; the parenthesis is in the original quote.
21 Ramsden, op cit, pp61, 63, 65.
22 Martel, op cit, esp. pp389, 392, 393, 397,399.
23 A. J. P. Taylor, *The Struggle for Mastery in Europe,* p364.
24 Carter, op cit, pp189-94.
25 Andrew Roberts, *Salisbury – Victorian Titan,* pp622-4.
26 Norman Rich, *Friedrich von Holstein* Vol II p578; the last quote is the author's paraphrase.
27 Roberts, op cit, pp691-2.
28 Carter, op cit, p246; the list was subsequently produced on appropriate occasions.
29 Holstein quoted in Rich, op cit, p584, also p580-1, Holstein's emphasis; Bülow quoted Carter, op cit, pp246-7.
30 Cf Harcourt-Solf exchanges, p119. James (op cit, p90) quotes *The Economist* 20 April 1912 stating that "if Germany is to go down in history as a Great Power", it "must also have its fair share of the territory". In the 1930s, the British were to offer former German colonies as sops to Hitler, who, as we know, was only interested in expansion into Eastern Europe. Before 1914, Germany was uninterested in European expansion and might well have been attracted by a more extensive colonial empire. See Charmley, op cit, for example pp142-3, 223-4 for the public opinion point.
31 J. A. S. Grenville, *Lord Salisbury and Foreign Policy,* p174-5.
32 Charmley, op cit, p274; Roberts, op cit, pp748-9.
33 Carter, op cit, pp263-4; Taylor, op cit, p389.
34 Quoted Rich, op cit, p615.
35 Ferguson, *Pity,* p51. "Had the real truth about French policy during the early months of the Boer War become known to the English [sic] government, the Entente would have been much more difficult to achieve." (Christopher Andrew, *Theophile Delcassé and the Making of the Entente Cordiale* p215.) When President Kruger toured Germany in December 1900, he was greeted with exultation by the people, but was snubbed by the Kaiser. This, like many of the Kaiser's Anglophile gestures, inflamed hostility to Britain (and to him) from German public opinion, as did his award in February 1901 of the Order of the Black Eagle to Field Marshal Lord Roberts, the victorious British commander in South Africa.
36 Grenville, op cit, p317; Julian Amery, *Life of Joseph Chamberlain* Vol IV, p152.

37 Rich, op cit, p576; Charmley, op cit, p257.
38 Rich, op cit, pp649, 653; Charmley, op cit, p290 for last point.
39 Taylor, op cit, p397.
40 Rich, op cit, pp655-7.
41 Grenville, op cit, pp359, 362, 365.
42 Rich, op cit, p655; Grenville, op cit, p355, 368; Rich, pp674-5, respectively.
43 Amery, op cit, pp158-61, 195.
44 The Edinburgh/Bülow episode is in Amery pp167-76.
45 Marsh, op cit, p507.
46 Charmley, op cit, p301; S. R. Williamson *The Politics of Grand Strategy: Britain and France Prepare for War 1904-14*, pp15, 17. Admiral Tirpitz, who pushed for the enlargement of the German navy, sometimes spoke as if he never intended the battle fleet to be used (in the various pre-1914 crises he said the navy was not ready). Bülow tried to persuade the Kaiser to rein in naval spending, he resigned in 1909 having failed over this. Yet Britain won the naval race: by 1914 she had 20 Dreadnoughts to Germany's 13.
47 Baron Hermann von Eckardstein, *Ten Years at the Court of St James 1895-1905,* pp228-30; Amery, op cit, pp179-80; Charmley, op cit, p306.
48 Amery, op cit, pp202-3.
49 Andrew, op cit, pp181, 185-6.
50 Ibid, pp195-6.
51 Ibid, pp202-5, 207, 209.
52 During it, France's other main ally, Russia, was severely pre-occupied: Port Arthur surrendered in January 1905, Russia was defeated at Mukden in March, the Baltic fleet was destroyed at Tsushima on 27 May; and revolution starting in January climaxed in October 1905.
53 Andrew, op cit, pp280-1, 287.
54 Ibid, pp284-5.
55 Rich, op cit, pp707, 733.
56 Grey quote in S. Williamson, op cit, p82; for contrast with Lansdowne policy, Charmley, op cit, pp 321, 324, 327, 332. Among the documents referred to by David Owen in *The Hidden Perspective: the Military Conversations 1906-14* is one by Lord Sanderson, just having retired as Permanent Under-Secretary at the Foreign Office, dated 2 February 1906, describing how he told the French ambassador that "I thought that if the Cabinet were to give a pledge which would morally bind the country to go to war in certain circumstances, and were not to mention this pledge to Parliament, and if ... the country suddenly found itself pledged to war in consequence ..., the case would be one which would justify impeachment." (Quoted, p61.)
57 Zara Steiner, *The Foreign Office under Sir Edward Grey,* pp32-3, in F. H. Hinsley (ed) *British Foreign Policy under Sir Edward Grey.*
58 Quoted Taylor, op cit, p479, and elsewhere.
59 C. Clark, op cit, p325; Steiner, *Britain and the Origins of the First World War* (hereafter *Origins*), p183.
60 Steiner, *Origins*, p43; C. Clark, op cit, p162, from which the earlier quotes come; Charmley, op cit, p250 for the last. Owen, op cit, pp77-8, quotes criticisms of Crowe's indictment of Germany by Lord Sanderson.
61 Ferguson, *Virtual History* p241. His encouraging Delcassé during the Morocco crisis with "belligerent talk"(C. Clark, op cit, p160) was referred to above.
62 S. Williamson, op cit, p96; Ferguson *Virtual History,* p 252.
63 C. Clark, op cit, pp161, 165-6; S. Williamson, op cit, pp157, 250.
64 Taylor, op cit, p445.
65 Ferguson, *Pity,* pp59-61.
66 Bülow to the German ambassador in St Petersburg, quoted Taylor, op cit, p455, Carter, op cit, p370.
67 Steiner, *Origins*, p90.

68 Beatty, op cit, p223.
69 Carter, op cit, p394. As in 1905, we see Jules Cambon, brother of Paul and French ambassador in Berlin, "warning when it became clear that his prudent policy of consulting with Germany and taking limited action in Morocco was being ignored." Hayne, op cit, p215.
70 C. Clark, op cit, p209-10, S. Williamson, op cit, p150; Taylor, op cit, pp469-70.
71 C. Clark, op cit, pp210-11; S. Williamson, op cit, p155.
72 Keith Jeffery, *Henry Wilson – A Political Soldier,* p90. Cf Owen, op cit, pp103-6, for a report by Colonel Fairholme of a detailed conversation with Foch in early April 1911, which referred to Russian weakness, Germany's likely advance through Belgium, and the need for the French army to have the clearest "previous assurance that it could count with certainty on the arrival of the British contingent". The latter was for tactical reasons and for the earmarking of railway lines and rolling stock. "A British contingent despatched at a later moment than as above might probably just as well stay away."
73 S. Williamson, op cit, pp313-6. Hankey, who opposed military commitments, told the First Lord that Wilson "has a perfect obsession for military operations on the Continent. He spends his holidays bicycling up and down the Franco-German frontier; he has preached this gospel at the Staff College for years; has packed the War Office with staff officers who share his views." Jeffery, op cit, p91.
74 Whereas "the French Army never based its mobilisation plans upon definite British assistance; with the two navies the situation was quite different." With the "forging of a virtual Anglo-French naval alliance," there were very detailed joint plans, such as for the Far East and elsewhere. S. Williamson, op cit, p324.
75 Vote details T. Wilson, *Decision for War,* pp149, 156n, in British Journal of International Studies I 1975.
76 S. Williamson, op cit, p157.
77 Williamson, op cit, pp256-7. See Owen, op cit, p169, for the Foreign Office "finessing away of Haldane's agreed form of words with the Germans". Also, ibid, pp177-8 for discussion of whether Asquith should have moved Grey (most unlikely): "Grey did not want an agreement with Germany. To do so in 1912 would have upset the French, indeed there was no worthwhile agreement that would not have upset the French." Owen judges that "The Haldane Mission undoubtedly offered the best opportunity to avoid war with Germany during Asquith's premiership" (p177).
78 Williamson, op cit, p 258, referring to Bertie's "personal campaign to frustrate the policy of his own government … nothing new for the ambassador who, during the Agadir crisis, had on several occasions failed to inform – or rather had misinformed – the French government about Grey's views on a Moroccan port." Also C. Clark, op cit, p319-20.
79 C. Clark, op cit, p330.
80 Ibid, pp328-31.
81 Steiner, *Origins*, p93.
82 C. Clark, op cit, p322-3; Steiner, *Origins,* p119.
83 Steiner, op cit, pp119-20. T. G. Otte in *Detente 1914: Sir William Tyrrell's Secret Mission to Germany* Historical Journal, March 2013, pp175-204, argues that the revival of Russian power and probing created the context for the Anglo-German *rapprochement* after 1912.
84 C. Clark, pp322-3. Owen also describes Tyrrell's movement towards Germany: he had previously taken the view that "the real cancer at Berlin is Bülow … I despair of decent relations with Germany as long as he has a finger in the pie" (Otte, op cit, p188). Tyrell hoped to meet Jagow in 1914, but this was frequently postponed for innocuous reasons and finally overtaken by the July 1914 crisis. See Otte, op cit, passim.
85 Ibid, p267. Two Grand Dukes were both married to Montenegrin princesses. At the end of January 1914 Kokovtsov was dismissed by the Tsar; he was succeeded by Goremykin, a figurehead: Krivoshein, a Germanophobe, who had been campaigning against Kokovtsov since 1913, held the real power even though he was Minister of Agriculture.
86 McMeekin, *July 1914,* p385.

A. J. Balfour from *Struwwelpeter Alphabet*

Duke of Devonshire from *Struwwelpeter Alphabet*

LORD HUGH DE CECIL PROTESTETH
AGAINST TARIFF REFORM.

Austen Chamberlain

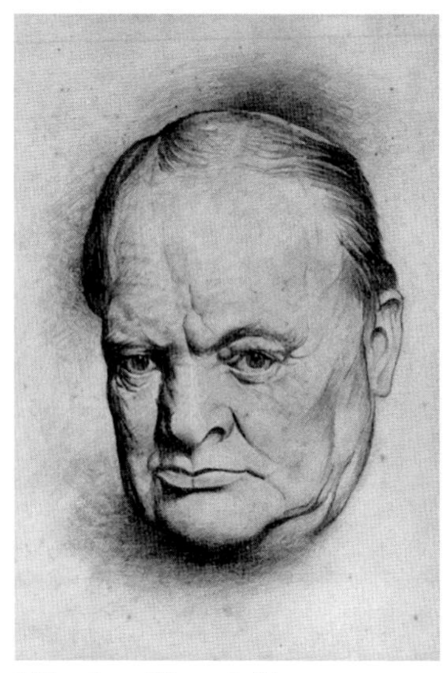

Winston Churchill

Leo Amery

Prince von Bülow

The Kaiser

Field Marshal
Sir Douglas Haig

Europe before the First Balkan War 1912-3

SIR JOSEPH DE BIRMINGHAM DEFIETH THE LORD VON BULOW OF ALMAINE

SIR JOSEPH DE BIRMINGHAM GOETH TO GUILDHALL.

The Bülow-Chamberlain clash of 1902

KING EDWARD THE SEVENTH VISITETH THE CHEVALIER LOUBET IN PARIS.

The Anglo-French Entente

Lloyd George

Baron von Eckardstein

Opposite page:
The Balkans in 1914-5

THE
BALKAN STATES
Railways thus.
Natural Scale 1:3,300,000
Miles
50 40 30 20 10 0 50
BLACK SEA
ÆGEAN
ARCHIPELAGO
SEA
TURKEY IN ASIA
SEA OF MARMARA
EAST RUMELIA
THRACE
MACEDONIA
UPPER MOESIA
ROUMELIA
BULGARIA
Balkan Mts
ALBANIA
EPIRUS
GREECE
MONTENEGRO
IONIAN ISLANDS
CORFU (To Greece)
CONSTANTINOPLE
ADRIANOPLE
Philippopolis
SOPHIA
SALONIKA
MONASTIR Bitolia
JANINA
GALLIPOLI
Sistova
Plevna
Lovatz
Tirnova
Shumla
Varna
Burghas
Kostendil
Uskub
Pristina
Prisren
Scutari
Dibra
Ochrida
Larissa
Trikkala
Kavala
Drama
Enos
Rodosto
Kirk Kilisse
Lule Burgas
Midia
Thasos
Samothraki I.
Imbros I.
Lemnos I.
Mitylene or Lesbos
G. of Saros
G. of Salonika
Athos
Pindus Mts
Sub. Tel.
Sub. Tel. to Odessa
Bosphorus or Str. of Constantinople

Bethmann-Hollweg

Right: Sir Edward Grey

Emir, later King, Feisal

King Habibullah of Afghanistan

87 P. H. S. Hatton, *Harcourt and Solf: the Search for an Anglo-German Understanding through Africa 1912-14* European Studies Review I, No 2 (1971), pp123-6, 129.
88 Ibid, pp132-3: the proposals for the Portuguese colonies are illustrated in the map on p503 of A. J. P. Taylor's *Struggle for Mastery in Europe.*
89 Ibid, pp133,135, 137, 139, 142 144; the last quote from Taylor, op cit, p514. See footnote 84.
90 Paul Schroeder, Journal of Modern History 1972, *World War One as Galloping Gertie: A Reply to Joachim Remak,* pp340-41; final point, Charmley, op cit, pp351, 377.
91 Schroeder, op cit, p338.
92 Lieven, *Towards The Flame: Empire, War and the End of Tsarist Russia*, p8.
93 The Austrian ambassador in London, Mensdorff, tells his departing German colleague, Lichnowsky, that he hopes to stop on in London, which he does for nine days until driven out by the press, just as his British counterpart, Bunsen, stays on in Vienna until 13 August. Emil Ludwig, *July 1914,* pp213-5.
94 McMeekin, *July 1914,* p206; last quote is in the author's words.
95 Ibid, pp237-44. The Latin is a legal phrase, meaning literally "on the threshold", or "at the start".
96 Ibid, pp281-2 This was after Goschen, the British ambassador in Berlin, had warned him privately that Britain would not stand aside if France was drawn in. Watson, op cit, p47. Jagow described the Hapsburgs as "an Atridite dynasty, moving from catastrophe to catastrophe". He was not present when the Kaiser and Bethmann issued the "blank cheque" to Count Hoyos, the Austrian emissary. (Otte, op cit, 201.)
97 Watson, op cit, pp36-7.
98 McMeekin, *July 1914,* p74. The Straits were important to Russia because most of her exports, especially grain, were too bulky to send by rail and remain competitive. Lieven, op cit, p75.
99 C. Clark, op cit, pp510, 517.
100 McMeekin, *July 1914,* pp401, 403.
101 MacMillan, op cit, p478.
102 C. Clark, op cit, pp530-1; McMeekin, *July 1914* pp342, 348-9. MacMillan shows how mobilisation schedules were altered throughout the war: the chief of the German General Staff's Railway Section said after the war that he and his men could have swiftly made plans to mobilise only against Russia (op cit, p301).
103 C. Clark, op cit, pp532-5; McMeekin, *July 1914,* p348fn.
104 McMeekin, *July 1914,* p360.
105 One suggestion is that Britain might have ignored the Belgium issue if Germany had just invaded without all her ultimatum paraphernalia. Some Ministers, including Churchill and Lloyd George, said Britain would not regard a transit as a casus belli so long as the Germans stayed south of the Sambre-Meuse line, keeping clear of the strategic area round Antwerp. Churchill, noted then for his "belligerent stance" remarked "I don't see why we should come in if they only go a little way into Belgium." C. Clark, op cit, p494.
106 Ferguson, *Virtual,* pp267-70, 273.
107 Barnes and Nicholson, op cit, I p103, being Amery's diary for 1st August 1914.
108 Ferguson, *Virtual History* (p278) quotes Crowe: if the Central Powers "crush France and humiliate Russia, what will then be the position of a friendless England?" Ferguson robustly replies: "better than that of an exhausted England in 1919."
109 Watson, op cit, p107.
110 Ibid, pp139, 156, 158; MacMillan, op cit, p596.

CHAPTER FIVE
War and Peace: The Middle East

"Squiff-Grey-K(itchener). Even the Bosh could not carry that load."
(Sir Henry Wilson to L. S. Amery, 18 December 1915, Barnes and Nicholson, op cit, I p126.)

"In his view the Western Front was a candle that burned all the moths that entered it."
(Lord Milner, minutes of the Committee of Prime Ministers, 31 July 1918, quoted David R. Woodward *Lloyd George and the Generals* p 324.)

"I am so convinced that Palestine will be a rankling thorn in the flesh of whoever is charged with its Mandate, that I would withdraw from this responsibility while we yet can."
(Curzon to Balfour, 20 August 1919, quoted Margaret MacMillan *The Peacemakers* p435.)

Mistaken Allied Strategic Options 1914-17

Volumes have been produced, and doubtless are yet to come, in the debate over Allied strategy, especially in 1915-17, as well as wartime diplomacy relating to a possible compromise peace. This chapter points to possible missed opportunities in both the military and diplomatic field, briefly explaining why things went as they did. The longer the war and the greater its cost, the more greedy the Allies, if victorious, would be at the peace-making. Thus, Britain obtained a new (and not wholly desirable) empire in the Middle East.

Douglas Haig as Commander-in-Chief from late 1915 and William Robertson as Chief of the Imperial General Staff were fanatical "Westerners", convinced that the war could only be won on the Western Front in France, and that the British Empire's military resources should be concentrated there. The rival Liberal leader to Asquith, Lloyd George, tried at times to challenge this determination. He did not succeed in removing Robertson until February 1918 – by which time most of the crucial decisions had been taken and the casualties incurred.

The opposite view was to question the prospects of breaking through the trench system in France; instead, Germany's weaker allies should be eliminated. In early 1915 the Cabinet was persuaded by Churchill to undertake the Dardanelles expedition, which dominated much of the Imperial war effort that year. Its dismal failure did not win support for more of the same. These attacks were, perhaps, a close-run thing. The naval assault terminated in panic after three battleships had been sunk by mines on 18 March; it is now known that the Turkish forts were at that time running out of ammunition. Then troops landed, but the element of surprise had been lost and the Turks were reinforced. A further landing in Suvla Bay on 6 August achieved surprise and was scarcely opposed, but the opportunity was lost through incompetence. Finally, after paltry gains, the whole Allied force was evacuated at year-end, almost without loss.

To the historian, possessing knowledge about the real strengths and intentions of the enemy unavailable to contemporaries (there was no Bletchley then), it appears doubtful whether there was an easy solution to be had in France and Flanders. Equally apparent, however, is a much more cold-blooded approach. At every stage during the First World War (with a risky period in the winter of 1917-18 when Russia was withdrawing from the war and the United States had hardly brought its manpower to bear), Britain and her allies heavily outnumbered the Central Powers, in population, in military strength, and in financial and commercial resources, though not decisively in commodities like steel production. Given the weakness of her three allies, how well could Germany use her formidable armaments and forces, her skill, and most importantly, her ability to shift reserves across internal lines? Germany usually defeated the Russians (and the latter's Balkan allies), inflicting much larger numbers of casualties than she herself suffered. Much more rarely, Germany suffered more casualties than she inflicted (for example, at Mons). What Germany could not survive indefinitely was a succession of large scale battles of attrition in which she, with a population of 67 million, suffered roughly equal – or even slightly lower – casualties as Britain and France, which had a combined population (excluding their overseas Dominions and colonies which were playing a steadily increasing role on the Western Front) of over 87 million (and this equation excludes Russia up to mid 1917 and the US after that point). Those great holocausts, Verdun, the Somme and Passchendaele, cost the Germans not far short of the total lost by the Anglo-French. For success in this strategy of bleeding Germany white, the Entente – and, since the French flinched from the ordeal in early 1917, increasingly Britain – had to suffer casualties unprecedented in her history.[1]

With deadlock at Gallipoli, the remainder of the Anglo-French war effort in 1915 was made in France, with attacks in Artois and Champagne at grievous human cost: the BEF in France suffered over 270,000 battle casualties in 1915. As Sheffield remarks: "It was not simply a matter of acquiring the appropriate technology (which in 1915 the BEF did not have); it was also a matter of developing appropriate methods (or tactics) of using the technology in an effective fashion, which was achieved by 1918."[2] The British were not only very short of shells, but swiftly discovered that shrapnel , as opposed to the then rarely used high-explosive shells, failed to cut the enemy wire or flatten trenches. The politicians in London were reliant on the optimistic reports from the generals, though gradually attrition ("killing Germans") replaced break-through as a strategic objective. So the attrition school cold-bloodedly regards the Somme as a success. The Germans could ill afford to lose experienced officers, NCOs and men; it "degraded the quality of the German army", while "the British, by contrast, lost mostly green soldiers while those who survived the holocaust benefited greatly ... by gaining experience."[3]

Why were French and later British troops thrown away in large numbers in the West when smaller numbers, coming to the help of the brave Serbs in 1915, and the perhaps less brave but not insignificant Rumanians in 1916, might have tipped the Balkan balance in the same way that it was tipped in the autumn of 1918? The huge difference with 1918 was that Russia was, most formidably despite great losses, still in the war in 1915-16. Of course, there was huge political pressure to try to regain French territory lost in 1914 but if the strategic direction, particularly in Britain, had been as cold-blooded towards such sentiment as it was towards casualties, it might have perceived that in 1915 the Balkan arena might well have been decisive.

Even before 1914 was out Lloyd George and Maurice Hankey, now Secretary of the Cabinet's War Council, both argued the case for reinforcing Serbia along the railway from Salonika to Belgrade.[4] The other "big beasts" of the War Council, Churchill and Kitchener, the Secretary of State for War, were both sceptical about the frontal attacks in the West. Churchill did not want anything to diminish his Dardanelles project and Kitchener did not want to quarrel with Joffre. However, Kitchener added that it was "very desirable" to send troops to Serbia – "ultimately we might send an army of 500,000 men to Serbia, and if the Dardanelles were open we could maintain it there" – but "he was not quite sure that the right moment had arrived."[5]

Lloyd George argued "I am fairly confident you will not get these Balkan States to decide until they see khaki."[6] Those opposed to diverting troops from the West claimed that all would be well with Serbia when it expected to face German attack in the autumn of 1915. As late as 23 September, when Lloyd George suggested to the Dardanelles Committee that 40,000 British troops in the Dardanelles be transferred to Salonika to help Serbia, that Athens should be told both this and that eventually four times as many would be sent, Kitchener sniffed that the German threat to Serbia was exaggerated. The Committee agreed to send a small Anglo-French force to Salonika; this began to land on 5 October, but the same day the pro-Allied Premier of Greece, Venizelos, resigned on account of the opposition of King Constantine, who was married to the Kaiser's sister. On the same day, Austro-German forces occupied Belgrade; they were swiftly joined (13 October) by the Bulgarians, attacking from the east. While the small British force merely advanced to the Bulgarian border, the French pushed north towards Nish.

Carson, who resigned as Attorney General on the issue, and Lloyd George were the main critics: the latter later wrote " We were warned early in 1915 that the Germans meant in confederation with the Bulgars to wipe Serbia out … When the attack came, we had not purchased a single mule to aid the Serbians through Salonika."[7]

During 1915 we see extravagant, but not totally unrealistic pressures from Leo Amery, Unionist backbench MP, visiting the Balkan capitals. Serving on General Rawlinson's staff in 1914 and early 1915, Amery drew up for Kitchener a plan to reinforce the Serbs and advance into the Hungarian plain. This was similar to a plan put forward by Lloyd George a few weeks later. Amery was then despatched by General Callwell, Director of Operations at the War Office, on a special mission to study road, rail and river communications in the Balkans to facilitate the advance of the British army towards Hungary "once the Dardanelles had been forced."[8]

At the end of April Amery described Greece as "the neutral which is more friendly than any other and to whom Germany can offer nothing", and argued that "if we send out six divisions at once we shall probably add the whole Greek army of 250,000 or so to our side, but risk drawing Bulgaria in against us ... If we send out not six but twelve divisions, then not only Greece but Bulgaria as well will probably join us ... and Rumania will be free and willing at once to launch her whole army into Transylvania." Six weeks later, in Bucharest, he wrote that "our diplomacy has ... failed here also, and Rumania which when I left three weeks ago was on the verge of coming in, has now quite cooled off."[9] Might this have worked? Possibly, especially if accompanied with a sensible diplomatic approach to Austria-Hungary, but all her assailants were greedy for annexations. The historian Charles Cruttwell argued that a Balkan campaign, reinforcing Serbia, would have had a "critical" effect on Austria when Italy joined the war on 23 May 1915 and might at least have disrupted the great Austro-German attack on Russia which began at the start of May.[10]

Strategic western domination was repeated in 1916, otherwise marked by the indecisive battles at Verdun, on the Somme, and on the Isonzo, and Brusilov's remarkable but temporary defeat of Austria in southern Poland. This latter finally tempted the Rumanians off the fence (on 27 August). In April the British rejected a French proposal for an offensive against Bulgaria from Salonika. The French, sensitive to the fate of Rumania, persisted, and on 9 October there was a "long tirade" by Lloyd George at the War Committee. Robertson argued that Rumania was not in danger; if she "made her dispositions properly she ought to be all right".[11] In fact, with the Germans and their allies invading from north and south, southern Rumania was conquered and Bucharest fell to the German cavalry on 6 December.

Likewise 1917 saw hecatombs of Allied losses, both in the French spring offensive in Champagne (the failure of which led to widespread mutiny in the French army) and the futile British attack in the autumn towards Passchendaele. While this was happening, the Germans and Austrians came near to knocking Italy out of the war at Caporetto.[12]

Lloyd George, as the new Prime Minister in December 1916, had in his new War Cabinet of five, some powerful allies against Haig and Robertson. This influence had little impact during 1917, because, to encourage other influential Unionists to join his government, Lloyd George had been obliged to promise that he would keep Haig as Commander-in-Chief of the BEF, a promise reinforced by his appointing the generals' friend Derby as War Secretary. Furthermore, Lloyd George had disparate objectives. Instead, he pressed for Britain and France to send heavy guns to support Italy, which might have helped – and for an attack from Egypt to capture Jerusalem – which fell in the autumn of 1917. These successes were hardly going to affect the balance in Central Europe.

Wartime Diplomacy – A Compromise Peace?

All the Allies were gradually tempted to compensate for their huge losses by developing territorial greed. This, and the rash promises made to them by their partners, destroyed the chances of a negotiated peace with Germany's allies. Thus Austria-Hungary, Turkey and Bulgaria stayed in the war until overwhelmed in its final weeks.

Asquith proclaimed at Cardiff, 2 October 1914, that the British Empire had no desire to expand. Within weeks, in secrecy, this innocence was to be undermined, with Lord Hardinge (the Permanent Under-Secretary at the Foreign Office), in correspondence in spring 1915, envisaging the whole of Asia with the exception of Japan and its position in China (and presumably also French Indo-China) as a "satrapy" (Rothwell's word) of the British and Russian empires.[13] Thus we see Grey encouraging Russia during the winter of 1914-5 to claim Constantinople, in order to keep her in the war despite her reverses. This commitment would scupper any early Allied peace approaches to Turkey. Likewise, the Treaty of London in May 1915, which brought Italy in on the Allied side, said Italy "will receive" Trentino and Trieste and large specified territories in Dalmatia. And in 1915 Rumania was offered what Sir Arthur Nicolson termed "practically one half of Hungary".[14]

The diplomatic history sees Bulgaria as Germany's weak link: "Of all the [Central Powers] Bulgaria was the only one which could, at almost any time after its entry into the war ... have had peace merely by asking for it; a peace, moreover, which satisfied most of her territorial ambitions ..." A Foreign Office report in August 1916 recommended giving her the "contested" (with Serbia) zone in Macedonia and also Turkey in Europe outside Constantinople. To detach Bulgaria would enable munitions to be sent to Russia, and as Hardinge wrote, "it would be the end of Turkey."[15] By the end of 1916 Bulgaria had occupied most of the territory it wanted and began to consider a separate peace based on this. She made feelers to Russia, which were rejected, then to the other Entente members. The Bulgarians loathed the Turks, but she wanted also Serbian Macedonia and some Greek territory, which posed difficulties. During the early autumn of 1916 hopes concentrated on Bulgaria, but it was recognised that a large force would have to be sent to protect Bulgaria from attack from Turkey and Germany, each facing a crucial breach to their communications. By October the Bulgarian Committee of National Defence had split into two and King Ferdinand had reportedly lost all interest.[16]

The Aubrey Herbert[17] episode in 1917 showed divisions in the Foreign Office over seeking peace with Turkey. Herbert liked Turks, had a low opinion of Arabs, and the Foreign Office accepted his offer to go to Switzerland to sound out the Turks on peace. George Clerk of the Foreign Office set out Britain's terms in a note of 31 July: Britain should get the Basra vilayet, with independence for Arabia and for the Baghdad vilayet, "real autonomy" for Syria and Armenia with the Allies exercising some supervision, and a "special position" for Palestine. Herbert returned after conversations with a close friend of the Grand Vizier, Talaat: the Turks wanted the Entente to drop annexations, and support "autonomy" for the Arab and Armenian areas under *Turkish* suzerainty. This, Herbert believed, would enable Talaat to depose Enver Pasha who was "incorrigibly pro-German".[18]

There were "very serious efforts to negotiate peace terms;" even Lloyd George (hostile to Turkey) backed them and was supported by Milner. One was through the British legations in Switzerland and Greece and the other was more bizarre. Lloyd George tried to make contact with Enver via Sir Basil Zaharoff, a Greek-born arms dealer, then one of the richest men in the world, and a friend of Bonar Law, who believed Enver might be bribed. Half a million dollars were offered to one Abdul Kerim (an agent of Enver's) and one and a half million to Enver himself, with the peace terms similar to those offered by Herbert to Talaat. These initial sums were deposited in the two Turks' accounts in Switzerland; the eventual total envisaged was 10 million dollars. In February 1918 Zaharoff, through Kerim, heard from Enver (all three being in Switzerland) that he could do nothing more as Talaat refused to cooperate. Enver returned his deposit, Kerim kept his.[19]

Later moves involved Philip Kerr, Lloyd George's private secretary, in Switzerland to coincide with a POW conference in Geneva where the Turkish delegation was led by Mouktar Bey, another close associate of Talaat. During January 1918, however, Mouktar showed little inclination to discuss peace terms. As Rothwell concluded: "In reality, the Austrians and the Turks were now adopting exactly the same attitude, that of severing their channels of communication with Britain and their other enemies in anticipation of a German victory in France."[20]

Britain's attitude to Austria-Hungary was ambiguous: a "residue of good will for Austria ... survived in Britain to the end of the war contrasted with the fierce hatred of Germany through society ... There was never to be any question of a compromise peace with Austria-Hungary being unacceptable on principle".[21] During the first two years of the war this was dormant, negated by the territorial ambitions of Russia, Serbia and Italy. After the death of the Austrian Emperor Franz Joseph in November 1916, there was a belief that the Emperor Karl wanted peace, and a Foreign Office paper in February 1917 argued that a separate peace with Austria was essential to shorten the war. In fact Karl and his Foreign Minister Count Czernin were only interested in a general peace.

With the Bolshevik revolution driving Russia out of the war, the winter of 1917-8 coincided with renewed approaches. Lord Robert Cecil, a Foreign Office minister who was sympathetic to the survival of the Hapsburg monarchy (a view not shared by his chief, Balfour) told St Loe Strachey (13 November 1917) that "the Slavs have never shown the slightest capacity for self-government". Talks took place in Switzerland between Smuts and Count Mensdorff (the Anglophile Austrian ambassador in London in 1904-14), with Smuts convinced that military victory for the Allies was "improbable" even as late as 1919-20 and therefore keen on a strong Austria as counterpoise to Germany. He thought Austria-Hungary should cede Trentino to Italy, grant cultural autonomy to Trieste, cede Bukowina to Rumania and possibly Herzegovina to Serbia. The Austrian and Russian sectors of Poland could be united into a "third state" of the Hapsburg Monarchy, with Serbia and Montenegro as its fourth![22]

While the Smuts-Mensdorff talks went well on a personal level, Mensdorff made it clear that Austria would not desert Germany while the war continued. A moderate speech by Lloyd George on war aims led to a suggestion that Czernin would like to meet Lloyd George. With caution being urged in case this was a German propaganda trap, the War Cabinet agreed on 18 January 1918 that Czernin be offered a meeting with Smuts. On the 28th, however, Balfour reported that he had not sent this telegram because he wanted to consult with Orlando, the Italian Prime Minister who was in London (this would be a conversation hardly friendly to the idea of an approach to Austria). On 6 February Balfour invited the US President Wilson to pursue the matter. Milner and Hankey sent messages to Lloyd George on 27 February and 2 March criticising Foreign Office delays. The American approach made sense in that the US was not committed by secret treaties to Italy, although Wilson might not have supported the survival of the Hapsburg monarchy against the counter-claims of the various subject races. However, by the end of March Austria had clearly cooled and decided to place her hopes in the success of Germany in the West.[23]

What, if anything, of the Germans? A friend of the King of Denmark was told "that one could not treat with the Germans on the same footing as one would another enemy. They had placed themselves beyond the pale and could only be treated as criminals."[24] On 19 July 1917, the Reichstag passed a Peace Resolution calling for a peace of reconciliation, and Bethmann's subsequent conversations with Vatican diplomats gave the Holy See the idea that Germany was prepared to restore Belgium. This upset the German High Command who demanded (and obtained) Bethmann's resignation. Hindenburg and Ludendorff, now in full control, saw victory as the best way to peace.[25]

1918 – The Germans Choose the Wrong Strategy?

After three years of Allied wastage on the Western Front, in 1918 it was the German turn to be bewitched. Lord Milner stated in mid 1918: "In his view the Western Front was a candle that burned all the moths that entered it."[26] The 100 divisions which Germany had on the Eastern Front could, when peace with

Bolshevik Russia was made, be used elsewhere. The question was, where? The Germans should have been sensitive to the plight of their weaker allies. If reinforcements had been sent south, the collapse of the Bulgarians[27] and the Turks in the autumn of 1918 might have been avoided.

Relief for Austria-Hungary and a major blow to the Allies would have been delivered by a spring attack on the Italian front. The style of attack actually delivered by the Germans in France, could well, directed as it would have been at predominantly Italian forces, have brought Italy to an armistice. The German High Command chose otherwise: to concentrate on a final effort in the West. Interestingly, Prince Rupprecht of Bavaria, one of Germany's most competent generals, commanding the northern group of armies in the West, favoured another strike at Italy. He, and Crown Prince Wilhelm of Prussia – the Kaiser's heir, commanding the central group, "were both unconvinced" about an offensive in the West, "and their staff officers shared their scepticism."[28]

There is no evidence that the Germans seriously considered either the Italian or other, more exotic, Eastern options. Indeed, between November 1917 and March 1918 they moved 8 divisions – their total – from Italy to the West. Only 33,000 men remained in Macedonia, and a mere 4500 in the Ottoman territories, although large forces remained in the Ukraine.[29]

So the Austrians had to attack alone in Italy in June 1918. Initially they found Italian morale unsteady and took thousands of prisoners, but their attack was held and rain swelling the River Po prevented heavy guns crossing. With the Italians counter-attacking, the offensive was halted after eight days and the bridgeheads were abandoned. It was a severe blow to Austrian morale and contributed to the collapse later in the year.[30] If German manpower, logistics (bridge and pontoon building) and aircraft had been available to the Austrians, it is not difficult to conclude that the Italians might have been forced back on Venice and Milan, and possibly out of the war. Albeit with some difficulty, a general compromise peace might have resulted.

There was one other, rather far-fetched operation, which the British were terrified of, and which might well have brought them to the conference table in 1918. The Brest-Litovsk treaty of 3 March 1918 gave the Germans control of the Ukraine, while Turkish and German forces had been moving into the Caucasus states. Enver Pasha had ambitions for dominions in Turkish-speaking central Asia; for this he raised an "Army of Islam" which contained most of Turkey's remaining good troops. As early as 22 March 1917, Balfour and Austen Chamberlain warned the War Cabinet of a possible German threat to the Persian Gulf and to India. As the evidence of Russian collapse grew, British intelligence chiefs became more alarmed. In November 1917, Arnold Toynbee, then the Foreign Office Political Intelligence Department's Near Eastern expert, warned: "... The Berlin-Bokhara line through Asia Minor and Northern Persia ... would seriously threaten India ..." Lord Curzon, Chairman of the War Cabinet's Eastern Committee, warned as late as June 1918 "The real and tragic nature of the disaster in Russia was not so much the increase in forces to the Germans in the West as it was opening the East to a new campaign ..." Colonel A. W. Knox, former chief British military attaché to Russia, warned that the German threat was "something more real to fear" than the traditional Russian one, "for German brains and energy are more effective than Russian".[31]

The threat was exaggerated, but faced with it, Henry Wilson, who had replaced Robertson as CIGS in February 1918, ordered an advance from Baghdad into north-west Persia. This was Dunsterforce, about a thousand officers and men in 750 Ford vans and cars under Major-General L. C. Dunsterville.[32] Wilson also emphasised the need "to get Japan to ... act with the greatest possible energy and with the greatest possible strength". But the Japanese were then mainly interested in eastern Siberia – four thousand miles from northern Persia!

Even Haig was obsessed by the threat to Turkestan and India, while the Germans in France were "noisily massing men and equipment in front of [him]."[33] After it became clear that the Germans were having their last throw of dice on the Western Front, those in London could not resist the wider dimension, as displayed during the meetings in June 1918 and after of the Imperial War Cabinet. This consisted of the Prime Ministers, or their deputies, of the Dominions, with India represented by the Secretary of State and three "assessors," alongside the British War Cabinet. Milner, now Secretary of State for War, on 9 June warned Lloyd George "We must be prepared for France & Italy both being beaten to their knees. In that case, the German-Austro-Turco-Bulgar bloc will be master of all of Europe & of Northern & Central Asia ... The fight will now be for Southern Asia ..."

Leo Amery was now political secretary at the Supreme Allied Command at Versailles, thus personal representative of Lloyd George and Milner there. In a memorandum on "War Aims and Military Policy" dated 15 June, Amery endorsed these fears, adding that even if the German attack in the West stalled, the Allies "had no reasonable prospect" of "acquiring ascendancy over the Germans till the autumn of 1919 or the spring of 1920" – a time-schedule that was widely believed at that time. Amery assumed continued attrition in the West but success in the East, with Britain ejecting the Turks from Syria and Mesopotamia, securing Persia and the Caucasus and, with the help of the USA and Japan, holding the Germans in Russia at the Urals or "even Lake Baikal".[34]

In a letter to Lloyd George of 8 June, Amery used the expression "we can call a New World into being to redress the balance of the Old". From all that is known of Amery, it is unlikely that he was thinking of the American input; much more likely was what he described in another letter as "that Southern British World which runs from Cape Town through Cairo, Baghdad and Calcutta to Sydney and Wellington."[35] Whether this world had the resources or the patience to undertake the huge task envisaged is debatable.

In a footnote added many years later to his diary entry for 16 July, Amery writes "it was on this day, I think, I was told to make plans for carrying on the war if France and Italy were out." In his memoirs, he says this may have been at the end of June or in mid-July when "very disquieting news had come in on the state of French and Italian morale if there should be a reverse". In a paper that was never completed, he analysed how much equipment could be evacuated from France: "vast depots of munitions and stores would have to be abandoned." Europe would be lost "except possibly Greece … [we] could wage the war more effectively in the East and release more men for shipbuilding and munitions – the 1940-43 situation in fact."[36] It was not a cheerful prospect.

As David Woodward declares on his final page, "can anyone seriously argue that the 'Westerners' could have achieved the same results (viz, Allied victory) in 1918 if the Germans had remained on the defensive, protected by the Hindenburg Line with their reserves intact?"[37] In his planning for 1918, Ludendorff said Germany had strength for only one main blow,[38] yet as the saga unfolds, he is seen to strike out repeatedly like Brer Rabbit in Uncle Remus's story of the Tar Baby!

While the German attacks from March to June put the Allied defence in great danger at times, in fact the Germans were gradually throwing away their numerical advantages. In the March offensive and subsequently, they resorted to mass attacks rather than infiltration, and thus incurred large casualties, including many well-trained storm troopers.[39] Their advances simply increased their supply problems in eventually three huge vulnerable salients, which would never be as strongly fortified, as defensible, or even as comfortable as the Hindenburg Line from whence they started. There were signs of indiscipline and drunkenness, following their captures of stores including wine. The sight of the abundance of British supplies was itself demoralising. "The German fighting methods that had seemed so formidable had evolved surprisingly little … were being applied less skilfully, and being halted faster and faster."[40]

For a month after mid-June there was a tactical stalemate, while German morale was affected by the failure of these great and costly strokes to bring the prospect of peace any nearer. Ludendorff's final onslaught, on 15 July against the French, mainly consisting of a pincer movement on Reims. Even this was not intended to be the last; that, to gratify Wagner-lovers, was codenamed 'Hagen' and was destined for the British. But the French knew the time and place of the Reims attack; they carried out a tactical withdrawal and then, on 18 July, counter-attacked. This was the turning point: 'Hagen' never happened.

Other factors ensured a decisive turn of the tide. American troops were now flooding in: by the end of September 39 US divisions were in France – each larger than the Anglo-French divisions. The modernisation of Allied tactics was bearing fruit: from the summer of 1918 tanks, and particularly the light and faster ones (the "Whippets") played an increasingly important role, in cooperation with artillery, machine gunners and the RAF. All this skill culminated in the British (and Imperial) counter-offensive east of Amiens on 8 August: 1904 Allied aircraft faced 369 German. Surprise was achieved: on the first day the attackers advanced up to 8 miles – far more than any other day on the Western Front, suffering 9000 casualties – low by comparison to other battles, while the Germans lost 27,000 including 12,000 prisoners. Ludendorff called 8 August a "black day for the German Army". He offered his resignation to the Kaiser who rejected it but agreed "the war must be brought to an end". The Germans were slowly, but surely, driven back towards Brussels.[41]

Crucial for the fate of Germany was that of her weaker allies. As a Poirot or Morse would have said, "the key is in the dates". A successful Allied attack from Salonika concluded in a cease fire on 29 September, with Bulgaria's weapons, ammunition, military transport, roads and railways put at the disposal of the Allies. They thus advanced through Serbia on Hungary, reaching the Danube on 1 November, and also towards Constantinople.[42] Allenby attacked in Palestine on 19 September, taking the weak Turkish forces opposing him by surprise. Cavalry, armoured cars and aircraft took part in the pursuit, resulting in three-quarters of the Turkish forces being taken prisoner. Damascus fell on 1-2 October, Beirut on 8 October, and Aleppo on 29 October. Meanwhile, another army advanced along the Tigris, forcing the surrender of the Turkish Sixth Army on 30 October, and occupying Mosul. Turkey signed an armistice the same day.[43]

The Italian Prime Minister, Orlando, delayed until he could see that an offensive was necessary "while Italy could still benefit from it". The 29th October saw the battle begin to go in Italy's favour, with Austrian morale and discipline breaking down. As with Germany a few days later, disorder at home determined the outcome. By late October national councils were taking power in Cracow and in Prague, while that in Zagreb declared the independence of the Serbs, Croats and Slovenes. Meanwhile Rumania invaded Transylvania. With Hungary also facing invasion from the south, on 24 October the Hungarian Government called on all units in Italy to return home. Even German-Austrian units refused orders. Italy did not concede an armistice until she had occupied Trent (1 November) and Trieste, amphibiously, on the 3rd. Meanwhile, in eastern France, German thoughts of forming an "Antwerp-Meuse" defensive line was doomed by the Franco-American attack in the Argonne, which crossed the Meuse on 7 November, and cut the crucial Lille-Metz railway at Sedan. The last days of the war saw cease-fire talks matched with revolution brewing in Germany.

Peacemaking in 1919: Rewarding Italy

Italy sought much but was deeply disappointed with her gains. This was to have damaging consequences for Britain, two decades later. By the secret Treaty of London in April 1915 the Entente promised Italy, if she would join the war on their side, Trieste and Trentino, a large part of Slovenia and the northern part of the Dalmatian coast, numerous islands, the port of Valona in Albania and a protectorate over central Albania, with the prospect of substantial parts of Asia Minor if Turkey were defeated.

While the mainly Slav populated Dalmatian coast had only small enclaves of Italians in some ports, the whole of it had belonged to Venice until her conquest by Napoleon. At the Peace Conference, the Serbs showed signs of being prepared to trade away Dalmatia and Istria to get more territory to their north and east; Pasic, their Orthodox Prime Minister, cared little for accumulating Catholic Croats and Slovenes. The Italians pointed out that while the western shore of the Adriatic had few natural harbours, the eastern Adriatic had good harbours, protected by reefs and islands. Italy threw away that strong position by incompetence and by exhibiting excessive "greediness", according to Lord Robert Cecil, who added "as a result ... it is now literally true that Italy has not a friend in Europe except ourselves ..." Italy's tactics "were irritating, transparent and frequently inept."[44]

Italy was opposed by France (the "Latin sisters"), which wanted a strong Yugoslavia as a brake on Germany, while Clemenceau despised the Italians, who "think they deserve the entire globe".[45] President Wilson alone actually believed in national self-determination, and was very suspicious of the Italians from the start of the Conference. Thus, the only one of Italy's claims that was settled easily was that for Trentino and South Tyrol. They wanted to move the border with Yugoslavia down the coast towards Split. The hostility to this was such that Balfour commented "The Italians must somehow be mollified, and the only question is how to mollify them at the smallest cost to mankind."[46] A very stormy meeting between Wilson and Orlando on 14 April led, ten days later, after a statement by Wilson to the press rejecting the Italian claims, to Orlando leaving for Rome. In reprisal, the Italian press claimed that Wilson had been bribed by the Yugoslavs or, most improbably, had a Yugoslav mistress.[47]

On 19 June, the Orlando Government fell, largely as a result of losing these arguments in Paris. The new Government was more moderate, agreeing that Fiume should become a neutral city, but in September 1919 it was occupied by the poet and nationalist D'Annunzio. The Yugoslavs agreed to the Treaty of Rapallo in November 1920, whereby Italy obtained the whole Istrian peninsula, Zadar and a few small islands, and Fiume (Rijeka) became a free state. By Mussolini's treaty of Rome in January 1924 Italy obtained Fiume, while Yugoslavia obtained its suburb of Susak as a port.

Italy had, of course, also been promised large, though undetermined, areas of Asia Minor. There were no communities, whose interests she might claim to protect: "in terms of Woodrow Wilson's self determination principles, there was no reason for Italy to occupy any part of Asia Minor at all."[48] Starting from March 1919, on the grounds of restoring order, Italian troops began landing at Adalia (Antalya), also occupying Marmaris. By the Treaty of Sèvres, eventually imposed on the Sultan of Turkey on 10 August 1920, Italy was allocated a vast "zone of influence" including the south-west and much of the southern coast of Asia Minor. She did not have the strength to occupy this vast area, while Nitti, then Italian Prime Minister and Tittoni, the Foreign Minister, lost interest in Anatolian mandates, preferring to co-operate with the Turks to get access to coalmines and other commercial opportunities in the area.

If Italy had achieved a more generous settlement, her democratic system of government might have survived, rather than fall to the Mussolini dictatorship. Mussolini was affected by jealousy of France and Britain, virtually from the start, and especially during the mid to late Thirties.

Wartime German Subversion in the Islamic World

Once Turkey joined the war in late 1914, the Sultan, in his capacity as Caliph of Islam, declared *jihad* or holy war against the Allies. Little *jihad* occurred, but it led to the reversal of the traditional British view about preserving the territorial integrity of the Ottoman Empire. The Middle East was crucial to Britain because, if a hostile power secured a substantial base there, the Suez Canal, India and links to Australasia would be threatened. Some rather obscure activities by Germany during the War gave powerful backing to security concerns. The story of Germany's rather futile attempts to subvert parts of the area between Algeria, Abyssinia and Afghanistan, in the first half of the War, is worthy of John Buchan at his best, and merits brief reference.[49]

The most exotic of the German attempts related to Northern and Eastern Africa. German groups were sent to raise French Algeria, without any effect. There were various early attempts – all equally unsuccessful – to block the Suez Canal, for example by sinking a large coal-filled German freighter: seamen on the ship betrayed the plot to the British. A German naval officer tried to cross into Egypt with a party of Germans "disguised as an Arab comedy troupe" to sabotage British fuel depots; they were caught.

One of the more ambitious was directed at Abyssinia, where one Frobenius was to take orders to German diplomats in Addis Ababa to encourage an invasion of the Sudan, or alternatively, of the Belgian Congo and Kenya. However Frobenius did not leave Damascus until January 1915 and was arrested by the (still neutral) Italians in Eritrea. In the summer of 1915, the 19 year old Abyssinian ruler Lij Iyasu began an infatuation with Islam, in which he was encouraged by the German legation. He sought an anti-British alliance with the Somali rebel Sayyid Muhammed Abdullah, known to posterity as the "Mad Mullah". Wilfred Thesiger, father of his renowned namesake, then British minister in Addis Ababa, forged a close alliance with the pro-British Prime Minister Habte Giorgis. Together, in September 1915 they produced a revolution which deposed Prince Iyasu. A few months later, with the help of aircraft, the British crushed a revolt in Darfur by a local sultan carrying out *jihad.*

The Germans also aimed to send via Turkey a mission to persuade Habibullah, King of Afghanistan, to attack India, but this was delayed by the Turks. Fears that Turkey intended to seize Persian territory did not encourage Persian collaboration. The leaders of two groups for Afghanistan, Niedermayer and Hentig, met in

Teheran in June 1915. Allied policing was such that the bulk of Niedermayer's group had to stay in Isfahan, while the others eventually reached Kabul on 1 October. Habibullah was friendly to them and even, on 24 January 1916, signed a draft treaty which promised Afghanistan's entry into the war on the German side in return for money and munitions. The absence of a telegraph line to Persia meant that a messenger had to take the draft treaty overland to Constantinople, which he did not reach until July. Whatever Habibullah's original intentions, he went cold on the idea of entering the war; the Germans left Kabul empty-handed.

In Persia itself, after early German successes at Shiraz and Bushire in July 1915, the latter was relieved on 8 August by 500 Anglo-Indian cavalry. The Persian government then asked Germany for a large loan, but the local diplomat's telegram only reached Berlin on 9 October, and then the Persians began to haggle. In November the Russians moved on Teheran, and the Shah refused to sign the treaty with Germany. The German supporters fled, failing to form a Government in exile in, of all places, Qum. Another group left Isfahan, was attacked by robbers in the desert and in April 1916 staggered into Shiraz where the British, having regained control, arrested them. Other German agents who had been trying to raise Persian Baluchistan were captured.

In accordance with the Kaiser's curse when Britain's declaration of war was made adamant ("if we are to bleed to death, at least England shall lose India"), the Germans tried to infiltrate India by various routes. They had some part in the Indian garrison mutiny in Singapore of 15 February 1915 and an abortive rising in the Punjab on the 19th. Later in 1915 they planned to free prisoners from the Andaman Islands and with them attack the Indian coast, but a German agent named Kraft sold the details to the British. Further trials took place in Burma of pro-German Indian nationalists who admitted subversion. In April 1916 the (neutral) US authorities raided an office in New York occupied by the German consul, seizing papers which were used in 1917 at the trial in San Francisco of 35 people including 9 Germans and 17 Indians on charges of using the US as a base for promoting rebellion against the British in India: "the trial delivered the death blow to the Indo-German movement in America."[50]

The British had been fortunate: these various efforts had not exactly been pursued with Prussian efficiency and largely petered out after 1916. Even attempts to carry out larger scale joint German-Turkish operations, such as in 1917 when the Germans sent to Palestine a heavily-armed Asia Corps, were plagued by the arrogance of the German officers, and their ignorance of Turkish language and culture: the Turks "even occasionally attacked and murdered" Germans.[51]

Allied Plans for the Middle East: the Balfour Declaration

Whatever views Britain might have previously had regarding the Ottoman Empire, as the War progressed "only a few disagreed that Britain could protect its position in India and the Middle East from pan-Islamism and a German-ruled

Turkey by not only defeating the Ottoman Empire but (by) dismembering it." Salisbury saw this during the 1878 Turkish crisis: how could Britain retain the loyalty of Indians "if they know Russia is to be dominant on the Tigris and the Euphrates?" This now coincided with Britain's recognition that in order to neutralise any *jihadist* tendencies among the Arab tribes, she might encourage those same tribes to fight Turkey.[52] It would have been naïve to suppose that Britain and France would not seek to control the Middle East, by whatever means seemed suitable.

Making deals with Arab leaders, in particular Sherif Hussein of Mecca, required negotiations with the French over their territorial requirements. These opened in London on 23 November 1915 where Georges Picot, an experienced French diplomat, fought stubbornly for long-standing French ambitions in Syria, resisted by the British Foreign Office on behalf of their aspirant Arab clients. Picot proclaimed "To promise the Arabs a large state is to throw dust in their eyes. Such a state will never materialize."[53] It was agreed that Lebanon, mainly inhabited by Christian Maronites who looked to France anyway, "enlarged by as many non-Christian areas as it could safely dominate", would go direct to France. From this base, France "could keep a watchful eye over a Syrian interior ruled by a loose federation of emirs – each 'assisted' by a French resident – under the nominal sovereignty of the Sharif of Mecca".

In August 1914, Sir Mark Sykes MP had become Kitchener's adviser on "oriental" affairs in the War Office, and he had just returned from intelligence gathering in the Middle East convinced "that an Arab rising would sooner or later take place". He now dominated the British input, and he and Picot swiftly gained both mutual respect and genuine friendship. By making concessions, such as removing the coastline of Lebanon and Syria from the Arab state to French control, and by conceding Mosul to the latter, Sykes obtained French agreement on the Syrian question.[54] However, they disagreed abruptly over the future of Palestine, with both sides demanding it. So a compromise was made; in the draft "Sykes-Picot" agreement signed on 3 January 1916, Palestine, except for Haifa and Acre which would go to Britain to provide the port and railhead for her oil pipeline from northern Mesopotamia, was to be a "Brown Area" under an international administration, the precise form of which was to be decided after consultation with Russia and later with Italy and Islamic representatives.

Otherwise, France would establish "such direct or indirect administration or control" as she wished over a "Blue Zone" from Cilicia east to the Persian border and down the Mediterranean coast as far as Acre, while Britain received similar rights in a "Red Zone," including Basra and Baghdad, in southern Mesopotamia. The area between the Red and Blue zones was to form "an independent Arab state or a confederation of Arab states" divided into "A" and "B" zones within which France and Britain respectively would have exclusive rights to provide advisers and economic assistance. The French zone included the major inland cities of Syria, while the British zone largely consisted of the deserts of northern Arabia, ranging from what later became Jordan to central Mesopotamia.

With hindsight, the whole original Sykes-Picot agreement might appear to have two large, linked, advantages for the future stability and the security of British power in the Middle East. First, with the Arabs obtaining sovereignty over the Syrian interior, they would not have felt betrayed, as they did after 1919, and they might have been more inclined to acquiesce in not having, or expecting, sovereignty in Palestine, and less embittered about a modest Zionist influx there. Second, these Zionist communities in Palestine (a small minority of the population) would be subject to international control, with fewer illusions about an eventual Zionist state (particularly as France and Italy were unlikely to be sympathetic to Zionist aspirations). Quite apart from the damage to her reputation, Britain, in particular, would have been spared some of the burdens and tensions in her Palestine mandate, which steadily got worse during the Twenties and Thirties, were to culminate in war with the Arabs and terrorism from the Zionists, and then, with Britain out of the way, conceivably endless war and terror between Arabs and Zionists.

It is worth also noting, at this juncture, that there have never been any firm boundaries, corresponding to nationality, language or religion, in the Middle East. Syria and Mesopotamia, as the world has been brutally reminded in the 2010s, are congeries of tribes, divided between Sunni, Shia and other Muslim groups, with scattered groups of Christians and Jews – both now largely disappeared.

Cheating and greed by and between the Allies was to increase, and eventually destroy the Sykes-Picot agreement. The French Syria lobby strongly opposed the proposal for an international regime for Palestine, while a conference on 19 April 1917 saw the British, French and Italians accept "a formal agreement embodying the international administration of Palestine." Sykes at first favoured this international regime, but as 1916 passed "the Zionist movement gradually strengthened its hold on his religious and romantic imagination. Above all, it came to impress him as the most effective means for bringing Palestine under a British protectorate."[55]

Many factors were now moving towards the most decisive act this somewhat indecisive man is now associated with – the Balfour Declaration proposing a National Home for the Jews in Palestine. It certainly seemed a good idea at the time. During 1915-17 the Zionist cause attracted support in London from a variety of potent individuals. Lloyd George had been born in Manchester, the home to Britain's largest Jewish community after London (both Balfour and Churchill had been MPs for Manchester seats). Having once been retained as the British lawyer for the Zionist movement, with his Welsh family upbringing, Lloyd George remarked that he recalled the names of the ancient kings of Israel better than he did those of England or even the "kings" [sic] of Wales. He told the Cabinet in 1915 that it would be an outrage to let the Christian Holy Places fall into the hands of "Agnostic,

Atheistic France."[56] While Grey wrote in March 1915: "Palestine might be given to Belgium, Christian, Liberal and now noble Belgium," Lloyd George was less romantic. At a Downing Street Conference on 3 April 1917, he "suggested that the Jews might be able to render us more assistance than the Arabs" and clearly supported "securing the addition of Palestine to the British area".[57]

Lord Milner, member of the War Cabinet, had sympathised with Zionism from early life, as did various of his "young men", now in positions of great influence: William Ormsby-Gore, Leo Amery, and Philip Kerr, Lloyd George's private secretary. And General Smuts, "on loan" in the British War Cabinet, "had expressed very decided views as to the strategic importance of Palestine to the British Empire".[58]

In early 1917 these pressures were to coincide with powerful, albeit temporary, reasons for the Allies attracting Jewish support. Tsarist Russia had increasingly persecuted her large Jewish population, driving many into emigration. Hence, the international Jewish community took a jaundiced view of the Entente side in the war: Jews in the United States had successfully blocked the Russian government's attempts to raise money on Wall Street.[59] An argument which became relevant after the US entered the war was that President Wilson was expected to disapprove strongly of the secret territorial deals the Allies had made, so the latter "would have to validate their claims to a position in the post-war Middle East by sponsorship of oppressed peoples, such as Jews, Arabs and Armenians."[60] And during 1918, Lloyd George came to the conclusion that the Sykes-Picot agreement "was quite inapplicable to present circumstances {and} altogether a most undesirable agreement from the British point of view", as it was British (and Imperial) forces that had almost entirely produced the victory over the Turks.[61]

In 1897 the first Zionist congress in Basle saw 200 delegates adopt the Basle programme: "to secure for the Jewish people in Palestine a publicly recognised, legally secured homeland." Palestine was then under Turkish rule. They very nearly found another location for a National Home. Their leader, Dr Theodore Herzl, met Joseph Chamberlain as Colonial Secretary in October 1902 and suggested interim locations "in the hope that Palestine would eventually become available." With Prime Minister Balfour's support, Chamberlain eventually offered, at a meeting on 24 April 1903, to set up an autonomous Jewish colony in British East Africa. Herzl agreed and the Foreign Office was sympathetic. At the 6th Zionist Congress at Basle in August, Herzl supported the Chamberlain idea but his "arguments swayed heads but not hearts". He won the vote but Chaim Weizmann organised powerful opposition because of the apparent abandonment of Palestine. In September the Russian Zionists at Kharkov rejected the scheme. By December the Chamberlain offer was postponed because of concerns about African feelings, some expressed in a House of Commons debate on 20 June 1904. By then, Chamberlain had left the Government over Tariff Reform.[62]

In many ways this was another lost opportunity, for the Jews, Britain and East

Africa. For Britain and the Jews it made sense for Palestine not to be the only refuge. This became clear in the Thirties when Britain, under Arab pressure, had to restrict Jewish immigration into Palestine at a time when the Jews were increasingly desperate to escape from Germany. The populist jibe would be "accepting that Britain did an injustice to the Arabs of Palestine, why double it by inflicting another injustice on the Africans of Kenya?" This fundamentally misunderstands the practicalities of the issue. With Palestine not the only refuge, there would have been less pressure on land and the perceived rights of the Palestine Arabs. East Africa is a far larger area than Palestine, and it is likely that Jewish immigration there would have brought huge benefits for agriculture and commerce (as, indeed, subsequently happened in Palestine).

And most importantly, Britain intended to remain in East Africa as the sovereign power, seeking to ensure equity between the various ethnic groups, including Asians. Independence in tropical Africa was not envisaged, until the very different circumstances of the late 1950s, and it would have been important for the administrating power not to be unduly beholden (as, sadly, it became) to a small group of British settlers. Jomo Kenyatta (or Idi Amin) would have found Jewish settlers rather less biddable than the genteel British or the peaceful Gujaratis!

Back in 1916-7, as pressure mounted on the British Government to issue a declaration endorsing Zionist objectives, there was conflict within the movement between the idealists and the realists. Arthur Ruppin wrote in his diary on 31 December 1916. "I want to settle about one million Jews in Palestine within ... 30 yrs". The draft declaration prepared by Harry Sacher on 2 July 1917 proposed "The British Government declares that one of its essential war aims is the reconstitution of Palestine as a Jewish State," but he was told by a colleague "If we want too much we shall get nothing." Sacher replied "We must control the *State* machinery in Palestine; if we don't the Arabs will ... The State must be Jewish."[63]

On 23 August 1917 the Zionist claims were challenged by Edwin Montagu, the most senior Jew in Lloyd George's government. He circulated a powerful memorandum, declaring that "Zionism" had always seemed to him "to be a mischievous political creed", threatening the position of Jews like himself who were fully assimilated in British public life: the declaration could only increase anti-semitism and create injustice to the Arabs.[64] The War Cabinet discussed Montagu's view on 3 September, and in the absence of Lloyd George and Balfour, decided to postpone issuing a declaration. Over the next few weeks, the war situation deteriorated: the Russians beginning to collapse, with the Germans taking Riga, little progress in Flanders, and the Italians routed at Caporetto.

Balfour told the War Cabinet on 4 October that the German Government was making "great efforts to capture the Zionist movement". On the morning of 31 October, the War Cabinet agreed to issue the Balfour Declaration (it was issued on 2 November), after these words of explanation by Balfour: "As to the meaning of the words 'national home' ... he understood it to mean some form of British,

American or other protectorate, under which full facilities would be given to the Jews ... to build up, by means of education, agriculture and industry, a real centre of national culture and focus of national life. It did not necessarily involve the early establishment of an independent Jewish State, which was a matter for gradual development in accordance with the ordinary laws of political evolution." That "not necessarily" speaks volumes as an example of Balfourian weasel words.[65]

1919-23: The Fate of Syria and Survival of Turkey

As Balfour observed in 1919 "We had not been honest with either French or Arab ... it was now preferable to quarrel with the Arabs rather than the French, if there was to be a quarrel at all."[66]

1919-20 saw Britain under great pressure, with revolt in Punjab, trouble in Afghanistan, a serious revolt in Egypt and another one in Mesopotamia, plus riots in Jerusalem. With Curzon advising leaving both Syria and Palestine "while we yet can," Lloyd George refused to give up Palestine (it could not be given up, he said, "without great loss of prestige"[67]). But he instructed the new Secretary of State for War, Churchill, to slash costs in Mesopotamia and evacuate Syria. In October 1919, Feisal, who had led the Arab Revolt against Turkey in 1917 and was still notionally King of Syria[68], was called to London and told to settle with France on the best terms he could obtain, with Britain cutting his monthly subsidies in half, leaving the remainder to be paid by France. At the San Remo Allied Conference in April 1920 the French mandates (giving control under League of Nations auspices) for Syria and Lebanon and the British mandates for Palestine and Mesopotamia were duly agreed.

Gouraud, the French commander in Lebanon, and de Caix, leader of the Syria lobby in Paris, were unsympathetic to Feisal, who at first rejected any compromise, urging complete independence for Syria, denying the French access to the Damascus railway (needed to reinforce their troops in Cilicia fighting the Turks) and doing nothing to check guerrilla raids from Syria into the French coastal zone. Eventually, the French, with tanks and aircraft, advanced on Damascus. Feisal's forces were routed on 24 July 1920 and he was deposed. The French Prime Minister uncompromisingly proclaimed that Syria would be held by France: "the whole of it, and forever".[69]

In fact, one of Britain's rather necessary successes in 1941 was to defeat the Vichy French in Syria, who were, in co-operation with the Axis powers, threatening the whole Allied position in the Middle East. After the war, Britain insisted on independence for Syria and Lebanon. The former swiftly drifted into hostility to the West, and both have experienced tragedy in more recent decades.

So far as the remainder of Turkey was concerned, the Treaty of Sèvres of August 1920, was a fantasy treaty imposed upon a fantasy regime, as the Sultan's government had become. The only areas of Anatolia to remain independent under the Sultan were to be the north coast. Armenia, extending to the coast west and east of Trabzon, was to be independent,[70] while Kurdistan was to be autonomous. Otherwise, the southern half of Anatolia was divided into three: a small district round Smyrna to go to Greece; a large area placed under Italian supervision, with a somewhat smaller zone under French supervision. The Turkish nationalists rejected Sèvres and their leader, Mustapha Kemal, rallied his forces, crushed the Armenian separatists and made an alliance with the victorious Bolshevik armies in the Caucasus. With the Italians making peace with the Kemalists, the only countries to fight the nationalists were France and Greece. The French underestimated them, and were defeated, with heavy casualties, at Marash and Urfa, in the spring of 1920. In June 1921 they agreed to recognise the Kemalists as the government of Turkey, and evacuated Cilicia.

The Greeks, encouraged but not helped by Lloyd George, had advanced deep into Anatolia and maintained their position there for over a year. Massing his forces in secrecy Kemal attacked on 26 August 1922; the Greek forces were routed and driven back to Smyrna which was brutally sacked and burnt. Greek folly, greed and incompetence (in November the Greek Prime Minister and five of his ministers were tried and shot by their own people) had doomed the once large and wealthy Greek community in Anatolia, which was deported to Greece.[71] The Treaty of Lausanne of 24 July1923 created the borders of modern Turkey, burying all evidence of Sèvres.

Aftermath in the British Mandates: Palestine

The linkage between Syria and the Arab attitude to the "Jewish Home" is indicated in a MS note Feisal had added to his 3 January 1919 agreement with Weizmann: he would only "carry out what is written in this agreement" on condition that "the Arabs obtain their independence" in Syria.[72]

The British leaders were not short of warnings about the contradictions implicit in their policy. On 16 January 1919 Curzon, about to become Foreign Secretary, reported to Balfour on his meeting that day with Sir Alfred Money, the Chief Administrator of Palestine, "his main point, and that of Allenby, is that we should go slow about the Zionist aspirations and the Zionist State ... A Jewish Government in any form would mean an Arab rising ..." Curzon added "I share these views, and have for long felt that the pretensions of Weizmann & Company are extravagant and ought to be checked."[73] Two months later, Curzon wrote again to Balfour (25 March 1919): "I told you some time ago that Dr Weizmann had departed altogether from the modest programme upon which he had agreed with you ... and that the ambitions of the Zionists were exceeding all bounds." He quoted from a programme agreed by a conference of Zionist leaders in England "absolute control of immigration, immediate control of water rights ... Jewish nationalisation of all public land and of the surplus land of all private estates exceeding a certain size ... complete control of all public works."[74]

Curzon was by no means alone. Allenby, now High Commissioner in Egypt, defended the growing anti-Zionist feeling in a letter to Curzon: "a large section of Moslem and Christian opinion in Palestine ... views Zionist aspirations with deep suspicion ... Jewish propaganda has increased in strength and confidence."[75] Gilbert Clayton, Allenby's chief political officer, is criticised by Fromkin for professing to believe in Zionism but "seemed to define it in its narrowest possible sense: the fostering of an expanded Jewish community in Palestine that could serve as a cultural and sentimental center for Jews throughout the world, but within a British administered, multi-national Palestine that would not become a Jewish state." The value of this sentence in Fromkin's account is that it neatly explains the divide between those who accepted the Balfour Declaration in its literal sense, complete with the reassurances to Arabs, and those, including Balfour himself at times, who saw it as code for the fullest implementation of the Zionist political creed.[76] While many of the British administrators in Palestine (and elsewhere in the Middle East) undoubtedly belonged to the first group, the Zionists themselves left little doubt as to their ambitions.

The Arab response was crude but typical – demonstrations which swiftly developed into riots. The first serious manifestation came in early 1920: first in February and then more seriously in April at the Muslim festival of Nebi Musa. The British took four days to quell the violence, 5 Jews and 4 Arabs were killed, and about 250, mostly Jewish, injured. It was the shape of worse to come; it led immediately to the end of military rule in Palestine, and the appointment as governor of Sir Herbert Samuel (a Jew, but as Curzon acknowledged "sensible").

The main theme in inter-communal relations in Palestine was the amount of Jewish immigration, which prompted Arab fears for the future control of the territory. Arab violence in Jaffa on 1 May 1921 led Samuel to order immediate temporary suspension of Jewish immigration. Churchill (now Colonial Secretary) telegraphed Samuel on 14 May "the present agitation is doubtless engineered in the hope of frightening us *out of our Zionist policy* ... We must make concessions on their merits and not under duress."[77] During the next two years the idea of firmer limitation developed, to the dismay of the Zionist leaders who had hoped for freedom of immigration. In July 1921, with immigration practically at a halt, Weizmann complained that the British government was "whittling down the Balfour Declaration". Yet when, at the Imperial Conference on 22 June 1921, Churchill was asked by Arthur Meighen, the Canadian Prime Minister, whether a Jewish National Home meant giving the Jews the control of the government in Palestine, Churchill's reply was alarmingly consistent with his Zionism: "if, in the course of many years , they become a majority in the country, they naturally would take it over."[78]

Meeting in Balfour's house with Weizmann on 3 June 1921, the latter quoted Samuel ruling out "mass immigration". Weizmann said it was "a negation of the Balfour Declaration", and to Churchill's further queries, replied that the Declaration "meant an ultimate Jewish majority", whereas Samuel's words "would never permit such a majority to eventuate." Gilbert adds that the minutes of this meeting indicate that Churchill "demurred at this interpretation", while Lloyd George and Balfour, both also present, agreed "that by the Declaration they had always meant an eventual Jewish State."[79]

The Cabinet on 17 August discussed whether to give up the Mandate (H. A. L. Fisher, President of the Board of Education, proposed "offering it to America"). Under pressure from the Premier, it was decided to retain the Mandate, "the honour of the government was involved in the Declaration made by Mr Balfour", and another conclusion read "that the Arabs had no prescriptive right to a country which they had failed to develop to the best advantage".[80]

While this detail was not known to either of the embattled communities in Palestine, it is clear to us, the reader, that Britain was on "a hiding to nothing". At no stage did an authoritative person define more closely, and more "prudently," to use Curzon's word, Britain's programme, which would inevitably rule out a "Jewish State".

There was one battle the Zionists never won. Within weeks of the 1918 Armistice, Arnold Toynbee advised the Foreign Office on 2 December to include in Palestine the area east of the Jordan on the grounds that "the Zionists have as much right to this no-man's land as the Arabs, or more".[81] This was not done, and by the summer of 1921 Abdullah, Feisal's brother, was governor of Transjordan, as it was called. Harold Philby, the great Arabist and explorer, became Abdullah's new official adviser, and Colonel F. Peake began organising a Bedouin force of regular troops under British command (it later became the Arab Legion). Even Churchill falls foul of Fromkin's disappointment, as his "temporary [sic] decision not to encourage – or even allow – the building of a Jewish National Home in eastern Palestine ran counter to the provisions of the Mandate, he decided to change the terms of the Mandate ..."[82]

The Times had been a strong backer of the Balfour Declaration. In early 1922 it ran a series of articles seeking to explain Britain's growing unpopularity in Palestine, adding "it is an interesting experiment, but the question is whether we have counted the cost."[83]

Further evidence came in a House of Lords debate on 21 June 1922, when a motion, opposing the Palestine Mandate, was carried by 60 votes to 29. It was a low profile affair, involving as speakers a cross party group of peers, most of whom had been Governors in India or the Dominions, but what was significant is that the newly enobled Lord Balfour, defending the Government's policy towards the Mandate, most definitely did not convince. He typically and flippantly concluded: "It may fail. I do not deny that this is an adventure. Are we never to have adventures?"[84] Putting the motion was Lord Islington, a former Unionist MP who had switched to the Liberals in 1905, and served as a junior Minister for Colonies and then India in 1914-6; he said that the Mandate was unacceptable because it "directly violates the pledges" made in October 1915 and reaffirmed by Allenby at the end of the war. Another speaker, Lord Sydenham, a cross-bencher, who as George Clarke had been the Secretary of the Committee of Imperial Defence 1904-7, referred to Joseph Chamberlain's offer of Uganda to Herzl; the latter, he said, had accepted it, but "extremists" had opposed it. If the East African project had been implemented, he said, "we should have been saved much trouble and great expense and at the present time some real danger."[85]

As Elizabeth Monroe stated: "The question of numbers was, throughout, the core of the Palestine problem." The fear that Jewish immigration would never stop was the cause of Arab revolts and rioting; several hundred Jews and Arabs were killed and wounded in the summer of 1929 after a riot at the Wailing Wall. Monroe adds: "From 1930, they [the British] lost control of the situation in Palestine, because they started to vacillate, and the two communities took advantage of the vacillation to become so obstreperous that the British were reduced merely to holding the ring."[86]

The evidence of this last statement was immediate: following the 1929 riots and advice from the High Commissioner, Sir John Chancellor, the Ramsay MacDonald government published a White Paper in October 1930 that proposed limiting Jewish immigration. It panicked when the Zionists and their supporters accused the Government of breaking the terms of the Mandate, and the White Paper remained a dead letter. With the coming to power of Hitler, Jewish immigration increased hugely, from 9500 in 1932 to 42,000 in 1934, and 61,000 in 1935, bringing the Jewish population of Palestine to 355,000 – a quarter of the whole. In 1936 an Arab rebellion broke out, directed at Britain as the mandatory power; it lasted until 1939. During the Second World War Britain had to maintain her substantial garrison in Palestine, facing opposition both from Arab nationalists led by the Grand Mufti of Jerusalem, who collaborated with the Axis Powers, and Jewish terrorists who assassinated the High Commissioner for Egypt, Lord Moyne, in November 1944.

Aftermath in the British Mandates: Mesopotamia/Iraq

Carrying peacetime dominion almost as far as Mount Ararat certainly seemed an extreme example of British over-extension. As part of the right-wing campaign against the cost of keeping so many troops in the Middle East, the *Morning Post*, in March 1923, urged disposing of "the *damnosa heritas* of Palestine before we become too embroiled", but argued that it was "impossible to jettison Mesopotamia because of Turkey."[87] This was long before Britain could begin to see Turkey as a neutral or even as a friend. Indeed, the treaty of Lausanne did not resolve the Anglo-Turkish dispute over Mosul, which continued through the next two years, accompanied by threats and occasional force, before being resolved, in favour of Britain and Iraq, in late 1925.

As the strategic rationale declined, that of oil increased. Very little reference was made, in the wartime exchanges about Britain's quest for Mandates, to the oil factor. Its existence in Mesopotamia was known, but exploitation did not start until 1927 (in 1920, Middle East oil made up only 1% of world production). Only when the Cabinet in July 1918 faced a paper by Admiral Sir Edmond Slade entitled "The Petroleum Situation in the British Empire" did Hankey, as Cabinet Secretary, start considering whether the retention of the Mesopotamian oilfields should be ranked as a major war aim. Slade argued that "the Power that controls the oil lands of Persia and Mesopotamia will control the source of supply of the liquid fuel of the future."[88]

Britain's post war presence in Mesopotamia started badly, as the result of serious mishandling by the officers in charge locally, and indecision in London.[89] The "popular" High Commissioner, Sir Percy Cox, had been moved to Teheran, where he spent two and a half years. His "overconfident" deputy, Arnold Wilson, "who believed that the country's destiny was as a colony of India" was left in effective control of policy. Under Wilson, political officers behaved "arbitrarily", with some true, and more rumoured, stories of "rough justice". In May 1919 Wilson dismissed Arab hopes of autonomy in Baghdad as "moonshine"; Gertrude Bell, whose letters to her family describe in detail her work in the country, later saw this episode as "the turning point", after which the locals would resort to force. T. E. Lawrence predicted trouble in September 1919 "if we do not mend our ways," and attacked Wilson through a letter to *The Times*, saying the latter's last minute concessions to the Arabs were "belated, insincere, incomplete".[90] A recent historian states that it was "almost incredible" that no progress was made in meeting Arab desires in the two years after the Armistice, with "seemingly interminable wranglings and procrastinations."[91]

In early 1920, the Kurdish north remained in some chaos (four British officers had been murdered there in late 1919). The Sunni Arab notables in Baghdad felt they were "excluded ... from power even more" than under the Ottomans, while among the Shia tribes of the centre and south, the British "were resented as the gatherers of tax and the breakers of custom."[92] As a foretaste of the folly of the 2003 invaders, the British had sacked the Arab officials who had run the country for the Ottomans, replacing them with their own.

To make matters worse, the British military now only had a tiny mobile force to patrol such a huge area. In the spring and early summer of 1920 more British officers and officials were attacked and killed, with the Arabs having accumulated large quantities of abandoned Turkish rifles and ammunition during the latter stages of the war. Ramadan was in June, always a difficult time when occurring in the summer. The establishment of an Arab government under Feisal in Damascus stimulated impatience at the British failure to allow a similar development in Baghdad. Thus, when Feisal was proclaimed King of Syria in March 1920, a nationalist congress of Iraqis in Damascus declared Iraq independent and Abdullah, Feisal's brother, its ruler.

The British forces were taken by surprise at the fact that the rebels were well armed, very mobile, and "directed by skilled brains".[93] Sunni and Shia came together and the revolt ranged from the frontier with Syria down to the lower Euphrates, with a *jihad* proclaimed against Britain in the Shia holy city of Kerbela. By mid August a group of rebels felt confident enough to set up a provisional revolutionary government in Najaf. Rather like the Indian Mutiny of 1857, it was really a series of uncontrolled risings: Baghdad was scarcely affected, Basra, Kut and Mosul not at all. But the revolt brought "almost total anarchy to the countryside."[94] While the British speedily secured the main centres, it was not until October that many of the cut-off Euphrates towns were reoccupied, and not until early 1921 that order was restored in the countryside. This all cost the British forces, mainly Indian, nearly 2000 casualties, including 426 dead; over 8000 insurgents were killed, and the total cost of suppressing the revolt was put at £40 million.[95]

In other respects, the British responded with good sense and alacrity: Wilson was recalled, to be replaced by Sir Percy Cox. Churchill, Colonial Secretary since New Year's Day 1921, summoned a conference in Cairo in March. Bell and according to her, Cox, both came to Cairo with a definite programme and found it "coincided exactly" with what Churchill proposed. Feisal would be King of Iraq, while Churchill expected the RAF to keep the peace by the threat of aerial bombardment. Feisal's brother, Abdullah would take over as emir in Transjordan.[96]

Feisal proved acceptable to the Sunni notables in Baghdad; he landed at Basra on 21 June, with the Council of Ministers on 11 July agreeing that he should be king. A plebiscite took place in early August; with British official pressure thrown into the balance for him, 96% of the electorate assented to his election as King of Iraq. He was crowned on 21 August. When they needed to, the British could move fast.

Churchill displayed typical ruthlessness, telling the Cairo conference that "if Feisal knew that not only his father's subsidy and the protection" of Mecca and Medina from Wahhabi attack, "but also the position of his brother in Transjordan was dependent on his own good behaviour", he would be easier to manage. In 1922 he added "All the time he takes our money, he will have to take our directions ... he will be a long time looking for a third throne."[97] The newly elected Constituent Assembly did not ratify the treaty with Britain until June 1924, adding that it would be null and void if British efforts to get Mosul included in Iraq were to fail.[98] Britain was to come near to war with Turkey over this northern border in the autumn of 1924. The League of Nations arbitrated Mosul's fate in July 1925, assigning it to Iraq.[99]

The main theme of the "peace-making" half of this chapter has been over-extension, but it is clear why Britain succumbed to the temptation of occupying both Palestine and Iraq. In fact, the arrangements made in Iraq in the mid Twenties were moderately successful for three decades. Kwasi Kwarteng judges that the

Hashemite dynasty "would, in the long run, produce as many problems as it supplied solutions," as Feisal was a Sunni, in a Shia majority country.[101] The Sunni, however, whether under the Ottomans or the post 1958 dictators, or in-between, have tended to predominate in Iraq. Feisal proved to be a reasonable monarch. Iraq and its population were never going to be easy to govern, as its chequered history after the "revolution" of 1958 indicates. There was a military-led rebellion in 1941 encouraged by the Germans and Italians. If Hitler had truly perceived its potential, which he failed to because his eyes were fixed on Soviet Russia, Britain might have been severely embarrassed and possibly swept out of the Middle East: faced as she was by Rommel, the loss of Crete, the Vichy French in Syria, and Axis subversives in Persia. In fact, it was vigorously and speedily suppressed by initially tiny British and Indian forces.[102] The tragic and very different saga of the 1958 revolution will be reached in the Epilogue.

FOOTNOTES

1 After their huge casualties of 1914-15- totalling 2 million, of which 1 million were killed or missing – the French became more economical with their manpower, with "flexible and imaginative tactics … effectively coordinating their artillery with their infantry" at Verdun and the Somme. (Woodward, op cit, p147.)

2 Gary Sheffield's *Forgotten Victory*, p119.

3 Ibid, p186.

4 The French politicians were always more sympathetic to helping Serbia, and in November 1914 Briand, the Minister of Justice, wanted an army of 400,000 men to be sent to Salonika. The French Cabinet, then and later, drew back from challenging Joffre "who had achieved dictatorial control over strategy." (Woodward, op cit, p 34.)

5 Sub-committee minutes, 28 January 1915, quoted Woodward, op cit, p35. Also ibid, pp44-5.

6 Ibid, p39.

7 Lloyd George to the director of military operations, 2 September 1916, during the Rumanian crisis. Woodward, op cit, p104.

8 Amery, *My Political Life*, Vol II, p47- 50; the last quotation in Amery's words.

9 Amery to Milner, 27 April, Amery to Mrs Amery, 7 June 1915; Barnes and Nicholson, op cit, pp113, 117.

10 *The Role of British Strategy in the Great War* (1936), pp38-9.

11 Woodward, op cit, p104.

12 The Germans had intended this attack to be on a limited scale and had transferred fewer than half the divisions the Austrians requested. Their success surprised them, but they lacked lorries and horses for a rapid advance.

13 V. H. Rothwell *British War Aims and Peace Diplomacy 1914-18* (OUP 1971), p23.

14 Ibid, pp25 and 57.

15 Ibid, pp120, 123: the Hardinge memorandum is dated 23 August 1916.

16 Ibid, p140.

17 Herbert, half brother of the 5th Earl of Carnarvon who opened Tutankhamun's tomb, and *'The Man who was Greenmantle'* (biography by Margaret Fitzherbert), was Unionist MP for Yeovil until his death in 1923; before 1914 he had been offered the throne of newly independent Albania. His daughter Laura married Evelyn Waugh.

18 Rothwell, op cit, pp135-6.

19 Ibid, p171-78 for this saga.
20 Ibid, p184.
21 The arch foes of Austria-Hungary had little influence in the Foreign Office until the setting up of the Political Intelligence Department in early1918; this included all the friends of the subject races, such as Robert Seton-Watson.
22 Rothwell, op cit, pp161-3.
23 Ibid, p170.
24 Ibid, p66.
25 Ibid, p100.
26 Minutes of the Committee of Prime Ministers, 31 July 1918, quoted Woodward, op cit, p324.
27 By the autumn of 1918, the Germans had withdrawn their infantry from the Salonika front (though they still crewed the heavy artillery) and the Bulgarians resented their abandonment. David Stevenson, *With Our Backs to the Wall,* pp143-8.
28 David Stevenson, *With our Backs to the Wall: Victory and Defeat in 1918*, pp312-3.
29 Ibid, p91, also German documents in Lutz (*The Causes of the German Collapse*), pp53-4. Germany needed to be sure of her food supplies from the Ukraine. In September 1918 the Austro-Germans together had 600,000 troops in the Ukraine.
30 Stevenson, op cit, pp98-105.
31 These quotes in Benjamin Schwartz, *Britain's Perception of a German Threat to her Eastern Position in 1918,* in Journal of Contemporary History, vol 28 (1993), pp103-22, which powerfully assembles the evidence, more of British concern than of actual German machinations.
32 Major-General L. C. Dunsterville *The Adventures of Dunsterforce* (1920), passim. Dunsterville hoped to rally "White" Russian support but by the time he reached Baku, he found most Russian units had been Bolshevised. A Turkish advance forced him to withdraw in, ironically, September 1918, weeks before the Turkish collapse.
33 Woodward, op cit, p284.
34 Schwartz, op cit, pp111-2, Woodward, pp316-7.
35 Woodward, op cit, p315; L. S. Amery *My Political Life*, II, p161.
36 Barnes and Nicholson, op cit, I p227, Amery memoirs, op cit, II p158. Smuts shows how widespread was this pessimism, even six days after the beginning of the Allied counter-offensive in France. He feared the Germans would retire slowly in the west, while expanding in the east: "Nobody concerned in this war except ourselves has any interest in Asia ... If the Turks get to Transcaspia and if this wave extends even to Afghanistan, our position in Asia is very much endangered. He thought it better to accept a compromise peace in the west." Minutes of Imperial War Cabinet, 14 August, quoted Schwartz, op cit, p116-7.
37 Woodward, op cit, p336.
38 Stevenson, op cit, p41.
39 Tim Travers, *How the War was Won*, pp51-3, 86-8, 99, and 108.
40 Barrie Pitt, *1918-The Last Act,* pp108-9, 222. Stevenson, op cit, p111.
41 Evidence of the British success lies in these statistics: the French, Americans and Belgians took 196,700 prisoners between 18 July and 11 November. With a significantly smaller army, Haig's forces captured 188,700 prisoners.
42 Stevenson, op cit, pp143-8, 509.
43 Ibid, pp149-55.
44 MacMillan, *Peacemakers*, pp295, 301.
45 Christopher M. Andrew and A. S. Kanya-Forstner, *France Overseas,* pp186-200.
46 MacMillan, op cit, p302.
47 Ibid, p310.
48 David Fromkin, *A Peace to End All Peace,* p392.
49 The principal source for the following paragraphs is Donald McKale, *War by Revolution – Germany and Britain in the Middle East in the Era of the First World War* (Kent, Ohio 1998).

50 McKale, op cit, pp189, 216.
51 Ibid, pp212-3.
52 Ibid, pp171; Salisbury quote, Charmley, op cit, p161.
53 Christopher M. Andrew and A. S. Kanya-Forstner, *France Overseas*, p90.
54 See Christopher Simon Sykes, *The Man who Created the Middle East* (a biography of the author's grandfather, Sir Mark), pp255-8. Christopher Andrew and A. S. Kanya-Forstner describe how, at the start, as a Catholic and an imperialist, Sykes had sympathies for the aspirations of French missionaries and the French colonial lobby, but loathed the "organised corruption" of international – chiefly French – finance in pre-war Constantinople and he detected an "occult French financial force" behind their Syrian ambitions. Like his patron Kitchener, Sykes would have preferred to buy the French out of Syria by concessions in Africa: Syria, Palestine and Mesopotamia "could then be put" under the temporal rule of the Sultan of Egypt and the spiritual rule of the Sharif of Mecca, each guided by British advisers! Op cit, p94.
55 Andrew and Kanya-Forstner, op cit, p96. Chapters 12 and 13, pp267-310 of Simon Sykes, op cit, describe this growing Zionist influence on Sir Mark and his work with leading Zionists on what became the Balfour Declaration. His role included securing the nominal support of the French Foreign Ministry for the Zionist aspirations.
56 MacMillan, *Peacemakers,* p426; Andrew and Kanya-Forstner, op cit, p65.
57 Rothwell, op cit, pp26-7 and Simon Sykes, op cit, p280, respectively.
58 Fromkin, op cit, p281-3.
59 James Barr, *A Line in the Sand,* p33.
60 Fromkin's words, p287. Barr sums up: "he [Lloyd George] decided that support for the stateless Zionists' aspirations was a good way to thwart French ambitions in the Middle East and silence Wilson simultaneously" (op cit, p35).
61 Cabinet papers quoted in Simon Sykes, op cit, pp306-7.
62 This whole episode is in Fromkin, op cit, pp273-4, and Martin Gilbert, *Exile and Return,* p60. A fuller account is in Julian Amery, *Life of Joseph Chamberlain* IV, chapter lxxxvii. Here it is pointed out (pp264-5) that the territory envisaged was not "Uganda" – the location referred to in subsequent debate, but part of Kenya between Nairobi and the Mau Escarpment, later known as the "White Highlands", and on which Amery comments (in 1951!) "there is no better white man's country anywhere in the Tropics".
63 Gilbert, *Exile,* p98.
64 Gilbert, *Exile,* p99, Fromkin, op cit, pp294-5.
65 This last quote from Gilbert, *Exile,* p107, preceding narrative from ibid, pp96-107.
66 Barr, op cit, p82 quoting Balfour in Colonel R. Meinertzhagen *Middle East Diary,* 30 July 1919, p26.
67 Ibid, p86.
68 Simon Sykes, op cit, p307, shows that the flag of King Feisal was flown over Damascus and Aleppo, when these fell in the autumn of 1918: however, Allenby ordered it taken down again in Beirut after strong French objections.
69 Andrew and Kanya-Forstner, op cit, pp218-9.
70 After the US Senate had rejected ratification of the Treaty of Versailles and adherence to the League of Nations, Wilson delayed proposing a US Armenian Mandate until 24 May 1920: the Senate rejected this a week later.
71 The consequences of this for the survival of important traces of Byzantine religious and secular buildings, for example in Cappadocia, originally researched by Gertrude Bell before 1914, are important for Western civilisation but clearly for another study. See *The Thousand and One Churches*, by W. M. Ramsay and G. Bell. Hodder and Stoughton, 1909.
72 Gilbert, *Exile,* pp117-8.
73 Ibid, p119.
74 Ibid, p 120-1. Curzon's words. It had little effect on Balfour: on 5 July he stated that land purchase should continue but "as far as possible, preferential treatment is given to Zionist interests" (ibid, p122).
75 Ibid, pp129-30; Allenby to Curzon 19 April 1920.

76 Fromkin, op cit, p445. The nuances are aptly summed up by Curzon who wrote to Allenby on 16 July 1920 "I should never, myself, have made the Balfour declaration", adding his intention "to give it the narrower and more prudent rather than the wider interpretation." Gilbert, *Exile,* p131. See Sir Ronald Storrs' *Orientations;* he was Military and then Civil Governor of Jerusalem in 1917-26. Pages 396-456 describe the tensions between the Zionists and the British administration during the early 1920s.
77 Gilbert, *Exile,* p133. My italics.
78 Ibid, p135.
79 Ibid, p136; Gilbert, *Winston Churchill,* Companion Volume IV, part 3, p1559.
80 Gilbert, *Exile,* pp136-9.
81 Ibid, p115.
82 Fromkin, op cit, pp512-3.
83*Times* 11 April 1922, quoted Fromkin, op cit, p525.
84 Lords Hansard, 21 June 1922, col. 1018.
85 Ibid, cols 1000, 1019. Sydenham added, with antiquarian accuracy, that "Palestine is not the original home of the Jews. It was acquired by them after a ruthless conquest."
86 Elizabeth Monroe, *Britain's Moment in the Middle East,* pp80-1, 86. Referring to the Balfour Declaration, she states: "Measured by British interests alone, it was one of the greatest mistakes in our imperial history" (p43).
87 Monroe, op cit, p143.
88 Charles Townshend, *When God Made Hell: The British Invasion of Mesopotamia and the Creation of Iraq* 1914-1921, p435.
89 This indecision, perhaps a polite term, is effectively described in Peter Sluglett, *Britain in Iraq 1914-32 (*pp18-32): "divergences of opinion between the India Office and the Foreign Office, the India Office and the Residency at Baghdad, within the India Office and within the Baghdad Residency as well" (p22).
90 Barr, op cit, p110; Townshend, op cit, p449.
91 Sluglett, op cit, p25. It is worth noting that Mesopotamia's previous independent rulers were probably Nebuchadnezzar and the unfortunate Belshazzar, as after them it formed part of Persian, Hellenistic, Roman, Caliphate or Turkish dominions.
92 Philip Ireland, *Iraq –A Study in Political Development* (1937) states that the "revolt was primarily reaction to the efficiency of British administration … its thoroughness and even its probity were unfamiliar, irksome and unnecessary". The British actually collected taxes, in contrast to the Ottoman regime, where the tribes were "left to enjoy an almost taxless and uninterrupted existence". Quoted Townshend, op cit, p 475.
93 Townshend, op cit, pp464-5, 470.
94 Barr, op cit, p472; Sluglett, op cit, p34.
95 The 426 figure is the one given by Kwasi Kwarteng, *Ghosts of Empire,* pp24-5. Townshend estimates 900 British and Indian troops were killed.
96 The RAF was used only sparingly in suppressing the revolt, but aeroplane wireless proved vital for communications. The RAF was used effectively over later border skirmishes with rebellious Kurds and Turks in 1924-5. Sluglett, op cit, pp184-92.
97 Townshend, op cit, pp483, 488 .
98 Townshend, op cit, pp491-2.
99 In the longer term, the British failed to protect the Kurds; more immediately, they failed to protect the small numbers of Christian Assyrians who were massacred in 1933 (Townshend, pp524-6).
100 Townshend, op cit, pp 520, 522.
101 Kwarteng, op cit, p26.
102 See Geoffrey Warner, *Iraq and Syria 1941,* passim. Also Barnes and Nicholson, op cit, II, pp653-8, 678-89.

CHAPTER SIX

Tariff Reform – Further Frustration and Belated Triumph 1918-32

For fifteen years after 1914, the Tariff Reform cause languished. Other concerns dominated: the War and then the Peace, Ireland, and the Middle East. Then Baldwin blundered into a premature protectionist election in 1923, and following defeat he retreated from the policy. Backbench pressure remained and built up just before the 1929 election. Most of this campaigning was for domestic protection only; the full Chamberlain programme, to give the Dominions substantial trade preferences, thus implying food taxes, was kept firmly in the background. Even so, advances in domestic protection would undoubtedly have contributed to the demolition of Free Trade doctrines.

Bonar Law's speech as party leader to the National Union on 30 November 1917 reiterated the party's commitment to Tariff Reform. As a parallel to the coupon arrangement for the post war December 1918 election, enabling Lloyd George's supporters to contest 150 seats without official Unionist Opposition, Carson arranged an agreement between Lloyd George and Law by which economic development was to be emphasised without reference to Tariff Reform or Free Trade. In his leader's letter to candidates, Law stated that "Our policy does not include a tax on food, but ... it does not of course interfere with the granting of a preference on any article ... on which...we have imposed a duty ... We must face all these questions with new eyes ... without any regard to theoretical opinions about Free Trade or Tariff Reform."[1]

Coalition 1918-22

Corelli Barnett sums up Britain's unenviable economic position shortly after the end of the war: "Her traditional exporting industries, decrepit as they were, had succumbed to foreign competition. Her new industries, the fruits of wartime expansion and still immature, had withered in the blast of renewed Free Trade imports from ... German and American competitors. In June 1921 the number of unemployed passed two million."[2]

The measures taken to counter this were minimalist. The "McKenna duties", introduced in September 1915 by the Liberal Chancellor, Reginald McKenna, imposed a 33.3 % duty on luxury imports: gramophones, clocks and watches, cinema film and, importantly, motor vehicles. In 1919 these had Imperial Preference added. More ambitious was the Safeguarding of Industries Act of 1921, prompted by the discovery that Britain was dependent on Germany for certain supplies to "key" industries. It imposed a five-year duty of 33.3% on nine categories of items (including optical glass, laboratory porcelain, other scientific instruments, hosiery latch needles, metallic tungsten, synthetic chemicals and certain electrical products) with Imperial imports exempt. It put a similar duty on imported goods shown to be "dumped". The proportion of industry covered was very small but the importance of these measures lay in "their inroads on Free Trade ideology."[3]

Nine applications for an anti-dumping duty were received by the Board of Trade and two of the earliest – over glass bottles from Holland and vulcanised fibre from USA in 1922 – got as far as committees, but failed to prove that imports were below the cost of production in the countries of origin. In March 1922 Baldwin divided the Cabinet on party lines and prevailed by a narrow margin: duties were imposed on fabric gloves from Germany, domestic and illuminated glassware from Germany and Czechoslovakia, aluminium, wrought enamelled holloware and gas mantles. Applications from larger industries such as machine tools, silk, and worsted dress goods were turned down without an inquiry.

One historian explains the problem facing this piecemeal approach: in Europe and the USA a general tariff offered something to everyone except the producer of the raw materials. With partial safeguarding "it became rational for even the most rabidly protectionist manufacturer to oppose a safeguarding application from a related industry or trade."[4]

The 1918-22 Parliament saw occasional proposals for "fusion" between the two coalition parties, quietly encouraged by Law because he thought Lloyd George was valuable as Prime Minister. By March 1922 the National Union led by its chairman Sir Alexander Leith "was close to open insurrection against the continuance of the coalition." This Conservative opposition to the coalition was caused not specifically by a desire for Tariff Reform, though Die-hards wished it, as by a growing opposition to Lloyd George, his methods and associates, and issues like Ireland, culminating in the murder of Field Marshal Sir Henry Wilson MP on 22 June 1922.[5]

With Government by-election defeats piling up, on 19 July Austen Chamberlain, acting party leader during Law's absence abroad, was told by Sir George Younger and Leslie Wilson, party chairman and Chief Whip respectively, of severe disquiet in the ranks. A further meeting with junior ministers and whips saw Lloyd George described as "tarnished goods". On 17 September the coalition leaders met at Chequers and decided on an election. Leslie Wilson warned Chamberlain that over 180 constituency associations were prepared to support independent Conservative candidates.

The tipping point for the coalition came with the Chanak Crisis in the Dardanelles, with Lloyd George deciding to resist Kemal Ataturk's forces. Churchill asked the Dominions for contingents: their response was lukewarm. There was a press storm of opposition, especially as Churchill, provoking Gallipoli memories, was involved. The British commander at Chanak defied the Cabinet and talked to the Turks; an armistice there was signed on 12 October.

Law was in regular communication with Derby, Salisbury, Younger and other lieutenants: all opposed another coalition election, but several were Free Traders. Baldwin was by mid October "very much a ringleader of the insurgency".[6] On the 16th Amery assembled the Chief Whip and 15 junior ministers for lunch at the Metropole where they resolved unanimously that the Conservatives should go to the country "as an independent party". Law, encouraged by his doctors over his health but very diffident about returning to active politics, lunched with Baldwin and Davidson. Baldwin said to him "Well, you are leaving all the white men on the beach. They can't get on without you to lead and it means we shall just all sink out of politics and we shall leave it to those who are not as honest."[7] This, his biographer thought, probably led Law to go to the party meeting at the Carlton Club on the 19th and speak in favour of coming out of the coalition, a view which won by 186 to 87, and produced the resignation of Lloyd George. The impact of chance in politics is supported by Bridgeman's remark regarding Law: "If he had not come I think we should have won. If he had spoken for Coalition I am pretty sure we should not". Both Baldwin and Lloyd-Greame were known to have expected defeat at the meeting.[8]

Amery, it seems, advised that "this next election would be run really on one issue, a change of Government, and that it was not desirable to confuse it by putting Tariff Reform as such in the forefront." During the campaign on 7 November Law pledged against "any fundamental change in the fiscal system of this country" during the forthcoming Parliament. The results of the election were decisive: Conservatives 345 seats with 38.2% of the vote, Labour 142 with 29.5%, Lloyd George Liberals 62 seats with 11.2 % and the Asquithians 54 seats with 17.5%. The relative survival of Lloyd George Liberals was because they and Conservatives cooperated in 160 seats and conflicted in 55.[9]

The 1923 Election and Opposition in 1924

Over the next twenty-four months, the key relationships were between those who revolted against the Lloyd George coalition and served as ministers under Law and Baldwin, who succeeded the dying Bonar Law, and a small group continuing to support that coalition: Austen Chamberlain, Birkenhead, Balfour – and Winston Churchill, still a Liberal. Those who were bitterly opposed to the return of Lloyd George, in particular Baldwin, allowed this to dominate his manoeuvrings round the "former coalition ministers" and various attempts to "re-unite" the Conservative party. There is little doubt of the mutual loathing of the two factions, with the coalitionists tainted by the sale of honours scandal. Baldwin hated "the private immorality of the 'First Eleven' [which] ... appeared to confirm the public corruption of Coalitionism." The defeated coalitionists scorned the personnel of the Law ministry as the "second class brains." Amery, one of the prime organisers of the mutiny, was described as "the son of a Salonika Jew whose name was

Himry."[10]

In October 1922 unemployment stood at 1.4m – 12.3% of insured workers, and stayed roughly at the same level during 1923. In July 1923 Gretton sent Baldwin a petition, signed by 103 Conservative backbenchers, on the need to extend Imperial Preference at the Imperial Economic Conference. Lloyd-Greame, President of the Board of Trade, wanting to extend the McKenna duties to silk, lace and tyres, raised this in Cabinet on 2 August. He was opposed by the Cabinet's Free Traders, but the episode helped to influence Baldwin towards the need for change. A three hour conversation with Baldwin at the end of August in Aix left Amery with the impression that "Stanley is evidently convinced [Protection] has got to come and is only seeing how he can get round the corner."[11]

Baldwin's espousal of Protection at the party conference at Plymouth on 25 October had a "high politics" aspect: it was intended to separate the Protectionist followers of Austen Chamberlain from the Free Trade of Lloyd George. Baldwin had decided to change tack suddenly on 6 or 7 October.[12] Neville Chamberlain and he agreed that the Law pledge debarred food taxes but not the extension of the McKenna duties.[13] After a few extra duties in November an education campaign would lead up "to a more thorough-going programme" by the time of an election. At Chequers on 13-15 October Baldwin, Amery, Chamberlain, Ormsby-Gore and Davidson agreed that Baldwin should "announce a whole-hearted policy of protection and preference at Plymouth, but meet the House and impose such McKenna duties as we could in November and give the country a chance of understanding what it is all about by postponing the election until after the middle of January."[14]

Various people were told in the meantime, the Cabinet not formally until 23 October. Thus Baldwin told Amery that "he ought to say nothing at Plymouth which would cause things to drift towards the immediate election or lay us open to the charge of levity in the matter." Amery "entirely agreed ... it would be very undesirable to create the election atmosphere immediately."[15] Baldwin was getting advice against an immediate election from others: Bridgeman was anxious for a proper agricultural policy to be developed and for Central Office to have time to prepare literature. Gretton, a Die-hard leader, wrote to Baldwin (24 October) that an immediate election "would be suicide for the party and much worse the temporary eclipse of a great policy," while Sir Reginald Hall MP, the party's Principal Agent, argued that to rush an election then or in January would give "most of the cards to the other side." If, however, they let safeguarding run for a year they would "be in clover". And Edward Wood was against a January election on account of "January fox hunting."[16]

At Plymouth, Baldwin declared "... If we go on pottering along as we are we shall have grave unemployment with us to the end of time, and I have come to the conclusion myself that the only way of fighting this subject is by protecting the home market." Whether food taxes should be included in the policy was not resolved until 21 October, and then negatively. And Milner's Tariff Advisory

Committee, intended to draft schedules of duties on manufacturing goods, was not established until mid November; thus it had not reported by election day. Chamberlain told his sister on 21 October that Baldwin was worried and vacillating, but came round to "my view that it would not do to rush an election next month." The public should be educated on the basis of new safeguarding duties "and so lead up to an election in a year or 18 months".[17] The Cabinet on the 23rd agreed to extend the McKenna duties "but to take the verdict of the country within six months." That of the 29th reported that Baldwin "intended to make clear that he had no desire to rush the country into an election."

Disastrously for Tariff Reform, Baldwin then appears to have lost control of the process. His speech in Manchester on 2 November was so Protectionist that Derby, a Free Trader, believed "an early general election was inevitable". Cabinet on 9 November saw Curzon attacking the policy and its effect on foreign affairs, and obtaining support from Salisbury, Cecil, Devonshire, Cave and Novar, none of whom was pressing for an election. At this meeting Amery expounded his view of "gaining the four or five months interval for education" and introducing a pre-election Budget, while challenging the other parties to oppose it. This would include "reductions on tea and sugar, the abolition of the Corporation tax, and possibly even something off income tax". In a letter to Baldwin dated 5 November, he had explained: "Every Free Trader would in fact be put on the defensive to explain by what fresh taxes he is to make the Budget square if he forgoes the tariff revenue."[18]

Amery added in his diary, which for the weeks after 8 November was dictated on 6 January 1924 on the basis of notes in his pocket book: "we should have had a 'tariff in being' as a standard afterwards. I fear after I made my appeal that morning I gave it up and when it was merely a question between January or at once I was quite prepared to accept the view that the sooner we went ... the more we should secure a verdict on the broad issue." On the 9th, Worthington-Evans and other "electioneering experts all ruled ... out" the early Budget idea as impracticable, and Baldwin's "own mind was setting towards an early election." Chamberlain reported "on the whole the majority were for January but I think Stanley has made up his mind for December. The party chairman and Reggie Hall want it at once, so do Worthy and Jix."[19]

With recognition that the Government was rapidly losing the initiative, Baldwin met Chamberlain, Amery, Lloyd-Greame, Worthington-Evans, Hall and Jackson, the party chairman, on the evening of the 11th. The following day he requested a dissolution from the King, who tried, in vain, to dissuade him.

Baldwin was not successful, at this time, in securing the formal support of the leading Chamberlainites. Austen was told of the policy on 12 October by Neville; he welcomed it but told his sister of his fear that the female voters were likely to panic over dear food. On the 23rd Neville told him that food taxes were "off"-Neville clearly believed that they were not excluded permanently, but his brother claimed that without food taxes the "gilt was off the ginger-bread ... Father's policy with all that part left out for which he cared most."[20]

Derby did not want to fight another election, as he had fought 1922, with Birkenhead sniping at him in Lancashire. There was, however, strong opposition to Birkenhead in Central Office: Sanders reported that "The Ulster men ... would not take the Whip" if Birkenhead were in the Government.[21]

Conservative Central Office forecasted a UK total of 351 seats[22] and its final prediction on polling day, 6 December, was a majority of 95. Neville Chamberlain expected one of 60 or 70, *The Times* one of 90, and the *Morning Post* one of 120. In the event, 258 Conservatives faced 191 Labour MPs and 158 Liberals – a minority of 93. Only eleven Conservatives had stood as Free Traders, mostly in Lancashire, where they were beaten. "The failure to do anything substantial for agriculture enabled Liberals to present themselves as the alternative governing party in some agricultural seats."[23] Despite the exclusion of food taxes, the Conservatives were bombarded by the "dear food" smear, enabling the re-united Liberals to inflict havoc. Along with Labour, they won all the West Yorkshire and East Lancashire seats where wool or cotton was a significant employer, with the Conservatives losing nine seats out of the ten in Manchester and Salford, including a sensational Liberal win in Exchange, regarded as the barometer of commercial Manchester. Aylesbury, Blackpool, Chelmsford, Sevenoaks and Tiverton went Liberal in 1923, having stayed Conservative in the wipe-out of 1906.[24] Britain had to face another decade under "Free" Trade.

Neville Chamberlain and Amery were blamed by several for the disaster. Above all, Baldwin became the target of various plotters, aiming to replace him and form a "mugwump" (Amery's word) Liberal-Conservative coalition to keep out Labour. According to Austen Chamberlain, Asquith "could not under any circumstances" support Baldwin, but was prepared to give "benevolent support" to a Balfour-Austen Chamberlain ministry. Rumours circulated that Birkenhead, Balfour, Derby, William Joynson-Hicks, Beaverbrook, Rothermere and Austen himself were prepared to work with Liberals, while Cecil, Younger, Strachey and Gretton – three Free Traders and a Die-hard – were "not prepared to cut off Baldwin's head and make Austen Chamberlain king."[25]

Crucially, the King's view was that Baldwin had the largest party; he should meet Parliament and it should be Parliament which turned him out. Balfour called on the King on the 9th, and was told that the King saw no reason to amend his May 1923 judgment, when Baldwin was preferred to Curzon, that the Prime Minister should be a member of the Commons. Balfour accepted this, and by the 10th Baldwin agreed with the Amery-Bridgeman line excluding coalition with the Liberals whom the Conservatives "hated much worse than Labour."[26]

Thus collapsed the "Birkenhead plot", founded on the belief that Baldwin was about to resign (which on the 8th December had been the case.) From a Tariff Reform point of view, this was the best it would get. The Cabinet meeting to discuss the King's Speech on 18 December saw only Amery, Neville Chamberlain and Bridgeman opposed to weakening on protection. A group emerged, described by Self as "pragmatic Protectionists," never favourable to Free Trade but inclined to call for postponement of the tariff issue: Hoare, Lloyd-Greame and Joynson-Hicks. Amery had done a "rough draft" for the speech reiterating commitment to Tariff Reform. This was accepted by the Cabinet of the 18th, with Curzon and "one or two others" wanting this passage dropped. Most followed Cave in wanting the tariff policy to be reasserted but in an "unprovocative" manner.[27] By 13 January even Neville Chamberlain was happy with a diluted final version; we see the first signs of a gap opening up between him and Amery who wanted a more combative stance. On 21 January, the Conservatives were defeated in the Commons by Labour with Liberal support, and on the 22nd MacDonald took office with the first Labour Government.

Amery's view included this largely accurate prophecy: forcing the Liberals to "face the necessity of supporting Labour … is bound to mean their eventual break-up and disappearance as a party", with the Conservatives absorbing "as much of the carcass as we can secure".[28]

After a further series of manoeuvres, the Chamberlainites Balfour, Balcarres, Birkenhead and Austen himself attended the meeting of the Shadow Cabinet on 7th February, indicating the end of the possible alternative to Baldwin's leadership. Baldwin gave control of discussion to Austen who declared himself in favour of the Hoare mid-December approach "this was the maximum practicable advance at that juncture." He was supported by Balfour, Birkenhead and Curzon. Amery and Bridgeman resisted but to no avail. While Neville Chamberlain opposed making this decision binding at the next election, he took a "much more acquiescent view" than Amery.[29]

So to the party meeting of Peers, MPs and defeated candidates on 11 February, Baldwin declared: "However mistaken on a long view of economic facts the electorate has been, the country as a whole decided in a sense hostile to our main proposal … which had implied in it the creation of a general tariff, and in those circumstances I do not feel justified in advising the Party again to submit the proposal for a general tariff to the country, except upon clear evidence that on this matter public opinion was disposed to reconsider its judgement of two months ago." Safeguarding, he added, might be extended, and a call to abandon Protection as such was shouted down.

Although, as we shall see, the backbench pressure for movement on the issue built up in the later Twenties, the home market was left largely unprotected for the next eight years, with economic and electoral consequences. More importantly, from the wider Imperial viewpoint, there was no prospect of substantial movement on Preference during this time. How much the experience of yet further delay, since the Chamberlain programme was first launched in 1903, and the absence of any clear expectation of change, contributed to disappointment and pessimism in the Dominions, it is difficult to assess. The elements of bitterness, impatience and money-grubbing which characterised the Ottawa negotiations of 1932 might have been a result.

A significant episode in this short period of Opposition was the progression of Churchill. Self traces his return to Conservative beliefs – by January 1923 he admitted he was a Conservative apart from being "sound on Free Trade, almost fanatical."[30] This progression was temporarily punctuated by the Westminster Abbey by-election on 19 March 1924, which he contested against Otho Nicholson, the official Conservative. Austen Chamberlain advised Baldwin to assist Churchill, and at a meeting of ex-ministers on 6 March Austen threatened to speak for Churchill if Neville or Amery spoke for Nicholson; in Amery's words, "it is quite clear that he wants Winston to get in at all costs". The Whips prevented Douglas Hogg from speaking for Nicholson and Baldwin warned Amery against doing so ("I ... found him so miserable about the whole business ... he said that if I insisted on speaking ... it would bust up the whole party"). Churchill was defeated by only 43 votes. He was adopted as "constitutionalist" candidate by Epping Conservatives in September, where he was returned in the October 1924 election.[31]

After the Conservative triumph in that election, Sir Robert Horne, a mild protectionist, refused the post of Chancellor. Baldwin then offered it to Neville Chamberlain, who asked for Health in the hope that he "might be a great Minister of Health but ... not likely to be more than a second – rate Chancellor". This enabled Baldwin literally minutes later to realise his "ideal plan" and offer the job to Churchill – to the amazement of Churchill and everyone else.[32]

The 1924-9 Baldwin Government

Before 1914, instead of meeting the challenge of competition by developing newer product lines, Britain had found new markets for old products and promoted demand in those markets by exporting capital. This process slowed down in the 1920s, even though actual growth saw an acceleration over 1899-1913. Britain was troubled by disappointing exports and thus high unemployment in the old staples of cotton, shipbuilding and coal. She was especially disadvantaged by Churchill's much vaunted return to the gold standard in 1925 – involving a substantial revaluation of sterling. By some measures, using retail prices, sterling might have been between 20 and 25% overvalued in 1925-6. This hit exports. The world economy boomed between 1925 and 1929 but Britain was excluded from this growth, while she also suffered from increasing competition from recovering Germany, France and Belgium, all with undervalued currencies.[33]

While Churchill denied that the gold standard was relevant to the 1925-6 coal dispute, which led to the General Strike, this was powerfully refuted by Maynard Keynes in the "*The Economic Consequences of Mr Churchill*" published in Beaverbrook's *Evening Standard* in 1925. Churchill speedily changed his tune: when Amery criticised the gold standard policy in April 1927, Churchill privately accepted the criticism, did not admit this to Amery, but "when Niemeyer attempted to defend it, Churchill paraphrased Amery in reply". Years later Churchill criticised Montagu Norman, the Governor of the Bank of England, for drawing him into "the biggest blunder" of his life.[34] A modern parallel to the 1925 decision would be the decision of Greece and other Mediterranean countries to enter the euro at an overvalued rate of exchange; this had devastating effects on all of them.

Back in the Twenties, British industry was changing its mood. A Federation of British Industry (FBI) mission to the US led by Colonel Vernon Willey, the FBI president, in November 1925, was full of praise for US economic success provided by its huge home market. After the war the US had adopted the Fordney-McCumber tariff – the so-called 60% tariff – pushing import duties to a height unequalled in American history or almost anywhere else in the developed world, while simultaneously Herbert Hoover, at the Commerce Department, gave aggressive support to US exporters. Willey toured FBI branches advocating amalgamations and cartel agreements to secure maximum economies of scale, leading to higher wages. He was a wool textile owner and a Free Trader, but he, Sir Alfred Mond, founder of ICI, and Sir Ernest Petter, pioneer engine builder responded to realities: the American example strengthened the case for protecting the home market and developing the Empire.

Boyce describes a "flood of literature," including Andre Siegfried's *America Comes of Age* (1927), J. Ellis Barker's *America's Secret* (1928), George Peel's *The Economic Impact of America* (1928) "some of it hostile, much of it sensational". "Thinly veiled anti-Americanism" was displayed in the Commons debate on Cinematograph Films Bill on 17 March 1927, which the Government frankly explained was to combat the Americanising influence of Hollywood films on British consumer taste and the broader impact on the Empire.[35]

The new Conservative Government predictably displayed timidity on both aspects of Tariff Reform. Although Amery became Secretary of State for Colonies and Dominions and an Imperial Economic Policy Committee was established to discuss details of Imperial Preference policy, "Churchill's success in out-manoeuvring Amery on the fiscal question throughout the 1924-9 Ministry rested upon his appearance of studied moderation in contrast to his opponent's petulant fanaticism".[36] Churchill recommended the implementation of the 1923 Imperial Conference undertakings in the form of non-tariff preferences: financial assistance to marketing in the UK through the establishment of the Empire Marketing Board. This did not have a great impact owing to the paucity of resources, with Cabinet on 11 February 1926 deciding to reduce the grant of £1m as it thought it could not be "wisely spent" – so the EMB only obtained £500,000 for 1926.[37]

The Government had "no definite proposals to put forward" for Empire marketing at the 1926 Imperial Conference, and were determined to avoid any further commitments, while 1927 saw Churchill making threats to the EMB's projected surplus of £600,000. By the Cabinet meeting on 20 July 1927, Amery's feud with Churchill had hardened, with a threat to resign, deterred by Neville Chamberlain's mediation. There was an interlude as Amery went off on his Empire tour – South Africa, Australia, New Zealand and Canada – from July 1927 to February 1928 – the first time a British minister had embarked on such an enterprise. In late 1928 Cunliffe-Lister, President of the Board of Trade – for departmental reasons- supported Churchill in another budgetary attack on the EMB: "the real trouble is that both of them hate the EMB and want to wreck it. Neither of them and, as far as I can make out, very few of the Cabinet attach any importance to the fact that this money fulfils a pledge to the Dominions."[38] In April 1929, the Cabinet accepted Amery's proposal to increase the sugar preference to relieve colonial distress caused by a fall in world sugar prices, despite Churchill's opposition, but the latter persuaded them to postpone a final decision until after the election.

There had been pressures from farmers and the NFU[39] throughout the 1920s, with Government opposed to either subsidy or protection. The Agriculture White Paper of February 1926 offered "orthodox, even trivial palliatives." A duty on imported malting barley had been recommended by the backbench Unionist Agricultural Committee, and the Minister, Edward Wood, proposed it to the Cabinet Committee in October 1925. He then went to be Viceroy of India and Walter Guinness, his successor, as a brewer, was less sympathetic. Cabinet in mid April 1926 rejected a duty.

In 1927 the NFU launched a campaign calling on county branches to pressure MPs for help for cereals, suffering from weakening world prices. George Courthope MP, chairman of the backbench Committee, argued for extending safeguarding to agriculture. Guinness replied that safeguarding was "unsuitable" for agriculture, because of the difficulty of proving unfair competition; there was also the commitment against food taxes. The Council of Agriculture carried Courthope's proposal at its quarterly meeting in May 1927 by over 2 to 1.[40] At the NFU annual meeting in January 1928, a Suffolk farmer praised Lord Milner's perspicacity in seeing that "we are approaching a new political alignment in which the division of the future will lie between the producer and the financier."[41]

Despite "undiplomatic" support for a barley duty from Davidson, party chairman, as well as Amery and Bridgeman, the Government remained opposed. In January 1929 the NFU AGM threatened to withdraw support at the coming election and set up a fund to sponsor independent candidates. However, Churchill's Budget, announcing that agricultural derating was advanced from October to April, at a cost of £2.75m, "almost immediately repaired the alliance between the Conservative party and the farming community" – however temporarily.[42]

Baldwin announced during the 1924 election campaign "we may hold ourselves at liberty to safeguard any efficient industry in which unemployment may be caused by unfair competition of any kind." In early February 1925 a short White Paper *Safeguarding of Industries: Procedure and Enquiries* proposed that before a Safeguarding Committee was appointed on an application, the industry had to be of "substantial importance" and suffering "exceptional" foreign competition affecting employment, and this had to be "unfair". An enquiry could be refused if the industry was not efficient or if a duty would impact on employment elsewhere. In May the Board of Trade recommended a duty on lace embroidery; this was carried in Cabinet with a protest from Churchill. Later in 1925 duties were granted to leather and fabric gloves, gas mantles, wrapping paper and cutlery, while applications from glove fabric, glassware, brooms and aluminium holloware were rejected.

Over the next four years the Government received 49 applications for safeguarding (several more were headed off by the Department): only 9 were successful. Some were rejected because the industry was of little significance, some, like steel, because it was too important.[43] Churchill told the Liberal C. P. Scott that the Government "would not go much further ... there wd be no protecn [sic] for iron and steel ... if iron and steel ... were interfered with he shd resign."[44]

Britain had declined from being the leading world steel producer in 1880 to being by 1914 the world's largest importer of iron and steel. Excess capacity had been created during the war and the return to gold did further damage. Its application for safeguarding came before Cabinet on 22 June 1925. Churchill had relied on "frightening Baldwin with the implications of such an Enquiry," as steel was a fundamental raw material of industry, but Cunliffe-Lister opposed him, with support from Amery and Neville Chamberlain. The outcome was not a normal safeguarding enquiry but a wider investigation under the newly established Committee of Civil Research.

Eleven meetings of this took place, with ministers and officials present, examining witnesses. Churchill adopted a "hectoring tone", with "an ill-tempered squabble" with a witness. On 12 October he was "cross-questioning the iron industry representatives and trying to trip them up". On the 20th he exploited the opposition to a duty from the Chairman of the Steel Re-Rollers Association (a "miserable fellow called Scarf" according to Amery.)[45]

After the final meeting on 19 November the Committee concluded that there were three methods of assistance – tariffs, subsidies and amalgamation with rationalisation. The first would inevitably "constitute a substantial advance towards a general tariff". The industry had made it clear that it was not interested in subsidy as a panacea. The favoured solution was regional amalgamations with the banks exerting pressure, but Cunliffe-Lister and Amery wanted a safeguarding enquiry. Worthington-Evans gave qualified approval to an enquiry; Balfour had been sympathetic to one in July, but was now opposed. The three civil servants – Hankey, Warren Fisher and Sir Richard Hopkins, Chairman of the Inland Revenue, true to their ideological training, were also opposed. Baldwin had announced at the meeting on 12 November that "on merits, and without reference to political considerations, he was satisfied that the application ... ought to go to a safeguarding enquiry." When Cabinet discussed the matter again on 18 December, it was agreed they could not refer the application to an enquiry without being prepared to accept its recommendations! On this basis, Baldwin told the Commons on the 21st that an enquiry was rejected.[46]

Of 167 furnaces in blast at the end of 1924, only 129 survived by September 1925, while France and Belgium were expanding their furnace capacity. The General Strike and the long coal stoppage were disastrous to the industry, with only 5 furnaces in blast by the end of September, by which time there was "practically no production" in the heavy sectors. Unemployment in the industry doubled to 56%.[47]

The steel industry was divided in its evidence to the CCR, as was the Engineers' Association, the FBI, and the Chambers of Commerce; a pro-safeguarding motion passed at the Hull meeting of the Association (ABCC) in September 1926 but only by 34 chambers to 32. The move in industry towards protection only happened in the late Twenties. After 1926 much of the steel industry's opposition to tariffs disappeared – GKN, the largest importer of semi-finished steel, opposed tariffs in 1925, but supported them in 1928, and by then the engineering industry as a whole supported safeguarding of iron and steel. In April 1928 the ABCC accepted Birmingham Chamber's resolution that the extension and simplification of safeguarding was "vitally necessary". In January 1929 Sheffield Chamber had a ballot on safeguarding of iron and steel; a total of 515 members voted in favour, 46 against, with a response rate of 62% of the membership.[48]

The Empire Development Union, under the presidency of Walter Long, formed in late 1921, was absorbed in 1925 by the Empire Industries Association, which settled its debts. The EIA was "commonly regarded as the most dynamic and influential Tariff Reform group of the period 1925-29". By late in 1926 EIA propaganda developed the scale that was to be characteristic of 1927-31, under Sir Henry Page Croft MP as Chairman. By 1929 EIA speakers were addressing 60 meetings in Manchester and the North West each month; 4 million pamphlets were issued that year.[49]

The Conservative party conferences at Scarborough in 1926 and Cardiff in 1927 saw solid support for the EIA; Cardiff saw two resolutions passed calling for a simplification of the safeguarding process and "immediate steps to safeguard the steel industry" to save it from "partial extinction". A revival of criticism of the gold standard was triggered by McKenna's address as chairman to the annual meeting in February 1927 of Midland Bank shareholders; he contrasted the US's "great and increasing prosperity" to Britain's "six years of trade depression and unemployment of almost unparalleled severity", and called for a thorough inquiry into the Bank of England's operations.

Little recovery took place during 1927, yet on 20 July the Cabinet refused a request from the heavy section of the Steel Industry to review their application for safeguarding. They sent Baldwin a memorial in April 1928 arguing that the circumstances were "so entirely new and exceptional ", but were rebuffed when they met him on 21 June. In December 1927 Croft sent Baldwin a memorandum signed by 257 Conservative backbenchers urging immediate action on safeguarding. With no response, Croft wrote again in February 1928 saying 304 MPs believed electoral defeat could be avoided only by speeding up the machinery of the Safeguarding White Paper; the same month saw a strongly worded resolution passed by the National Union's Central Council under Gretton's chairmanship.[50] In July 1928 a deputation led by Croft repeated the demand, to no avail. Meanwhile, Amery met Baldwin on 7 May, "blowing off ... steam on the general position" – Baldwin "was as usual silent, sympathetic and friendly but gave no real indication". Amery was planning to speak at the EIA Albert Hall rally on 15 May – the 25th anniversary of Joseph Chamberlain's 1903 speech. Under advice from Neville Chamberlain he decided against doing so.[51]

Matters brewed towards a pre-summer recess crisis. On 9 July the Cabinet committee, in Churchill's absence, found Cunliffe-Lister "vigorously in favour of dealing with iron and steel straightaway ... even the timid Guinness supported him". Davidson, the party chairman was "obviously impressed ... still more I gather when he went up to the 1922 Committee afterwards and found them clamouring for immediate action ..." Baldwin met Amery two days later: "he took the view that there could be no possible question of dealing with iron and steel this side of the next election."[52] Then Joynson-Hicks, the erratic Home Secretary, in a speech at Romsey on 28 July, implied that safeguarding would be applied to steel in the next Parliament. On 1 August Cabinet began with Baldwin pronouncing on "the desirability of letting the safeguarding leaven work with as little advertisement as possible ..."[53] It was agreed that Baldwin should issue "some sort of announcement" before the recess.

A meeting to discuss this took place the next day. Before it, Amery agreed with Chamberlain that the former should "open the case against our inaction" while the latter "should lie low and steady the position afterwards". Acknowledging that "no one was asking for a general tariff or food taxes", Amery "gave what I thought was the kind of formula" that would calm the party "viz ... a simpler and more effective safeguarding procedure and no efficient industry excluded." This was supported by Cunliffe-Lister, but Guinness's "usual nonsense" that steel protection would upset the farmers' vote ("distressed about his fences") was "dismissed ... as absurd" by Bridgeman. Hogg, confusedly "declared that the whole unemployment was due to Free Trade ... the essential thing was to say as little about it as possible and avoid letting protection become an issue at the election." Churchill acknowledged that iron and steel could not be excluded from a safeguarding inquiry ("he thought it would lose us a great many votes but did not see how we could get out of it.") The agreed policy would be set out by a letter from Baldwin to Eyres-Monsell, the Chief Whip.[54]

This letter was published by the press on 5 August. Unfortunately, in respect of what was ruled out, Baldwin substituted the ambiguous and catch-all word "protection" for what had been agreed should be "general tariff." Thus he prolonged the row. Most were not too concerned; but Amery's "histrionic response ... was predictable, solitary and exaggerated."[55] Amery wrote Baldwin "a very strongly worded letter" saying he held himself free to act independently in the autumn. In fact Amery was "quite disarmed" over Baldwin's intentions when they met on 24 September. He further found that Neville Chamberlain "had not liked the letter which he thought must have been drafted by Bobby Monsell, who is not a friend on this matter ... we agreed that no irrevocable harm had been done. "[56]

Self comments, accurately, that Amery's criticisms were too verbose –his 10 April 1927 letter to Baldwin consisted of 23 handwritten pages – and they were too frequent to be taken seriously. He quotes Baldwin telling Neville Chamberlain "he has no grip on the House; no-one pays any attention to him", and Neville thought Baldwin "would go much further if Amery could be kept from nagging at him."[57] However, Amery would be proved right by the political outcome and it is likely that, in the circumstances of the time, he was right about the economics, as indicated by Chamberlain's line in Opposition after the 1929 Election. In 1927-8, perhaps, Chamberlain was more the humble supporter of his leader. And, of course, the deference shown then to the party leader, whether in office or Opposition, contrasts massively with modern times!

The 1928 party conference at Yarmouth, like most pre-election Conferences, saw the party calm down. Yet it passed another resolution for safeguarding iron and steel. In his speech, Baldwin did not use the notes prepared by Amery but he corrected the August mistake by speaking of the specific exclusion of a general tariff rather than "protection". Then the wire trade put in an application for safeguarding. Croft continued to stir: on 12 November 200 Conservative MPs passed a resolution in favour of a duty on iron and steel, and on the 14th Croft harried the Government during a debate on safeguarding. That day, the Government announced proposals to modify the safeguarding procedure.

Arthur Pugh was the General Secretary of the Iron and Steel Trades Confederation, which had previously remained uninvolved. With a decline of membership from 117,547 in 1921 to 52,296 in 1928, it set up a committee to examine the case for a tariff, under pressure from members. In early 1929, the Cabinet decided to tell Pugh there would be no further investigation. A changed trade union view was also seen in the woollen industry. In 1923 and 1925 the woollen industry unions stood aloof from applications for safeguarding. With woollen imports doubling and unemployment at more than 25%, a union proposal in January 1928 to support safeguarding was headed off by Philip Snowden, Labour's Chancellor in 1924 and again in 1929 – an avid Free Trader. On 1 December the union agreed to support a joint application with the employers, in spite of Snowden. The inquiry found in favour of the industry and Churchill's attempt to challenge this was overruled in Cabinet on 9 May 1929. However, with Cunliffe-Lister and Baldwin "wobbling" over publication, "it was left for the PM to consult the Central Office and they decided against."[58]

Despite his criticisms of Amery, Self cites abundant evidence, including absenteeism in Commons votes, to show the state of the Conservative party. They went into the 1929 Election "listless, demoralised and internally divided". "Bemused candidates" failed "to exploit the full potential of derating" – Churchill's solution to unemployment. Self cites copious evidence that "after four years at the Treasury, Churchill's standing with Baldwin, the Cabinet, the Parliamentary party, and the Treasury was at its nadir."[59]

At the same time, Herbert Hoover won a landslide Presidential election victory in November 1928. Sir Arthur Balfour, a Sheffield steel manufacturer, an old acquaintance of Hoover, said he would start "an economic offensive against us all the world over". It was in this context that Baldwin warned MacDonald, shortly before the latter defeated him, "the American money power is trying to get control of some of the natural resources of the Empire. They are working like beavers."[60]

Reaping the Whirlwind 1929-31

Campaigning under the slogan "Safety First", the Conservatives lost 152 seats, while Labour gained 136, and the Liberals a mere 19- the three parties ended with 260, 287 and 59 respectively. MacDonald formed his second government.

The economic weather began to change for the worse. The Board of Trade's seasonally adjusted index of industrial production (100 in 1924) fell from 115 in the third quarter of 1929 to 104 in the second quarter of 1930. The proportion of insured workers unemployed rose from under 10% in the summer of 1929 to 15% in May 1930. Protectionist views in industry hardened, with several large Chambers of Commerce conducting polls of members. In a May 1930 poll of the Manchester Chamber 2343 out of 3941 members voted; 607 clung to Free Trade, while a total of 1736 voted for some form of tariff. This was a huge transformation for what had been only a few years earlier a bastion of Free Trade. In June the Bradford Chamber voted 7 to 1 in favour of protection, Leeds by 497 to 37, while in July 96% of respondents in the British Engineers' Association favoured protection.

There were hopes that the World Economic Conference in early 1930 would produce a tariff truce, but the Dominions, looking for tariff increases rather than cuts, refused to attend, and the FBI, ABCC and London Chamber joined the protectionist EIA and the National Union of Manufacturers in opposing British participation. The USA would only send observers. Only 30 nations attended and only 18 signed the convention in March. In March 1930 the US Senate, after long debate, passed the Smoot-Hawley Tariff Bill, with rates of 46.4% on cottons and 59.8% on woollens.[61]

From February 1930 Keynes favoured tariffs to raise prices and profits and revive business confidence. In May, Hubert Henderson, secretary to the Economic Advisory Council (established in January 1930 to advise the government) suggested a revenue tariff to finance industrial rationalisation. In October, the majority of the Committee of Economists, a sub-committee of the EAC, including Keynes, Henderson and Josiah Stamp, recommended protection; this in a profession which had almost been completely Cobdenite. Twenty leading City bankers met on 2 July 1930 at Hambros to draft a manifesto: it referred to "bitter experience" over the previous four years and accepted that Britain should look to the Empire: "Trade protection was the price the City was prepared to pay to maintain sterling as a world currency."[62]

The TUC economic committee proposed "in particular circumstances where it is desirable to help a specific trade, a tariff may be justifiable ...": an attempt in General Council to delete this was defeated 17 to 5. In July a Cabinet Committee chaired by Addison reported in favour of a home wheat quota; at full Cabinet the Chancellor, Snowden, ensured its rejection, while MacDonald "lay low". Rooth concludes "But for the presence of Snowden, the Labour Government would almost certainly have introduced protectionist measures in 1930." The Liberal Summer School in August 1930 saw attacks on Free Trade from E. D. Simon, a Manchester machinery manufacturer and MP, referring to "the tremendous revulsion of opinion" against keeping Free Trade in a protectionist world, while another Mancunian called on Liberals to "get away from the Free Trade slush".[63]

So the years 1929-31 saw the Labour Government trying, in vain, to cope with the economic blizzard, the Liberals meandering in the wilderness, and the Conservatives facing challenges and divisions, including several by-election split votes. The political future of the country would not begin to become apparent until the autumn of 1931.

Lord Beaverbrook launched his peculiar but fanatical Empire Crusade with his article "Who is For the Empire" in the *Sunday Express* on 30 July 1929, advocating free entry for all Empire food and taxes on non-Imperial food. This was a more extreme and impractical version of the full Tariff Reform programme. He launched the United Empire Party which challenged official Conservative candidates in by-elections. Baldwin's Albert Hall speech in November 1929 was "the first step towards disassociating the party from previous inhibiting pledges and declaring a 'free hand' on fiscal and Imperial questions."[64] Progress was slow: Baldwin's Coliseum speech of 5 February 1930 proposed safeguarding for iron and steel and textiles, but offered nothing to agriculture although wheat prices were collapsing. After meeting Beaverbrook, Baldwin stated at the Hotel Cecil on 4 March 1930 that food taxes should face a referendum. Beaverbrook was privately assured by Neville Chamberlain that the referendum idea would be buried, but refused to share a platform with Baldwin at the large Empire Day rally at the Crystal Palace in April 1930. The other Press Lord, Rothermere, opposed food taxes and Baldwin's policy on India. Baldwin returned their hostility with interest: to call them "swine ... was to libel a very decent, clean animal."[65]

Neville Chamberlain aspired to the leadership. He had removed Lord Percy as chairman of the newly created Conservative Research Department and then removed Davidson and became party chairman too. Supported by Hoare, Amery,

Austen Chamberlain and Cunliffe-Lister, Neville used a CRD committee to develop "emergency" and "scientific" industrial tariffs and agricultural quotas not simply as protection but to stimulate rationalisation and marketing arrangements. Exasperated by Baldwin's "want of inspiration and decision,"[66] he pushed Baldwin towards a bolder policy, especially after a Rothermere candidate had polled very well against the Conservatives in the Bromley by-election in September.

At the 1930 Imperial Conference, the Cabinet majority led by Snowden opposed the offer by Richard Bennett, the Canadian Prime Minister, of reciprocal preference: "Snowden's brutal rejection ... caused great offence to the Canadian and Australian delegates." Bennett's offer was dismissed by Thomas, Dominions Secretary, as "humbug". Snowden lectured the Dominion Premiers in "his usual haranguing style."[67] This all helped to sour the atmosphere for the Ottawa Conference two years later.

Conservative critics pressed Baldwin to accept Bennett's offer. On 14 October the Conservative Business Committee accepted Chamberlain's programme, with Churchill alone dissenting; it dropped the referendum and advanced over agricultural protection, targeting foreign imports of fruit, vegetables, and malting barley. A programme of an emergency tariff on manufactures and a "completely free hand" to negotiate preferences with the Dominions was accepted at a second Caxton Hall meeting of MPs, peers and candidates on 30th October 1930, while a Gretton-Page Croft motion against Baldwin's leadership was defeated by 462 votes to 116. This helped to neutralise the victory on the 31st of the Empire Crusade candidate in the South Paddington by-election.

Early 1931 saw the leadership drama climax. For the East Islington by-election Neville Chamberlain persuaded one Beaverbrook candidate to withdraw in favour of the official Conservative; then a new Crusader candidate stood and pushed the official Conservative into a poor third place. This persuaded Neville that it was impossible to work with Beaverbrook. Then Churchill resigned from the Business Committee, in part because he opposed policy on India; he calculated that both Rothermere and the Die-hards would support him on India though not on food taxes. And the party managers inside Central Office turned against Baldwin: "crucially, the collective leadership cracked." While Hailsham was the candidate of the Right, Austen, Hoare and Cunliffe-Lister supported Neville. On 1 March, Baldwin was about to resign, deterred only by his friends Davidson and Bridgeman.[68] On 5 March Neville and Hailsham agreed that either would serve under the other. But also on the 5th came the news of the Irwin-Gandhi pact, which produced a "tremendous revulsion of feeling" in the party against Churchill and the Die-hards.[69] On the 12th, Baldwin swept the Die-hards aside in a Commons debate on India; he gave his famous "prerogative of the harlot" speech in the St George's by-election on the 17th, and on the 19th his candidate Duff Cooper won, thus marking the defeat of the Beaverbrook campaign.

European Parenthesis

Before Europe was overwhelmed by the 1931 slump, and then by Hitler's accession to power, a campaign had begun with fascinating implications for the post-1945 world. Herriot, the French Prime Minister and Foreign Minister had in January 1925 told an enthusiastic Chamber of Deputies that he wanted to see a "United States of Europe". The Mayrisch committee, named after a prominent Luxembourg industrialist, brought together leading French, German, Belgian and Luxembourg industrialists and opinion formers, who designed a European Steel Cartel in September 1926. Count Richard Coudenhove-Kalergi, of Austro-Hungarian and Japanese parentage, created the Pan-Europa Society in 1922. This was supported by Aristide Briand, who headed eleven French ministries between 1909 and 1929, and was Foreign Minister from 1925 until his death in 1932. The idea also appealed to German industrialists and to Gustav Stresemann, Briand's great German counterpart, who was Foreign Minister from 1923 until his early death at age 51 in 1929. *The Economist* supported the idea – "the tendency of modern times is towards greater political and economic aggregations," but recognised that Britain, because of her Imperial connections, could not take part. The concept lacked detailed substance; Briand spoke in September 1929 of "some kind of federal bond" in Europe, primarily economic. On 9 September Stresemann gave Germany's qualified support; on 3 October he died. His successor, Bruning, needing nationalist support, was unsympathetic.

The British government made a cold response: as Boyce exclaims "That a British 'socialist' government should condemn Europe to face its worst economic crisis in modern history without any practical means of co-operation, for the sake of free trade, a special relationship with the US, the exemplar of unregulated capitalism, and the maintenance of the British Empire was not a little ironic."[70] The crunch came over a proposal for an Austro-German customs union, in the spring of 1931. This would be paralleled by the Oslo Convention of December 1930, and then the Ouchy Convention in 1932, aimed at trade co-operation between the three Scandinavian countries, the Netherlands, Belgium, and Luxembourg, with Finland planning to join in 1933. The Board of Trade emphasised legal objections to the Austro-German proposal, so Austria decided not to proceed. Within weeks she faced the collapse of the Kreditenanstalt, her largest commercial bank. By now, Britain was leaning strongly towards Imperial protectionism. This did not rule out a European dimension, but Britain could not have joined in a European preferential arrangement "without cogent and effective leadership, something it manifestly lacked."[71]

Amery was one of the Britons attracted to Coudenhove's ideas. The two first met in June 1926 and he and Churchill are found "battling freely" about Pan-Europa on 4 November 1926; Churchill "is an out and out European and regards the combination of England, France and Germany as the pivot of the world's peace", while Amery argued "that we were not European though a useful link between Europe and the new world outside".[72] Amery attended a Pan-European conference in Berlin in May 1930, where "my chief part was to make quite clear both our sympathy and our inability to take part in any Pan-European union," and another one in Basle in September 1932. He met Coudenhove frequently; the two of them lunching together with Churchill in February 1938. Amery explained to Coudenhove on 9 June 1931 that Austen Chamberlain and Arthur Henderson, the former and present Foreign Secretaries, took the view they did on Europe, not because they were stupid but because "mentally we are much too far from Europe ever to enter wholeheartedly into its policies".[73]

The 1931 National Government and Tariffs

Back in Britain in July 1931, there was talk of coalitions. About 12 Liberals had regularly voted independently of the rest, and in late June various including Sir John Simon resigned the whip: Simon was attacked by Lloyd George for leaving "the slime of hypocrisy in passing from one side to another."[74] There was nothing inevitable in the actual formation of the National Government or in the personnel included. Indeed, there was a degree of smoke and mirrors throughout, especially how a "doctors' mandate", a temporary arrangement to handle an emergency, turned into a decade-long government. No wonder Amery was sceptical – to put it mildly!

The initial British response to the European crisis was to raise bank rate, eventually to 4.5% on 30 July. The Governor of the Bank, Montagu Norman, and Treasury officials warned MacDonald and Snowden of a "real danger" of sterling being forced off gold; the pound began to fall in early August. By 23 August MacDonald was disgusted by Labour opposition to his and Snowden's proposed austerity programme, required by foreign bankers, and the King told him, with reference to the Conservative and Liberal leaders (Samuel acting for a seriously ill Lloyd George), that he would "advise them strongly" to serve under MacDonald. Baldwin, however, disliked coalitions; he preferred to form a Conservative government and get Liberal help in passing emergency legislation, probably not at this stage including tariffs, through the existing Parliament. That evening the Cabinet received news that the US bankers required them to cut unemployment benefit. Eleven ministers including MacDonald and Snowden would accept, but nine were opposed; so they unanimously agreed on resignation. On the evening of the 23rd MacDonald told the King of this; the King replied that Samuel and Baldwin would accept him as the "national" Prime Minister.

At the Buckingham Palace Conference of party leaders on the 24th the King pressed hard for this "National" Government. Baldwin, who had told his wife the previous evening that he expected to form a government on his own, was obliged to tell his monarch that "in the circumstances ... at that time there was nothing for anyone in my position to do but promise full co-operation." But "the National Government would be an emergency arrangement, not a party coalition but a 'co-operation of individuals', restricted to the budget programme."[75]

Keynes complained that the main problem, the balance of payments, could only be cured by one of four measures: tariffs, reduction of money incomes, exchange and capital controls with pressure on France and America to enforce sensible international credit policies, or devaluation. The Government had chosen none of these, but had produced a programme which he estimated would increase unemployment by 400,000. To an all party meeting of MPs on 16 September he described the austerity programme as not just "wrong" but "perfectly mad", while ministers' fears of depreciation were "quite barmy".[76]

Pressure continued to build for tariffs. A Manchester Chamber of Commerce statement to *The Times* of 15 September had a "marked impression on MPs."[77] Simon that day declared the emergency as a reason to "abandon ... the system of free imports", while Hore-Belisha and other Liberal MPs announced that "Free Trade had ceased to count". The Invergordon naval "mutiny" of 24 September forced Britain off the gold standard.[78] Samuel claimed that this made a tariff unnecessary as it checked imports and encouraged exports; while Liberals remained opposed to dogmatic protection, Liberal ministers would assent to tariffs if these were shown to be "indispensable" to restore the trade balance.

There were only four Conservatives in the National Government. Baldwin and Chamberlain were, perhaps too conveniently, joined by Cunliffe-Lister with "experience at the Board of Trade" and Hoare because he "had worked closely with Chamberlain during the August crisis". So Amery was excluded, to be told later by Baldwin that MacDonald had objected ("too uncompromising views").[79] Amery, anyway, was in Italy when the first moves towards coalition were made, only returning home by the 25th when it was virtually formed. His reaction was sour, even before his exclusion was confirmed: "Even Neville may be influenced by City panic and by the idea that it is our duty to 'save the pound' ..." He added "It all seemed to me silly and endangering everything that I had worked for ... Neither Neville nor Sam (Hoare) have the comprehensive grasp or the clearness of purpose not to let themselves be frightened by the bankers in such a crisis ... To find that even Neville loses his head and sells the pass in the first fortnight of serious crisis ..."[80]

On 29 August, after talking to Joynson-Hicks, he notes "the real secret of it all is ... SB's instinctive reluctance to face the responsibility of forming a government of his own" – here, as we have seen above, he was wrong. Next day he looks to Hailsham as an ally "in helping to bring the thing to a conclusion fairly soon." On 8 September he refers to Commons "fireworks" from Mosley, "who was free to make the speech I should have liked to make, pouring contempt on the whole of this economy nonsense," while the 10th saw Snowden's Budget, "the very worst type of Cobdenite Snowdenish finance." He thought devaluation would have enabled the Government to "scrap most of the cuts."[81] His critique resembles Keynes's, with more of a tariff emphasis, but was probably not practical politics.

Amery's detailed diary shows his varying moods: relief at being excluded, or resentment at exclusion and surviving hopes of office, and his continued policy suspicions (largely misplaced); for example the suggestion that "our people" had not insisted that Runciman studied the CRD tariff which Cunliffe-Lister had left in the Board of Trade.[82] Williamson opines that this attitude was "extreme and absurd" and quotes Neville Chamberlain telling his wife (26 August 1931) that Amery was "as tiresome as could be". But there is also evidence of Chamberlain colloguing with Amery, sympathising with his exclusion and promising to help. On 26 January 1932 we see that Beaverbrook "seems now definitely to regard me as the next leader of the Party and coming PM", though Williamson exaggerates in adding that Amery was "vain enough to believe him."[83]

Pressure for an election was irresistible. Parliament was dissolved on 7 October for an election on the 27th. The Simon Liberals decided to form a separate group, issuing their own manifesto and sponsoring 40 Liberal National candidates, most of which had a good chance of winning because they ran in strong Liberal areas, in most cases without Conservative opposition. The Samuelite Liberals tried to get Lloyd George's co-operation but he refused. They campaigned more against Protection than Socialism, and the Conservatives retaliated: only 19 Conservative candidates withdrew to help Samuelites, whose leader, described as the "twisting eel,"[84] was opposed by a Conservative candidate in Darwen. The EIA was rigorous about the terms of supporting non-Conservatives. Four days before the poll Lloyd George advised Liberals to vote for any Free Trader available, even if a Socialist.

The successful Conservatives totalled 470, with 35 Simonite National Liberals, as compared to 13 National Labour and 33 Samuelites. On 29 October Baldwin told the Business Committee that Conservatives "could not expect to be represented in the Cabinet in strict proportion" to their numbers. He insisted on the Chancellor being a Conservative. Hankey advised making Baldwin Chancellor because he "was not such an extreme Tariff Reformer as Neville Chamberlain." MacDonald at first wanted Runciman as Chancellor but by 5 November he had appointed Chamberlain. He opposed having Protectionists at both economic departments, so Runciman got the Board of Trade.

On 10 November Runciman proposed an Enabling Bill to put a 10% duty on excessive imports. This was more modest than Chamberlain would have liked but Runciman would not accept the CRD three-decker tariff of 10%, 16.7% and 33.3%. So Chamberlain reluctantly accepted a wide 10% revenue tariff and the Abnormal Importations Bill received Royal Assent on the 20th. Conservative MPs, the NFU and other agricultural interests protested at the omission of food, so Gilmour, the agriculture minister, obtained the parallel horticultural measure, with duties on various imported fruit, vegetables and horticultural products deemed to be luxuries. On 11 December this received Royal Assent. "Proposals were presented to Parliament so rapidly that they did not have Cabinet approval."[85]

Runciman gradually detached himself from Free Trade Liberal pressures, and Chamberlain outmanoeuvred the Free Traders on the Committee on the Balance of Trade established in early December. By the penultimate session on 13 January 1932 all the members except Thomas (who was persuadable) and Samuel had accepted his proposals. At the final meeting on the 18th Samuel and Snowden submitted separate memoranda of dissent.

The conclusion of the Committee was a flat-rate tariff with selective taxes on non-essentials. Cabinet on 21 January endorsed this, while Runciman accepted the tariff on pragmatic grounds, as did Thomas, Sankey and Simon. When it seemed that the Free Traders were set to resign, leaving MacDonald even more dependent on Conservatives, Hailsham proposed an "agreement to differ", approved by Sankey and Simon and then accepted by the Free Traders, who remained silent during discussion and recorded their dissent in the Cabinet conclusions.

Chamberlain's speech in introducing the Import Duties Bill on 4 February got massive approval on account of his references to his father, while Samuel's "really nastily delivered" attack was seen as "an outrage on good taste", leaving the lobbies like a "hornets' nest".[86] By the end of February the Import Duties Bill was law.

Cabinet agreed in principle to the Ottawa Preparatory Committee's recommendation for a Dominion wheat quota, as a bargaining card at the forthcoming Ottawa Imperial Conference, especially to help the Canadian hosts thereof.

Thus an ideological, as well as fiscal, revolution took place, 29 years after Joseph Chamberlain launched his great campaign, with remarkably little public and Parliamentary dissent.

Ottawa and After

For decades, starting with Canada in the 1890s, the Dominions had granted preferences in trade to Britain and received very little in return. By the end of the 1920s the Dominions were meeting more competition from Argentina over livestock and Scandinavia over dairy products; Australia and New Zealand were losing market share. The Imperial Conferences of 1923, 1926 and 1930 had been replete with economic questions "almost beyond resolution without a fundamental reorientation of British fiscal arrangements."[87] While Drummond sums it up as "Dominion importunity, and British intransigence", Sir Robert Vansittart, in early 1932, declared "one reason for our loss of weight since 1926 has been that the 'foreigner' ... has been secretly anticipating the gradual dissolution of the Empire, and some of the Commonwealth delegations have not at times exactly discouraged the idea."[88]

The 1932 Ottawa Conference was a continuation of the 1930 Conference which had postponed discussion of trade matters. Writing to Bennett, the Canadian Premier, on 4 March, Amery said that the Import Duties Act "had broken down the idea that raw materials, even more than foodstuffs, are absolutely taboo".[89]

Britain sent to the Dominions detailed schedules of goods on which she would like tariff concessions, and when no progress was apparent, a chaser telegram was sent on 9 May to say that free entry, granted under the Import Duties Act, would only be continued if concessions were forthcoming from the Dominions.

Bennett set great store by the conference; failure would lead to a Canadian-US agreement. Canada eventually produced a list of 7000 items not made there on which Canada would not tax the same items imported from Britain. As an example of the lack of detailed homework done by the Canadians (Bennett's Cabinet was divided and subject to various protectionist pressures from industrial supporters), none of this material reached British officials in time: Bennett only sent his requests to London on 11 July, two days before the British sailed. Officials in Ottawa complained that 12 days before the conference, several key matters, including the appointment of the Canadian delegation, needed ministerial authority. On foodstuffs other than meat Britain was prepared to give Australia a good deal – better than Australia had asked for – but no one gave this soothing information to the Australians. Similarly, "when they sailed for Quebec, the [British] delegates were divided": their hopes "unrealistic", their plans "unmade".[90] Cabinet divisions meant that very little policy was decided beforehand.

Seven British Cabinet ministers attended. Thomas was originally intended to lead, but after having one row with Bennett at the 1930 conference, and another, fuelled by alcohol, in February 1932 with Howard Ferguson, the Canadian High Commissioner, Baldwin instead was made to go, in order to lead the delegation. He insisted on not participating in detailed negotiations, so the brunt of these fell on Neville Chamberlain and Hailsham.

The conference lasted 31 days between the preliminary session on 20 July and the final one on 20 August – 112 meetings in all, concluding in a final night of hard bargaining. Relations were jeopardised from the start by Bennett's low opinion of all the British delegation, including Chamberlain, who in turn attributed most difficulties to "the personality of Bennett".[91] He "made his contempt" for the British delegation all too apparent in an interview on 9 August. To the British Bennett had "the manners of a Chicago policeman and the temperament of a Hollywood film star."[92] This tension coincided with the crunch-point of the conference. With some concession to Bennett being politically necessary, the British, after hesitation, conceded both a grain duty and free entry to Dominion flour. This made it more difficult for them to give way on a meat duty. On this the negotiations almost failed. Here Bruce from Australia was the combatant: he twice threatened to break off, while Baldwin talked him into remaining.

In private conversations with his colleagues Chamberlain made it clear that if the conference broke down because of a refusal to put a duty on meat, he would resign. Faced with this, Thomas telephoned MacDonald and agreed to drop his own objections but was reminded that if a meat duty was imposed, five other ministers would resign. So a quota on British meat imports was resorted to: by 17

August Australia and New Zealand had accepted this, with an agreement that foreign sheepmeat and frozen beef imports would be cut back so that by mid 1934 they would be at 65% of the 1931-32 level. This agreement to regulate foreign meat imports was to involve British ministers in continuing discussion and dispute and an embarrassing later attempt to mollify Argentina, the importer most affected. There would be no duties on Empire supplies for five years. Then followed agreements on both butter and cheese – the British agreed to raise duties against imports to please New Zealand – and new or higher duties on foreign fruits, including canned and dried fruits. As food taxes were political dynamite, quotas and supply restrictions were surer ways of raising prices; because they were less familiar, they were less politically dangerous.[93]

Amery, attending as an representative of various lobbies (including agriculture, sugar and timber), seems to have burnt his boats with his colleagues. His efforts to persuade them to accept a meat duty (which Baldwin, in typical fashion, had previously implied was no difficulty),[94] had the result of persuading them that he was responsible for Dominion truculence. The Diary does show him trying to mollify both Bennett and Bruce,[95] but on the 17 August he received a letter from Neville "in which he accused me of wrecking the Conference by inciting the Dominions to make impossible requests etc. If he knew how little 'inciting' I have done …" The same day Fabian Ware told him that Chamberlain "had more or less collapsed" from exhaustion, with Hailsham having to bear the brunt, but the following day Hailsham, also "utterly exhausted," had spoken to Ware "most bitterly about me". On the 24th Bennett himself told Amery that the British delegation "were very bitter against me, having concluded … that I had been the chief instigator of opposition to them".[96] Fairly or unfairly, this tension excluded Amery from benefiting from the ministerial resignations which followed in late 1932, and added to the rifts on a variety of issues which developed between him and ministers during the Thirties. These are described in the Diaries, explain the curious title he gave to his third volume of memoirs (*The Unforgiving Years*), and culminate in the greatest and most decisive speech of his life in May 1940, during the debate on the Allied defeat in Norway, and directed at Chamberlain.

Was Ottawa a success? Such intense negotiations, whether over trade or wider economic issues, are commonplace in the modern world. They were fairly unique in the Twenties and Thirties: "one is reminded that no British minister or civil servant in living memory had been involved in such trade negotiations," which of course could not have happened while the UK was bound to Free Trade.[97] Some British officials thought the delegation was too large. "Also it would be desirable, if such an occasion ever occurs again, to have something vaguely resembling a policy before we start … in the end Bennett and Bruce made up our minds for us."[98]

Even so, it was a definite achievement to construct seven major trade agreements in 31 days, but it constitutes yet another reason for deploring the delay in reaching this point. With a positive approach among British politicians and officials (which manifestly did not exist even in 1932), an Ottawa might have taken place years or decades earlier, to be followed up by more harmonious gatherings, before the prospect and then the actuality of another world war intervened.

Reading the agreements, Amery comments "a substantial advance has been made, far beyond anything one could have expected twelve months ago." He gave the chief credit to Bennett, while "our crew ... were too divided in instinct and tradition to have any real view as to what it was they were out to create." Thus "there is little love lost between most of our people and Bennett, and the Civil Service go home very anti-Dominion and vice-versa."[99] These tensions may have played a damaging role over the ensuing decade, contributing to Dominion reluctance to commit to resist German incursions into Eastern Europe in the late Thirties, and perhaps to British reluctance to understand Australasian concerns about their vulnerability in 1941-2. However, as Amery stated, in the economic and commercial field a "great change in our national and Imperial policy had taken place" and if it was betrayed during the war and post-war years because it was not expounded or defended as such, that was not apparent in 1932.

Almost certainly as a consequence of the agreements, British recovery in the Thirties was stimulated by an increase in Empire trade: between 1930 and 1938, British exports to the Empire, as a proportion of total exports, rose from 43.5% to 49.9%, while her imports increased even more markedly, from 29.1% to 40.4%. With imports of manufactures and of food and drink rising only marginally, and imports of raw materials rising by 82% between 1931 and 1937, Amery argued that there "could be no more convincing proof of the expansionist effect of our domestic tariff and of the Ottawa agreements taken in conjunction."[100]

More recent economic historians are rather more restrained. Drummond calculates that, in contrast to the Twenties when the Empire drew a decreasing proportion of imports from the UK, Ottawa slightly reversed this trend, with a direct benefit of around 3.5% of UK exports in 1933 to 5.4% in 1937, and that the Agreements increased British output by £26m (0.5%) in 1933 and £56m (1%) in 1937. British imports from the Empire were remarkably stable in proportion during the 1920s, rose sharply in 1932 and continued to rise thereafter: to 7.2% and 10.3% of total British imports in 1933 and 1937 respectively.[101] These crude figures do not tell the whole story. By boosting industrial confidence and by integrating Britain and the Empire more fully in a dynamic sense, Ottawa had a far greater effect on output and employment than the figures measure. So the worst unemployment in Britain was increasingly confined to the "black spots" of coal mining and shipbuilding. Those in work benefited from the fall in the cost of living following a fall in international prices, while Britain experienced a resurgence of house-building (helped by low interest rates) and the growth of "new" industries, such as motor vehicles, partly based on the rising real incomes of the employed.

There followed the inevitable political consequences. On 28 August 1932 a memorandum from Samuel argued that the national economic crisis had passed, Ottawa should be denounced, and the Free Traders should resign. Snowden told MacDonald on the 29th "The Ottawa agreements are the final and complete triumph of the Tory protectionists." On 8 September the Samuelite leadership in both Houses agreed to resign from the Government without going into Opposition. Neville Chamberlain was adamant that they could not have another agreement to differ; if Samuel went "I should rejoice for he is a most uncomfortable colleague".[102] At Cabinet on 28 September, both Samuel and Snowden failed to impress potentially sympathetic colleagues; they resigned "in an acrimonious atmosphere."[103]

The Simonites benefited: some were promoted, and they moved into informal alliance with the Conservatives: they did not formally unite until Woolton's Cheviot agreement of 1948, and had a separate whip until 1966. The Samuelites were greatly diminished in the 1935 election, gaining fewer than 1.5 m votes and 21 seats; Samuel himself was beaten at Darwen.

The Start of the American Challenge

UK political tensions on tariff related matters did not cease. The Dominions, especially Australia, expressed frustration at British reluctance to exclude foreign suppliers from her market: Chamberlain told the Cabinet in May 1936 that the Dominions were beginning to realise that their markets in Britain for agriculture were limited as the UK "in years to come, would take a diminishing rather than an increasing share of their products." Thus they needed to develop secondary industries.[104] Britain made trade treaties with Germany, which, predictably, had no effect on Hitler's longer-term schemes, and with two important food suppliers, Denmark and Argentina. These were condemned by the *Daily Express* and by Amery who said that while the letter of Ottawa was preserved "the whole spirit of the Ottawa agreements is ... contradicted by the conclusion, and even by the language of these agreements."[105] Austen Chamberlain led the opposition to the German treaty, and 7 out of 12 Birmingham MPs voted against it.

At the World Economic Conference in June 1933, Britain insisted that there was no question of Britain returning to the gold standard without settlement of war debts. In April the US had left the gold standard; the dollar depreciated. Cordell Hull, the US Secretary of State, displayed his obsession with tariffs: "everyone became weary of Hull's lengthy, rambling sermons ..." Then followed President Roosevelt's "bombshell" message of 3 July rejecting any thought of currency stability, with Chamberlain telling the Cabinet that same day that it was "couched in language which could not fail to give deep offence to almost every other delegate at the Conference" .[106]

While Britain had ruled the Ottawa agreements as outside the scope of the conference, the US objected to the trade agreement with Argentina. The US subsequently sought a trade agreement with Britain so as "to use what leverage they possessed to undermine the (Ottawa) system." This became a portent of the way the US "were to use their growing power in an attempt to … undermine the regional and imperial system Britain had built in the 1930s."[107]

Cordell Hull had an "awesome faculty for transmuting American interests into universal moral principles," describing the Ottawa agreements as "the greatest injury, in a commercial way, that has ever been inflicted on this country since I have been in public life." The State Department started its anti-Ottawa preparations in the summer of 1934 by setting up the British Empire Committee, with a twofold strategy: to make agreements with the separate Dominions and pursue bilateral negotiations with the UK. So the US delayed a trade treaty with Canada until after the 1935 elections, calculating accurately that they would get more from a victorious Mackenzie King than from Bennett, the defeated Prime Minister (in fact, the Ottawa agreements limited Canada's freedom of manoeuvre). Hull intensified his pressure on Britain in 1936, encouraged by Sir Robert Lindsay, the British ambassador. Rooth sums up the realities: "Hull's remonstrations might have led to nothing more than a rising tide of resentment in Whitehall if the deteriorating European situation had not created a second set of forces that pushed the British government towards *rapprochement* with the US." Lindsay was backed by Eden, then Foreign Secretary, who wanted the goodwill of the US government and public opinion in the event of a major crisis in Europe.[108]

Long haggling took place during 1937 and 1938 over maize, timber, and tobacco, with Britain wanting to safeguard the Rhodesian trade in the latter. The Foreign Office wanted agreement, but "there was pressure for a strong stand" in Cabinet, by Oliver Stanley, Runciman's successor at the Board of Trade, and Simon, former Chancellor and Foreign Secretary, who declared "it was impossible to say that the treaty, as it now stood, was one which on balance would be approved by the commercial community."[109] Eventually Hull "grudgingly" recommended the agreement to Roosevelt telling Joseph Kennedy, the new US ambassador in London, that "the present offers represent the ultimate limit to which the British are prepared to go …"

So these trade agreements between Britain, the US and Canada were signed in Washington on 17 November 1938. Britain participated with "extreme reluctance", with "huge doubts … harboured about the whole enterprise". There was no British Cabinet minister at the signing, and a Foreign Office official commented that the agreement was "highly unsatisfactory from the point of view of our foreign trade and our inter-imperial commercial relations." The American tariff barriers even when reduced remained high, giving the US an enormous trade surplus with Britain, while "British protection stood virtually intact at the end of 1938."[110]

A theme in the Epilogue will be the further American pursuit of this policy in wartime.

FOOTNOTES

1 R. J. Q. Adams, *Bonar Law,* pp276, 278.

2 Barnett, *The Collapse of British Power,* p269.

3 Forrest Capie, *Depression and Protection: Britain Between the Wars,* p41. By contrast, in 1921 India obtained fiscal autonomy. Through protection cotton, iron and steel, paper and sugar industries flourished. With the cotton tariff raised to 25% in the early 1930s, by 1939 India was 86% self sufficient in cotton goods. Only 4% came from Lancashire.

4 Andrew Marrison, *British Business and Protection 1903-32*, p292.

5 Adams, op cit, pp288-93.

6 Adams, op cit, p321.

7 According to Mrs Baldwin's account ("Recollections of a Cabinet-Breaker's Wife" in Davidson papers), quoted Adams p324.

8 Adams, op cit, p328; Robert Self's LSE thesis, published as *Tories and Tariffs: The Conservative Party and the Politics of Tariff Reform 1922-32* by Garland Publishing Inc, pp24 and 35. Self describes his work as "a study of 'high politics': of the politicians who mattered ... the prominent few in close and continual interaction".

9 Amery diary, 20 October 1922, Barnes and Nicholson, op cit, I p307. M Kinnear, *The Fall of Lloyd George: The Political Crisis of 1922.*

10 Self, op cit, pp22n and 19. The far-fetched jibe about Amery (his mother was Jewish) is from Joan to Eddy Balfour, n d, quoted Self p19.

11 Amery diary, 30 August, op cit, p344.

12 Self (op cit, pp167-9) describes the evidence that Lloyd George, returning from America, was planning to adopt Tariff Reform, and this influenced the timing of the Plymouth speech. Hence Baldwin's remark "Dished the Goat, as otherwise he would have got the party with Austen and FE".

13 Neville Chamberlain diary, 10 October, cited Self, op cit, p87.

14 Amery diary, 14 October, op cit, p349. Alan Clarke in *The Tories: Conservatives and the Nation State 1922-97* states no election was necessary: the tariff measures necessary to deal with the worst structural unemployment could have been achieved by "extending the scope of the tariff mechanisms already in existence" pp40-1. Baldwin however might have regarded it as sharp practice.

15 Ibid, 22 October, p351.

16 Self, op cit, p99.

17 Baldwin speech, *Times*, 26 October 1923; Self, op cit, p100.

18 For Derby, Self, op cit, p104. Amery to Baldwin 5 November; Barnes and Nicholson p342.

19 Amery diary, 2 and 9 November, op cit, pp354-5. "Jix" is Joynson-Hicks. For Chamberlain, his diary 9 November, quoted Self, op cit, p107.

20 Letter to Neville Chamberlain, quoted Self, op cit, p181.

21 Self, op cit, p207.

22 T. Jones *Whitehall Diary*, 4 December, quoted Self, p227.

23 Cowling, op cit, p331. The Liberals won 43 of the 80 seats where agriculture employed more than 30% of the population. Michael Kinnear, *The British Voter,* pp43-4.

24 The quote is from the *Manchester Guardian* of 8 December, see Trevor Wilson, *The Downfall of the Liberal Party 1914-35,* pp259-60.

25 Self, op cit, p239; Amery to Baldwin 8 December; Younger to Cecil 11 December, quoted ibid, p255.

26 Amery to Baldwin, 8 December 1923 quoted ibid, p263.

27 Amery diary, 18 December 1923, Barnes and Nicholson, op cit, p362.

28 Amery diary, 8 December 1923, op cit, p361.

29 Amery diary, 7 February 1924, op cit, pp367-9 and Self, op cit, pp304-6.

30 C. P. Scott diary, 18-20 Jan 1922 quoted Self, op cit, fn p323.

31 Amery diary, 6, 7, 8 and 14 March, op cit, pp372-3; Self, op cit, pp321-4.

32 Neville Chamberlain to Ida, 26 October; Chamberlain diary 1 December; Self, op cit, p385. This extraordinary episode is described by A. Clark, op cit, pp52-3 and as Appendix One the extracts from Chamberlain's diary for 5 and 6 November 1924.
33 Tim Rooth, *British Protectionism and the International Economy: Overseas Commercial Policy in the 1930s,* pp24, 41.
34 Robert Boyce, *British Capitalism at the Crossroads,* p91, pp138-9. Sir Otto Niemeyer was a senior Treasury, and later Bank of England, official.
35 Boyce, op cit, p118.
36 Self, op cit, p391.
37 "Austen ... queering the pitch badly by suggesting" £250,000: Amery diary 11 February 1926, op cit, p 442.
38 Amery diary, 28 November 1928, op cit, p573.
39 Changes in the pattern of landownership caused by the decline of prices towards the end of 19th century led to the formation of the National Farmers' Union, originally by tenant farmers, then shifting towards owner occupiers who controlled 11% of farmland in 1913, and over 33% in 1927. NFU membership rose from 21,000 in 1914 to 120,000 by 1929. Boyce, op cit, p11.
40 Rooth, op cit, p43, Self, op cit, p413.
41 Boyce, op cit, p152.
42 Self, op cit, pp 415,418.
43 Rooth, op cit, p41.
44 Scott diary, 30 June-1 July and 13-4 November 1925 quoted Self, op cit, p435.
45 Amery diary, op cit, pp416, 420, 423.
46 Self, op cit, p450.
47 Ibid, p454.
48 Rooth, op cit, pp39-41; Marrison, op cit, p29.
49 Marrison, op cit, pp360-74.
50 Self, op cit, p459.
51 Amery diary, op cit, p543, expressing his regret at his decision both then and later.
52 Amery diary, 9 and 11 July, op cit, p554-5.
53 Neville Chamberlain to his sister, quoted by Self p465.
54 This narrative and quotes from Amery's diary, op cit, pp560-2.
55 Self, op cit, p467.
56 Amery diary, 24 September 1928, op cit, p563-4.
57 Chamberlain diary, 1 July 1927 quoted Self, op cit, p462.
58 Amery diary, 9 May 1929, op cit, p595.
59 Self, op cit, pp488, 493, 502.
60 Boyce, op cit, pp183-4. The Baldwin quote is in Thomas Jones *Whitehall Diary* II, for 8 March 1929.
61 Marrison, op cit, p396.
62 Boyce, op cit, p253; Philip Williamson, *National Crisis and National Government* pp68-9.
63 Rooth, op cit, p53-4, Boyce, op cit, pp264, 255.
64 Self, op cit, p520.
65 Quoted by P. Williamson, op cit, p126, from Headlam diary 20 Feb 1930.
66 P. Williamson, op cit, p128.
67 Quotes from narrative by Boyce, op cit, p273.
68 P. Williamson, op cit, p186; A Clark, op cit, pp98-9.
69 P. Williamson, op cit, p189.
70 Boyce, op cit, p250.
71 Boyce, op cit, pp321, 329.
72 Amery diary, op cit, I pp457, 477.

73 Op cit, II pp70, 162, 282, 414, 455, 554.
74 Quoted in P. Williamson, op cit, p251.
75 Middlemas and Barnes, *Baldwin*, pp628-9; P. Williamson, op cit, p342.
76 P. Williamson, op cit, p371.
77 Ibid, p389 fn.
78 Both the Russian revolution in 1917 and the German one a year later had started as naval mutinies! Sterling fell from par ($4.86) to around $3.85 at end of the week, and to $3.20 in December but swiftly recovered in early 1932.
79 Amery diary, 10 November, II p219. Key officials like Hankey and Tom Jones disliked his views.
80 Amery diary, op cit, II pp191-2, and footnote p191 for later holograph note to the entry for 15 August "I have often wondered since if I could have done anything to prevent the Coalition if I had returned at once. I think not."
81 Ibid, II pp195, 196, 199, 200, 202. Mosley had left the Labour party and formed the New party in March 1931.
82 Ibid, II, pp222-4.
83 P. Williamson, op cit, pp358, 476, 477; Amery diary, op cit, II pp217, 220, 221, 228.
84 Austen Chamberlain to his wife, 14 October, quoted P. Williamson, op cit, p451.
85 Rooth, op cit, p64.
86 Respectively quotes from an Elibank letter, an Austen Chamberlain letter, and a Neville letter all from Self, op cit, p690.
87 Self, op cit, p701.
88 Ian Drummond, *Imperial Economic Policy,* p171; Rooth, op cit, p71.
89 Barnes and Nicholson, op cit, II p232.
90 Drummond, op cit, pp193, 200, 217.
91 Rooth, op cit, p86.
92 This phrase was used by Chamberlain, Baldwin and Cunliffe-Lister, all quoted by Self, op cit, p722. With Chamberlain, Bennett "behaved ... like a pig", Chamberlain letter quoted ibid p723.
93 Rooth, op cit, pp90-4, 99.
94 Diary, 16 July, II p242, also p256.
95 Ibid, pp246, 249, 251.
96 Ibid, pp253-5. Hailsham and Chamberlain were 60 and 63 respectively in 1932.
97 Drummond, op cit, p284.
98 Dominion Office officials' exchange, 22 August 1932, quoted Rooth, op cit, p96.
99 Diary, 24 August 1932, op cit, p256.
100 L. S. Amery, *The Awakening,* pp65-6.
101 Drummond, op cit, pp286-8.
102 Letter 30 August, quoted Self, op cit, p739.
103 P. Williamson, op cit, p514.
104 Rooth, op cit, pp319, 321.
105 Diary 1 May 1933, op cit, p293; Rooth, op cit, p158. Also Barnes and Nicholson, op cit, pp263-4.
106 Rooth, op cit, pp165, 167, 171.
107 Ibid, pp321, 288.
108 Ibid, 284, 286, 290-1. The Hull quote is from Congressional hearings on the renewal of the trade agreements in 1940, quoted in R. Gardner, *Sterling – Dollar Diplomacy,* pp18-9.
109 Conclusions of Cabinet meeting of 19 October 1938, quoted Rooth p302.
110 Ibid, pp284, 306.

CHAPTER SEVEN

The Japanese Challenge

"We must at all costs avoid the simultaneous antagonism of Germany, Japan and Italy."

(Sir Maurice Hankey, 1935, quoted Paul Haggie *Britannia at Bay – The Defence of the British Empire against Japan 1931-41* p101.)

During the Thirties, British strategists took the view that the British Empire could fight Germany if needed, and possibly both Germany and Italy, but hardly a contest with Japan as well. One historian acknowledges that the British public and much of the international community had "an entirely inflated idea of the role that Britain had the capacity to play in the far eastern area."[1] As was to be seen in 1941-2, most people underestimated Japan's strength and skill. However, the Thirties saw considerable efforts to avoid Japan joining other potential enemies. In contrast to Nazi Germany, Japan's ruling group was more balanced between those favourable to, and those hostile to, Britain and the US. The militarists only began to achieve dominance by the late Thirties. The story of how we failed to avoid war with Japan is, however, complex.

New research has emerged on how sadly Britain was misled, particularly by the Italians. Count Dino Grandi, Italian ambassador in London, was helped by Sir Joseph Ball, Director of the Conservative Research Department and master of intelligence. Thus Grandi had privileged access to Chamberlain's office, constantly misled Chamberlain with hopes of peace and compromise, and helped to contrive the fall of Eden as Foreign Secretary in February 1938. Some time elapsed before Baldwin admitted to an "intelligence failure" over German rearmament "we were completely misled on that subject."[2]

With Japan, Britain's appeasement must sit with the fact that the Japanese military treated Chinese civilians and prisoners barbarously, just as they were equally foul after 1941 to Allied service prisoners and civilians. These factors were not high-profile before 1941, partly because there was no evidence of Japanese ill-treatment of prisoners during the Russo-Japanese war of 1904.

Non Renewal of the Anglo-Japanese Alliance and the Twenties

There were early tensions during and after the First World War. Some in Britain were critical of Japan's failure to play more of a part in the war against Germany. Japan was disappointed when her attempts to outlaw racial discrimination in the League of Nations covenant were defeated. In discussions over setting up a consortium to handle the future of China, including Japan's claim to a special position in Manchuria and Mongolia, Britain sided with the USA. Prince Ito remarked (August 1919) "we had anticipated that the US would oppose our claims … but it was a great shock that Britain, our ally, … went so far as to oppose us." Younger Japanese politicians became reluctant to accept the post war order.[3]

The US saw the Anglo-Japanese Alliance as "nothing more than a device to permit Japanese expansion in East Asia." While Canada supported the US, France and Holland wanted the Alliance renewed, as their Far Eastern possessions were almost defenceless; so too did the Southern Dominions. The British ambassador in Tokyo warned of resentment were it not renewed; Curzon echoed this. Initially the Cabinet decided to renew it, but for a shorter period than ten years, and to ask the US President to call a Pacific Conference ("a favourite British cure-all of miraculous efficacy."[4]) With a strongly pro-American delegation led by Balfour and including, as First Lord of the Admiralty, Lord Lee of Fareham, married to an American, in December 1921 the Washington Conference ("one of the major catastrophes of English history"[5]) agreed to replace the Alliance with a four power treaty (signed February 1922) between Britain, the USA, Japan and France.

The Japanese Government accepted this "calmly" with "resignation" but also "a great sense of loneliness also permeated the Japanese delegation." Sir Robert Craigie, later British ambassador in Tokyo, judged Japanese "face" to have been affected by the "unnecessarily formal and abrupt" procedure in terminating the Alliance. Japanese revisionists used this to arouse anti-British feeling in the late 1930s; they argued that Britain had thrown the Alliance away "like an old pair of shoes". The Japanese navy – traditionally pro British – was aggrieved. Prior to this Japan had relied heavily on Britain for naval technology; subsequently Germany began to take Britain's place.[6]

China aroused international concern, and Britain remained a prominent interventionist there. After virtually a century of chronic decline, the Ching dynasty fell in 1911 and the country became a republic. Republican status did not protect this vast country from the divisions, at times amounting to anarchy, which traditionally marked the fall of a dynasty. Inevitably, Japan wished to step into the vacuum. After the first president, General Yuan Shi-kai, died in 1916, northern China fell under the control of war lords, supported by Japan, whereas Chiang Kai-Shek's Kuomintang, in the south, was trying to re-unite the country, aided by substantial Soviet assistance and "anti-imperialist" (ie anti British) propaganda. Some Britons wanted to work with Japan when anti-British boycotting in the Shanghai-Hankow area intensified in 1925-6, while Japanese army leaders also wanted Anglo-Japanese co-operation. War Minister Ugaki noted in his diary (5 December 1926) "It now appears that Great Britain regrets the dissolution of the Alliance. It seems to me that they want to put [it] back together again …"[7]

The British Government asked Japan on 20 January 1927 to assist in protecting the foreign concessions in Shanghai, but the Japanese Foreign Minister Shidehara rejected the use of force to defend foreign interests. So Britain acted alone and sent an army of 13,000. The US also refused British requests for troops, though we see American and British gunboats shelling Chinese forces in March 1927. In May 1927

Japanese forces went to Shantung, partly to protect Japanese residents but also as part of joint action with Britain, a fact welcomed by the British Chief-of-Staff General George Milne and by Austen Chamberlain, the Foreign Secretary. A Japanese military memorandum stated (June 1927) "we must co-operate with Britain in dealing with Soviet Russia's aid to the Chinese revolutionary movement, and in the conduct of our policy in support of the moderate groups in China," while a Japanese diplomat argued that Japanese-British co-operation was possible because their interests in China were "identical, being purely of an economic nature."[8]

Professor Nish summed up the inter-war British position: "There continued to be advocates of a return to some sort of alliance, agreement or understanding with Japan in the 1920s and 1930s. But they were generally silenced by what was going on in China – and perhaps by the wagging finger of the United States in the background."[9] That should not surprise, but what should is that during the winter of 1928-9 US-British relations were frequently on the Cabinet agenda, with Churchill vigorously opposed to appeasement of the US over naval limitations. Apart from Churchill no one was prepared seriously to contemplate open conflict with the US, but Esme Howard, British ambassador in Washington, had to explain to Baldwin that such a war would mean at the very least US absorption of Canada and the West Indies, the break up of the Empire, soaring food prices and massive opposition from the British public. Churchill acknowledged "however foolish and disastrous such a war would be," adding cheekily that all that would happen "is that they would blow off steam in a few programmes of aggressive cruisers ... and we should find in a few years a strong reaction ... in the US against unnecessary expenditure and a *strong revival of Anglo-Japanese association*".[10]

Manchuria and Shanghai

There was no dissent in Japan about consolidating control over Manchuria; debate concerned degree and timing. The Minseito party, in power during most of the Twenties, favoured caution, wanting to keep on terms with Britain and the USA. The navy supported this, while the army wanted a more vigorous and inevitably unilateral policy. The latter view grew with economic deterioration after 1927 – an occupation of Manchuria had been narrowly averted in 1928. The Chinese nationalists there provoked intervention by infractions of Japanese treaty rights, and Japan subsequently claimed she was trying to protect the province from Soviet encroachment. In 1929 the Red Army, by launching a land and air assault on a Chinese war lord in Manchuria, showed it was far stronger than had been imagined. As far as the British War office was concerned, Japanese aggression there did not threaten British interests but strengthened Japan's ability to contain Russia.[11]

In 1930 the Japanese Cabinet tried to reduce the army by four divisions: the Prime Minister, Hamaguchi, was seriously wounded by a fanatic and died soon after. His loss, and that of Ugaki, the War Minister, through illness, contributed to the occupation of Mukden and South Manchuria in September 1931 and the extension of Japanese control over the whole province, which was set up in March 1932 as an independent state called Manchukuo. The army based in the Kwantung peninsula had acted in defiance of the Cabinet.

On 7 January 1932 the US Secretary of State, Henry Stimson, told Japan that the US would not recognise this "new order." The US expected Britain's support, but Britain's Foreign Secretary, Sir John Simon, merely hoped that Japan would respect the principle of the "open door" for trade in Manchuria. Not only did President Hoover rule out sanctions, he was described by Stimson himself as being "opposed, in every fibre of his being, to any action which might lead to American intervention in the struggles of the Far East. In this view he had the support of the American people."[12]

Japan welcomed the British line on Manchuria, noting that Britain had few interests there, and recognising, at a Tokyo cabinet meeting on 27 August 1932, that Britain was mainly interested in Shanghai, the Yang-tse region and Southern China –"accordingly, it would be reasonable for Japan to pay due respect to the British position in those areas" in the hope and expectation that Britain would support Japan over Manchuria. This was proposed by Foreign Minister Uchida and endorsed by the Japanese Cabinet.[13]

Two developments disturbed this *modus vivendi*. First, the "Shanghai Incident", in early 1932, involved a further Japanese incursion, this time close to Britain's zone of interest. The Japanese did not help their cause by, for example, brutal dive-bombing. A ceasefire was achieved, largely by British initiative, in May 1932. While some Foreign Office officials feared Britain would need to stand up to Japan "there is little evidence in the British records of positive friendship ... or sympathy for the Chinese nationalists ... resentment at Chinese boycotts in the 1920s seems to have bitten very deep into the British subconscious."[14]

The second development was the intervention of the League of Nations. Simon persuaded the League to send out a Commission of Inquiry under Lord Lytton. The Lytton Report, published that October, was critical of the Chinese for their subversive activities, but also critical of Japan's action, and recommended the restoration of Chinese sovereignty. Sir Frank Lindley, British ambassador in Tokyo " had urged ever since the Shanghai fighting that Britain should retain the goodwill of Japan and that this was of far greater account than 'a handful of Chinese politicians who are here today and gone tomorrow.' " But as Simon told the Cabinet, Britain had a duty to the League, though he added "we must not involve ourselves in trouble with Japan." Oswyn Murray, the Admiralty Secretary, also thought it wiser to keep on good terms with Japan, arguing whether "a China consolidated on anti-Communist lines under Japanese control might not be preferable to an anarchic and Communist-penetrated China."[15]

The Report was discussed by a special League Assembly in December 1932. Simon showed his anxiety to keep Japan in the League and to avoid isolating her. Professor Nish states: "My conclusion is that Britain – and with her the Empire –

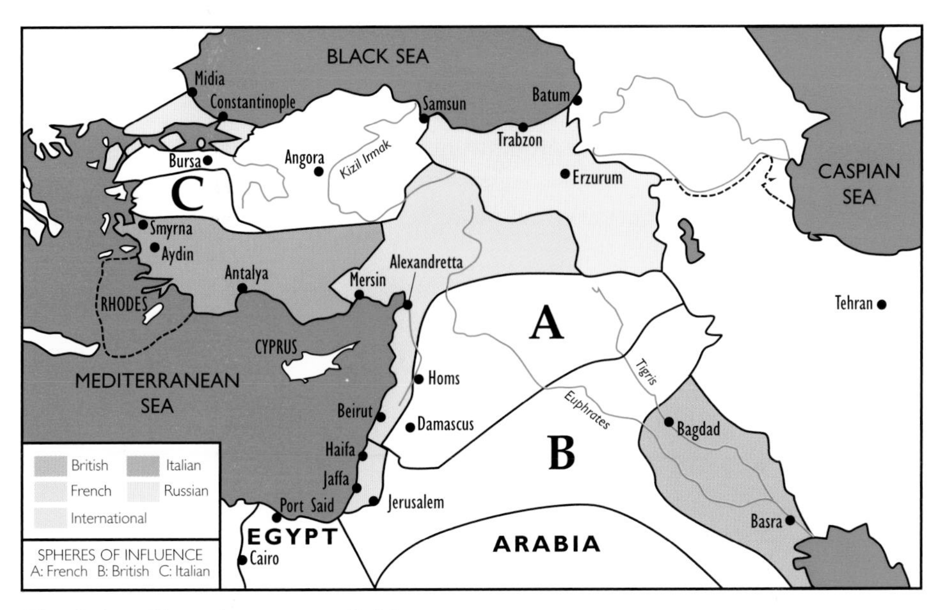

The Sykes-Picot Agreement 1916

Sir Mark Sykes

Dr Chaim Weizmann

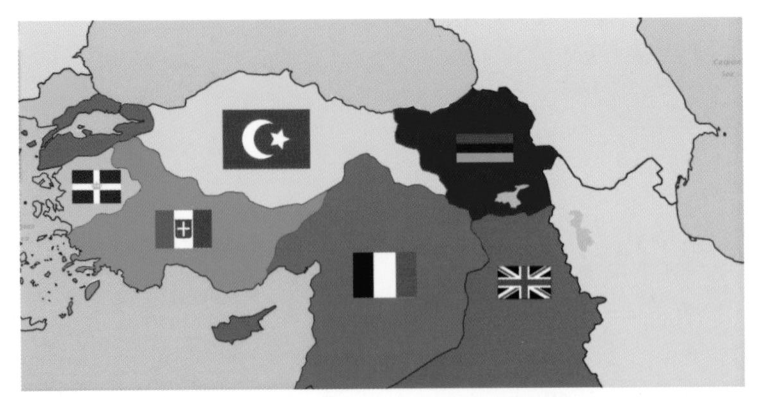

Turkey partitioned by the Treaty of Sèvres 1920

Persia

Talaat Pasha

Left: Enver Pasha

Aubrey Herbert

Count Mensdorff

Stanley Baldwin

Sir Herbert Samuel

Dr Theodore Herzl

Sir John Simon

Stanley Bruce of Australia

Ramsay MacDonald

Philip Snowden

Richard Bennett of Canada

U.S.S.R.
Inner Mongolia
Sea of Japan
KOREA (JAPAN)
JAPAN
East China Sea
PACIFIC OCEAN
TAIWAN (JAPAN)
Hong Kong (U.K.)
PHILIPPINES
INDOCHINA
South China Sea

Top left: Neville Chamberlain

Top right: Sir Warren Fisher

Left: Chinese territory occupied by Japan December 1941

Opposite page: The Western Pacific, showing the extent of the Japanese mandate

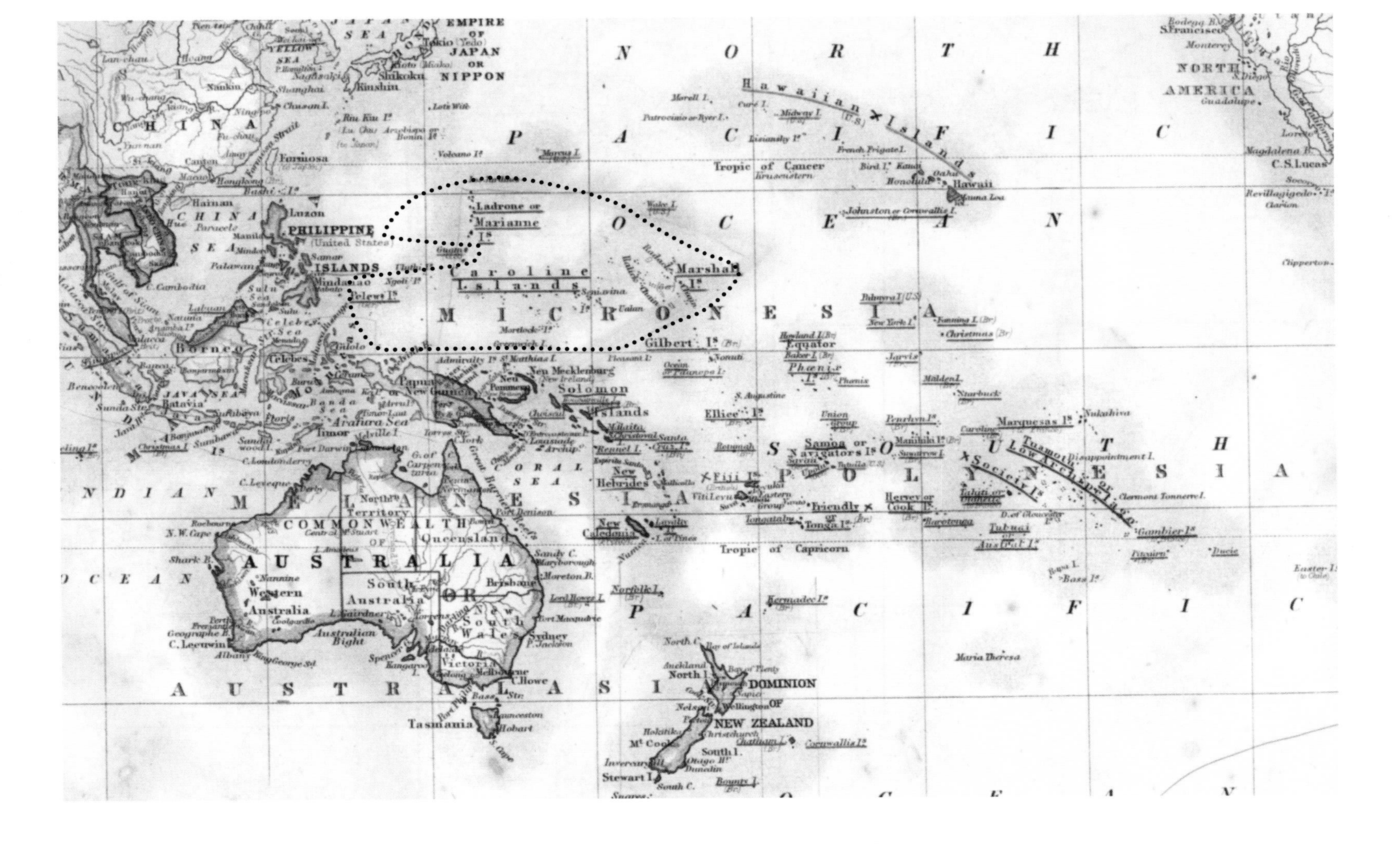

NORTH PACIFIC OCEAN
EMPIRE OF JAPAN OR NIPPON
CHINA
CHINA SEA
PHILIPPINE ISLANDS
(United States)
Formosa
Luzon
Mindanao
Borneo
Celebes
Java Sea
Timor
Arafura Sea
Papua or New Guinea
Ladrone or Marianne Is
Caroline Islands
Marshall Is
MICRONESIA
Gilbert Is
Solomon Islands
Hawaiian Islands
Hawaii
Honolulu
Tropic of Cancer
NORTH AMERICA
S. Francisco
Ellice Is
Samoa or Navigators Is
Fiji Is
New Hebrides
New Caledonia
Friendly
Tonga Is
Society Is
Marquesas Is
Low Archipelago
Gambier Is
POLYNESIA
MELANESIA
Tropic of Capricorn
CORAL SEA
COMMONWEALTH OF AUSTRALIA
Northern Territory
Queensland
Western Australia
South Australia
New South Wales
Victoria
Tasmania
Sydney
Brisbane
Melbourne
Hobart
Australian Bight
DOMINION OF NEW ZEALAND
North I.
South I.
Wellington
Auckland
Stewart I.
INDIAN OCEAN
AUSTRALASIA
PACIFIC

Hirota Koki

Yoshida Shigeru

Ernest Bevin

Sir Anthony Eden

went to tremendous pains to work out through private manoeuvrings and official committees some settlement with Japan in a spirit of compromise." Despite all this, on 24 February 1933 the Assembly voted: 42 members for the report, Japan alone opposing it. After that, as Nish adds, "there was no move to approach, persuade, cajole Japan to stay within the League".[16] So in March 1933 Japan left the League, blaming Britain for this mess because Lytton was British: "whatever Simon's equivocations", Britain had exercised the leading role in the League's handling of the matter.[17]

Manchuria became an issue in British politics. The Conservative Right and the right-wing press supported Japan. Leo Amery in the Commons pointed to Japan's "very powerful case based upon fundamental realities," including what Japan spent to defend Manchuria from Russia in 1904-5 and her subsequently defending the railway system from Chinese guerrilla attacks. "Our whole policy in India [and] Egypt stands condemned if we condemn Japan."[18] Amery reported a conversation with Eyres-Monsell, First Lord of the Admiralty, who said that the Liberals in the Government were hostile to Japan "but when he had convinced them that in case of trouble Japan could clear the sea of us all the way to Aden they toned down."[19]

Britain's Defence Dilemma; the 1933-5 discussions

The 1922 Washington Treaty prescribed a ratio in capital ships of 5:5:3 between Britain, the US and Japan, to apply across the globe, whereas Japan's foreseeable interest lay only in the Western Pacific; equally, while the US's interest was larger, it was not then global. Britain agreed not to build or fortify a base east of Singapore and the US agreed not to fortify the Philippines or Guam: the price for Japan agreeing to an inferior naval ratio. To allay anxieties arising from the ending of the Anglo-Japanese Alliance, a committee chaired by Churchill in 1922 recommended a fortified base at Singapore. Progress was typical of the "locust years", with work suspended by Labour in 1924 and 1929. There were further delays in 1928 and doubts whether to continue work on Singapore at all. An inspection remarked on the "deplorable" state of the defences there.[20]

The essential complement to a strongly fortified base was an effective battle fleet. But the tonnage of the British fleet had almost halved since 1914, while those of the US and Japanese fleets had greatly increased. After 1931 it was expected that Japan would reject naval limitation in the Pacific when the time to renew the Treaty came in 1935. Britain had 15 capital ships, 12 dating from 1915-7; three of these would be continually absent for large-scale repairs. With the size of the Japanese air force rapidly approaching that of the major powers, at the end of 1934 it was decided that Singapore on completion – which did not occur until 1938- should be kept on a care and maintenance basis, "capable of functioning fully in six months from an emergency occurring."

This ended Admiralty plans to station heavy naval units at Singapore in time of peace. Planners were warned that Britain could not rely on receiving accurate or timely intelligence of the collection, despatch and movements of Japanese military expeditions or of Japan's main fleet, judging from the experiences of 1931-2.[21] Singapore was 2500 miles from Japan, but Britain's nearest naval base, in the Mediterranean, was 6000 miles away. And Britain's cruiser forces – vital for an extended maritime campaign – had been "unwisely" limited to 50, 20 fewer than deemed essential, because of Ramsay MacDonald's wish to conciliate the USA.

In March 1934 a revealing conversation took place between Admiral Sir Frederick Dreyer, C-in-C China station, and the Commander of the US Asiatic Fleet, Admiral F. B. Upham. The latter talked of American withdrawal from the Philippines; he did not think the US needed a fleet in China waters, and it was awkward having Japanese mandated islands on his flank, making his ships very vulnerable to air attack. It was better for US to get out "before they were kicked out". Upham implied that it was Britain's responsibility to police the Far East; to Dreyer saying that the Dutch were worried about the Indies, Upham riposted "oh, the British will look after them".[22]

However, the policy-makers in London had to face financial and political realities. The Conservatives lost East Fulham, in a by-election in October 1933, on an enormous swing, over the disarmament issue championed by the victorious Labour candidate; 1935 was to see the "Peace Ballot". Sir Robert Vansittart at the Foreign Office argued that Britain should guard against all risks but "it would cost too much money and far too many votes."[23]

In November 1933, as the CID was discussing its report on the annual review by the chiefs of staff, Neville Chamberlain tried to remove certain powers from the potential enemies list; he wanted Japan to be added to France, the US, and Italy. Britain, he said, had received no adequate compensation for the termination of the Anglo-Japanese Alliance and her position in the Far East had been rendered more precarious without it. Within the cabinet Thomas, the Dominions Secretary, Hoare the India Secretary and others were "bemoaning the loss of the Anglo-Japanese Alliance." At the Defence Requirements Committee, Chamberlain argued that there was "... much to be said for the view that our subservience to the United States in past years has been one of the principal factors in the deterioration of our former good relations with Japan and that, before the naval disarmament conference in 1935, we ought thoroughly to reconsider our attitude."[24] He was thinking of a bilateral pact with Japan, possibly an agreement over spheres of influence in China, which would recognise Japan's position in the north but secure Britain's in the south. Importantly, he saw this as a means of limiting defence spending, aware that excessive spending away from the shores of Britain might both jeopardise economic recovery and lose votes.

In papers put to this Committee in January and February 1934, Sir Warren Fisher, Permanent Secretary to the Treasury, assumed that Germany was "the supreme ultimate national risk" (the phrase "ultimate potential enemy" was also used) and argued against the danger of a two front war. "It is an imperative and pressing need for us to effect a genuine and lasting reconcilation with her [Japan]. And this latter we cannot do by futile insistence that we won't permit her to have such naval weapons and in such quantities as she may think necessary", thus he did not want Britain to align with the US against Japan at the Naval Conference. It was vital to remove the impression that the British were "morally spineless sychophants of the USA" which had "bamboozled" Britain into renouncing the "invaluable asset " of the Anglo-Japanese Alliance. It was necessary to dispel Japan's impression of the British as "servile adherents" of the US. The USA regarded Asia "as an excellent object of exploitation by themselves, and view Japan as a serious impediment"; it would suit the US if Britain got "embroiled with Japan". An accomodation with Japan would be less urgent if US support were forthcoming but that was "the very last thing in the world" which could be counted upon. The end objective was to make Germany realise that "we intend to have available for immediate concentration our maximum force in the event of their engineering any future cataclysm in Europe."[25]

At Cabinet on 14 March Chamberlain's desire for a rapprochement with Japan was supported by Simon, Hoare, Lord Sankey, the Lord Chancellor and Eyres-Monsell, First Lord, who thought it would make the naval conference easier. Thomas thought Australia and New Zealand would favour it but warned of opposition in Canada. MacDonald feared any pact would be seen in the US as an alliance, while the Foreign Office argued the bad effect on Russia and China and the offence to the League of Nations Union with its 1 million members. On the 19th Simon presented the Cabinet with a document on Anglo-Japanese relations which was less encouraging than the tone of the meeting on the 14th, listing more disadvantages than advantages (obviously, the Foreign Office had got at it). "An Anglo-Japanese understanding, raising the prestige of the power universally regarded as America's principal enemy [sic], would obviously 'come as a shock to the Government and people of the United States'. "[26]

What, however, was the USA prepared to offer? A Foreign Office naval expert wrote (17 April 1934) of a "tendency on the part of the Americans to get us to pull the chestnuts out of the fire for them in connection with this question of the Japanese ratio.This our people are not in the least disposed to do ..." Chamberlain remarked on 28 July "we ought to know by this time that the USA will give us no undertaking to resist by force any action by Japan short of an attack on Hawaii or Honolulu. She will give us plenty of assurances of goodwill especially if we will promise to do all the fighting but the moment she is asked to contribute something she invariably takes refuge behind Congress." Vansittart summed it up characteristically: "The US are mostly futile or disloyal" over co-operation, adding "we have Germany to consider as well. The Americans haven't". And Chamberlain told his sister Hilda in 1937, it was "always best and safest to count on *nothing* from the Americans but words."[27]

Dodd, the US ambassador in Germany told Phipps, his British counterpart, that Roosevelt was inclined to make closer working with Britain in Europe "contingent upon greater co-operation with the USA in the Far East." Vansittart remarked: "As to co-operation with the USA in the Far East I hope we shall be very careful, almost obstinate in fact. I know what the USA mean by that – they want *us* to get in wrong with the Japanese instead of them. They would let us down at every turn."[28]

The debate over relations with Japan was paralleled by one over which of the Services should receive budgetary priority if and when rearmament started, and this had important implications for Britain's military performance in 1939-41. Apart possibly from Japan, Britain was the only power after 1918 under pressure to be strong in all three Services. In addition to traditional reliance on the Navy, she knew that the war had been won on land in 1918 by an unprecedented military effort, and that the air was becoming increasingly vital; hence Baldwin's grossly pessimistic statement, reflecting contemporary orthodoxy, that "the bomber will always get through".[29] As Chancellor and then Premier, Chamberlain took the view that the public would more readily accept preparations against possible aggression from Germany than preparations against Japan. So he wanted to increase air forces, especially those based at home, but curb Naval and Army spending. While Fisher argued that adequate land forces should be maintained to secure the Low Countries, Chamberlain doubted whether Britain could despatch forces to Europe fast enough (his view did not change until after Munich in 1938). Resources should be concentrated on the Air Force, he said, while the Army might find itself assisting Belgium while the French were "sitting contentedly in their own perfect defences". While this was an ironic commentary on what actually happened in May 1940, few could have predicted it in 1934.[30]

On 4 and 15 May 1934 the case for upgrading the air programme was led by Chamberlain. It encountered significant opposition. Harding, the Permanent Under-Secretary at the Dominions Office, criticised to Hankey (21 June) Chamberlain's emphasis on Germany rather than the Far East: "the whole weight of expert opinion … realises full well that the Achilles heel of the British Empire is the Far East". Chamberlain was "juggling with the whole security of Hong Kong, Singapore, India and even, conceivably, South Africa" in order to make a show against Germany. In Europe, he said, Britain would have allies; it was doubtful whether she would have any in the Far East. Hankey supported a strong Navy and a major role in the Far East. He sent a memorandum to MacDonald, copied to Baldwin. Singapore was more valuable with a strong Navy to defend it, and Hankey warned against Fisher who had "never been sound about the Navy or understood the defence question in the Pacific".[31]

At the Committee on 5 June, Eyres-Monsell for the Admiralty said Japan was in a truculent mood – "a sort of Elizabethan period of expansion". At meetings in July, principally on the 24th, Chamberlain said Britain could not afford the expenditure involved in fighting both Germany and Japan. Monsell, with singularly misguided predictions, said "Germany was unlikely to be a menace for some time. She might ... never be a menace at all ... The danger from Japan was an hourly danger; a danger which was always present ... It must surely be wrong to abandon our sea power and to create at the same time what would merely be a municipal Air Force [sic]." Eden gave Monsell his backing, deploring Japan's arrogance; she represented "the greatest menace at present ... (it was) impossible to know where her madness might lead."[32]

There was an important outcome of these debates on defence priorities during the Thirties. "Contrary to Churchillian mythology, Chamberlain must be credited with having established within only 18 months of Hitler coming to power the foundations of aerial rearmament against the Third Reich." This was despite the Air Ministry doubting whether Germany could present a serious risk before 1942: they would have preferred expansion over 20 rather than 5 years! Where Chamberlain was at fault was curbing expenditure on the Army. Public opinion, he believed, was influenced by memories of 1914-8.[33] By December 1937 the Army was placed last in order of commitments after air defence, trade protection and overseas security. Between 1936 and 1939 Palestine held more troops than were available for Europe. Nothing was done to bolster French resolve until the staff talks of April 1939, and this neglect was to have dire consequences in 1940, when the collapse of France proved almost fatal to Britain, as well as leaving Indo-China open to Japanese occupation.

Seeking a *Modus Vivendi* 1933-35

China was decisive in preventing harmony between Japan and the USA. China attracted some 6% of total British investment overseas, in contrast to only 1% for the US; Asiatic trade was then of little importance to the US economy and the US had larger total investments in Japan. Naturally, there was US concern at possible Japanese threats to supplies of rubber and tin from Malaya and the Dutch East Indies. "But much of America's concern for East Asia sprang from confused moralising rather than a hard-headed assessment of US interests", and the US saw itself as having a special protective role in China. In the Thirties this became a major obstacle to any Anglo-Japanese *rapprochement*.[34]

Much depended on the advice from the diplomats on the ground. The ambassador in Tokyo until 1934 was Sir Francis Lindley; the pro-Japanese tone of his despatches during the Manchurian crisis had been criticised in Whitehall. He was succeeded by Sir Robert Clive, but both relied on George Sansom, the commercial counsellor, whose views were regarded as those of a man "labouring under a sense of grievance against Japan."[35] Clive's successor, Sir Robert Craigie, was even more pro-Japanese, while the emissaries in Nanking took a pro-China view.

The hopes of a diplomatic breakthough coinicided with the appointment in 1933 of Hirota Koki as Japanese Foreign Minister.[36] To Simon's message of goodwill to him, Hirota's reply referred to the "disastrous blunder" of abrogating the

Anglo-Japanese Alliance. At a ministerial meeting on 16 April 1934, Chamberlain argued that there was "room for both the Japanese and ourselves." What China needed was development: "Can we not leave you free to supply capital in one area while we are free in another?"[37]

"The notion that warlords in North China could be induced to oppose Chiang (Kai-Shek) and support Manchukuo had blossomed among local Japanese army commanders ...," and this led in 1932-3 to the occupation of parts of Inner Mongolia. Through the Hopei-Chahar Provincial Council, Japan sought to separate from Nanking the provinces of Hopei, Chahar, Shansi, Suiyuan and Shantung. The warlords did not want Chiang's rule in their domains and collaborated with Japan.[38] The nature of the divided opinions is shown by a report from Peking in spring 1934 that 30% of Chinese political leaders were in favour of rapprochement with Japan, 50% apathetic and 20% relentlessly opposed.

Some Japanese leaders were afraid that reconstruction would enable China better to resist. This was illustrated by the controversial "Amau statement" by a senior Japanese diplomat in April 1934. Japan, he stated, had a special mission to maintain order in East Asia and oppose foreign interference in China. Britain, however, argued for the principle of equal rights; Lancashire and Midlands MPs were hostile to any suggestion that Japan was claiming the Chinese market. Hirota tried to reassure Lindley that he did not approve of the Amau statement; the Japanese ambassador in London told the British that it was a bad blunder, and other senior Japanese criticised it. But the later publication of Japanese documents makes it clear that Amau was taken "almost verbatim" from a Hirota instruction to the Japanese legation at Nanking.

Sir Robert Clive, the new ambassador, reported Hirota telling him that Japan was ready to sign non-aggression pacts with Britain and the US. Simon favoured this idea but wondered what would Japan want in return. The recognition of Manchukuo might be acceptable, but granting a free hand in China was more difficult. Ann Trotter sums up the view of the far eastern section of the Foreign Office: "any non-aggression pact that Britain might be prepared to conclude with Japan would fail to satisfy her, while the type of pact that Japan would like would be too dangerous for Britain to accept".[39]

During his August 1934 holiday in Perthshire Chamberlain encouraged Simon to appreciate the "special distinction" of a "Simon-Hirota pact". Meanwhile Simon's Foreign Office worked up its objections; a pact might encourage Japan to attack Russia, which the officials saw acting as a restraint on Germany. Eventually Simon decided to pursue the Hirota-Clive conversation. While Hirota "implied" that Japanese proposals, that is, naval parity with the British and US fleets, might be acceptable to Britain but not to the US, Britain recognised that Japan's denunciation of the 1922 Washington Five Power Treaty was inevitable. The Japanese navy "genuinely feared that Japan was vulnerable to an attack by the United States." Talks continued and then Japan gave formal notice of termination on 29

December 1934. Britain, for her part, "had no wish to accept the Japanese rejection as final and continued to discuss ways of 'keeping Japan in the ring'."[40]

The FBI and Leith-Ross Missions and the Yoshida Episode 1934-6

The next initiative lay with British industry: on behalf of the Federation of British Industries (FBI), Lord Barnby, FBI president in 1925-6, and briefly MP for a Bradford seat, in the autumn of 1934 headed a group to visit Japan and Manchukuo. It consisted of Guy Locock, former diplomat and since 1932 Director of the FBI, Sir Charles Seligman, director of Seligman Bros, bankers, and Julian Piggott representing the Iron and Steel Federation. The Japanese organised an audience with the Emperor. The mission paid an eight-day visit to Manchukuo where there were some suggestions for British investment in railways, implying a first step to recognition. The International Trade Bureau of the Japanese Foreign Ministry wanted to open the Manchukuo market to Britain, but the army opposed this.[41]

The mission reported back in Britain in December, expressing a fear that British exporters might lose the Manchukuo market because of non-recognition: the British share of trade there had increased by 50% during 1933. It had high hopes of a "substantial scale" of business including a big trade deal over steel with Mitsubishi, but nothing came of this. As the Foreign Office predicted, once it was clear that no political concessions were forthcoming, the mission was left "like some Western Madame Butterfly waiting ... at its Midland lattice for the Japanese Pinkerton." Locock wrote to Horace Wilson, the chief industrial adviser to the Government, that "a very small advance on our part would have a great effect."[42]

While the Foreign Office and the Treasury circulated to ministers papers with opposed views, the Board of Trade circulated Locock's letter to Wilson, with a covering note by its President, Runciman, stating that the mission "believe that ... Japan desires an understanding with us ... which might begin with co-operation as regards China." Locock's letter claimed that Sino-Japanese relations would improve from an Anglo-Japanese understanding, as Japan was disturbed by her isolation. To this Sansom quoted Sir Frederick Whyte, political adviser to the Kuomintang Government from 1929-32: "When I hear British businessmen in Shanghai say 'if we back Japan she will pull the chestnuts out of the fire for us', my only answer is that when the operation is complete there will be no British chestnuts left". And the Foreign Office memorandum was dismissed by Warren Fisher as "a revised version of the Book of Lamentations". The Treasury view was "if we refuse to consult and cooperate with Japan (bringing in America, of course) and China sinks into economic chaos, an isolated Japan may take military measures there," with consequences for Britain's trading interests.[43]

Next, in 1935-6, followed a mission by Sir Frederick Leith-Ross, chief economic adviser to the British Government from 1932 to 1945. Described as "essentially the brain child of the Treasury," the idea was that Britain and Japan would grant a joint loan to Manchukuo, with the Government of Manchukuo paying it to China as indemnity for the loss of the province, in return for Chinese recognition of Manchukuo. If the Leith-Ross approach had been in the form originally conceived by Chamberlain, with emphasis on reducing economic friction with Japan, and had not contained an insertion by the Foreign Office about the future of China, it was thought that the Japanese might have reacted more positively; the negative response by their Government has been criticised by some post-war Japanese historians.

On his way to Tokyo, Leith-Ross composed grand ideas of a peace treaty between China, Japan and Manchukuo, with each undertaking not to intervene in the others' political admininistration. He knew many in the government circles in Tokyo, but the Vice-Minister of Finance did not believe China would recognise Manchukuo until the great powers had done so. And public opinion in Japan might not think recognition of Manchukuo was worth paying money for. The Japanese response uses words like "doubtful" and "unconvinced", while expressing good will. In China Ross found a conviction that public opinion would not tolerate recognition of Manchukuo. By the end of 1935 his mission was deadlocked in China, while the Foreign Office was embroiled in Abyssinia; Vansittart told Ross to drop the idea of Nanking recognising Manchukuo which would "cut no ice" and lead into "deep waters".[44]

The Japanese army was suspicious of the government's policy of Sino-Japanese reconciliation and claimed that the Chinese had made several violations of the truce in the North. It threatened to extend the demilitarised zone to include Peking and Tientsin. And it was concerned about Soviet subversion, with the Comintern congress in summer 1935 designating Japan, along with Germany and Poland, as the main targets of subversion, and the Soviet army openly boasting of its ability to fight on eastern and western fronts. Clashes were taking place along the Soviet border with Manchukuo. 1934-5 also saw the "Long March" of Chinese Communist units from South-East China, where they were facing annihilation by Chiang Kai-Shek, to Yenan in Shensi, where they could obtain Soviet supplies through Mongolia. There, they built up strength and advocated a united front with the Kuomintang against Japan.

Japan tried to create an anti-Communist zone, promoting in 1936 a "Mongolia for the Mongolians" campaign. Longer term, the army regarded war with the Soviet Union as inevitable, and made plans to move on Vladivostok and Ulan Bator in Outer Mongolia. Meanwhile, in September 1935 the Japanese Ministers of Foreign Affairs, War and Marine agreed on political and economic co-operation between Japan, China and Manchukuo, joint defence against sovietisation and complete suppression of all anti-Japanese and anti-Manchukuo activities.[45]

Hirota told Clive that, in the absence of agreement on naval matters, Japan would be ready to conclude non-aggression pacts with America and Britain.[46] Simon warned that this would be opposed by the US, Chinese, Russians and Dutch, but Chamberlain wanted to go ahead. Craigie, at the Foreign Office but soon to be appointed to the Tokyo embassy, asked Norman Davis, an American delegate, about a political understanding with Japan as a means of preventing her from breaking from the naval talks. Davis said he had found Roosevelt doubtful of the wisdom of this in view of Japan's attitude to China. Craigie made a similar suggestion to William Phillips, US Under-Secretary of State, who "made it clear that there could be no question of the US doing anything which would look as if China was being abandoned to her fate." Joseph Grew (the US ambassador in Tokyo) told Clive that there was a possibility that the US would consider a political agreement, if this would make it easier for Japan to accept the existing naval ratio: "he said that the President, who had always been a big navy man, would never yield about the necessity for American naval superiority to Japan". The British ambassador in Washington was "not so sanguine" about all this; neither the Roosevelt administration nor US public opinion would tolerate anything "which would imply that Japan's actions had ceased to be condemned."[47] So the Japanese delegates withdrew from the London Naval Conference when it reassembled on 13 January 1936.

Hoare, appointed Foreign Secretary in June 1935, asked whether it might be possible to reach an agreement with Japan over spheres of influence in China, recognising Japan's position in the north but securing Britain's in the south. The Far Eastern department commented: "Co-operation of the kind which would be welcome to Japan would mean supporting her in a perfectly unscrupulous pursuit of exorbitant claims," and as Vansittart drily remarked " we shall get no consideration from Japan till we are stronger. It will then be less worthwhile to offend us."[48] Hoare was clearly attracted by this form of *realpolitik;* hence his attempt to partition Abyssinia with Italy, in agreement with his French counter-part Pierre Laval.

A parenthesis here is required about the Hoare-Laval episode, the failure of which made a settlement with Japan more essential. Italy was concerned about German threats to Austria and Mussolini had in January 1935 signed an agreement with France featuring Austria, the demilitarisation of the Franco-Italian frontier, where both parties had maintained large numbers of troops, and the future of Abyssinia. A similar agreement was planned for Britain, with Grandi the Italian ambassador in London proposing definition of economic spheres of influence in Abyssinia, together with (possibly) a naval agreement covering the Mediterranean. The British were dilatory, being confused by the demands of "collective security" and their compromise proposals were rejected in Rome, where Mussolini ordered the invasion of Abyssinia in October 1935. The League insisted on sanctions which Britain agreed to apply. First sanctions applied to armaments, loans and credits. After 6 November the League's Sanctions Committee endorsed an oil embargo. This made war with Italy more likely and the US refused to co-operate. "The Hoare-Laval Plan only became a reality when Roosevelt's government would not embargo oil."[49]

With the Italians facing unexpectedly hard Abyssinian resistance, it was thought they would welcome a partition agreement, which was negotiated by Vansittart. Under it, Italy would gain much of Ogaden and Tigre, with economic influence over southern Abyssinia, leaving Abyssinia with its historic heartland and a guaranteed but narrow corridor to the sea. Before it could be presented to Mussolini (and there is, of course, the doubt whether he would agree, or keep to anything promised), the Pact collapsed in mid December 1935, following a press leak in Paris and a public outcry, led by bishops in Britain and the Left in France. After inept handling, intensified by illness, Hoare resigned on 18 December as Foreign Secretary. A. J. P. Taylor argued that it "was a perfectly sensible plan" which would have "ended the war; satisfied Italy, and left Abyssinia with a more workable, national territory." Without the Pact, and with Eden, devoted to the League, as new Foreign Secretary, Britain was further enticed down the route of threatening an oil blockade on Italy. Barnett argued the obvious: alienated, Italy "would be a potential enemy astride England's main line of imperial communication."[50]

A new Japanese ambassador, Yoshida Shigeru, arrived in London in June 1936. He was attracted by British culture and his father-in-law was a leader of the pro-British group in Tokyo; Yoshida became Japan's first significant post-war Prime Minister from 1948-54. He encouraged the belief that moderation in Tokyo was increasing, and made an "obscure proposal" for co-operation in China, with Japan in charge of law and order and Britain in charge of irrigation and flood control! The Foreign Office saw this as displaying Japan's fear of isolation. Yoshida put to Chamberlain suggestions that he thought might lead to a definite understanding, including the "open door", and foreign rights and interests in China – British concerns – and the Japanese *desiderata*: financial and political aid to China, as suggested by Leith-Ross, checking the spread of Communism, and closer financial relations. If all this made progress, the naval conference might be revived. The Foreign Office claimed that Britain "could not afford to flout the moral sense of the British or American people or world opinion by appearing as an abettor in the spoliation of China by Japan".[51]

Clive in Tokyo was warned that Yoshida was "rather bold" and likely to put forward his own ideas. While Yoshida had influence with the immediate advisers of the Emperor, he was not popular with the army which had refused to accept him as a cabinet minister. Eden, as Foreign Secretary, discussed ideas with Yoshida, but argued that Britain could not accept obligations contrary to the covenant of the League or act against the interests of the US and China. This view should not surprise: Eden was close to Sir Alexander Cadogan, who had been minister to Peking in 1933, and ambassador there in 1934. Cadogan had witnessed the activities of the Japanese army in China "which made him distinctly sympathetic to the Chinese." He was recalled in early 1936 to become Joint Deputy Under-Secretary; he soon became Permanent Under-Secretary, with a key influence on policy towards Japan in 1936-8.[52]

It "proved impossible to penetrate the smokescreen of unexceptionable platitudes and find out whether Yoshida really had anything to offer."[53] The draft reply to Yoshida was extensively amended by Chamberlain and Leith-Ross, in the face of Foreign Office protests, and the result left scope for negotiation. However, Yoshida was described as finding it "embarrassing" – perhaps evidence that he had exceeded his instructions. Indeed, it was believed that he either did not dare tell his Government of the British reply or that he had already indicated that this would be more favourable than it was. The Foreign Office regarded him as "extremely tiresome" and "very crooked" and Clive dismissed as "nonsense" his claim that the document he sought from London would strengthen the chances of a more liberal government in Japan.[54] One historian suggests that Chamberlain had changed his stance since 1934, and failed to inject vigour into the Yoshida discussions.[55]

In early 1937, Japan's concern over war with Russia intensified and there were clashes along the Amur River in the summer. Hence hopes of *rapprochement* with the West survived: the new Prime Minister, Hayashi, told the Diet on 15 February 1937 that he had "no faith in a pugnacious foreign policy," while the new Foreign Minister, Sato, regarded as friendly to Britain and the US, criticised Japan's policy in Asia and hoped, in a speech in the House of Peers, that negotiations with China might be conducted on the basis of equality. Meanwhile, Australia thought London had "not been enthusiastic enough" in responding to Yoshida's overtures. Australian agriculture had obtained relief during the depression by exporting to Japan, and Sir John Latham (External Affairs Minister and Deputy Prime Minister), who had led a mission to east Asia, "described the chaotic conditions in China and argued that Japan gave at least some degree of security to those in Manchuria." While London took offence at Australia questioning British Government policy, Stanley Bruce, Australian High Commissioner in London from 1932-45 (previously Australian Prime Minister 1923-9), was critical of Foreign Office rigidity: "His views did not derive from sympathy for Japan but from concern for the security of Australia."[56] Bruce urged on Eden a proposal for a Pacific regional understanding and non-aggression pact to include Japan and the British Empire, and at the Imperial Conference in May 1937 the Australian Prime Minister, Lyons, obtained support from his fellow premiers for this. It ran into the sand when full war between Japan and China started.

War Between Japan and China 1936-8

Important changes were taking place in both China and Japan. During 1936 a national movement of opposition to Japan grew throughout China. In October a Japanese-trained "independent Mongolian army," attempting to occupy part of Inner Mongolia, was routed by the Chinese after a week-long battle at Palingmiao. Next month Chiang Kai-Shek broke off talks with the Japanese ambassador in China. Aiming to crush the Communists, on 7 December he flew to Sian in Shensi to launch the final onslaught. He was arrested by a local warlord who obliged him to abandon the fight against the Communists in favour of agreeing to a united front between the Kuomintang and the Communists against Japan. On this basis, Chiang was released on 25 December.

1936 also saw a change of direction in Japan though it was not unanimous and not known to Britain. A ministerial conference on 7 August 1936 approved the navy's aims for southward advance ("advance and development in the South Seas" and "securing footholds for the empire on the Asian continent"). Professor Hosoya quotes other sources which believed that war with China made a clash with Britain inevitable; one minister believed Britain and the US were "separable" ("it's inconceivable that the Americans would be willingly made a cat's-paw of the British.")[57] Perhaps less significant than it seems, on 25 November 1936 Japan joined the Anti-Comintern Pact with Germany and Italy, her aim being to secure the appearance of allies if relations with Britain and the USA worsened.

An indication of how Cordell Hull, US Secretary of State, viewed these matters came via a conversation he had with Lord Tweedsmuir (formerly John Buchan), Governor-General of Canada: "if the great democracies, led by Britain and America, would offer [Germany] help in getting her economic situation stable she could be detached from her ... alliance with Italy and Japan." This suggested that Hull, a fanatical internationalist, disliked most the countries which had affronted the League (which the USA had refused to join), rather than the sinister but then clever Hitler. It was assumed in the US that "appeasement in Europe would leave Japan morally and politically isolated, thus forcing Tokyo to conclude a just peace with China." Thus "appeasement would not only establish an Open Door order in Europe but would also prevent the construction of a Closed Door system in the Far East."[58]

One alarming factor operating in Japanese politics at this time was assassination. Between November 1930 and February 1936 nine highly placed politicians were assassinated, and there were a further four attempts where the victim was wounded or escaped. The most significant was 26 February 1936 coup attempt, in which two former prime ministers and three admirals were murdered. Most of the victims were moderates, opposed to aggressive military action. Despite the failure of the coup and the execution of the perpetrators, the February Incident had the effect of significantly increasing the military's influence over the civilian Government.[59] So when the selection of Hirota as Prime Minister was made and he began to assemble a Cabinet, General Terauchi, the new Minister of War, made clear his displeasure with some of the selections. Hirota gave into these demands and changed his appointments. The service chiefs could cause a Government to fall at their pleasure, as happened to Hirota himself in February 1937 when Terauchi resigned; his successor, Hayashi, fell at the end of May 1937 after army opposition to Foreign Minister Sato's conciliatory policy towards China.

Two conclusions by Ann Trotter give a rather pessimistic, but credible, view of the efforts to secure an Anglo-Japanese agreement. After referring to the increased political difficulties in Tokyo after February 1936, she states: "Hindsight ... suggests that, while there were men in Japan who were well disposed towards Britain and moderate in their political outlook, they were never capable of, or interested in, challenging the general trend of Japan's national policy." And, as for the British, they "felt that they were left with no alternative but to sustain the bluff and play for time."[60] It is difficult to disagree with these conclusions, and not easy to argue that a more positive approach by Britain before 1937 might have changed the course of events. The preservation of peace until the end of 1941 was itself an achievement, but the signs of a tragic conclusion steadily built up.

On 7-8 July 1937, Japanese and Chinese forces clashed at the Marco Polo Bridge, near Peking; Lee argues that this was not engineered by the Japanese army.[61] Escalation of the Marco Polo Bridge Incident was not inevitable, and a ceasefire and compromise were agreed on 11 July. Tokyo wanted a local agreement but Nanking refused to accept this – "it had become clear that Chiang Kai-Shek was determined to preserve what remained of his authority in Northern China."[62]

The aftermath was gradual but wretched. At Cabinet on 9 July, the Army Minister Sugiyama recommended that three divisions be sent to China: this was opposed by Foreign Minister Hirota and Navy Minister Yonai and did not pass. Over two weeks a decision to mobilise was reached and then cancelled three times: one thinks of Russia in July 1914. The final agreement to send three divisions was taken on 20 July, only after claims from the field army that Chinese forces had attacked. By the end of July the Japanese controlled Peking and Tientsin: they subsequently advanced across the North China plain. On 9 August two Japanese marines were shot dead in Shanghai by the Chinese. Fighting broke out, with both sides reinforcing this front. On 26 August the British ambassador in China, Sir Hughe Knatchbull-Hugessen, was seriously wounded when Japanese planes strafed his car on the road between Nanking and Shanghai.

On August 21 a Sino-Soviet mutual assistance agreement was signed, with the Russians sending ammunition, equipment, military advisers and planes to China. Important strategists on the Japanese General Staff, a moderate body, feared that further warfare in China would weaken their preparations to combat Russia; they wanted a diplomatic settlement. But mainland army commanders believed Nanking would be easy to take and this would destroy Chiang's will to resist. In October Chiang told the British that Japan's terms were not "worth serious consideration" – he wanted complete sovereignty in North China. So the Japanese stiffened their terms, calling for China to pay an indemnity.[63]

By the end of September, 15 Japanese divisions had been sent to China; the piecemeal approach contributed to heavy casualties on both sides during the long battle for Shanghai, stalemated for weeks. Frustrated by this ordeal, the Japanese troops received deliberate encouragement to commit atrocities from their generals and officers, hence the massacres of civilians and disarmed soldiers inflicted on their march towards Nanking and, more dramatically, in the "Rape" of Nanking when it fell in December. Anti-Japanese feeling was developing in Britain and anti-British feeling increased in Japan; in 1938-9 there were widespread anti-British demonstations in Japan. Craigie warned the Foreign Office of a "real and growing danger" in the "bitter hatred" towards Britain fuelled by "a compound of mysticism and nationalism."[64]

As Lee states "The shaping of the Chamberlain Government's response to the East Asian crisis was left to the permanent officials of the Foreign Office, who were sympathetic to the Chinese and quite unsympathetic to the Japanese". Eden, as Foreign Secretary from December 1935 to February 1938, was "if anything more 'anti-Japanese' than the Foreign Office staff". And while Chamberlain had wanted conciliation of Japan in 1934, by 1937 he "was no longer thinking seriously in those terms". His Government "gave surprisingly little sustained consideration during ... 1937-39 to a policy of appeasement in East Asia".[65]

Diplomatic exchanges continued. The civilians in Tokyo held to the hope that Britain might mediate towards peace in China. This featured in a discussion between vice-ministers in the Foreign, Army and Navy Ministries on 28 February 1938. At first they had wanted Germany to mediate but attempts in late 1937 had failed. Germany, both before and after Hitler's coming to power, had been a strong supporter of the Kuomintang; she had a profitable trade with China, and the Foreign Ministry, General Staff and business circles sympathised with China. Germany then moved closer to Japan, recognising Manchukuo in February 1938 and withdrawing military advisers from China in May.

Despite his Japanese sympathies, Craigie admits that the military extremists had sabotaged peace conversations with the Chinese after the Marco Polo Bridge conflict: "There was nothing official about these conversations but they did at least indicate to me that, had it not been for army intransigeance, a war which was to run into its ninth year could have been terminated in its fourth month."[66] The spring of 1938 saw a threat by the army to sidetrack Tokyo's Ministry of Foreign Affairs from any say in China; Hirota resisted this, but in May he preferred to resign as minister rather than accept further curtailment. Craigie "saw him go with genuine regret."

Bradford Lee has a slightly varying view. Konoye, the new Prime Minister, doubted the wisdom of Hirota's January 1938 statement that he would not deal with Chiang Kai-Shek, therefore removed Hirota, while Ugaki accepted this post on condition he could start peace talks with China; these were kept secret from the West. Ugaki was also to facilitate talks with Britain. Talks took place between Ugaki and Craigie between July and September 1938, with Craigie resisting demands for Britain to cease assistance to China. In face of the failures in the Chinese and British talks, the army forced Ugaki out in October. The hard-liners insisted on a China Affairs Board to run policy on China. In Craigie's view, this "ended the last determined attempt to curb the activities and policies of the Japanese military in China".[67] In December Konoye demanded that the Chinese recognise Manchukuo, allow Japanese troops to be stationed in inner Mongolia and other points and cooperate with Japan in trade; Chiang rejected all these.[68]

The Foreign Office believed the Japanese economy was weak and that she would be unable to defeat China; this was based in part on analyses from Sansom, who however reported in June 1938 that Japan was "not even partially exhausted". Meanwhile, the British resisted working with Soviet Russia to assist China. Stalin granted China credits in March and July 1938 amounting to US $100million; he had an estimated 250,000 troops and 870 aircraft east of Lake Baikal. In July fighting between the Soviets and the Japanese broke out at Changkufeng on the Manchukuoan-Soviet border, ending in a truce on 11 August after heavy Japanese casualties.[69]

Towards Pearl Harbour 1938-41

1939 saw the Japanese expanding in China, where their October 1938 offensive on Canton alarmed Hong Kong. They annexed Hainan island in February and the Spratly and Paracel islands (menacingly, between the Philippines and Indo-China) in March. Tokyo issued a statement "in the name of" Prime Minister Konoye on 3 November 1938 declaring Japan's resolve to build a new order in East Asia, designed to minimise Western and Communist influence in China and build a Pan-Asian movement under Japanese leadership.[70] In November 1938 British and Chinese interests agreed to build a railway from Burma to Yunnan; in December the Burma Road was completed. By the spring of 1939 approximately 1000 tons of supplies were going into China this way during the dry season.

Extraordinarily, frail hopes for amity remained alive. The Foreign Minister from 1936-39 was Arita – Craigie thought he wished to avoid a war with the West. Germany pressed Japan to join the Anti-Comintern Pact; Konoye was happy to join it as an anti-Soviet alliance but Berlin wanted it directed at all other powers. Konoye, Arita and the navy were firmly opposed to anything which threatened war with Britain or the US. Konoye resigned in January 1939 but his successor Hiranuma also demurred over this. Negotiations between the three powers dragged on; eventually Germany and Italy lost patience and signed the Pact of Steel in late May.

The chapter heading in Craigie's memoirs at this point was "Two Moderate Governments August 1939 to July 1940". Prime Minister Abe and the Foreign Minister Admiral Nomura "both impressed me with their desire to put matters on a better footing with Britain and the US."[71] In October 1939 the Abe Cabinet sent to Shanghai its "Guidelines" for peace which would have made North China an independent state and turned Hainan into a depot of the Japanese navy. Meanwhile, in the late summer of 1939 the US gave six months' notice to denounce the America-Japan treaty of Friendship and Commerce. The world of commerce was horrified but the US was incensed by the continual bombing of numerous religious missions marked with the US flag in China.

During the summer of 1939, a crisis over Japanese pursuit of Chinese fugitives into the British concession at Tientsin, which the Japanese then blockaded, "brought Britain and Japan nearer to conflict than at any previous time in the twentieth century." Whitehall was divided over how to respond and reluctant to let Craigie negotiate. However, during June-July Craigie skilfully negotiated with Arità a settlement in which "Britain gave greater recognition to the Japanese presence in China than she had given hitherto."[72]

Within the Tokyo War Ministry and the General Staff, opinion was divided in 1937-9 between expansionists and anti-expansionists. One of the "army heroes" of the original Manchurian occupation stated in 1938 that the real threat came from Soviet Russia, and that the Japanese should not become overextended in China. The Japanese were angered by Germany making the Molotov-Ribbentrop pact while Japan was engaged in hostilities with Russia ("one of the worst jolts ever suffered by Japanese diplomacy", as Craigie later wrote: a "wave of revulsion toward Germany swept Japan.")[73] The earlier clashes on the Soviet-Manchukuo border in 1938 had culminated in the Japanese defeat at Nomonhan in August 1939. This cost Japan around 20,000 casualties; her force was greatly outnumbered by the Russians in men and equipment, while Tokyo refused to reinforce or extend the fighting to a wider front.

When the Abe government fell in January 1940 it was succeeded by "one of the most homogeneous and best-balanced cabinets of recent times" headed by Admiral Yonai. It stated that its policy towards the European War – at that time in its "phoney" phase – was "non-involvement", and that "the Cabinet was opposed to that policy of adventure and armed aggression which the German government had so long been urging upon Japan." Craigie added "Had the European war taken a different course in 1940, I believe that a reaction against the extremes and follies of the last three or four years would have set in."[74]

With the fall of France the position hardened: in June 1940 the Yonai Cabinet fell after army pressure on 16 July. Konoye formed a further government: the moderates thought he alone could ride the storm, while the extremists "liked his totalitarian dilettantism."[75] While Konoye told Tojo, his War Minister and Matsuoka, his Foreign Minister, that he was opposed to a military alliance with the Axis, a new army-navy consensus agreed in conferences of 26-7 July 1940 that Japan should bring the China "incident" to a speedy conclusion and then expand to the south. Meanwhile stalemate continued: the Chinese moved industry from the coast to Chungking, and a belt of no man's land was created between the two forces. Guerilla activities against the Japanese developed, requiring her to maintain one million troops in China.

The Japanese thought that if Wang Ching-Wei, who was a genuine revolutionary and former associate of Chiang Kai-Shek, gave his prestige to a peace movement, it might diminish China's will to resist. Wang left Chungking in December 1938 for Hanoi and arrived secretly in Shanghai in May 1939. After long negotiations, he set up a collaborationist government at Nanking in March 1940. The Wang initiative, however, did not break the deadlock; the Japanese were disappointed that no uprisings in Yunnan and Szechuan took place. *The China Quagmire* concludes: "China's ability to continue its resistance with such unity for four years after the Marco Polo Bridge Incident was a surprise to Japan, which grew increasingly uncertain and apprehensive about the outcome of the struggle." The Nationalist army was able to fight well, while Chiang's control over it was strong. Despite careful Japanese work, "the local military cliques did not revolt against Chungking's authority as anticipated."[76]

British plans over war in the Far East faced a dilemma. Talks with the US Admiral Leahy in June 1939 brought home to the US the absence of any Royal Navy battle fleet in the Pacific. There was also no guarantee that if Britain put economic pressure on Japan the US fleet would guard British possessions against Japanese retaliation.[77] In July 1940 – the most desperate of times – the Cabinet asked the Chiefs of Staff for an appreciation if Japan attacked the Netherlands East Indies. The Chiefs explained that the two assumptions which had governed their 1937 view had both been falsified; these had been that any threat would only be seaborne and that Britain could send a fleet of sufficient strength east. Japan's moves south, her likely development of airfields in Thailand and possible occupation of Indo-China, and the increased range of her aircraft, would enable her to attack Malaya overland.

The Chiefs had already concluded that the maximum force Britain could send to the Far East, given home and Mediterranean demands, would be two capital ships, designed to secure the Indian Ocean and deter the Japanese from moving towards Australia. If the Japanese fleet moved south in strength, Britain would leave Singapore to be invested. Churchill told Australia and New Zealand in August 1940 that if Japan set about invading them, Britain would cut her losses in the Mediterranean and "sacrifice every interest, except only the defence and feeding of this island" to send a fleet big enough to frustrate the Japanese.[78]

All this assumed that the US would be uninvolved. Any glance at the map would suggest that the US, with its interests in and responsibilities for the Philippines, would be highly unlikely to let the Japanese rampage unchecked all round that archipelago. An earlier display in the Pacific of Anglo-American collaboration might have deterred Japan from rash courses; but the US was still dogmatically against foreign entanglements.

Churchill himself had unrealistic expectations; he thought the Japanese were unlikely to enter the war and that, if they did, their efforts would be confined to naval raiding of trade routes. He minuted in November 1940 "The Japanese Navy is not likely to venture far from its home bases so long as a superior battle fleet is maintained at Singapore or at Honolulu." Both British and Americans thought there would be time after a Japanese declaration of war to make dispositions. However, British-US staff talks in February 1941 in Washington indicated that the US would not reinforce its Asiatic Fleet at Manila (which had no capital ships).[79]

The Japanese Cabinet in 1940 had aimed to establish an "East Asia Co-Prosperity Sphere," to comprise Japan, China and Manchukuo. Their appetite grew, and Foreign Minister Matsuoka told reporters that the "Greater East Asia Co-Prosperity Sphere" must naturally take in Indo-China, Thailand and the Dutch East Indies. Nish argues that it was difficult to interpret what Japan's intentions were to the south "because of the vagueness of Japan's pronouncements and the imprecise nature of the Japanese language" – the term "southern ocean" describes the colonial territories of South East Asia but not Australia or New Zealand. Wilder dreamers certainly applied the concept to Malaya, Burma and ultimately India and Australia.[80]

These dreams were encouraged and facilitated by the German victories in June 1940, which made realistic the prospect of occupying French Indo-China. The Japanese navy believed that attacks on Malaya, wished by the army, would cause the US to come to Britain's aid. Matsuoka believed a firm stand by the Axis would deter the US, so Japan joined the Tripartite Pact with Germany and Italy on 27 September 1940. Having appeased Japan by closing the Burma Road to supplies to China in June 1940, Britain in October told Japan that she would not continue to close it, and she announced a loan of £10m to China while inviting Chinese troops into Burma.

On 23 September the Vichy Government agreed to Japanese occupation of North Indo-China. Matsuoka visited Moscow, Berlin and Rome in March-April 1941, then Moscow again where he signed, on 13 April, a Soviet-Japanese treaty providing for each party to be neutral if the other was involved in war with a third power. There was no consultation by the Germans before they attacked Russia on 22 June; indeed Matsuoka had been told by Hitler that no attack was contemplated so long as Russia abided by the Nazi-Soviet pact. Matsuoka then tried to get Cabinet agreement for Japan to attack Russia in the rear but the majority opposed this and he was forced into retirement in July. Craigie remarked that if Germany had attacked Russia a few months earlier – or Japan had had foreknowledge of this – "It is my belief that … no Neutrality pact would have been concluded with the USSR and Japanese troops would not have marched into South Indo-China in July 1941." Their first thrust would have been against Russia.[81]

A border feud between Thailand and Indo-China gave Japan the pretext to move further south, with naval forces sent to Saigon and Bangkok in early 1941. On 23 July it was announced that Vichy had granted Japan naval and air bases in South Indo-China and the right to move troops there. The progress towards international conflict was rapid. The US reacted immediately by freezing Japanese assets and imposing an oil embargo. Britain, the Dominions, and the Dutch East Indies, all followed suit. While the consequences for Japan were potentially grave –

her navy oil stocks would last for 18 months, the army's for only a year – she must have realised that the occupation of South Indo-China could not be justified by her war with China and would be seen as tantamount to Pacific aggression. Haggie states that it was "clear from the records of 1941 policy conferences in Tokyo that the question of whether Japan could hope to win a struggle against Britain and the US was never faced; instead Japan moved confusedly towards war with its leaders in a mood of resigned fatalism and a belief that material deficiencies could be overcome by superior martial qualities."[82]

Craigie reported a conversation with Amau, the Deputy Foreign Minister, on 17 September. Going back to the racial equality issue at the 1919 Paris peace conference, Amau lashed out – "Both British and Japanese authorities should be fully aware that Britain is an obstacle to Japan's natural development. We would like to say frankly that the British should try to keep in mind what they might do if they were the Japanese."[83]

The handling of the sanctions made war not only inevitable but likely sooner. Leith-Ross, now at the Ministry of Economic Warfare, pointed out that the Chiefs of Staff were urging postponement of conflict with Japan "which hardly suggested that the application of drastic sanctions was wise," – indeed, it was "not carefully prepared but improvised". Britain and the US might have temporised the sanctions if they had appreciated the full power of Japan: "The efficiency and hardness of the army ... the superiority of the Zero fighter, [and] the high degree of competence of the navy." Meanwhile the Chiefs of Staff "shared his [Churchill's] contempt for the Japanese as the Asian equivalent of Italy."[84]

The Americans had broken the Japanese "Magic" codes, and were thus aware of the Japanese decision on 2 July to move south rather than attack Russia. In the 1930s the US had not regarded the defence of the Philippines as a priority but by mid 1941 this had changed. With General Douglas MacArthur in command there, there would be reinforcements of men and aircraft. This was to be completed by spring 1942, so talks with Japan in Washington had to be spun out. Unfortunately, "hawkish, middle-level bureaucrats" in Washington wanted to block Japan's applications for oil purchases, and "by September ... the Administration was effectively enforcing a complete oil embargo on Japan." This was "likely to force Japan to an early decision for peace or war."[85]

Likewise the British needed time, planning that only when a balanced fleet, based on Ceylon, had been created by March 1942 would this move into the danger zone at Singapore. Churchill, however, insisted on rapidly sending an aircraft carrier and two modern capital ships to Singapore. He cited the parallel of the *Tirpitz* in the north Atlantic which, he said, was "doing to us exactly what a K[ing] G[eorge]V [class battleship] in the Indian Ocean would do to the Japanese navy. It exercises a vague, general fear and menaces all points at once."[86] So the *Prince of Wales* and the *Repulse* and the aircraft carrier *Indomitable* were despatched to Singapore, to be followed later by older battleships and then in early 1942 by other capital ships, cruisers and destroyers. Unfortunately, the *Indomitable* was delayed by an accident in the Caribbean – whether, if present, it would have survived the disaster that overtook the other two is debatable.[87]

After Nomura's arrival as Japanese ambassador to the US in February 1941, talks began. Konoye, who was "desperately anxious to avoid war with America," encouraged these and in early August offered to meet President Roosevelt. The army forced a compromise at an Imperial Conference on 6 September: war preparations would be completed by early October, and if by then no diplomatic solution had been reached, Japan would decide. Nomura proposed a Konoye-Roosevelt meeting to Roosevelt on 17 August. Roosevelt initially accepted and Grew, the US ambassador in Tokyo, argued that the US should not weaken Konoye's already frail power base. But Grew's influence had weakened and Hull and his Far East advisers took a very different view: no summit could take place unless Japan accepted the US's fundamental principles. This reply was sent to Tokyo on 2 October. The Konoye offer eventually leaked in Tokyo and as a result of a hostile reaction Konoye and his Cabinet resigned on 18 October. His successor was hard-liner General Tojo: at an Imperial Conference on 1 and 2 November it was decided to give the diplomats until the end of November.

Nomura offered on 20 November that Japan would withdraw from South Indo-China if the US would end its freezing order. The Americans were attracted as they needed the winter to reinforce the Philippines, but Hull proposed a Japanese evacuation of all Indo-China, apart from a small force in the North, and a modified freezing order. Reynolds states that Hull "was adamant that Japan must abrogate the Tripartite Pact"; he was also "obsessed with the question of Japanese withdrawal from China. " On 26 November Hull decided to abandon hopes of a deal, having discovered from intercepted Japanese cables that they planned imminent attacks. He also discovered that a large Japanese force had embarked at Shanghai and was moving south towards Luzon. Neither the US or UK expected the attack on Hawaii. The Hawaii task force left Japan on 25 November but it and the other attacks could have been halted up to 24 hours beforehand.[88]

The Disaster at Singapore

British service attaches in Tokyo had long been dismissive of Japan's military proficiency. This "owed much to the continuing belief in racial stereotypes of the Japanese," and contributed to the view that Britain could take a stronger line with Japan, shown during the summer of 1941. From 1933, both the Japanese army and navy began large scale rearmament and training. No recognition was made of the technical advances made by the navy, for example in developing torpedos. An enthusiast for the Japanese military, Malcolm Kennedy, claimed in *The Problem of Japan* (1935) that it was behind Western armies in equipment and training. Others were even more critical, claiming that Japan lacked men and aircraft for a long war, while her industrial base was too small. The British Admiralty welcomed these reports, and emphasis was given to Japanese reverses in China in 1939-40. Anthony Best concludes that if intelligence on Japan had been more accurate there might have been a "less confrontational, more flexible policy" towards her, and war "might have been averted."[89]

Warnings pointing to possible disaster at Singapore, where 80,000 unwounded prisoners were taken by a exhausted force almost a third of this strength in February 1942, had been accumulating for years. Churchill had a "misconception" of the strength of the base; years of misuse of the word "fortress" made it sound like Verdun.[90]

Chatfield, the First Lord of the Admiralty, thought that Singapore might hold out for six months without the fleet; in March 1938 the CID accepted a figure of 70 days before relief. The British tended to believe that as the Japanese had never fought against a first class power in the air, they would be ineffective there. It was decided in September 1940 to make "some start in re-equipping the obsolete Far East air force." "Grudgingly" Churchill sanctioned this. It reassured the British public but did not alter the facts, hence shocks "when the bluff was finally called." Most of the aircraft – only 158 in all – were outdated Buffalo fighters, virtually eliminated in the first two days of Japanese attack. [91]

During the Shanghai crisis of early 1932, the Japanese had landed a division, in 48 hours – 10,000 men, 60 guns, 15 tanks, other equipment, including 12 crated aircraft – all from 16 medium sized transports totalling 66,000 tons. The British observers remarked that for them to do the same would require 215,000 tons. "The neglect of such demonstrations of Japanese military capability was ultimately going to cost the British dear." Malaya Command in 1937 was impressed by Japanese combined operations in China and began to think actively of defence. "It is equally clear that this caused friction with the civil authorities" and these ideas lapsed when General Sir William Dobbie was relieved as GOC Malaya in 1938. At a conference in June 1939 British and French commanders in the Far East warned that Singapore was very vulnerable, and the Admiral commanding the Australian squadron recorded the reactions of the staff officer dispatched to the Singapore conference in October 1940: "Very depressed about the lethargy, lack of co-operation and ineptitude there ..."[92]

The British eventually established that it was possible, though hazardous, to land troops on the east coast of Malaya in the winter monsoon season. Yet in January 1941 the newly appointed Commander-in-Chief Far East Air Chief Marshal Brooke-Popham (he was removed from the command at the end of December 1941) claimed that the Japanese had never made a seaborne landing or engaged in bombing against concerted opposition. David Margesson, the War Secretary, said when the attack on Malaya came: "The Japanese can only be rated in the fifth class and this has been amply demonstrated in the fighting against the Chinese." The British "whistled into the wind, imagining that the storm would somehow hit Thailand instead." And the *Prince of Wales* and the *Repulse* (Force Z) should have been withdrawn "when it was clear that the bluff of which they were a major part had failed."[93]

There is a slender argument that Admiral Phillips' Force Z was merely unlucky: if, instead of sailing into the range of the Japanese torpedo bombers, it had, as Churchill suggested "vanish[ed] into the ocean wastes" to act as "rogue elephants" it would have maintained a general threat to the Japanese and might have averted the disaster of the Battle of the Java Sea at the end of February 1942.[94]

Following the fall of Singapore, Japanese submarines moved freely throughout the northern and eastern expanses of the Indian Ocean. In March 1942, Japanese aircraft carriers raided shipping in the Bay of Bengal and bases in Ceylon. After severe losses, including *Hermes,* the only British aircraft carrier in the Indian Ocean, the British Eastern Fleet was forced to retreat to Kilindini, near Mombasa, in Kenya. If Japanese submarines had been able to use bases on Vichy-held Madagascar, Allied communications would face dire threats. Britain responded with alacrity, with Operation Ironclad, the seizure of the port of Diego Suarez near the northern tip of Madagascar, on 5 May 1942, followed that autumn by the occupation of the whole island.

Restraining Japan from all-out aggression against "the West", would have required a stronger leadership in Tokyo, making a more careful calculation of the military risks. Japan was expensively embedded in her war in China. Geography meant that any Japanese thrust south of Hong Kong must bring in the power controlling the Philippines, viz the USA. And although the USSR in fact remained neutral until August 1945, a glance at the map shows that Soviet bombers had the Japanese homeland within easy range, and her military forces virtually surrounded the Japanese forces in Manchukuo. For Japan, the risks of aggression were huge, but she was misled by American vacillation to conclude that the US would not mobilise her full weight in the event of war. For this error, she duly paid the price.

Of all the disasters since the start of the war, blame for the fall of Singapore can be directed at the planners and providers of equipment in the pre-war years for their serious inadequacies. But there was another factor, seen also in Crete earlier in 1941. There was a collapse of fighting capacity in the usually sturdy British soldier. And would resistance have been more vigorous if the British forces had known the fate of those surrendering? Alan Clark is scathing "... every ingredient attaching to it of a decadent empire in terminal decline," adding that 57,000 of the 85,000 surrendering would die in captivity "a loss of life not much different ... than if they had fought on the spot."[95]

There would have been less easily measurable consequences of a stand at Singapore. Instead, defeats in South East Asia during the winter of 1941-2 had important post-war consequences both for India, and for the future direction of Australia and New Zealand.

FOOTNOTES

1 Ann Trotter, *Britain and East Asia 1933-7* p4.

2 See Richard Aldrich and Rory Cormack, *The Black Door: Spies, Secret Intelligence and British Prime Ministers,* HarperCollins 2016, pp63 and 75. Also William C. Mills *The "Secret Channel" to Italy,* International Historical Review 2002, pp278-317.

3 Citations in the name of (Ian) Nish, Hosoya (Chihiro) or (Peter) Lowe are from chapters authored by them in *Anglo-Japanese Alienation 1919-52: Papers of the Anglo-Japanese Conference on the History of the Second World War,* edited by Ian Nish. This from Hosoya pp5-6 and Nish, p28.

4 Barnett, op cit, p264. Barnett (op cit, pp255-72) describes the strength of American influence on senior British statesmen, like Churchill, Balfour and Austen Chamberlain (expressions like "infatuation", "myth-making", "sentimentalising" are used).

5 Ibid, p272. Alan Clark, op cit, p260 says it "signalled the start of Britain's decline as an Imperial power in the Far East."

6 Hosoya, op cit, pp8-9, the quotes, except where otherwise attributed, are his paraphrasing; Sir Robert Craigie, *Behind the Japanese Mask,* p13.

7 Hosoya, op cit, p11.

8 Hosoya, op cit, pp13, 15.

9 Nish, op cit, p27.

10 Robert Boyce, *British Capitalism At The Crossroads,* p182; the Churchill quote (my italics) from Martin Gilbert, *Winston S. Churchill,* Companion Vol V, part 1, p1034 Cabinet memorandum entitled *Cruisers and Parity*, dated 20 July 1927. By the spring of 1929 negotiations for a new naval agreement began to progress.

11 Anthony Best, *British Intelligence and the Japanese Challenge in Asia 1914-4,* p99.

12 Quoted in R. Bassett, *Democracy and Foreign Policy: A Case History: The Sino-Japanese Dispute 1931-3,* p144. In Simon's words, when Britain did act with the USA she was left with "the brunt of the work and the blame." (Trotter, op cit, p11.)

13 Quoted Hosoya, op cit, p17.

14 Nish, op cit, p38.

15 Paul Haggie, *Britannia at Bay – The Defence of the British Empire against Japan 1931-41,* pp38-9.

16 Nish, op cit, pp41-3.

17 Barnett, op cit, p305. During the 1935 meeting of Commonwealth Prime Ministers, Lyons of Australia suggested the recognition of Manchukuo: Simon replied that this could not be done "In so far as the matter was one for the League of Nations, this country would have to act as a good member of the League." Ibid, p348.

18 Commons Hansard, 27 February 1933.

19 Amery diary, 16 September 1932, Barnes and Nicholson, op cit, p282.

20 Haggie, op cit, especially pp6 and 34.

21 Ibid, pp37 and 46.

22 Peter Bell, *Chamberlain, Germany and Japan 1933-4,* p89.

23 Ibid, pp4, 34.

24 Trotter, op cit, p42.

25 Bell, op cit, pp92-3.

26 Bell, op cit, pp70-1, Trotter, op cit, pp42-4.

27 Trotter, op cit, p53; Bell, op cit, pp56, 140, 165. Last quote dated 17 December 1937. Compare Baldwin's complaints about the US during the Manchurian crisis "you will get nothing out of the Americans except words. Big words, but only words". C. A. MacDonald, *The United States, Britain and Appeasement 1936-9,* p14.

28 The quotes from Bell, op cit, p55.

29 Baldwin's speech was on 10 November 1932. By 1939 planners were expecting raids on a scale of 700 tons per day, even a "knock-out blow" against London of 3500 tons. In fact the heaviest load

dropped on Britain during the war was 1000 tons in an April 1941 raid; most raids fluctuated between 40 and 300 tons. Dilks ed, p105.
30 Bell, op cit, p112, Trotter, op cit, p90; Haggie, op cit, p72.
31 Bell, op cit, p125, Trotter, op cit, p96.
32 Quotes in Bell, op cit, pp125, 133, 136-7.
33 Bell, pp151-7.
34 David Reynolds, *The Creation of the Anglo-American Alliance 1937-41,* p59.
35 Trotter, op cit, p36.
36 Hirota became Prime Minister in 1936-7. He opposed Japanese excesses in China, but seemed to share responsibility for them. His execution in 1948 was a contentious outcome of the Tokyo war crimes trials.
37 Trotter, op cit, p54.
38 J. W. Morley editor: *The China Quagmire – Japan's Expansion on the Asian Continent,* pp 30, 144.
39 Trotter, op cit, pp73, 79, 85, 97, the last quote on p98.
40 Ibid, pp101-2, 112.
41 Hosoya, op cit, p20.
42 Trotter, op cit, p122 for both quotes.
43 Ibid, pp126-8.
44 Ibid, pp151-3.
45 Ibid, pp162-3; Shimada Toshihiko *Designs on North China,* in *The China Quagmire,* p196-7.
46 Clive despatch, 5 July 1934 quoted B. J. C. McKercher *Transition of Power: Britain's Loss of Global Pre-eminence to the United States 1930-45,* p196.
47 Trotter, op cit, pp174-5, the "actions" being Manchuria and creeping aggression.
48 Haggie, op cit, pp92-3.
49 McKercher, op cit, p223.The Dominions, notably the former Australian Prime Minister W. M. Hughes and the usually docile New Zealanders warned Britain against the sanctions path (Barclay, op cit, pp110-13). American oil exports to Italy and its African colonies, the bases for the invasion, increased by thirty-five times during the last five months of 1935, compared with the same period in 1934 (Medlicott, *The Hoare-Laval Pact Reconsidered* in Dilks, ed, op cit, p131.
50 A. J. P. Taylor, *The Origins of the Second World War,* p128; Correlli Barnett, op cit, pp352-3 and p356. Vansittart "believed that the front against Germany should be preserved at the expense of Abyssinia , which was a lost cause." (Haggie paraphrase of his view, op cit, p85.) Vansittart described the incompetent handling of the Pact by officialdom in London and Paris in *The Mist Procession* pp539-43.
51 Trotter's paraphrase, op cit, p193.
52 Nish, op cit, pp44-5.
53 The words in quotes are Trotter's, p195.
54 Quotes in Trotter, p198.
55 Bradford A. Lee, *Britain and the Sino-Japanese War 1937-39,* p15.
56 The passages in quotes are from Nish's account, op cit, pp48-9.
57 Hosoya, including quotes, op cit, pp58-9.
58 C. A. MacDonald, *The United States, Britain and Appeasement 1936-9* p40. The first quote is from Tweedsmuir to Chamberlain, 25 October 1937, the other two from MacDonald's analysis.
59 In November 1936, Churchill, previously pro-Japanese, noted in an article in the *Evening Standard* that if war occurred in Europe, Japan would start one in the Far East; the murder of political opponents "has been for some years accepted practice".
60 Trotter, op cit, pp215-6.
61 Lee, op cit, p15.
62 Trotter, op cit, p203.
63 Lee, op cit, pp38, 50, 58.

64 Quoted Lee, p112. British opinion on sanctions against Japan was sharply divided, with the predominant official view being that sanctions could only be considered if the US gave firm assurances of support. Australia, Canada and South Africa all sent messages opposing sanctions.
65 Quoted ibid, 206, 219-20.
66 Craigie, op cit, p51.
67 Lee, op cit, p140; Craigie, op cit , pp60, 62.
68 Lee, op cit, pp152-4.
69 Ibid, pp124-7, 137.
70 Hosoya, op cit, pp64.
71 Craigie, op cit, p78.
72 Peter Lowe, in *Anglo-Japanese Alienation,* p105-7.
73 Ian Nish chapter, in *Crisis and Controversy,* edited Alan Sked and Chris Cook, p132; Craigie, op cit, p71, Lee, op cit, p202.
74 Craigie, op cit, p81, presumably referring to the period 1936-39.
75 Ibid, p92, last quote.
76 Usui Katsumi, *The Politics of War* in *The China Quagmire,* ed Morley p424.
77 Haggie, op cit, pp141, 164.
78 Ibid, pp150,178, 180.
79 David Reynolds, *The Creation of the Anglo-American Alliance 1937-41*, pp223-4.
80 Nish, in *Crisis and Controversy*, pp134-6.
81 Haggie, op cit, p199; Nish , op cit, p136, Craigie, op cit, p119.
82 Haggie, op cit, p203.
83 Quoted Hosoya, op cit, p73; Hosoya described this as "abandon(ing) the usual diplomatic language" and expressing "the resentment of many years."
84 Lowe, op cit, p115, 118-9; Reynolds, op cit, p224. Some British officers, notably the military attaches in Tokyo in 1940-1 gave warnings about Japanese strength and skill, which were "disregarded". Comparing British and Japanese naval aircraft, Barclay states "the discrepancy in quality was horrifying" (op cit, p121).
85 Reynolds, op cit, pp235-6. 249 B17s – the US "wonder weapon" – were destroyed on the ground in the Philippines on 8 December.
86 Quoted ibid, p240. Alan Clark disagrees, pointing out that the Japanese were able to threaten "a full-scale fleet action". Op cit, p255.
87 Haggie, op cit, pp186-7.
88 Reynolds, op cit, pp244-47.
89 Antony Best, *British Intelligence and the Japanese Challenge in Asia 1914-41*, pp43, 116-9, 145, 159, 168. Last quote p187.
90 Haggie, op cit, p180. See Richard Lamb, *Churchill as War Leader: Right or Wrong?* pp185-95 over the weaknesses there, especially Wavell's warnings about the inadequacy of the armaments and that many troops were of "doubtful value"; also the palpable failure of Duff Cooper's mission ("inept", "careless", "deplorable impression") to improve things there.
91 Haggie, op cit, pp106, 134, 185; also Barclay, op cit, pp158,160, 163.
92 Lee, op cit, footnote p171; Haggie, op cit, pp30, 120, 192; *Automedon* point, Best, op cit, p163.
93 Best, op cit, pp150, 169, 190-2.
94 This, though not the Java Sea point, in Lamb, op cit, p181. Lamb argues (p342) that Churchill should have revised the plans to defend Malaya (always a Cinderella objective, well behind the Middle East) once the Japanese had occupied Indo-China.
95 Clark, op cit, pp262-3.

EPILOGUE

Victory's Price: "The Steady, Grinding March of Decline"[1]

"The idea of the Commonwealth as a vehicle of post-imperial world influence had been fiercely promoted; it was hard to repudiate. It had helped to anaesthetise British public opinion against the pain of decline ..."
(Darwin, *The Empire Project,* p641.)

"... India's continued association with the Commonwealth does not help us in any way ... She will not agree to any co-ordinated foreign policy. She is definitely hostile to our colonial policy. She reserves the right to stab us in the back at any moment at the United Nations."
(Lord Salisbury, writing to Lord Swinton, 22 April 1949, quoted in Partha Sarathi Gupta *Power, Politics and the People: Studies in British Imperialism and Indian Nationalism,* p306.)

"These people could never run an empire."
(remark about Americans, attributed to J. M. Keynes, quoted Richard Bassett, *The Last Imperialist: A Portrait of Julian Amery*, p157.)[2]

This links the effects of the war on Britain's ability to retain her power and influence in key areas of the globe. For the sake of argument, it advances certain counterfactuals – might events in one or more cases have turned out otherwise? As in earlier chapters, it is hard to avoid a chilling sense of inevitability.

However dire the stakes, there was no alternative: in the words of the King's Speech in September 1939 "it is unthinkable that we should refuse to meet the challenge." Unlike the German leadership in 1914, it was clear to anyone who had the wit to see that Hitler and his clique were not only totally untrustworthy, but they personified evil. While some British leaders who favoured a deal with Hitler might have pleaded ignorance of the nature of his regime, historians, such as the late Alan Clark, who opposed British commitments to eastern European countries like Poland, have no such excuse. John Charmley has also sympathetically described the debates in Cabinet at the end of May over a possible compromise peace; Halifax favoured this and was close to resigning at the idea of continued resistance, denying that Hitler's terms would necessarily be intolerable. Churchill made an emotional appeal to all ministers and this clinched the matter but, as Charmley says "by a thin margin," adding "a growing number of people were to come to the conclusion" that Britain and her Empire would not emerge from the war "with anything except nominal independence." However, he adds the caveat "it was certainly better to be an American rather than a German protectorate."[3]

Germany was geographically close enough to Britain to pose a real threat, particularly after the fall of France. Having declared war, Britain was only likely to achieve peace with the Nazis if she disarmed herself, for example, by surrendering part of the RAF or the Navy. Grim fictional accounts of Britain and Europe after a Nazi victory are in Robert Harris's *Fatherland,* C. J. Sansom's *Dominion* and Len Deighton's *SS-GB.*

Even after 1941, the British Commonwealth and Soviet Russia were not able to mobilise the resources to defeat Hitler on their own; they needed finance and armaments from the United States. In the end, only full American participation in the war ensured victory – even so, Communism engulfed Europe as far as the Elbe. It was thus inevitable that international power would pass from the British domains to the USA.

Reference has already been made to the tardiness and misdirection of British and French rearmament. Britain, as we have seen, concentrated on Air Force rearmament rather than increasing naval air power, which might have avoided such disasters as Crete and Singapore. Opposed as they had been to war over the Sudetenland, the Dominions placed even less emphasis on re-armament: Canada in 1938 actually cut defence spending by $2 million. As for modern aircraft, manufactured in Britain, by June 1939 126 Hurricanes had been promised to Rumania, 24 Spitfires to Greece and 60 Spitfires and Blenheims to Turkey. None of these modern types went then to any of the Dominions. An embargo on the export of all military aircraft was later lifted to send Australia 88 Fairey Battles "unfit for action on any other front except possibly Abyssinia."[4]

Britain's heroic resistance in 1940 and various successes in 1941 – mopping up the Italians in Abyssinia and securing control of rebellious Iraq, Vichy-held Syria and semi-subverted Persia – might blind us to several of the mistakes in these earlier years, such as the "chivalrous" sending of forces to Greece in early 1941 which laid Wavell in Libya open to Rommel's counter-attack (intelligence was optimistic about holding in Greece and over the timing of Rommel's attack in Libya: it was wrong on both counts). This linked with the failure to send tanks to Crete or Singapore where they might have made a difference; many were understandably being sent to Russia, but many were sunk en route.[5] Inadequate and ineffective equipment contributed to defeats in Libya until late 1942.

Richard Lamb develops the theme of mishandling Vichy France. The Mers-el-Kebir episode, perhaps justified in the immediate circumstances of desperation, led to perhaps unnecessary French resistance at Dakar, and in Syria later. On more than one occasion Britain prevented Vichy from sending reinforcements to Indo-China, which might have enabled France to resist Japanese pressures to occupy.[6]

The Dominions had responded to Britain's danger, with Canada sending forces to Britain and the southern Dominions reinforcing Egypt; they resented, however, their forces being sent to Greece and Crete, without proper consultation and with heavy losses. Japan's onslaught put Australia and India in the front line. In the spring of 1942 London appealed to Canberra to order an Australian division returning from the Middle East to land in Burma (where it would almost certainly have been engulfed in the Japanese triumph); Canberra refused, and a tense exchange took place with Churchill. Even before this and the fall of Singapore, came the Australian Premier Curtin's gloomy and often reported remark "Australia looks to America, free of any pangs as to our traditional links or kinship with the United Kingdom" (27 December 1941).

For several months India faced grave danger. With aircraft from Admiral Nagumo's fleet attacking Ceylon, the Viceroy criticised "the concentration of virtually the whole of our heavy bombing force for use on the Continent and for raids which involve us in casualties of the order of 5 per cent of the bombers flown in any one night ... It will not surprise me at any moment to hear of a Japanese landing somewhere in south India ..." He hoped a few days later that "Winston has at last grasped that there is now no more than a sheet of paper between the Japanese drive westward and the German drive south east from Libya to the Caucasus."[7]

In fact, the Japanese turned back to the Pacific, towards their naval defeats in the Coral Sea and Midway in May and June, while the Germans concentrated on Stalingrad, that "Verdun on the Volga", rather than breaking through the Caucasus barrier. After El Alamein and Stalingrad in November 1942 had turned the tide, Allied progress in the West and Russia was slow but steady; in the Far East, however, Commonwealth attacks in Arakan in the spring of 1943 were defeated and the Japanese remained for many months threatening Australia from the north. Their final attempt to invade India was eventually decisively defeated at Imphal-Kohima (March-July 1944).

Brief reference might be made to other strategic and tactical vicissitudes: the failure, largely owing to inflexible application of the "unconditional surrender" policy, to produce an earlier Italian ceasefire, with the Allies occupying more of Italy and especially more of the Aegean islands; the failure to give adequate support to the non-Communist Chetnik resistance in Yugoslavia, owing to the malign influence of the Communist spy Klugman; the failure to invade Yugoslavia via Istria, helping to deny total victory to the Communist Tito. Many of these criticisms are now well established. More debatable might be the "unconditional surrender" policy towards Germany, reinforced by lurid rumours of the Morgenthau plan, requiring the disappearance of much of the German population. This helped the Nazis to recruit large reserves after their Normandy defeat, leading to firmer resistance, the reverse at Arnhem and the shock of the Ardennes offensive.

During the war, the idea of an Imperial War Cabinet, as existed in the First War, was firmly rejected by Canada's Mackenzie King, but a high level of contact was maintained, by modern communications and ministerial meetings, including a Prime Ministers' Meeting in 1944. After the war, Attlee raised Commonwealth defence co-ordination in the autumn of 1945 with Mackenzie King, who opposed it. By the early 1950s, Canada's trade was closely aligned with the US: only 9% of her imports, compared to twice that proportion pre-war, were drawn from Britain. Clearly, the USA had to be involved: in 1949, Canadian entry into NATO alongside Britain and the US resolved that dilemma.

In 1951 the ANZUS treaty was signed in San Francisco between the USA and Australia and New Zealand, both of which latter would have liked British involvement: the US opposed this.[8] At the same time, both in Australia and New Zealand mistrust of the USA combined with resentment at its ungenerous financial treatment of the UK. Hence Menzies offered Australia to the UK as a partner and test-ground for nuclear weapons, and was prepared in 1952 to send Australian troops to the Middle East if necessary. In the 1956 Suez crisis, the two southern Dominions supported Britain: "Like the Australians, New Zealanders expected the British to behave imperially, especially when it came to safeguarding the Suez route."[9]

As a major positive post-war factor, over 1,200,000 Britons migrated to the "white" Dominions, including South Africa, as well as to Rhodesia and Kenya, between 1946-54 (130,000 to Canada and 138,000 to Australasia in the three years 1946-9); half the intake of migrants into Australia were from the UK until well into the 1960s.

Underscoring practically everything Britain aspired to after 1945 was the dire economic position she faced. The cumulative shortfall on current account was £10 billion, with $15 billion owing to the US and £3 billion to sterling countries, especially India and Egypt. Could Britain substitute for her military exhaustion and her economic weakness, the flexibility and skill of diplomacy? Despite great diplomatic talents deployed, as a sympathetic modern historian has concluded: "The British found almost everywhere that their assumptions about retaining a premier influence in regions where they had previously exercised colonial or semi-colonial domination were belied by events."[10] Noting the exception of South East Asia, Britain was obliged to decamp from the three key regions of the Subcontinent, the Middle East and Africa, in each case failing to protect her allies while conceding much to her opponents. And while India has been a great success for democracy and capitalist-led prosperity, the same cannot be said of Pakistan, or much of the Middle East and Africa.

Denoument in India

In Darwin's view, "it is unlikely that the architects of British Indian policy between the wars would have considered British withdrawal in the immediate or foreseeable future as either necessary or desirable." The outcome in 1947 "constituted a devastating reversal for British plans and the almost complete defeat of pre-war policy;" the war had "damaged or demolished most of the instruments whereby the British hoped to control India's political development."[11]

After 1930, with provincial government in the hands of elected Indians, the

British hoped to oblige the political parties to come to terms with each other, and with the Princely rulers, while becoming absorbed in provincial bread and butter issues. Politics in the provinces would, they hoped, reflect the huge variations in interests, cultures and languages. They assumed special post-war links to Britain; India would need large numbers of Britons to help or advise over agriculture and forestry. They hoped that the Indian leaders would see that economic self-interest and the inability of India to defend herself would ensure a close military and diplomatic alliance with Britain to protect the Indian Ocean zone. The outcome was otherwise.

Unexpectedly, Congress emerged in the 1937 elections as the largest party in six out of eleven provinces. The declaration of war in 1939 was clumsily done without Indian consultation, causing these Congress ministries to resign. Congress rejected the "August Offer" in 1940, because Nehru wanted India to be free to leave the Commonwealth. Britain was seen to draw closer to the Muslim League because Muslims supported the war effort. The main Muslim majority provinces were Bengal, where more than half of India's industrial capacity was situated, and the Punjab, the main recruiting area. In rejecting the Cripps offer in 1942, Congress demanded concessions which would have jeopardised the war effort. Churchill, Amery and Linlithgow all thought this, and with some Americans fearing a revolution in India, even Roosevelt had doubts over Indian self-government. Linlithgow's ruthless and effective quelling of the Quit India rising in August 1942 "proved to most Americans, including Roosevelt, that in India the British could manage their own affairs and would resist to the bitter end any American interference."[12]

In 1942, it was feared that large parts of India would come under Japanese occupation, at least temporarily. Both then and later, nationalists were listening to German and Japanese radio broadcasts. The "Quit India" revolt was more spontaneous than centrally organised. Railways and telegraph lines were sabotaged, numerous British officials and servicemen were attacked and killed, while aircraft attacked crowds disrupting railways. On British estimates, perhaps conservative, 1000 were killed and 3000 wounded; 60,000 were interned. The Viceroy admitted that "we have so far concealed … for reasons of military security" the "gravity" and "density" of the disorders.[13].

Developments during the war made a looser, confederal, constitutional outcome, giving Britain the opportunity to remain holding the ring, less likely. Congress agitation for a centralised Hindu Raj caused the Muslim majority provinces to draw towards Jinnah's League as a form of insurance.[14] Pakistan became League policy at Lahore in March 1940. During much of the war, the League and other non-Congress parties functioned in provincial government, and the Viceroy's executive consisted overwhelmingly of Indians, though not sitting as party representatives. Even the Labour leader Attlee, Prime Minister in 1945, was unenthusiastic about the party leaders: he saw the risk of handing over the Indian people to wealthy controllers of political caucuses. As Secretary of State until 1945, Leo Amery wanted to build up the status of the Viceroy's Indian ministers and make them more credible as representatives of the Indian people without being dependent on political parties.

Amery's "pretty revolutionary" initiative (his words), launched in a letter to the new Viceroy, Lord Wavell, on 3 October 1944, was described by his sympathisers as "Home Rule for the Viceroy". Arguing that the main source of India's grievance was not the existing government in Delhi but remote control and interference from Whitehall and Westminster, Wavell, he suggested, should "announce the full independence of India under the present constitution". Wavell opposed it: he did not believe that the political parties could be by-passed; "even if Gandhi and Jinnah disappeared tomorrow ... I can see no prospect of our having more reasonable people to deal with". This view, he added, was shared by the Commander-in-Chief, all eleven governors of provinces and the senior members of the armed services. At a meeting of the Cabinet's India Committee on 5 March 1945 Simon said that Amery's scheme "appeared ... to leave the Viceroy in the air", while on 27 March Attlee objected to the substitution for ultimate British control of "a brown oligarchy subject to no control either from Parliament or electorate". Churchill, who tended to be ostrich-like over India's future, had taken the firm view in October 1943 that "victory is the best foundation for great constitutional departures". He minuted Amery on 30 May 1945: "no action or negotiation until the election has shown which party is in power."[15]

There was, however, plenty of evidence during 1945-7 that a multi-state solution might emerge. Linlithgow, Amery and Churchill had all expected at least three Dominions, with British authorities and forces providing coordination and security from a federal enclave. Staff at the Muslim university of Aligarh claimed that the Muslims of India were "a nation by themselves," envisaging the division of British India into three sovereign states, Hindustan, north-west India and Bengal. The largest Princely State, Hyderabad, they said, should also be recognised as sovereign, with the Carnatic coast of south-east India restored to it.[16]

A memorandum produced by Cripps, the Attlee Government's chief thinker on India, in April 1946, put forward two alternatives: an All-India union, in three parts – Hindu majority provinces, Muslim majority provinces and the States which would unite *for a minimum of compulsory subjects including defence, foreign policy and communications.* The second envisaged partition into Pakistan and Hindustan, with the States acceding to one or other *or remaining independent.* On 13 April Attlee cabled the views of the Chiefs of Staff who thought a loose All-India federation was far better than partition, which in turn was better than chaos. A year later this was still the thinking; in a staff meeting on 29 March 1947, the new Viceroy, Mountbatten, pointed out that there might be "a 'Dominion' of Pakistan, a 'Dominion' or 'Dominions' of the Indian States and a 'Dominion' of the rest of British India. *All these would be autonomous units*", with certain subjects reserved to "some form of central government."[17]

There was undoubted support for this flexible approach from the Conservative Opposition. After Churchill and Simon had met Jinnah in December 1946, the former opened a secret avenue for communication. Churchill was also sympathetic to the Princes. In January 1947 Sir Walter Monckton, acting for the Nizam of Hyderabad, approached Lord Templewood (previously Sir Samuel Hoare) to ask whether Conservative leaders like Cranborne, about to become Lord Salisbury, Eden and Butler would support appeals by Jinnah and the Princes for Dominionhood within the Commonwealth; for himself, Templewood replied affirmatively. In April 1947 Monckton was trying to acquire port facilities for Hyderabad in Portuguese Goa and visited Portugal for this purpose. In a memorandum sent to Lord Ismay, Mountbatten's Military Adviser, he argued that the States "had a living culture of their own, and were, in many cases, as well administered as the provinces." If the British government would maintain direct relations with Hyderabad State, Pakistan, Egypt and Saudi Arabia would recognise it. He sighed (a theme that might be replicated in this Epilogue) "How ready we are to appease our enemies at the expense of our friends."[18]

Three factors prevented the British from insisting on a flexible policy and, in line with their treaty obligations, safeguarding the rights of the Princes. These were: the critical shortage of British manpower in India, the rising tide of disorder and, perhaps most important, the need, particularly urged by the military chiefs, for retaining India in the Commonwealth with a defence pact.

The end of the war saw a growing shortage of British officials and police, with many due to retire. Likewise in the Army, there were many Indian officers and men whose insulation from nationalism had been broken, first, by the "serious blunder" of holding trials of captured Indian National Army soldiers (regarded as heroes by nationalists) in Delhi's Red Fort and, second, by their having to assist in restoring to the Dutch and French their colonies recaptured from Japan. At Dum Dum airbase members of Royal Indian Air Force refused orders and in February 1946 the Royal Indian Navy mutinied in Bombay.[19] By now Wavell and his advisers believed Britain could not hold on beyond the spring of 1948.

These weakened powers had to deal with a growing tide of inter-communal disorder. August 1946 saw the League's Direct Action Day; intending peaceful protest but leading to riots in Calcutta which, out of control for four or five days, saw 5000 dead and 20,000 injured, with 100,000 homeless. Later rioting in Bombay saw a curfew and 6000 arrests. Parts of East Bengal and Bihar in October saw large gangs of Muslims terrorising Hindus. In April 1947 the police in Bengal mutinied, with the Army having to disarm them. On 23 November 1946 Wavell told the India Secretary "we are very near what will amount almost to open civil war". A few months later, Ismay pointed to the "highly inflammable material" of private communal armies. The Muslim League National Guards paraded the streets of Lahore in military uniforms in January 1947. The Punjab Coalition ministry banned this; the ban was defied, then withdrawn and in March the Coalition collapsed. This was followed by inter-communal clashes.[20] Instead of seeking an agreement with the Sikhs over Pakistan, the League made no attempt at conciliation. Shahid Hamid, private secretary to Auchinleck as Commander-in-Chief, cites a report that the Sikh rulers were planning a civil war to establish Sikhistan and listed details of various Sikh rulers supplying arms round Amritsar.[21]

The third factor was that the British military chiefs saw Indian participation by treaty in a Commonwealth defence system as essential to upholding Britain's position in the Middle East, as well as her ability to support Australia, New Zealand and the Far East generally. This pious hope was not universally shared in Whitehall. In October 1946 Frank Turnbull, the India Secretary's Principal Private Secretary, circulated a draft letter to the Permanent Secretary at the Dominion Affairs department, questioning whether it was in the interest of the Commonwealth as a whole that India should remain within it. "Turnbull doubted whether, in view of India's lack of spiritual and racial kinship with the Dominions, this was really so. If India remained ... she would become a larger and noisier Southern Ireland and thus be 'more of an embarrassment than an asset'." From the Burma Office Sir Gilbert Laithwaite rather agreed – as with Southern Ireland the Commonwealth link might provide only a "paper relation" of little real use. One K. Anderson at the India Office (with foresight) saw "no reason to suppose" that India would accept or carry out "the broad unwritten obligations" of Commonwealth membership; she would seek to lead an Asiatic bloc that would be anti-British and anti-American, while the Colonial Office argued (with even more foresight) that India would be an awkward partner over colonial issues. The Foreign Office, typically, "attached importance to appearances": in Moore's words, it thought that India's departure from the Commonwealth "will be universally interpreted as a blow to British authority and prestige."[22]

Cripps, Attlee, the India Secretary and even Auchinleck disagreed with Wavell's proposal of phased withdrawal by the British, and this led to Attlee proposing to the King in mid-December that Wavell be replaced by Lord Mountbatten. On 18 February 1947 the Cabinet authorised the statement that British rule would end in June 1948. Nehru wrote to an Indian colleague in April "We must ... proceed on the assumption which is a practical certainty that India will go out of the British Commonwealth by the middle of next year."

This changed in May when Nehru spent a few days at Simla with Mountbatten. With Muslim pressure building up, Congress saw the need for a quick transfer to a stable central authority, while Nehru was anxious to keep Mountbatten as Viceroy to help influence the Princely States and the Forces. So on 13 May Mountbatten told London "I have omitted choice to Provinces for standing out independently ... I do not now like the idea of HMG giving them that choice." He added "we cannot avoid giving a lead to the Princes."[23]

Thus Nehru accepting partition was at the expense of the Princely States: as

Moore notes, "A main attraction of the dual Dominions deal to Congress was that it promised to banish the spectre of princely Ulsters." When in April 1947 Mountbatten referred to Attlee's instructions to enable States to become independent and negotiate freely with any confederation of provinces, Nehru, as President of the All-India States' Peoples' Confederation, a Congress satellite, stated that those who did not join the Constituent Assembly should be regarded as "hostile" states and be made "to bear the consequences of being so regarded." If Britain admitted the possibility of separate relations with States or groups of States then Congress was "likely to withdraw its application for Dominion Status" within the Commonwealth. On 10 June, Nehru threatened to "encourage rebellion in all States" that stood out from the Assembly.[24]

For a while there was tension between London and Delhi. On 24 May the Cabinet's India Committee, while accepting that Britain should facilitate "the exclusive association of the States with one of the new Dominions", also accepted that if a State stood aside from both Dominions, Britain would have to consider separate relations with it. On 10 May Attlee asked the Chiefs of Staff for their appraisal of the military implications of Dominion status being given separately to West Pakistan, Bengal and Travancore (a State in the south with a coastline): they replied in favour of Dominion status in all three. In contrast, as Moore adds "Mountbatten ... would be in breach of his understanding with Nehru if he failed" to draw the Princes into the Dominions, while "Congress might well refuse to endorse the deal."[25]

Some Princes did want to be separate Dominions, including the Maharajah of Bhopal, Chancellor of the Chamber of Princes, and the rulers of Travancore and Hyderabad. These three, along with Junagadh, started to pursue independence. On 17 June Mountbatten told Monckton, Bhopal and Zafrullah Khan, representing the League, that Congress would never have accepted partition if there were to be more than three Dominions. He now even refused to allow Bengal to vote for separate Dominion status, even to avoid its being partitioned. Meanwhile, Monckton encouraged Butler, Templewood, Salisbury, and Brendan Bracken to press the Government to establish direct relations with States which sought autonomy. However, Mountbatten told the Nizam of Hyderabad that as his state was militarily defenceless, landlocked and surrounded by the Indian Dominion, the Government could not accept any commitment to protect it.[26]

The House of Commons debated the second reading of the India Independence Bill on 10 July 1947. Attlee said when paramountcy lapsed the States would "regain their independence" but he hoped that "no irrevocable decision to stay out would be taken prematurely," while Harold Macmillan, leading for the Opposition, referred to a State's right to join a Dominion or enjoy "independent sovereign authority". Both he and Sir John Anderson (Governor of Bengal 1932-7 and a senior Cabinet member during the war) said they believed that the Government should enter into independent relations with States that requested them. During the Lords debate on the 16th, Listowel, the India Secretary, said the States would, after the lapse of paramountcy, "be entirely free to choose whether to associate with one or other of the Dominion Governments or to stand alone," adding "we do not, of course, propose to recognise any States as separate international entities." Questioned closely by Templewood, he conceded that if a State failed to enter a Dominion the question of international recognition would be "left open to be considered on its merits ..." Monckton was pleased with this, albeit ambiguous, outcome.[27]

Mountbatten insisted that accession by 15 August – the date fixed for independence – was urgent, implying that after it non-acceding States would be left to fend for themselves, while possibly facing rebellions of their subjects. Listowel was alarmed at this line, having promised that the Government would not apply pressure. A conciliatory response to him was drafted for Mountbatten, but after speaking to Menon of the Congress, he instructed his private secretary to "knock these arguments on the head".[28]

After independence, India eliminated every vestige of sovereignty from the Princes apart from privy purse allocations, and these were attacked four years later. The only States which did not accede in August 1947 were Hyderabad, Kashmir and Junagadh. Kashmir, with a Muslim majority population but a Hindu ruler (strongly supported from Delhi as the Nehru family originated from Kashmir), saw an invasion of irregulars from Pakistan and a short war lasting into 1948; the province remains divided and caused further wars and constant tension. Hyderabad had a Hindu majority population but a Muslim ruler. After a variety of turbulence, the state was invaded by Indian troops in September 1948: two divisions crushed resistance in four days. Junagadh, a small state in the Kathiawar peninsula, also had a Hindu majority; its Muslim ruler tried to accede to Pakistan. Delhi imposed an economic blockade and armed a Hindu liberation army which took control in November 1947. In July 1948 Churchill claimed that Britain's past pledges to the Princes entitled Kashmir and Hyderabad to choose their future by plebiscite under UN auspices. This never took place, Mountbatten subsequently claiming that Churchill refused to talk to him for years because of the States issue.

An estimated 10 million people changed lands that summer as a result of Partition; approximately 1 million were killed. Andrew Roberts, in *Eminent Churchillians*[29], is highly critical of Mountbatten as Viceroy, in particular, his bias towards Congress and India. For example, he is believed to have intervened in Sir Cyril Radcliffe's awards of partition boundaries to transfer the Ferozepur area, populated by Muslims but the location of much of the Subcontinent's military equipment, from Pakistan to India. Another change gave India a corridor to Kashmir through Muslim populated Gurdaspur. Roberts further refers to Mountbatten's unpreparedness, ignoring warnings, and incompetent handling of the announcement of the new boundaries, leading to dreadful massacres. According to Hamid, Auchinleck believed that if the original timetable had been adhered to, with independence in summer 1948, it might have been possible to reconstitute forces and avoid much bloodshed. He also quotes Sir Evan Jenkins, the capable Governor of the Punjab, warning Mountbatten that it would take four years to split the Punjab peacefully.[30]

There were further signs of scepticism towards India when it eventually became a Republic in 1950. True to their military illusions, the Chiefs of Staff still wanted to keep it in the Commonwealth. The older Dominions were critical: New Zealand did not want a "flabby Commonwealth with no guiding principle."[31]

Disasters in the Middle East

British power in the Middle East was seen as essential after 1945. Not only was there a need to reassure morale after the withdrawal from India, but the region had obvious strategic importance. Ernest Bevin, Labour's Foreign Secretary, saw in 1948 "… the need to build up a Commonwealth defence system which together with the Western (European) Union, would result in a bloc equivalent in strength to the United States or the Soviet Union."[32] Montgomery, the CIGS, agreed: he accepted the political case for evacuating Egypt but insisted on retaining Canal bases, as well as air bases in Libya and Transjordan and full military rights in Palestine. As Darwin perceives, "Britain's ability to use the Canal Zone and its bases … was its greatest surviving geo-strategic asset outside the Home Islands."[33]

The first agony was in Palestine, where Britain was in a no-win situation. The 1939 White Paper aimed to stabilise the balance of population at one-third Jewish and two-thirds Arab. These implied limits on Jewish immigration became impossible to sustain after 1945. President Truman (who "once candidly stated that his pro-Zionist attitude could be explained by his having no Arab constituents")[34] pressed for the admission of 100,000 Jewish refugees into Palestine in August 1945: if Britain had acted fast and accepted this as a final quota, she might have been able to resist further migration.

Britain's priority was to retain Arab support. As the Chiefs of Staff declared in July 1946 "All our defence requirements in the Middle East, including maintenance of our essential oil supplies and communications, demand that an essential feature of our policy should be to retain the co-operation of the Arab states …" She wanted the two communities to co-exist, rather than being partitioned into separate states, a course bitterly opposed by the Arabs. She could not rely on the UN, because both the US and the Soviet blocs at that time supported the Jewish ambitions. These, sadly, were reinforced by terrorism which further alienated the Arabs: the King David Hotel was blown up, with large cross-communal casualties, on 22 July 1946. Truman's statement of support for the Jews on the eve of Yom Kippur (4 October 1946), with Zionists publicising the part which expressed support for "the creation of a viable Jewish state," infuriated Attlee.[35]

1947 saw the peak of Britain's post war economic crisis, while Churchill complained about the cost of maintaining 100,000 servicemen in Palestine where order was only tenuously maintained. Bevin advanced his own plan in early 1947: the UN would prepare Palestine for independence as a bi-national state, with cantons of the two communities side by side. Both sides rejected this. In this deadlock, the Irgun hanged two British sergeants and booby-trapped their bodies in July 1947. After a visit by the UN Special Committee that summer, a majority of it voted for partition. All these events triggered the British decision to resign the mandate in September 1947 and evacuate by May 1948. And hardly anyone anticipated the extent of the Arab collapse in the war which then began.

The evacuation of Palestine hardened the British military reluctance to leave Egypt. While the Egyptian ruling class was usually reticent to encourage the populace against the British for fear of things getting out of control, their humiliation in the war removed such restraint, while Britain was blamed for her "betrayal" of the Palestine Arabs. And, as in a forest fire, disparate local outbreaks restricted the ability to fight the whole. With the US oil company (Aramco) in Saudi Arabia agreeing to a 50-50 share in the profits, this was the obvious course for the Anglo-Iranian Oil Company in Abadan. The latter delayed, fatally: Shuckburgh describes its chairman as "quite unconcerned with the national interest, and anxious only to squeeze the utmost out of Persia for his already bloated company."[36] It was nationalised by the insurgent Musaddiq in April 1951, with Attlee vetoing military action because the US feared Soviet retaliation in the north of Iran. While there was a coup in August 1953, promoted by the British and US intelligence services, and demolishing Musaddiq, this was no help elsewhere.

Evacuating Abadan brought repercussions: in October 1951 the Egyptian Government unilaterally abrogated the Anglo-Egyptian treaty of 1936. Disorders there increased: in January 1952, aiming to disarm auxiliary police, British tanks attacked a barracks killing 41 Egyptians. The following day saw massive anti-foreign riots in Cairo, with Shepheard's Hotel burnt down and 11 British deaths. In July 1952 a group of junior officers under Neguib and Nasser removed King Farouk. With the British garrison of 80,000 chiefly employed in defending itself, pressure grew from the US for Britain to evacuate the Canal Zone. Typical of unrealistic expectations at this time, both Britain and the US hoped Egypt would join the "Middle East Defence Organisation", directed at Russia.

While the US had been "generally amenable" to leaving Britain with the preponderant influence in the Middle East, after Eisenhower became president in 1953 and Dulles Secretary of State, they were concerned over the Cold War and increasingly saw Britain as not taking sufficient account of Arab nationalism. "To tie ourselves to the tail of the British kite in the Middle East ... would be to abandon all hope of a peaceful alignment of that area with the West," an US State Department official stated in June 1953.[37] Eden remarked in 1970 "the trouble with Dulles was that he regarded British and French interests in the Middle East as colonial and American interests in South East Asia, or anywhere else in the world, as virginal." After Abadan Leo Amery warned Eden of the need to show "that the lion has claws and teeth, as well as a tail to be twisted."[38]

Paradoxically, the Suez Group of 41 right-wing Conservative MPs saw the Middle East in terms of the domino theory, which later guided US thinking about South East Asia. Eden tended to agree. He then adopted what Dutton terms "a more moderate and realistic policy," setting him against Churchill who complained that Eden was "throwing the game away."[39] The whole episode was complicated by rivalry between these two prima donnas – Churchill knew that Eden was impatient to succeed him. The former suffered from ageing and the occasional stroke, but Eden also suffered from ill-health. While Shuckburgh argued that the Suez Canal base was a "prime example of an irritant which, with no clear benefit to ourselves, was poisoning our relations with the most influential Arab nation," Julian Amery later asserted that "one of the great heresies of contemporary thought is that a base is useless if situated amidst a hostile population."[40]

Churchill continued to be sympathetic to the Suez rebels. After a speech by Julian Amery on 17 December 1953, Churchill rang him to tell him he "agreed with every word": "Keep it up – you're on the right lines." He was attracted by Amery's view that the Zone could be held by 10,000 "teeth troops", but the Chiefs of Staff disagreed.[41] The Leo Amery diary (22 November 1953) records an anecdote of Churchill telling the Chief Whip of his reluctance to go to a party meeting to support Eden; he did go but insisted on speaking last "You see, I am not on our side". Churchill was at times brutal; referring to the security issue in the Zone in December 1953, he said "If they attack us, that would be war, and you can do a lot of things then."[42] After the withdrawal treaty debate on 15-6 May 1954, 14 Conservative rebels, including Amery and Enoch Powell, abstained. As Julian Amery said "it can be quite difficult to stay put in a place but it will be a damned sight more difficult to get back:" Australia, New Zealand, Canada and South Africa, as well as Israel and Iraq, and even the Indian Army general staff, all urged Britain to remain in the Zone.[43]

Eden's agreement with Egypt of July 1954 provided for the base to be maintained by British civilians for another seven years, with the right to return if Arab countries faced attack, though how these points could be guaranteed after evacuation might be questioned. Churchill in fact, wanted the US to back Britain staying in the Canal Zone; scared of obtaining a colonialist taint, Washington refused. Churchill began to hesitate over the costs of the base, and the fact that the Chiefs of Staff supported evacuation. Eventually he appears to have used the acquisition by Britain of the H-bomb to support Eden, arguing that it made the Zone base redundant. Darwin states "there is more than a hint that the H-bomb was a rabbit pulled out of the hat: it gave Churchill the escape route he ... needed".[44]

The Baghdad Pact began as a Iraqi-Turkish agreement in February 1955, with Eden as Premier in April committing Britain to it. Nasser hated the Hashemite Kings of Jordan and Iraq and particularly Nuri es-Said, the Iraqi premier; Cairo Radio attacked them ceaselessly. By raising trouble in Jordan he deterred it from joining the Pact. Tension was further raised by an Israeli raid on Gaza in February 1955 in which 38 Egyptian soldiers were killed. Shootings and reprisals continued on that border.

In September 1955 Nasser bought arms from the Soviet bloc; this infuriated the US. Congress, because of opposition from the Israeli lobby, the cotton lobby and the China lobby (Nasser had just recognised Communist China) would prevent the US financing the Aswan dam.[45] Days after the Aswan decision, with the final British troops leaving the Canal Zone on 26 July 1956, Nasser announced its nationalisation.

Perhaps Eden was already regretting the evacuation of the Zone. King Hussein of Jordan had suddenly sacked Glubb Pasha as commander of the Arab Legion in March 1956 – an act believed, erroneously, to have been inspired by Nasser. Suffering from a bad press and having performed badly in the Commons on 7 March, Eden told Shuckburgh " I was seriously to consider reoccupation of Suez as a move to counteract the blow to our prestige." Given the extraordinary way the Suez "Crisis" developed, Shuckburgh's diaries set the background, describing Eden as "completely disintegrated – petulant, irrelevant, provocative ... (and) weak," while after Eden's appointment of Selwyn Lloyd as Foreign Secretary: "it becomes daily more apparent that we have no Secretary of State. We have a rather nervous official ..."[46]

In planning his Suez coup, Eden was selective over US comments, welcomed those favourable to action but ignoring those unfavourable. Similarly, Gaitskell and Herbert Morrison, whose early reaction was very hostile to Nasser, never gave Eden a blank cheque, covering themselves by references to the UN and avoidance of force. With foresight, Macmillan argued that if Britain did not deal with Nasser "Nuri and our friends will fall."[47] After the crisis, Lloyd in the US sent Eden a telegram reporting that Dulles "deplored that we had not managed to bring down Nasser." Lloyd's posthumously published memoir states that Dulles said "Selwyn, why did you stop? Why didn't you go through with it and get Nasser down". Elsewhere Louis accepts that while Eden and Macmillan might have been correct that Dulles would have acquiesced, this was "certainly not" true of Eisenhower, "who was outraged"; the Anglo-French invasion coincided with the US Presidential election.[48]

Alan Clark describes Macmillan, whom Clark believed was plotting to succeed Eden, meeting Eisenhower on 24 September, making no mention of Suez himself; the absence of any mention by Eisenhower "did just allow Macmillan to report back to Eden that the US was supportive." Louis reports Macmillan's "celebrated misjudgement" in sending the telegram stating that Eisenhower was "really determined, somehow or other, to bring Nasser down."[49]

In an interview with Naim Atallah, publisher of *The Oldie* (22 November 1992), Julian Amery claimed that Allen Dulles, Director of the CIA at the time of Suez, told him "I don't understand why you didn't go on." President Nixon, who despite his weaknesses had a distinguished grasp of international affairs, later told

Amery "in retrospect, the US role in restraining Britain at the time was a major foreign policy mistake," adding that even Eisenhower shared this view.[50]

Churchill's own verdict, typically, has at least two versions. "I am not sure I should have dared to start; but I am sure I should not have dared to stop." That is how Hugh Thomas records it; the other version is more circumspect: "I would never have dared to do it without squaring the Americans and once I had started I would never have dared stop." This latter is supported by Lord Moran's record of Churchill's *ipsissima verba:* "One can't tell what one would have done, but one thing is certain, I wouldn't have done anything without consulting the Americans". Moran earlier records him saying "I cannot understand why our troops were halted. To go so far and not go on was madness."[51]

This author, aged 12 in 1956, then a vehement supporter of Eden, but now at 72 somewhat more circumspect, would look to that great but immoral genius Bismarck. His view was, if you are going to wage aggressive war, first get your victim to start it and, second, ensure your forces are capable of speedy victory. Bismarck achieved both in 1866 and 1870. Nasser was hardly seen as the aggressor in 1956, and Britain's military performance fell sadly short. The Service ministers were reluctant, Clark reports that the Chiefs of Staff were "defeatist", and the invasion armada took nearly six days to sail from Malta. The original COS plan was to attack Alexandria – then on 7 September this was switched to Port Said. This "cost ... heavily in time and initiative". And there are indications that Selwyn Lloyd, in the context of the Iraqi crisis of 1958, remarked that if the British had acted immediately over Suez (end July 1956), "it would have been accepted by world opinion."[52]

Comment since has been condemnatory, mainly on the grounds that the Anglo-French action affronted the UN, where "The British delegates were avoided as if they were lepers."[53] Nasser became a hero to Arab (and African) nationalists. France had been a very willing participant in Suez and a very reluctant withdrawer: so angry were some French troops with the British for giving way that they allegedly sold their weapons to EOKA terrorists in Cyprus as they were returning.[54]

Julian Amery later commented that the Suez debacle led to wars between Saudi Arabia and her neighbours, a series of Iraqi revolts, the destabilisation of Lebanon, the disastrous Egyptian invasion of Yemen, the rise of Gaddafi, the Soviet takeover of Aden and Ethiopia and the emergence of Palestinian terrorism. It is hard to deny an element of *post hoc, ergo propter hoc.*

The Suez failure indisputably led to the brutal Kassem coup in Baghdad in July 1958, with the slaughter of Britain's good allies King Feisal and Premier Nuri. Louis gives a powerful analysis, derived from contemporary diplomatic reports, of the political and social discontents which produced the Iraq army mutiny and revolution of July 1958. The key to this, which clearly took the British and their Baghdad allies by surprise, was "not that the British used force against Nasser, but that they consorted with France and Israel, 'the one regarded as the arch-colonizer and the other the arch-enemy of the Arabs.'" One explanation of the surprise was that the British military attaché "was at sea in larger political issues, such as the loyalty of the officer corps."[55]

The Retreat from Africa

As in India and the Middle East, the British suffered from a combination of misplaced benevolence, bad judgement, bad luck, and bad timing. Their African colonies had remained quiet before, during and after the 1939 war, until the prospect of political change unleashed hopes and fears. Discontent was present, over taxation, the low prices from colonial marketing boards, and attempts to improve native agriculture. Blacks in East and Central Africa feared – rightly – substantial post-war white immigration. Thus during the period 1955-1980 African affairs dominated the British press as they have not done since.

British power was collapsing by 1960, and vanished altogether by 1965. The white settler communities, were eclipsed but survived in Kenya and Northern Rhodesia/Zambia, and were later dramatically reduced under Mugabe's rule in Zimbabwe/Rhodesia. How large a white community – English or Afrikaans – will survive in South Africa remains to be seen.

Unrealistic hopes were widespread – carefully disguising a loss of nerve, as seen in this warning from Colonial Secretary Oliver Lyttelton to the Cabinet in September 1953 regarding the need for constitutional progress in West Africa, where failure "would bring to an end a settled government by consent and forfeit the goodwill towards the United Kingdom and the desire to retain the British connection which are common to all parties in the Gold Coast."[56] After his electoral triumph in 1951 Kwame Nkrumah, newly released from prison to became chief minister, was soon collaborating with Nasser and Nehru in a trio of anti-colonial campaigners, happy to seek support from the Communists.

In East Africa the British renewed their quest, started by Leo Amery as Colonial Secretary, and aborted by the 1929 Labour Government, for a federation with which the Africans in Tanganyika and Uganda would acquiesce and in which a multiracial but European–led Kenya would be dominant. They were wholly disappointed. Kenya endured the Mau Mau rural terrorist outbreak (largely a revolt of landless Kikuyu against their chiefs), with a state of emergency from 1952 until 1959. Partially because of an exaggerated threat to white civilians – the Kenya settlers were a powerful and well-connected lobby (the "officers' mess" compared to the "sergeants' mess" in Rhodesia) – there was a huge armed response, with 10,000 regular troops, and a large loyalist home guard among the Kikuyu. Atrocities occurred, mainly inflicted by Africans on Africans, but the British authorised over 1000 executions, while a total of 20,000 Mau Mau were killed. A Chequers meeting on East Africa in January 1959 took the view that internal self-government for Tanganyika and Uganda was at least a decade away and there was no timetable at all for Kenya.[57]

British Africa was now influenced by events elsewhere. Since 1954 France had been fighting a bloody and difficult war against the Nationalists (FLN) in Algeria. After coming to power in June 1958, de Gaulle stated there would be no independence. He made a U turn (autumn 1960), in which year most of the other French African colonies were granted independence.

The end of the Algerian war saw the first of several displacements of European settler communities in Africa. White terrorist reaction (the OAS) produced more terrorism from the FLN. Virtually the whole "*pied noir*" population of 1.4 million left, while Muslims who had been loyal to France were massacred. Horne judges that without the OAS, the departure of *pied noirs* could have been phased "more gently, less tragically."[58]

These events, the Soviet threat, and American concern put pressure on the British. After his 1959 General Election victory – colonial issues had been exploited by Labour but without effect – Macmillan made the liberal Tory Iain Macleod Colonial Secretary. In Darwin's judgement the records do not show that Macleod wanted to hand over to the African nationalists. However, he started a process that had that result.

Tanganyika obtained self-government in 1960 and independence in 1961, much more rapidly than Macleod had planned. Kenya, however, saw a prime example of British miscalculation. They aimed to build a coalition between moderate whites and blacks, and encouraged a "moderate" black party, KADU. As usual, the "baddies" won: the 1961 elections gave KANU the majority in African seats. After a new constitution removed nominated and European members, KANU won the first universal suffrage election by a landslide, in May 1963. Apart from Rhodesia, Kenya was the last British African colony to become independent, in December 1963.

In terms of size, economic potential and British emotional commitment, Central Africa was more important than elsewhere. Britain hoped to achieve racial partnership in the Federation, established in 1953 and described as a "new Dominion in the making". In November 1957 London promised that a predominantly white-ruled Federation's constitution would be reviewed in 1960 to see if independence might be granted. Alongside South Africa (where there were still hopes of cooperation) these would be Britain's regional allies, with air and sea links to Australia and New Zealand. Like Leo Amery in 1918, Darwin saw it as the "Southern British World."[59]

Britain failed completely to assure the Africans that an independent federation would not "become the Trojan Horse of an irrevocable settler supremacy." White liberal leaders said "Federation has been a rocket booster to African nationalism"; even chiefs opposed it.[60] London, however, hoped the settlers would accept sufficient African participation, through a highly complex franchise system, to justify internal self-government and then independence. Failure resulted as a consequence of miscalculation and misfortune. The British never defined or promoted their concept of "partnership". By late 1958 nationalism in Northern Rhodesia gravitated towards those under Kenneth Kaunda pledged to boycott the new multi-racial constitution, while in Nyasaland Hastings Banda started a struggle for majority rule. Darwin puts the question why nationalism was so much more successful after 1958 than in the fight against Federation in 1950-3, and attributes it to, first, urbanisation and better opportunities for nationalist political campaigning, second, the aggressive tactics of white trade unionists provoking militancy from black labour, and third, African fear of continued white immigration.

It all unravelled in Nyasaland, where the nationalists were accused of planning a murder plot; excessive force was used in repression, with 51 Africans killed. Not for the first time, and certainly not for the last, Whitehall naively resorted to the judiciary: here, it was the Devlin Inquiry, where London and the Federal Government expected a favourable outcome. Devlin judged otherwise in July 1959, indicating that most Africans opposed the Federation. Macmillan was "dumbfounded" and privately dismissed the findings as "perverse."[61] Again, the archives do not support the idea that Macmillan and Macleod wanted to abandon federation and hand power to the nationalists. "Even in hindsight, decoding British intentions is far from straightforward." [62]

The Monckton Commission was intended to produce a reformed Federation that would be supported by "moderates". Its report in October 1960 recommended sweeping and rapid changes, with devolution of power, leaving only external affairs, defence and broad economic policy to the Federation. Equally, it argued that this experiment in multi-racial partnership should not be allowed to fail. However, there was enough here to encourage the militants: the northern provinces, significantly, might be allowed to secede; not only should there be parity of representation for black and white immediately in the Federal Assembly, but also African majorities in these northern provinces, with drastic changes in Southern Rhodesia's racial policies. Even the location of the Federal capital should be reconsidered.

Sir Roy Welensky, the Federal Premier, warned Macmillan that nationalist success in the North would lead Southern Rhodesia to reject its new constitution. So in June 1961 a new constitution in Northern Rhodesia provided for a white majority and the South passed theirs in a referendum. With chaos in the Congo – many refugees passing through Southern Rhodesia – moderation collapsed. The end of emergency regulations in the North saw large and increasingly violent nationalist demonstrations. Later in 1961 Britain lost her nerve; she "gyrated".[63] Maudling, the new Colonial Secretary, retreated from the June proposals. In March 1962 the North obtained a constitution weighted towards an African majority, which was accordingly delivered in the elections of October 1962, while in December Sir Edgar Whitehead was swept away in the Southern Rhodesian elections by the more extreme Rhodesian Front.

At the same time South Africa became a Republic, and isolated herself because, having to re-apply for Commonwealth membership, which Asian and African members opposed, she had to withdraw in May 1961. In March 1963 London decided to dissolve the Federation. As a post-mortem, Darwin judged: "It is far from clear that even the political decisions taken after the end of 1959 were intended to have the consequences which actually followed from them."[64]

Instead of the pusillanimity emitted from London, perhaps there was a case for a more decisive, and simultaneously both brutal and generous approach. The various interests in each of the three parts of the Federation might have been firmly told that the British Government wanted it to continue, because it was in the best interest of the whole population. To this end, Britain would offer the two Northern provinces black rule with secure safeguards for minorities, economic aid for development and military protection against disorder, while the South would be permitted to run its own affairs. If the blacks refused to co-operate, after a period of trying to persuade and police the two northern provinces, Britain would accept the break-up of the Federation, abandon the North without any more money, and grant independence to the South on existing arrangements. If the whites (who wanted the Federation to continue) resisted, the same would happen, but with money for the North and without recognition of the government in the South. Macmillan was determined not to be drawn into an Algerian style war; even so, in these circumstances, Britain should have done what many wanted her to do over the fifteen years after 1965 – wash her hands of the matter. There would have been no pious legalities, no more earnest debates in Parliament, no economic sanctions, no hysteria.

Both South Africa and Southern Rhodesia attracted enormous sympathy in Britain during the 1960s and '70s, with many families having relatives there. The demographic position of whites in Rhodesia was much weaker (they were never much more than 5% of the population). While there was no strict apartheid and greater harmony with elements of the black population uninfected by the nationalist campaigners, there was a clear injustice, never remedied during the years of stability, over land apportionment, and the franchise was heavily weighted against blacks.

The dissolution of the Federation led in 1965 to the "unilateral declaration of independence" in Southern Rhodesia by the white settlers' Government. While the British Labour Government of Harold Wilson insisted on NIBMAR (no independence before majority African rule), it also refused to use force, both for internal political reasons and for fear of another Curragh Mutiny. Wilson resorted to economic sanctions which he said would work in "weeks rather than months." Some nations, such as West Germany, conducted business legally with Rhodesia until 1973, when Bonn joined the UN. France ignored sanctions, and Japan continued to accept more Rhodesian exports than any other nation, while Iran provided oil. The Portuguese government marketed Rhodesian products as its own and South Africa openly refused to observe the UN sanctions. The USA permitted

American firms to go on importing Rhodesian chromium and nickel.

There were two major attempts at a settlement; if either of these had succeeded, sanctions would have been lifted and Rhodesia (probably) would have remained capable of resisting attacks by African nationalist guerrillas. These latter were based in Zambia, and, after a revolution in Portugal leading to the evacuation of Portuguese African territories in 1974-5, in Angola and Mozambique. The terms offered at a meeting on HMS *Tiger* in 1966 were more favourable to the white settlers than the 1961 constitution but were rejected by an over-confident Rhodesian Government. The 1971 terms offered by the Conservative Heath government were even more generous and were accepted by the Rhodesian Government. They required consultation of the various communities, under the Pearce Commission, and were overwhelmingly rejected by the African population in 1972, while 98% of whites, 97% of coloureds and 96% of the Asians voted for the settlement. It was a close run thing, and more flexibility and imagination by the whites coupled with more determination by Pearce and company might have implemented a settlement very much better than the post 1979 outcome.

Rhodesia's struggle thereafter was heroic but doomed. Until the mid 1970s, there were more blacks in the Rhodesian armed forces and police than whites, and the two nationalist groups, ZANU and ZAPU, were as much at war with each other as with the Smith Government. Under Soviet encouragement, Cubans and East Germans intervened in Angola, and the position worsened. Perhaps this contributed to the demise of the Soviet Union: Angola's "unrecoverable" debt to Russia totalled $5billion by 1989, with 55,000 Cubans in Angola. These were withdrawn in 1988 as part of a deal but Castro resented Gorbachev's "betrayal" of international Communism.[65] Not wanting Cubans in Mozambique, South Africa insisted on a solution in Rhodesia in the late 1970s, while US President Carter insisted on sanctions remaining. Another "what if" occurs – what if President Reagan, with his strong sympathies towards whites in southern Africa,[66] had taken over before the Thatcher Government began negotiations for a settlement (he did so in January 1981)? Encouraged by the "internal settlement" and the election of the moderate Bishop Muzorewa as Zimbabwe-Rhodesia's first black Prime Minister in April 1979, the Rhodesians would have resisted any risk that London negotiations would have enabled an extreme nationalist political take-over.

British Conservatives in 1979 would have preferred international recognition of Muzorewa's Internal Settlement, which gave white MPs a veto over further constitutional changes for ten years and preserved white leadership in the civil service, judiciary, police and army. Such a solution was opposed at the Commonwealth Conference in Zambia in August 1979. Another Lancaster House Conference in late 1979 produced an agreement, leading to elections in February 1980. As usual, the results surprised the British, with Muzorewa only winning 3 seats, Nkomo 20 and Mugabe 57. Darwin comments "This was one further instance of the extraordinary delusion so characteristic of British policy during the colonial withdrawal from Africa – that there existed a natural constituency for what London blithely defined as 'moderation' ..."[67]

War in Matabeleland in 1983-4 saw Mugabe's North Koreans and Shonas killing perhaps 20,000 men, women and children. Mugabe abolished the reserved 20 white seats. With the seizure of white-owned farms, by 2007 it was estimated that 80-90% of whites had left; inflation soared to 5 billion%, and famine produced a halving of life expectancy. In 1980, even after sanctions, the country exported maize, tobacco and minerals all over the world, with a well-educated and highly-skilled work force. It is now (2016) one of the poorest countries in Africa.

The Decline of Commonwealth Economic Unity

Neither the advance of Tariff Reform towards its triumph at Ottawa during the first third of the century, nor the process leading to its disruption after 1940 make for easy reading. Both, however, are crucial to the central theme of this book and the second one has obtained even less attention than the first – perhaps because it tended to lack fiery political exchanges.[68]

Britain's pressing need after mid-1940 for US armaments and financial help provided an opportunity for Cordell Hull, Roosevelt's Secretary of State, to advance his ambitions. The naivety of these is shown by this remark as late as March 1944: "There will no longer be need for spheres of influence, for alliances, for balance of power ..." in the post-war world. Convinced that discriminatory economic collaboration between countries with political bonds or common interests tended inevitably to produce military conflict, he allied himself to those in the US who sought the dramatic expansion of American exports and economic influence.

On his return to Washington in November 1940 after Roosevelt's re-election, Lord Lothian, the British ambassador, told reporters "Well boys, Britain's broke; it's your money we want." He had also said, in a despatch to Halifax (29 April 1940): "The United States will not do much in this direction (ie loans, credits etc) until she is sure she has got our investments, our gold and any assets Overseas [sic] which are saleable in the United States ..."[69] Congress enacted the Lend-Lease Bill by 11 March 1941, providing that in return for these supplies, the USA should receive "some consideration which the President deemed satisfactory." So on 28 July 1941 Keynes was handed the first draft of Article Seven of the Mutual Aid Agreement and was told that its acceptance would preclude Britain from maintaining Imperial Preference. An attempt to pursue this was made when the Atlantic Charter was agreed between the British and US leaders in early August; Churchill, however, insisted on adding "with due respect for their existing obligations."

"There was hardly an occasion during the next two years (1943-5) when the American Government failed to attempt to consolidate and strengthen Article Seven" of the Mutual Aid Agreement.[70] The British response was confused and divided. The influential and forward-looking Tory Reform Committee proclaimed in its manifesto for the post-war world, *Forward, By the Right,* "Only if the

Commonwealth be regarded as an economic unit can it deal with America and Russia upon equal terms ... the nations of the Commonwealth should be free to order their economic relations with each other as are the States of America ..." Richard Law, later Lord Coleraine, Minister without Portfolio, who carried on a vigorous Cabinet debate on this issue with Leo Amery on 7 February 1944 attacked Amery's criticisms of the US proposals: "If it is our policy to make economic war upon the United States (and it is sheer humbug to pretend that this policy is anything else) then the United States will certainly make economic war upon us." In April Churchill slapped Amery down, saying he could not allow an Amery memorandum to be circulated to "nearly fifty Ministers" – "from its general tenor I gather it is calculated to cause a split in the Conservative Party."[71]

Despite these warnings, there was shock when, on 8 May 1945, President Truman abruptly terminated Lend-Lease aid to Britain except for use in the Pacific, contrary to Churchill's agreement with Roosevelt at Quebec in September 1944. Instead, the US made available the Washington Loan, requiring Britain to eliminate discrimination, especially preference. As the most formidable proponent of Commonwealth preferential union, Leo Amery was out of action during the winter of 1945-6 – not only was his party in Opposition and he without a seat in Parliament, but he was enduring the trial and execution for treason of his eldest son, John. In his diary, he cites Dean Acheson, then US Under-Secretary of State, commending the loan to his reluctant colleagues "by drawing a picture of the immense strength and prosperity of the British Empire which it would achieve on its own if the loan conditions did not go through."[72] 98 MPs of all parties, including 71 Conservatives, voted against the Loan, with the Conservative Front Bench abstaining.

Amery did have an alternative, put only to choice correspondents, and he later commented "The subsequent unconditional grant of Marshall Aid is ... some warrant for believing that a firm insistence on maintaining the right of the Commonwealth to have an economic policy of its own would not have been met by an absolute refusal."[73] Throughout the whole debate, he had welcomed support from the Labour side, especially Emmanuel Shinwell. He saw a warning by Bevin to Eden about "the adjustment of a proper equilibrium by the old free trade process of starvation".[74] Marshall's initiative was first made in June 1947, and enacted by the following April – after Western Europe had faced two years of utter deprivation.

International conferences between 1947 and 1950 set up the General Agreement on Tariffs and Trade (GATT). Tariff reductions were negotiated and some reductions, not large, of preferences also took place. Far more significant was the acceptance by Britain of a clause preventing any effective increase in preferential margins, despite inflation. This, in the view of Amery and his allies, prevented the expansion of Commonwealth trade along the lines laid at Ottawa. Because Britain agreed to join GATT, other European and Commonwealth countries did so. While Menzies and Holland, leading Australia and New Zealand respectively, were sympathetic to removing the GATT preference requirements, Canada, South Africa, India and Pakistan opposed such a step for a variety of reasons.

Conservative party conferences between 1945 and 1953 carried resolutions or amendments urging the revision of GATT to restore preferential freedom of action. Normally this had been accepted by the Minister or Shadow Minister replying, but after the 1952 Conference, the first in Government, Oliver Lyttelton, the Colonial Secretary, assured Amery "there is absolutely no support visible in any country of the Commonwealth for an extension of the preferential system or any alteration in GATT".[75] While Lyttelton gave a lukewarm acceptance to the anti-GATT amendment in 1953, the 1954 Conference saw Amery's amendment rejected in a vote, described in the official report as "a substantial majority", after a powerful speech by the President of the Board of Trade, Peter Thorneycroft. Amery died eleven months later, at the age of 81.

Amery also identified an insidious way in which the GATT rules may have fatally distorted the process of European unity. While outlawing the development of preferential arrangements, Article 42 of the Geneva Charter permitted the formation of a customs union. Not only did this require much more discrimination against the outside world than required by a mere preferential trading community – Commonwealth trade with Britain was the victim when Britain eventually joined the EEC – but customs union implied eventual political federation. There was no way the Commonwealth would federate politically – that had been decided in the first decade of the 20th century, if not before; but the pressure of an inflexible approach, unsuited to Britain, towards federation in Europe constantly created tension with Britain, and in 2016, helped to bring about Britain's decision to leave the EU.

Last Words

It is a well-established complaint that, after 1945, Britain failed to adopt the leadership of the European unity movement and mould it on the lines of British political tradition. At first, in the late Forties, Britain was dissuaded by the weak and unstable position of the main European states. Even when Marshall Aid began to transform their economies, the growing evidence that the Continentals saw unity in terms of supranational institutions further dampened British interest: "Throughout the 1950s, it remained an absolute orthodoxy of British policy that membership of such a community, or even of a European customs union, was fundamentally incompatible with Britain's Commonwealth links, her global commitments and even with her special relationship with the USA".[76]

At first, Britain relaxed in confidence that the European schemes, started at Messina in 1955, would fail. When it became clear that they would not, she tried to negotiate a free trade area permitting the free movement of manufactures but not of food stuffs, thus enabling her to maintain Commonwealth preference. The opposition of the French agrarian lobby, along with reluctance to dilute the ambitions of the Treaty of Rome of March 1957, and finally the return of General de Gaulle to power in June 1958, put an end to this "half way house" approach. The rest, in 1963, 1972 and 2016-17, is history.

Was the European project perceived by many of its earlier British supporters as a substitute for the gradually disappearing Imperial Commonwealth?[77] Was the constitutional and commercial structure of the European Community, resulting from GATT, as Leo Amery perceived, fatal to any continuous "wholehearted" consent by the British people to membership? And was the discrimination against ("old") Commonwealth trade and loyalty, which Europe seemed to require, an enduring source of discontent, not only in Britain but elsewhere? A highly placed Australian quoted, privately but in this author's presence, with some scorn in the autumn of 2016 words of that grand Europhile, Roy Jenkins, uttered in the circumstances of Britain's earlier Europhilia, and still apparently rankling – "the time of kith and kin foreign policy is over."

This is not the occasion to trace the experience of American "imperial" policy between the Fifties and the start of the 21st century. At first, hostility to British (and other) colonialism was paramount, but fear of international Communism swiftly gained equal place. Gradually the US began to discover, first, that the "imperial" burden was not a light one (Vietnam) and, second, that Britain could help. Hence Britain's doing various tasks well, usually with American moral support – in Malaysia, Jordan, the Gulf and Kuwait, then as late as 1982, the remarkable Falklands campaign. More recent episodes in the Islamic world, very much under US command, have been unpopular and unsuccessful. Strangely, recalling Suez, by the 21st century, it was the USA, one-sidedly backing Israel, desperate to civilise Afghanistan, and in 2003 barging into Iraq, with a deceived and reluctant UK in her wake. The image of the 18th century Spanish Bourbons, dragged into disastrous colonial wars "at the chariot wheels" of the French Bourbons, comes to mind.

And finally, a subject which hardly mattered even in the 1950s, but now causes alarm – reverse migration from the non-white Commonwealth and adjacent countries. This was well controlled during the 1970s and 1980s – apart from those most desperate and welcome entrants, the Asian passport-holders of East Africa – but after 1997, whether out of incompetence or malevolence, the flood gates have been opened. Are the great colonisers becoming the colonised? And while the former, in the 19th century, came from a powerful state with a strong economy, the latter in the 21st tend to be the casualties of self-rule.

FOOTNOTES

1 Sir Evelyn Shuckburgh, *Descent to Suez: Diaries 1951-56,* p214 for this phrase.

2 Bassett has told the present author that, while Skidelsky attributes (*John Maynard Keynes* Vol III, p414) a very similar comment to Frank Lee, a civil servant on Keynes's staff at a meeting in

September 1945, "Paul Bareau's original note of the meeting strongly implies this was also Keynes's view." Keynes's criticisms of American mismanagement of the negotiations are also in Skidelsky pp 110, 115 and 180.
3 Charmley, *Churchill: The End of Glory* pp399-407, last quotes p440.
4 Barclay, op cit, pp118, 124, 163. In August 1942 Spitfires arrived in Australia and helped in the defence of Darwin.
5 Lamb, op cit, 151.
6 Ibid, pp66-9, 123, 148, 153.
7 Linlithgow to Amery, 7 and 14 April and 1 May 1942, Barnes and Nicholson, *The Empire At Bay: The Leo Amery Diaries 1929-45*, p727.
8 Darwin, *Britain and Decolonisation,* hereafter *Decolonisation,* p149.
9 Darwin, *Project,* pp548, 576.
10 Darwin, *Decolonisation,* p335.
11 Darwin, *'Imperialism in Decline? Tendencies in British Imperial Policy between the Wars',* Historical Journal, vol.23, 1980 pp674-7, and Darwin, *Decolonisation*, pp85-6.
12 William Roger Louis, *Ends of British Imperialism: The Scramble for Empire, Suez and Decolonization* pp400-2. Hereafter *Ends.*(Note variation between American and British spelling of "decolonisation".)
13 Francis Hutchins, *India's Revolution: Gandhi and the Quit India Movement* p226.
14 The League did not control Punjab, where Sikander's Unionist party, mostly Muslim, but containing representatives of Hindus and Sikhs, governed. Sikander opposed incorporation in Pakistan and in the summer of 1942, with Sikh and Hindu leaders, he planned to petition the British for a separate Punjab Dominion. This was overtaken by the Quit India rising.
15 The sources for this paragraph are various introductory passages in Barnes and Nicholson, op cit, pp905 and 1007-15, drawing on documents in Nicholas Mansergh *The Transfer of Power* Vol. V.
16 R. J. Moore, *Escape from Empire – The Attlee Government and the Indian Problem*, pp22, 51-52.
17 Moore, op cit, pp89, 245. My italics.
18 Moore, op cit, pp207, 305, 308. Monckton was Solicitor-General in Churchill's 1945 caretaker government, and a Cabinet minister from 1951-7.
19 Moore, op cit, pp23, 39, 43. It was estimated that 75 ships and 20 shore batteries were affected by the mutiny, which was ended by Congress intervention. Hutchins, op cit, p287.
20 Moore, op cit, p175.
21 Maj-Gen Shahid Hamid, *Disastrous Twilight: A Personal Record of the Partition of India*, pp163, 169, 180.
22 Moore, op cit, p227-9.
23 Both quotes Moore, op cit, pp250, 281.
24 Ibid, pp290, 295, 301.
25 Ibid, pp307, 298. As Political Adviser to Wavell and then Mountbatten – the official link between the Viceroy and the Princes – Sir Conrad Corfield argued that Mountbatten was in danger of acting contrary to the spirit of the promises made in the Cabinet Mission Memorandum in 1946. He was ignored, and decided to seek early retirement, resolving in the words of H. V. Hodson that he and the Viceroy were "pulling in different directions" (Hodson, *The Great Divide* p359).
26 Moore, op cit, pp309-10.
27 Ibid, pp311-2.
28 Ibid, p312. Shahid Hamid's diary for the 25 July reports "Mountbatten addressed the Princes, overawed them and gave them hell. They ... are most depressed. They have no future." And on the 28th, describing a reception at Viceroy's House for the Princes "Those who had not signed the Instrument of Accession were taken individually to Mountbatten's study and received a dressing down." Op cit, pp210-1.
29 Roberts, op cit, pp95-6.
30 Hamid, op cit, pp237, 170.

31 Darwin, *Project,* p554 quoting a despatch from New Zealand of March 1949.
32 Quoted, ibid p544.
33 Ibid, p591.
34 Louis, *Ends,* p404.
35 Louis, *Ends,* p430.
36 Shuckburgh, op cit, p150.
37 Quoted David Dutton, *Anthony Eden: A Life and Reputation* Arnold 1997, p360.
38 Quoted ibid, pp355-6.
39 Ibid, p358.
40 Shuckburgh, op cit, pp210-11; Amery minute, in the context of Aden in 1959, quoted Brown and Louis, op cit, p344.
41 Louis, op cit, p622.
42 Shuckburgh, op cit, p121.
43 Last two points from Bassett, op cit, pp150-1; otherwise Barnes and Nicholson, op cit, Vol II, p1064, recording evidence from Amery family sources.
44 Darwin, *Project,* p598.
45 Louis, *Ends*, pp477, 651.
46 Shuckburgh, op cit, pp290, 327, 337.
47 Dutton, op cit, pp392, 396.
48 Quoted Louis, *Ends,* p662, from Lloyd's *Suez 1956: A Personal Account* p219; Brown and Louis eds, op cit, p342.
49 Clark, *The Tories: Conservatives and the Nation State 1922-97* p367, latter quote by Louis, *Ends,* p673.
50 Bassett, op cit, p155.
51 Thomas, *The Suez Affair* pp182-3; Martin Gilbert, *Churchill* VIII, p1222, note 2; Lord Moran, *Churchill – The Struggle for Survival 1940-65,* diary for 6 December 1956 and 26 November 1956 respectively, pp709-10.
52 Clark, op cit, p365; Louis, *Ends,* p633 reporting Robert Rhodes James biography of Eden: "contradictory, cumbersome and fatally slow military planning." And, pp821-2 for last point.
53 Louis's words, *Ends,* pp683, 696.
54 Alistair Horne, *A Savage War of Peace: Algeria 1954-62,* p163.
55 *Ends,* pp849-76; the last two quotes are from pp860 and 870.
56 Darwin, *Project,* p614.
57 Ibid, p618.
58 Horne, op cit, p545-7.
59 Darwin, *Project,* p626. See p138 (ref to 1918).
60 Darwin, *Decolonisation,* p272.
61 The words are those of James, op cit, p310.
62 Darwin, *Project,* pp627, 629.
63 Darwin, *Decolonisation,* p275.
64 Ibid, pp247-8.
65 These two points in James, op cit, pp322, 328.
66 Lord Carrington reported that Reagan opined "Well, of course, the South Africans are whites and fought for us during the war. The blacks are black and are Communists." Charles Moore, *Margaret Thatcher* Vol I p547.
67 Darwin, *Decolonisation,* p323.
68 A narration of the post 1940 process, by the present author, appears in the various introductory passages in Barnes and Nicholson, *The Empire at Bay,* pp702-9, 922-32, and 1051-58. Secondary sources used for these passages include R. Gardner, *Sterling-Dollar Diplomacy,* D. P. Calleo and B. M. Rowland, *America and the World Political Economy,* G. Kolko, *The Politics of War,* and C. Thorne, *Allies of a Kind* as well as L. S. Amery's, *The Awakening* and *A Balanced Economy.*

69 McKercher, op cit, p301.
70 Kolko, op cit, p282.
71 Quoted Barnes and Nicholson, op cit, pp 927, 929, 931.
72 Diary, 14 March 1946, quoted Barnes and Nicholson, op cit, p1052.
73 *A Balanced Economy,* p178.
74 The letter is dated 24 April 1942 and a copy is in the Amery Papers, quoted Barnes and Nicholson, op cit, p705.
75 Letter, 23 October 1952, Amery papers, quoted Barnes and Nicholson, op cit, p1055.
76 Darwin, *Decolonisation,* p232.
77 This very theme was the subject of a colloquium 'The Imperial Idea and the European Idea' in Birmingham on 8 July 1986, the 150th anniversary of the birth of Joseph Chamberlain, under the auspices of the Hughenden Foundation. Julian Amery and the present author gave papers, and the latter possesses a record of the proceedings.

BIBLIOGRAPHY

Adams, R. J. Q. *Bonar Law* Stanford University Press, 1999

Aldrich, Richard and Cormack, Rory *The Black Door: Spies, Secret Intelligence and British Prime Ministers* HarperCollins, 2016

Amery, Julian *Life of Joseph Chamberlain,* Macmillan, Vol IV, 1951; Vols V and VI, 1969

Amery, L. S. *My Political Life* Hutchinson, Vol I: *England Before the Storm. 1896-1914,* 1953; Vol II: *War and Peace. 1914–1929,* 1953; Vol III: *The Unforgiving Years. 1929–1940,* 1955

Amery, L. S. *The Awakening: Our Present Crisis and the Way Out* Macdonald and Co, 1948

Amery, L. S. *A Balanced Economy* Hutchinson, 1954

Andrew, Christopher *Theophile Delcassé and the Making of the Entente Cordiale* Macmillan, 1968

Andrew, Christopher and Kanya-Forstner, A. S. *France Overseas*, Thames and Hudson, 1981

Barclay, Glen St John *The Empire is Marching* Weidenfeld and Nicolson, 1976

Barnes, John and Nicholson, David eds *The Leo Amery Diaries* Hutchinson, Vol I, 1980; Vol II *The Empire at Bay,* 1988

Barnett, Corelli *The Collapse of British Power* Eyre Methuen, 1972

Barr, James *A Line in The Sand* Simon and Schuster, 2011

Bassett, Richard *The Last Imperialist: A Portrait of Julian Amery* Stone Trough Books, 2016

Beatty, Jack *The Lost History of 1914 – how the Great War was not inevitable* Bloomsbury, 2012

Beckett, J. C. *The Making of Modern Ireland 1603-1923* Faber and Faber, 1981

Belich, James *Replenishing the Earth – The Settler Revolution and the Rise of the Anglo-World 1783-1939* OUP, 2009

Bell, Peter *Chamberlain, Germany and Japan 1933-4* Macmillan, 1996

Best, Anthony *British Intelligence and the Japanese Challenge in Asia 1914-41* Palgrave Macmillan, 2002

Boyce, D G and Stubbs, J O *F S Oliver, Lord Selborne and Federalism* Journal of Imperial and Commonwealth History 1976

Boyce, Robert *British Capitalism at the Cross Roads* CUP, 1987

Boyce, Robert *The Great Interwar Crisis and the Collapse of Globalisation* Palgrave Macmillan, 2009

Brown, Judith M. and Louis, William R., eds *The Oxford History of the British Empire: The Twentieth Century* OUP, 1999

Brownell, Josiah *The Collapse of Rhodesia* IB Tauris, 2011

Cain, P. J., *Hobson and Imperialism* OUP, 2002

Cannadine, Sir David *Ornamentalism: How the British Saw Their Empire* Allen Lane, 2001

Capie, Forrest *Depression and Protection: Britain Between the Wars* Allen and Unwin, 1983

Carter, Miranda *The Three Emperors* Fig Tree, 2009

Chamberlain, Austen *Politics from the Inside: An Epistolary Chronicle 1906-14* Cassell, 1936
Charmley, John *Splendid Isolation: Britain and the Balance of Power 1874-1914* Hodder and Stoughton, 1999
Charmley, John *Churchill: The End of Glory* Hodder and Stoughton, 1993
Clark, Alan *The Tories: Conservatives and the Nation State 1922-97* Weidenfeld and Nicolson, 1998
Clark, Christopher *The Sleepwalkers – How Europe went to war in 1914* Allen Lane, 2012
Corfield, Sir Conrad, *Princely India* Indo-British Historical Society, 1975
Craigie, R. *Behind the Japanese Mask* Hutchinson, 1946
Crowe, Sybil, *The Berlin West Africa Conference* Longmans Green, 1942

Darwin, John *The Empire Project* CUP, 2009
Darwin, John *Britain, Egypt and the Middle East; Imperial policy in the aftermath of war 1918-22* Macmillan, 1981
Darwin, John *Britain and Decolonisation: the retreat from empire in the post-war world* Macmillan, 1988
Darwin, John *'Imperialism in Decline? Tendencies in British Imperial Policy between the Wars',* Historical Journal, vol.23, 1980
Davenport, T. R. H. *South Africa: A Modern History* Macmillan, 1977
Denoon, Donald, *The Grand Illusion; the failure of Imperial policy in the Transvaal colony during the period of reconstruction 1900-5* Longman, 1973
Drummond, Ian *Imperial Economic Policy* Allen and Unwin, 1974
Dunsterville, Major-General L. C. *The Adventures of Dunsterforce* Edward Arnold, 1920
Dutton, David *Austen Chamberlain: Gentleman in Politics* Ross Anderson Publications, 1985
Dutton, David *Unionist Politics and the Aftermath of the General Election of 1906: A Reassessment,* Historical Journal, 1979
Dutton, David *Anthony Eden: A Life and Reputation* Arnold, 1997

von Eckardstein, Baron Hermann *Ten Years at the Court of St James 1895-1905* E P Dutton and Co, New York, 1922
Elton, Lord *Imperial Commonwealth* Collins, 1945

Ferguson, Niall *Empire – How Britain Made the Modern World* Penguin, 2003
Ferguson, Niall ed *Virtual History* Papermac, 1998
Fischer, Fritz, *World Power or Decline* W W Norton, New York, 1974
Friedman, Bernard *Smuts – A Reappraisal* Allen and Unwin, 1975
Fromkin, David *A Peace to End All Peace* Phoenix, 2000

Gardner, R. N. *Sterling –Dollar Diplomacy* Clarendon Press, 1956
Garvin, J. L. *Life of Joseph Chamberlain* Macmillan, Vol III 1934
Gilbert, Martin *Exile and Return* Weidenfeld and Nicolson, 1974
Green, E. H. H. *Balfour* Haus Publishing, 2006

Grenville, J. A. S. *Lord Salisbury and Foreign Policy* University of London, Athlone Press, 1964

Grigg, John *Lloyd George: From Peace to War 1912-16* Methuen, 1985; *War Leader 1916-18* Allen Lane, 2002

Haggie, Paul *Britannia at Bay – The Defence of the British Empire against Japan 1931-41*, OUP 1981

Halperin, Vladimir *Lord Milner and the Empire* Odhams Press, 1952

Hamid, Maj-Gen Shahid Hamid *Disastrous Twilight: A Personal Record of the Partition of India* Leo Cooper, 1986

Hancock, Sir Keith *Smuts* CUP, Vol I 1962; Vol II 1968

Hatton, P. H. S. *Harcourt and Solf: the Search for an Anglo-German Understanding through Africa 1912-14* European Studies Review I, No 2,1971

Hayne, M. B. *The French Foreign Office and the origins of the First World War 1898-1914* OUP, 1993

Holland, R. F., *Britain and the Commonwealth Alliance* Macmillan, 1981

Horne, Alistair *A Savage War of Peace:Algeria 1954-62* Papermac, 1996

Howard, Sir Michael *British Military Preparations for the Second World War,* in *Retreat from Power: Studies in Britain's Foreign Policy of the 20th Century Vol I, 1906-39,* edited by David Dilks, Macmillan, 1981

Hutchins, Francis *India's Revolution: Gandhi and the Quit India Movement,* Harvard University Press, 1973

Hyam, Dr Ronald *Britain's Imperial Century, 1815-1914: a study of empire and expansion* (1976, 3rd edition 2002) and *Britain's Declining Empire: the Road to Decolonisation 1918-68* CUP, 2007

Ireland, Philip *Iraq – A Study in Political Development* Jonathan Cape, 1937

Jackson, Alvin *Home Rule: An Irish History* Weidenfeld and Nicolson, 2003

Jalland, Patricia *UK Devolution 1910-14: Panacea or Tactical Diversion?* English Historical Review No 94, 1979

James, Lawrence *Empires In The Sun: The Struggle for the Mastery of Africa* Weidenfeld and Nicolson, 2016

Jeffery, Keith *Field Marshal Sir Henry Wilson: A Political Soldier* OUP 2006

Jeffery, Keith *British Isles/British Empire; dual mandate/dual identity*, in *The British Isles 1901-51,* ed. Keith Robbins OUP 2002

Kendle, John *Ireland and the Federal Solution: The Debate over the UK Constitution 1870-1921* McGill-Queens University Press, 1989

Kennedy, Paul *The Rise and Fall of the Great Powers* Vintage Books, New York, 1989

Kinnear, Michael *The Fall of Lloyd George: The Political Crisis of 1922* Macmillan, 1973

Kinnear, Michael *The British Voter* Batsford, 1989

Kolko, G. *The Politics of War: Allied Diplomacy and the World Crisis of 1943-45* Weidenfeld and Nicolson, 1969

Kwarteng, Kwasi *Ghosts of Empire: Britain's Legacies in the Modern World* Bloomsbury, 2011

Lamb, Richard *Churchill as War Leader: Right or Wrong?* Bloomsbury, 1991
Lee, Bradford A. *Britain and the Sino-Japanese War 1937-39* Stanford University Press, 1973
Lieven, Dominic *Towards The Flame: Empire, War and the End of Tsarist Russia* Allen Lane, 2015
Louis, William Roger *Ends of British Imperialism: The Scramble for Empire, Suez and Decolonization* I B Tauris, 2006
Ludwig, Emil *July 1914* G P Putnam's Sons, 1929

Macdonald, C. A. *The United States, Britain and Appeasement* Macmillan 1981
McKale, Donald *War by Revolution: Germany and Britain in the Middle East in the Era of the First World War* Kent State University Press, Ohio, 1998
McKercher, B. J. C. *Transition of Power: Britain's Loss of Global Pre-eminence to the United States 1930-45,* CUP, 1999
McMeekin, Sean *July 1914-Countdown to War* Icon Books, 2013
McMeekin, Sean *The Russian Origins of the First World War* Harvard University Press, 2011
MacMillan, Margaret *Peacemakers* John Murray, 2001
MacMillan, Margaret *The War that Ended Peace* Profile, 2013
Marrison, Andrew, *British Business and Protection 1903-32* OUP, 1996
Marsh, Peter T. *Joseph Chamberlain: Entrepreneur in Politics* Yale University Press, New Haven and London, 1994
Martel, Gordon *The Limits of Commitment – Rosebery and the Definition of the Anglo-German Understanding* Historical Journal, Vol 27, 1984
Middlemas, Keith and Barnes, John *Baldwin* Weidenfeld and Nicolson, 1969
Mills, William C. *The "Secret Channel" to Italy,* International Historical Review, 2002
Monroe, Elizabeth *Britain's Moment in the Middle East 1914-71* Chatto and Windus, 1981
Moore, R. J. *Escape from Empire – the Attlee Government and the Indian Problem* OUP, 1983
Morley, J. W. editor: *The China Quagmire – Japan's Expansion on the Asian Continent* Columbia University Press, New York, 1983

Nish, Ian ed. *Anglo-Japanese Alienation 1919-52: Papers of the Anglo-Japanese Conference on the History of the Second World War* CUP, 1982
Nish, Ian *Japan and the Outbreak of War in 1941*, in *Crisis and Controversy,* edited Alan Sked and Chris Cook, Macmillan, 1976
Pakenham, Thomas *The Boer War* Abacus, 1979
Pakenham, Thomas *The Scramble for Africa* Abacus, 1991
Paxman, Jeremy *Empire: What Ruling the World Did to the British* Viking, 2011
Pitt, Barrie *1918 – The Last Act* Cassell, 1962

Ramsden, John *The Age of Balfour and Baldwin 1902-40* Longman, 1978
Ramsden, John *Don't Mention the War: the British and the Germans since 1890* Little, Brown, 2006

Rempel, Richard *Unionists Divided: Arthur Balfour, Joseph Chamberlain and the Unionist Free Traders* David and Charles, 1972
van Rensburg, Patrick *Guilty Land*, a Penguin Special, 1962
Reynolds, David *The Creation of the Anglo-American Alliance 1937-41* Europa, 1981
Rich, Norman *Friedrich von Holstein* CUP Vol II, 1965
Roberts, Andrew *Salisbury: Victorian Titan* Phoenix, 2000
Roberts, Andrew *Eminent Churchillians* Phoenix, 1994
Rooth, Tim *British Protectionism and the International Economy: Overseas Commercial Policy in the 1930s,* CUP 1993
Rothwell, V. H. *British War Aims and Peace Diplomacy 1914-18* OUP, 1971

Scally, Robert J. *Origins of the Lloyd George Coalition: The Politics of Social-Imperialism 1900-18* Princeton University Press, New Jersey, 1975
Schroeder, Paul *World War One as Galloping Gertie: A Reply to Joachim Remak* Journal of Modern History, 1972
Schwartz, Benjamin *Britain's Perception of a German Threat to her Eastern Position in 1918,* in Journal of Contemporary History, vol 28, 1993
Self, Robert *Tories and Tariffs: The Conservative Party and the Politics of Tariff Reform 1922-32* Garland Publishing Inc, 1986
Shannon, R. *The Crisis of Imperialism 1865-1915* Hart Davis, MacGibbon, 1974
Sheffield, Gary *Forgotten Victory: The First World War: Myths and Realities* Headline, 2001
Shuckburgh, Sir Evelyn *Descent to Suez: Diaries 1951-56* Weidenfeld and Nicolson, 1986
Sluglett, Peter *Britain in Iraq 1914-32* Ithaca Press, 1976
Smith, Jeremy *The Tories and Ireland* Irish Academic Press, Dublin, 2000
Steiner, Zara *Britain and the Origins of the First World War* Macmillan, 1977
Steiner, Zara *The Foreign Office under Sir Edward Grey*, in F. H. Hinsley (ed) *British Foreign Policy under Sir Edward Grey* CUP, 1977
Stevenson, David *With Our Backs to the Wall: Victory and Defeat in 1918* Allen Lane, 2011
Stewart, A. T. Q. *The Ulster Crisis : Resistance to Home Rule 1912-14* Faber and Faber, 1967
Sykes, Alan *Tariff Reform in British Politics* OUP, 1979
Sykes, Christopher Simon *The Man who Created the Middle East* William Collins, 2016

Taylor, A. J. P. *The Struggle for Mastery in Europe* OUP, 1954
Thorne, Christopher *Allies of a Kind: The United States, Britain and the war against Japan 1941-45* Hamilton, 1978
Townshend, Charles *When God Made Hell: The British Invasion of Mesopotamia and the Creation of Iraq 1914-1921* Faber and Faber, 2010
Travers, Tim *How the War was Won* Routledge, 1992
Trotter, Ann *Britain and East Asia 1933-7* CUP, 1975

Warner, Geoffrey *Iraq and Syria 1941* Davis-Poynter, 1974
Watson, Alexander *Ring of Steel – Germany and Austria-Hungary at War 1914-18* Allen Lane, 2014

Watt, D. Cameron *Succeeding John Bull: America in Britain's Place 1900-75* CUP, 1984
Williamson, Philip *National Crisis and National Government: British politics, the economy and Empire 1926-32* CUP, 1992
Williamson, S. R. *The Politics of Grand Strategy: Britain and France Prepare for War 1904-14* Harvard University Press, 1969
Wilson, Trevor *Decision for War* British Journal of International Studies I, 1975
Woodward, David R. *Lloyd George and the Generals* University of Delaware Press, 1983
Woodward, Sir Llewellyn *The Age of Reform 1815-70* OUP, 1962

INDEX

Peerages and knighthoods awarded after mention in this volume are not always included, while some names, mentioned only once in the text, are omitted.

INDEX